Ordinary Heroes

Ordinary Heroes

The Story of Civilian Volunteers in the
First World War

SALLY WHITE

AMBERLEY

This book is for my mum, with love and thanks for a lifetime of shared experiences. Since I started the research for this book her interest has spurred me on and her response to each fresh chapter helped shape the text. Her belief in me, and in this book, has never wavered. Alzheimer's disease is now stealing her, day by day.

It is also for my dad, 1927–2017, who did so much to encourage my early interest in history and archaeology.

First published 2018

Amberley Publishing
The Hill, Stroud
Gloucestershire, GL5 4EP

www.amberley-books.com

British Library Cataloguing in Publication Data.
A catalogue record for this book is available from the British Library.

ISBN 978 1 4456 7666 1 (hardback)
ISBN 978 1 4456 7667 8 (ebook)

Typeset in 10.5pt on 13pt Sabon.
Typesetting and Origination by Amberley Publishing.
Printed in the UK.

Maps by Thomas Bohm, User Design.

Contents

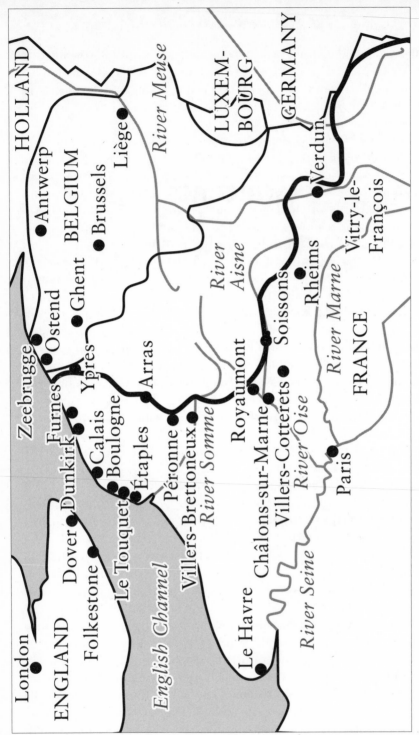

France and Belgium in 1918. The solid line shows the furthest advance of the German Army. (Thomas Bohm © Amberley)

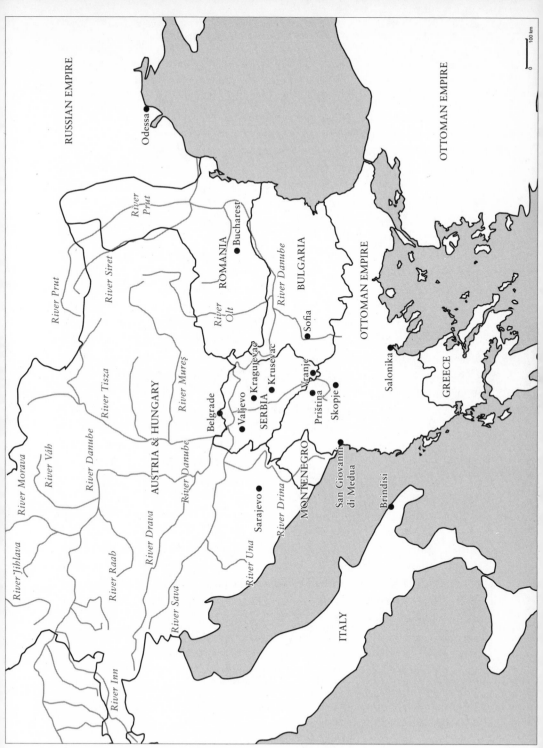

RUSSIAN EMPIRE

OTTOMAN EMPIRE

Odessa

River Prut

River Prut

River Siret

Bucharest

ROMANIA

River Danube

River Olt

BULGARIA

Sofia

River Tisza

AUSTRIA & HUNGARY

River Mureş

River Danube

OTTOMAN EMPIRE

Belgrade

Kragujevac

Kruševac

Vranje

Valjevo

SERBIA

Priština

Skopje

Salonika

GREECE

River Morava

River Váh

River Danube

River Drava

River Danube

MONTENEGRO

San Giovanni
di Medua

River Jihlava

River Raab

River Sava

River Una

River Drina

Sarajevo

Brindisi

River Inn

ITALY

100 km

0

The Balkans in 1914. (Thomas Bohm © Amberley)

Introduction and Background

This book grew from the discovery of a worn press cutting that confirmed Worthing's adoption of the French village of Richebourg l'Avoué in 1920. At that point, it was impossible to find anyone who had heard about the adoption, let alone the British League of Help for the Devastated Areas of France under whose auspices it was made. Realisation of the scale of trauma suffered by civilians in France and Belgium led to consideration of civilian experiences in Britain. This led to an awareness of the unacknowledged myriad of volunteers and charity workers without whom the war may not have been won and without whom the suffering would certainly have been far greater.

It is rare to find a book about the First World War that devotes more than a cursory couple of sentences to civilian volunteers. Even then, it is usually limited to references to female members of the Volunteer Aid Detachments, commonly known as VADs, with perhaps a slightly derogatory reference to knitting. In 1929, a Mrs C. S. Peel wrote about how large numbers of associations were set up and hospitals opened all over the country. She went on to say that a book might be written about all these activities which, as social life ceased to exist, absorbed the energies of people in all ranks of society. That book had not been written until now.

Men, women and children from all backgrounds devoted their time, energy and often money, to a range of schemes including, but not exclusively, making and sending comforts to soldiers and the sick and wounded, providing them with tobacco, cigarettes, eggs and vegetables, making medical supplies, collecting moss for dressings, entertaining and supporting convalescent soldiers and sailors, preparing parcels for Prisoners of War (POWs), giving hospitality to refugees, nursing, driving ambulances, and raising money.

Large numbers of middle- and upper-class women with time and energy to spare were among the first to offer their services. They were soon followed by mill and factory workers, who made dressings in their free time – or even arranged their shifts so that they could clean hospitals or help in hospital kitchens before or after a full day's shift. Men, who were in reserved occupations or who were too old or medically unfit for military service, ran committees, worked in hospital supply depots, drove ambulances, were on standby to help during air raids, knitted, invented, and played their part. William Wedgwood Benn wrote that such an outpouring of national energy had never been seen before. While everyone seemed to want to do something, and wanted to do it immediately, there was a lack of existing organisations to utilise all this energy. The remarkable thing was that order was brought to the maelstrom and that countless efficient and effective organisations took root.

It is difficult to give some kind of financial scale to what was achieved. The *Daily Chronicle* estimated that by February 1916, the British people had donated £29,000,000 to causes linked to the war. Most towns and cities did not collate records of how much was raised in their area.

The BBC's website shows that over five years, from 2010–14, the Children in Need Appeal raised nearly £226,000,000. Over the same period, the combined total raised by Comic Relief and Sport Relief was nearly £393,000,000. During this period, the UK population was around 63,700,000. Each appeal had the advantage of hours of global prime-time television coverage, countless articles, stunts, celebrity endorsements, and donations. By contrast, over almost five years – from 1914 to 1918 – The British Red Cross Society alone raised nearly £22,000,000. According to the Bank of England's Online Inflation Calculator, this equated to £1,120,000,000 in 2015. The British population was roughly 46,000,000 in 1914 and raised this money while enduring all the hardships and expense of being at war.

Fundraising underpinned everything. Incredibly detailed reports of who did what appeared regularly in newspapers alongside lists of donors and the size of their contribution. Newspaper reports often recorded the names of each and every performer and helper at the numerous fundraising events held in small communities and reported precisely how much each event raised. Publicising donations gave the donors a boost while encouraging other people to play their part. Relentless fundraising year in and year out, on a scale never previously achieved, was an endless challenge. As time passed, the cost of living rose and some people reached a point when they felt they could not go on responding to the numerous flag days, concerts, lecture tours, door-to-door collections, miles of pennies and appeals for money. Fundraisers themselves grew weary and short of funds.

Florence Upton, who wrote the popular series of children's books about a golliwog and two Dutch dolls, wanted to support the war effort but was not well enough to be an active volunteer. She therefore decided to sell the original dolls and golliwog, together with more than 300 of the original illustrations. They were sold at a special auction at Christies, in 1917, in aid of the Red Cross and raised more than £500. She was therefore able to achieve her goal of buying and equipping an ambulance for the Red Cross to send to France, emblazoned with the words 'Florence Upton and the golliwogs gave this ambulance'. The toys and illustrations were bought by Miss Faith Moore whose brother-in-law, Sir Arthur Lee, MP, gave Chequers to the nation for the use of the Prime Minister. Until a few years ago, the toys remained, somewhat bizarrely, in a glass case at Chequers to be enjoyed by nobody but politicians. They are now in the Bethnal Green Museum in London.

As well as money and time, people donated colossal quantities of goods. Donations, generally known as 'comforts', including new and second-hand clothes, footwear, fabrics, vegetables, fruit, eggs, cigarettes and tobacco, books, games, musical instruments and sports equipment poured in and added a vast amount to the value of the voluntary help provided.

With few exceptions, soldiers and sailors welcomed the efforts these workers made. Comforts helped them feel they were not forgotten, no matter where they were. Countless wounded and sick young men were grateful for the tender care they received at the hands of female medical staff. However, all this work also had a financial value, relieving the government of some of its responsibilities.

For the first year of the war, there was no overall system for providing comforts for servicemen. This resulted in widespread duplication and the waste of time, effort, and materials. Some groups, who began providing comforts, or more expensive items such as motor ambulances, showed a dramatic lack of understanding of circumstances in the warzone by trying to specify which regiment or group could benefit from their gift. Members of some well-established regiments were receiving a plentiful supply of parcels, while soldiers in some of the newer regiments got almost nothing.

Once it was clear that the war would not be over in just a few months, the Army Council acknowledged that there was an urgent need for an organised system. The scheme that was set up in October 1915 was led by the Director General of Voluntary Organisations (DGVO), Sir Edward Ward. It depended on a network of local organisations throughout Britain that made comforts and hospital requisites. Ward then arranged for them to be despatched to wherever they were needed most. He was an experienced manager and was keen to stress the need for different groups to co-operate with each other to maximise what they could achieve. He also recognised the importance of continuing the link between groups making comforts and soldiers from the same area.

There were eventually 276 local associations with a total of almost 2,000 groups and about 400,000 members. They provided more than 8,000,000 garments and surgical 'comforts'. Volunteers who worked regularly for one of the charities registered with the DGVO could apply for a badge after three months. Large numbers of these badges were issued and were highly valued by their holders.

Not wanting to disturb the existing systems that did work, the DGVO recognised Queen Mary's Needlework Guild, regimental associations, the Red Cross and the Order of St John of Jerusalem (Order of St John) as organisations that were outside his remit but with whom his staff would work closely. Both Queen Mary's Needlework Guild and the Joint Committee of the British Red Cross and the Order of St John registered their affiliated working parties to regulate and maximise productivity. Ward wrote to the Joint Committee to clarify that he would deal with combatants at the front and men in military hospitals; the Red Cross was to deal with auxiliary and voluntary hospitals. The Red Cross and the Order of St John also contributed help to military hospitals as requested by the DGVO.

At the same time that the scheme, and Ward's appointment, were announced, an appeal for help was made through the press. This urgent appeal was for mufflers and mittens, knitted according to the War Office pattern. The effect of the DGVO's work was soon apparent and he sent a representative to France to investigate how comforts were distributed and identify possible improvements. A very effective restructuring followed and a Comforts Pool was set up in each area of fighting. The DGVO sent requests for quantities of specific items to local associations and arranged for them to be despatched to the appropriate destination. Materials, including specially spun wool, were available through the War Office. Centralised buying significantly reduced costs, and the style and quality of all the articles local associations produced was standardised to reduce wastage. From 1916, the DGVO also provided comforts to Allied Armies including the French, Serbians, Russians, Italians, Romanians, and Americans.

At the end of the war, Ward wrote about the enormous positive impact all these comforts had on the morale of troops and recognised the 'noble self-sacrifice' shown by all the civilian volunteers.

The DGVO's remit was very specific and did not extend to charity fundraising or management in general and the Charity Commission only oversaw charities with permanent endowments. Before the war, there had been 35,000 charities in Britain. In 1916, the Government realised that the proliferation of charities could not continue without monitoring. It was, among other things, worried that the existing, informal, arrangements left charities vulnerable to mismanagement and fraud. It decided that all charities whose objects were linked in any way to the war would have to apply for registration. This was done under the powers of the War Charities Act 1916 and nearly 18,000 charities were subsequently registered. A further 6,492 charities, such as those aiming to provide comforts for a single POW, were exempt from registration. The Home Office clarified one area of confusion by stating that charities that were set up and managed by the proprietor or editor of a newspaper for the benefit of the forces or POWs were also exempt from registration.

Local councils were made responsible for registering charities, with the London County Council (LCC) taking a lead. The diligence and effectiveness with which they fulfilled this role varied considerably. Registered charities had to be run by a committee of not less than three people. They also had to keep proper minutes of their meetings and detailed, audited accounts, which were monitored by the registering authority. If charities did not comply with the regulations, they could be removed from the register.

Ward was initially concerned that the War Charities Act might have a negative impact on what his organisation could achieve and before the Act was finalised, he lobbied to have the organisations he worked with exempted from registration. He failed in his efforts and in reality, none of them had trouble getting registered – and registration did not affect the DGVO's work.

The office of the DGVO closed in April 1919, although some of the groups that had been providing goods for it continued a little longer, helping people in the devastated areas of France and Belgium and veterans or former POWs returning to this country. When war charities were wound up, they presented their final accounts to their regulating body and had to get the approval of the Charity Commission for how any residual funds would be allocated. The volunteers went back to try to pick up the threads of their previous lives.

We should recognise how much the recipients of charity have to 'pay' for what they receive by being gawped at and photographed. It is the same today but it is striking how widespread putting the recipients of charity on display was during and just after the war. Open days were held at hospitals, convalescent homes and homes for Belgian refugees to enable people to come and see how their money had been spent. It made them feel pleased with themselves, and probably more likely to give again if they were able to see neatly dressed children or rows of clean, carefully bandaged and duly appreciative recipients of their charity. The traumatised, shell-shocked, mutilated, and ungrateful were kept out of the way. Photographs of these visits, published in the newspapers, were regularly used as fundraising tools.

Whenever there is a disaster there are crowds of people who want to see what is going on. Battlefield tours were being offered by British and French organisations before the ink was dry on the Armistice. It is understandable that the bereaved wanted to see where their loved ones had died and to visit their graves. These people should not really be put together with the real tourists who went to France and Belgium in large numbers to look at the damage and to feel, with a shudder, what might have happened to their world had Germany invaded Britain. Some of these tourists were killed when they wandered into areas where shells had not yet been cleared. In the early days tourists had to put up with very rough conditions, after all, the local people had nowhere decent to live. We ought to remind ourselves how abhorrent it would have been to the French and Belgians to have these groups trampling over the ruins of their world and spectating as they took the first steps in rebuilding their lives.

When it came to raising money in Britain for reconstruction in France and Belgium, the organisers repeated time and time again that eyewitness testimony was invaluable, with photographs coming a close second. French mayors were often asked to supply pictures of their ruined communities to stir the consciences of the British, only to reply that nobody had taken any photographs. How different it is today when smartphones are clicking away at the first sign of a disaster, but it is equally repugnant for those whose lives have been turned upside down.

It is impossible to provide a comprehensive picture of the work done by all charities and civilian volunteers during and just after the First World War. This book focuses on British efforts but that is in no way to ignore or denigrate the enormous work done by volunteers from all over the world who worked both in their own countries and in the warzones. There were some remarkable collaborations between groups of different nationalities. The greatest of these may have been the feeding of Belgium led by Herbert Hoover. This book does refer to some of organisations from the British Colonies and Dominions, where they had a direct impact on the work of British organisations, but it would require another book to do them justice.

In recent years, we have come to recognise the damage that war does to service personnel and have begun to treat their invisible wounds. What we do not do adequately is to acknowledge that post-traumatic stress disorder does not affect only military personnel and members of the emergency services. Civilians living or helping in all the battle zones of the First World War suffered appallingly and many of them would have struggled, for the rest of their lives, to cope with their mental as well as physical scars. Some killed themselves, had breakdowns or found it impossible to fit back into 'normal' life. Their damage was not even dignified with the old term shell-shock.

At the end of the war, the Commander-in-Chief, Sir Douglas Haig, wrote to Sir Edward Ward expressing the gratitude he felt for all the civilian volunteers. He acknowledged that the volunteers, working to support the men on active service, had come from all classes and had sacrificed huge amounts of time, effort and money. He felt it would be impossible to praise them too highly or overestimate their achievements.

It is high time for us to recognise and appreciate what they achieved, compelled by duty, by love and, in some cases, by a sense of adventure.

'Guests of the Nation': Belgian Refugees in Britain

The First World War was a time of mass movements of refugees. It covered a vast area and involved civilians in a way no previous conflict had done. Between the summer of 1914 and the spring of 1915, more than 400,000 Germans from Eastern Prussia fled west to escape the Russian advance. At the same time, over 200,000 Jews headed for Vienna from Galicia, hoping the Austrians would protect them from the Russians. When Austria defeated the Serbian Army, almost a third of the Serbian population left their homes. An estimated 200,000 died during their journey to Corfu, Corsica and Tunisia. Some children were brought to Britain by the Serbian Relief Fund. More than 1,000,000 Armenians were deported from Turkey in 1915 and tens of thousands fled into Russia and parts of the Middle East. Poles, Latvians, Lithuanians, Ukrainians and Jews were all displaced by fighting between Germany, Austria and Russia, and some were exiled to the Russian interior by the Russians. It has been estimated that there were 6,000,000 wartime refugees in the Russian Empire. After the fall of Caporetto a huge number of Italians left the north of the country and became refugees in large Italian cities. France suffered a vast internal movement of people from the battle zone to the safer parts of the country.

While British people raised funds for Serbians, Armenians and other refugees, and doctors and nurses went to Serbia, Russia, Corsica and elsewhere to provide what help they could, it was a different movement of people that had the most serious impact on Britain. Within a few months of the German invasion, one in sixteen Belgians had left the country. Most of them had never seen a German, or even heard artillery fire, but fear is infectious. Rumours of German atrocities against civilians multiplied and the sight of pathetic columns of refugees followed by retreating Belgian and Allied soldiers spread panic. It was clear that being a civilian was no protection in this war. People from all backgrounds – rich city folk, miners and country people – were crowded together on the packed roads. Flemish- and French-speakers fled alongside each other in their determination to escape. Many headed for big towns such as Louvain, Liège or Brussels, only to find that they too would fall to the enemy. As the Germans did kill some civilians, deported others to Germany, pillaged and destroyed buildings, the panic snowballed out of control and refugees headed for the Channel ports or Holland in ever-increasing numbers. By the end of August, the civil authorities had to issue instructions to try to ensure that refugees would give way to retreating troops on the crowded roads. How effective these instructions were is open to speculation.

An appeal for help was made to the British Government in late August 1914. Winston Churchill was opposed to the idea of letting many Belgians come to Britain. He stated that we ought not to concern ourselves with merely helping Belgians avoid the unpleasant consequences of residing in Ghent and Bruges under German occupation. He believed there was no reason why the civil population of Belgium, not concerned in the defence of Antwerp, should come and live in England. He was in favour of bolstering Belgium's military resistance but felt it was not the time for charity. The Home Office underlined the fact that large numbers of refugees would be a serious source of embarrassment, and wanted to avoid taking responsibility for them. On 2 September, the Home Office said that if, for reasons of policy, Belgians were allowed to come into this country for refuge, they should be dealt with by charitable funds. However, they recognised that the Government was likely to have to give financial help at some point. Although it was said that helping the refugees would be a relatively inexpensive way of supporting an ally, the Government must have been horrified at the thought of yet another drain on its funds. On 9 September Herbert Samuel, later Home Secretary, announced in the Commons that the Government had offered 'the hospitality of the nation to these persecuted people'.

Transport was arranged for several thousand refugees to travel to Tilbury, Harwich and Folkestone. This was not enough and the exodus continued on such a vast scale that by 1 November three quarters of the population of the Yser area had left to escape bombardment. In the space of a few weeks, 1,500,000 Belgians left their homes and most ended up in France, Holland or Britain.

An enduring gulf opened up between the Belgians who had fled and those who had stayed in their homes. Criticism was not levelled at those whose homes had been burnt or bombed but at the wealthy bankers, industrialists and affluent upper classes who had left their fellow citizens to suffer under the invader. In January 1915 Edmond Picard wrote a diatribe mocking what he saw as the cowardice of the exiles and the opportunism of the businessmen whose flight to Britain was based on self-seeking financial opportunism. The Belgian authorities were keen to persuade people to stay put and the occupying Germans put up posters in the refugee camps in Holland to encourage key tradesmen – such as butchers, bakers and grocers – to return to Belgium. Some refugees feared that returning would seem like helping the enemy and felt staying in exile was a kind of resistance. In December 1914 the Ghent authorities voted unanimously to put a tax on people who had left their homes. This measure was resented by the exiles but was, understandably, more popular in Belgium. In January 1915 the Germans imposed this same measure throughout the country. Anyone who had spent more than two months out of the country since the start of the war and had not returned by March that year was subject to stringent taxation. Belgian troops were taxed, in absentia, at the highest level. Half the tax went to the government and half to the local authorities. If it was not paid, the tax could be recovered by the seizure of goods. A small number of the exiles did return to avoid the tax but it was not a major success; opposition was widespread. In some areas the Germans complained that the Belgian authorities were less than enthusiastic about collecting the tax.

There was a stark contrast between the resentment towards the exiles that was expressed in Belgium and the enthusiastic and sympathetic reaction with which the refuges from 'plucky little Belgium' were welcomed into almost every corner of Britain. Offers of hospitality also came from distant countries including Australia, the Argentine, Canada, the USA and South Africa. Chile offered to take 25,000 refugees. The Belgian authorities discouraged their people from accepting these offers and only a small number did so. In 1915 the Belgian authorities barred representatives of the Canadian Pacific Railway from entering the Uden refugee camp in Holland to persuade refugees to emigrate to Canada. The Belgian authorities were concerned that these potential hosts were not trying to help so much as wanting to attract workers that their economies needed. Potential hosts, such as Algeria, expressed their anger at the attitude of the Belgian authorities and turned to helping Belgians who had stayed at home instead. The host countries, primarily Britain and Holland, were left to cope alone.

Many of the refugees arrived with only the clothes they were wearing. Some did not even have shoes. The majority were ill-equipped, tired, hungry and traumatised. We now have a better understanding of the depth of trauma being a refugee creates. In 1914 there was only an ardent desire to meet the most immediate physical needs – recognition that enduring depression, anxiety, indecisiveness and apathy were the natural effects of their experiences was many decades in the future. One five-year-old refugee, called Emile, was so traumatised that he did not speak for many months after arriving in England. The refugees' stories brought some of the realities of war home to people in the host countries. It is clear that experiences became exaggerated as stories were told again and again, but they served a purpose, generating sympathy and increasing the refugees' acceptance in their host communities.

Once it became clear that there were more than a few thousand refugees Herbert Samuel, of the Local Government Board, sent Mr Reyntiens, and later Dr Farrar, to arrange for them to be shipped from Ostend to Britain. Dr Farrar's job was to check the refugees for infectious illnesses. These two men stayed in Ostend, working at full stretch until the Germans were close to the town, when they caught the last boat to leave. In 1915 the British Government decided to take some of the refugees who had fled to Holland through the Government Commission for Transportation of Belgians to the United Kingdom. Reyntiens and Farrar were sent to Flushing to select refugees who were healthy and who were likely to find work in Britain. Then they arranged to ship the selected refugees to Tilbury, using neutral shipping. They also arranged to transport the families of men who had already reached Britain. Their work finished in the latter part of 1915 due to diminishing applications for transport but the Consul General in Rotterdam still helped with transport for families working in Britain. By June 1915, 265,000 refugees had arrived. Some of the first arrivals had money to support themselves and took rooms in hotels or boarding houses. A *Times* journalist said that they carried with them the unmistakable air of Paris or Brussels and that you would not think they were refugees until you saw the expression on their faces. It was clear that some would only be able to support themselves for a short while.

On 14 October 1914 the Mayor of Dover received a telegram from the Local Government Board to say that about 5,000 refugees were due to reach Dover that evening and the mayor could expect co-operation from the military authorities. He was asked to do what he could to feed the refugees. A second telegram soon followed to point out that the military authorities could provide food but not milk. The Mayor was asked to secure milk and all possible shelter for the night.

Folkestone, in Kent, bore the brunt of the arrivals and nearly drowned under the deluge of traumatised, hungry and exhausted Belgians who arrived on its shore. In early September 1914 a report in *The Times* quoted people in Folkestone as wondering how they were to cope as the hotels and guesthouses were already full. Folkestone changed from being a typical seaside resort into a huge caravanserai. The report said most of the refugees were terribly poor and that the pier was perpetually thronged with people, as more and more boats arrived. The writer said London was full of soldiers and patriotism but Folkestone was dealing with the tragedy of people who had fled their homes. After the fall of Ostend, 26,000 refugees arrived in one week. Some had travelled for days with little food. They had crossed the Channel in every conceivable type of vessel. Few had any clothing, except the garments they were wearing. One white-haired old woman arrived in her carpet slippers, not having been able to grab her boots in her panic to escape. Their arrival brought home to British people, in dramatic form, the effect that war could have on a civilian population.

On 24 August 1914, when it was clear the influx of Belgians was not going to stop in the near future, the Belgian Committee for Refugees was set up from men who had already been helping. It was officially instituted at the French Protestant Church, Victoria Grove, by a Belgian Vice-Consul from London. The president was a Belgian who lived in Folkestone, who soon afterwards became Belgium's representative in the town. The committee was headed by the mayor, Sir Stephen Penfold. A few French-speaking boys from the Grammar School acted as guides to little groups of refugees on their way to the homes where they could be received. Interpreters for the Flemish-speaking refugees were harder to find.

The committee set to work to provide food and shelter. Some local churches undertook the responsibility of collecting food on certain days of the week; but the task was far beyond their powers. Volunteers in borrowed cars toured the town round the clock collecting food, which was taken to centres to be cooked and served. Hotel owners and shopkeepers helped generously, people gave or lent clothing, and beds were made in up in every available hall and school. A group of women met the boats and gave out food and hot drinks to the new arrivals. The Hon. Rose Hubbard and a group of women devoted themselves to coaxing a number of refugees who were so severely traumatised that they were scared to leave their boats to set foot on shore. Many of the older people were utterly prostrate after their journey, others were traumatised and some were sick. Giving appropriate help to these particularly vulnerable refugees was a priority; they were taken to the old Grammar School House, which was turned into a hospital and night hostel for about sixty people a night. A trained nurse and two VADs volunteered to take care of the patients and local doctors gave their help free of charge.

One of the first refugees to arrive in Folkestone was only a few hours old. Baby Elizabeth was born on the quay in Ostend, weighing only 2 lbs 4 oz. She then travelled to England in an open fishing boat. Amazingly,

Elizabeth not only survived but did well. Twenty-three refugee babies were born in a maternity home for refugees that was set up at 126 Sandgate Road and each baby and mother was given a complete set of clothes when they left the home.

It was soon apparent that dealing with the refugees was more than the local people could manage without help and the Local Government Board stepped in with financial support. It also sent Mr Basil Williams to Folkestone to run the organisation – but the bulk of the work continued to be done by volunteers. New arrivals were taken to St Michael's Hall for a meal, clothing and registration. The corporation later made the old Harvey Grammar School available. Various sub-committees were set up to manage clothing, food and finance.

Most of the refugees were sent up to London before being forwarded to hosts elsewhere in the country. Others, such as one group who went to Bexhill, were collected directly from Folkestone by their eager hosts. It was estimated that about 15,000 remained in Folkestone and they urgently needed warm clothing. An appeal was made through the press and a large quantity was quickly donated. However, the committee was determined to ensure that refugees who had been in social positions of influence in Belgium should not be offered second-hand garments, but should be enabled to buy new ones from local shops. In 1916 a tablet was put up in the Town Hall expressing the thanks of the Belgian refugees. Later, when many Belgian soldiers passed through Folkestone on leave, the committee also fed and cared for them.

Long-term homes had to be found for the refugees moving on from Folkestone. Before the war, there had been real concern that a civil war would break out in Ireland and the authorities in Ulster had prepared for the quick evacuation of large numbers of non-combatants. Women's organisations had quietly arranged that many of them would be put up in households in England. Lists of willing hosts were ready and the appropriate paperwork drawn up. Lady Lugard, who knew something of this preparation, thought the plans might be adapted for dealing with the Belgian refugees. The Ulster leaders quickly made their plans available and, largely thanks to the efforts of Mrs Alfred Lyttleton, the War Refugees Committee was promptly set up to put them into practice. It was a non-political organisation with Lord Hugh Cecil as chairman and Lord Gladstone as treasurer.

The War Refugees Committee started organising food, clothing transport and hospitality from an office in the Aldwych, in London, that lacked all furniture. General Building was owned by the General Accident Fire and Life Assurance Corporation, who made it available to the War Refugees Committee at a greatly reduced rent. A team led by Colonel Irving quickly took over a nearby empty skating rink. As well as housing a large luggage store, the rink held a nursery run by VADs, and a small shop selling basic necessities such as matches and shoelaces. The colonel allowed a Belgian barber to set up shop but later found that he was charging his customers while also taking an allowance from the authorities for serving them free of charge. There were large boards plastered with pictures of children who had been separated from their parents and a number of families were reunited in this way. Sadly, the rink was destroyed in a Zeppelin attack in October 1915.

When the War Refugees Committee made its first appeal for money and help, on 24 August 1914, there was an immediate and overwhelming response. On the first day alone 1,000 letters arrived offering hospitality to refugees. On just one day, 5,000 letters and 1,200 callers arrived at the War Refugees Committee's offices in the Aldwych. There was no precedent in British history for the work done by thousands of volunteers in those early days. Most of the volunteers were women, who gave their time and skills unreservedly. It has been said that if they had had more business experience before coming forward, some of the early confusion might have been avoided. However, this is a counsel of perfection and, given the circumstances and the deluge of refugees arriving in Britain, it is hard to overestimate their achievements. So many volunteers came forward that it was impossible to respond to all their letters or allocate them to appropriate tasks at the same time as dealing with the arrival of the refugees. This led to some frustration and disillusionment among people who had offered their services and who felt rebuffed when they were not immediately snapped up.

After giving their services for many months, some members of staff were no longer able to continue as volunteers and numbers dwindled. After an investigation into the situation in November 1915, the Local Government Board accepted a request from the War Refugees Committee that all the staff should be paid, albeit some at a nominal rate. It also agreed to cover the costs of administration. The Local Government Board also paid the rent and rates for the headquarters in the Aldwych, from 1916.

The scale of the organisation was such that a worldwide appeal was made for clothes and help. The War Refugees Committee set up a clothing depot, run by Lady Emmett, and by the end of March 1915 they had already given out nearly 1,000,000 garments. Herbert Samuel arranged for the Post Office and railway companies to hand over large amounts of unclaimed clothing. As the war progressed and prices rose, the government had to provide more and more of the funding for buying new clothes and boots. Every effort was made to buy goods at reasonable prices and the officer in charge regularly visited manufacturers to negotiate the best deals. The committee was careful to ensure that refugees did not claim too many garments and any application had to be countersigned by the secretary of a local committee. When the depot eventually closed, the remaining stock was sold by the Surplus Government Property Disposal Board and the funds were credited to the government account. Clothes that had been donated, rather than bought, were sent to Belgium for repatriated refugees.

Although offers of accommodation for individual families came from all over the country, the immediate need was for large-scale accommodation – primarily in London. The first offer of space for a hostel came when the Borough of Camberwell made the Dulwich Baths available to house 100 refugees. Another emergency hostel was set up in an empty shirt factory near Victoria Station. This was lent by the Army and Navy Stores and was clean but empty. In less than twenty-four hours it was ready to welcome the first batch of 250 refugees. A refuge at Hackney Wick was used as an observation ward for cases who were thought to have been in contact with infectious diseases and another was opened in Marylebone for those requiring special observation and treatment. The Salvation Army stepped forward to offer beds in its shelters, the London County Council lent Carrington House in Deptford and the *Morning Post* newspaper took refugees at Embankment House. Separate hostels for Jewish refugees were opened in Poland Street and the Manchester Hotel, where a kosher diet could be provided.

In October 1914 two enormous hostels were opened in London, the first at Alexandra Palace and the other at Earl's Court. The Local Government Board delegated running these hostels to the Metropolitan Asylums Board. When Alexandra Palace was turned into an emergency hostel, it could accommodate 5,000 people. Simply getting, erecting and making up this number of beds was an extraordinary feat; by September 1914 it had 1,000. Men were accommodated in the skating rink and the women and children were put in rooms on the first floor. The matron and her staff slept in the same area. The huge central hall was used as the dining room, where a weekly menu of stodgy, simple dishes was prepared by a Belgian cook. Recreation rooms were also provided and the men had a smoking and reading room in the palm house. The women were allowed to use the Venetian Garden. The refugees were allowed out of the grounds as long as they were back in the building for meals and at night.

When the groups of refugees arrived, hundreds of North Londoners turned out to welcome them with gifts and comforts. There is no doubt that curiosity also spurred many of the crowd to go to have a look at the new arrivals. There were many unaccompanied children who were allowed to play in the playground while English children watched them from beyond the railings. An appeal for clothing brought in 4 tons of donations. One headmaster was amazed that the day after he appealed to his pupils to try to bring in one garment each, they arrived with armfuls of clothing, much of which was almost new. The authorities also appealed, successfully, for tobacco, cigarettes and toys.

Earl's Court was run by Elizabeth Macdonald (née Morgan) and Dr Bruce, Medical Superintendent of the Western Hospital, Fulham. Earl's Court was an important exhibition centre; the last exhibition closed on a Wednesday evening and the first 400 refugees were accommodated there just twenty-four hours later. On the Sunday night, more than 1,700 people slept there with another 500 due the following evening. The refugees had to bathe in the nearby public baths, and one of the exhibition rooms was turned into a vast dining room with row upon row of tables. A hospital was set up in the oak-panelled Garden Room. It was carefully arranged with fresh muslin curtains, soft throws on the beds, with fresh flowers on the tables to add a splash of colour. Many of the patients were young children, some of whom sat up in their cots crying inconsolably in their strange surroundings. There was another ward for men. Some staff from the Metropolitan Asylums Board's hospitals volunteered to help at Earl's Court in their spare time. There were three resident doctors and a team of skilled nurses. Within the complex, there were also a crèche, a dispensary, a chapel with resident priests, schools, a large concert hall and, later on, a cinema. Dormitories were set up for women and children in the large halls and tier upon tier of rows of beds was set up for male refugees in the great amphitheatre. An appeal was made for good and useful clothing. They also asked for toys for the children but stressed the need for donations to be sent carriage paid.

Later in the war, Earl's Court housed many refugees who were unable to earn a living because they were unskilled, or sick. In order that they should have something to do, the authorities set up a number of workshops, which produced a range of articles such as army huts, shell cases, and military clothing. They also built cubicles for married women within the main buildings and in many of the large huts that dotted the grounds.

After the Armistice, Earl's Court again came into its own as a temporary shelter for many of the Belgians who were making their way home. It finally closed in July 1919. A post-war report described it as a Belgian village in miniature. An estimated 100,000 refugees passed through its doors.

Most refugees spent only a short time in these London hostels before being forwarded to hosts elsewhere in the country. However, those refugees who could not settle in their host area, or who caused problems, could be sent back to London. They were generally allocated to a new area but some troublemakers were kept in London. Most refuges closed in 1915 or 1916 but Poland Street and Earl's Court were retained until 1920. Mrs Alfred Lyttleton and Mrs Gilbert Samuel were in charge of allocating refugees to hosts. They also dealt with the delicate task of reallocating refugees when placement failed. The Belgian Army had a recruiting office in the same building and there was also a Labour Exchange where the Belgians had to register. There were notices in Flemish advertising vacancies, flats to rent, and furniture for hire. Staff operated a poste restante system for refugees.

In October 1914, Herbert Samuel decided that there should be a central register of refugees. The registration was carried out under the registrar, General Sir Bernard Mallett. The information collected included data about Belgian men of military age, which was passed to the Belgian authorities, and classified the refugees by age, gender and trade or profession. When this index was first opened to refugees seeking friends and relatives they had 20,000 letters of enquiry in one day. Volunteers carried out up to 4,000 searches a week. By June 1915, 265,000 Belgian refugees had arrived in Britain.

The War Refugees Committee rented and furnished some flats in London. The flats were then let to working refugees, who contributed towards their costs. At one point 1,200 refugees were housed in 210 flats. This system was popular with refugees who were then able to manage their own lives. When the refugees were repatriated in 1919, the furniture was sold and the money credited to the government account.

Although the majority of refugees were dispersed around the country, some remained in London. The War Refugees Committee believed the central refuges, including those at Earl's Court and Alexandra Palace, were not suitable for 'persons of the better class' and took hotel and boarding house accommodation for them until suitable hosts could be found. Private hostels provided some long-term accommodation and the War Refugees Committee set up others to provide temporary accommodation that was cheaper than hotels.

An appeal was made for further private hospitality in 1915, but offers fell short of those needed. The War Refugees Committee was then authorised to billet groups of refugees in seaside resorts, paying 10s per head per week. Medical costs were also met. Several resorts in Devon, North Wales and Blackpool took refugees. This scheme was a boon to boarding house keepers, but had its problems. There was little industry and therefore few employment opportunities in seaside resorts. Of the 2,090 refugees in Blackpool only 200 found work. A club and reading room helped alleviate the boredom of inactivity but it remained a serious issue. Some of the landladies were kind, but others were less than sympathetic to their new type of guest. One landlady thought a pound of meat a day was enough between nine refugees. Ladies of the local committee had to sort out this type of problem. After a while, the subsistence payments were raised to 11s a week. Further problems arose when different classes of refugee were put in the same boarding house. About sixty refugees a week changed accommodation.

Many of the children had fun, running free at the seaside, until two schools were set aside for their use. One was run by Flemish nuns and the other was secular. About twenty middle-class children were offered free places at a local secondary school. As is common among refugees, the children learnt English far more quickly than their parents did. When they were asked to compare schools in Belgium and in England, they showed an enthusiasm for sport and for the less rigid attitude of their English teachers. One boy concluded that Belgian schools gave a better theoretical education but that English schools gave a better preparation for later life. Many of the essays reflected how homesick the writers were.

Organisers soon found that class distinctions in Belgium were possibly even more rigid than in England. From the outset, there was a marked difference in the treatment of the Flemish-speaking peasant or working class refugees and those who were predominantly French-speaking and from a higher class. It was also apparent that host families wanted guests who came from the same class as they did. Local committees quickly found that it reduced problems in properties where groups of refugees were billeted together if they were all from a similar background.

The committee found that some of the middle class refugees were not only penniless but were much less likely than their working class compatriots to find employment. To meet their needs, flats in model developments in Battersea and Brixton were rented by the War Refugees Committee. The rents were from 5s 6d to 15s 6d a week. They were furnished at a cost of about £20 per flat and the furniture was then rented to the refugees at a rate that would cover the costs over nine months. Some of the refugees could not afford to pay for the hire of the furniture. They were given enough help to let them keep their families together and to 'maintain in exile the decency and privacy of home life'. About 1,100 people were housed under this scheme in London.

Lady Lugard, one of the people behind the establishment of the War Refugees Committee, was so concerned that differences should be maintained, that she founded eleven hostels or large boarding houses for better class refugees, members of the aristocracy and those 'who had occupied superior positions in Belgium'. They were run like private hotels. She also placed selected refugees in a number of large furnished houses in London's West End and was dedicated to fundraising for her guests throughout the war. More than 4,000 refugees were supported in this way. The Duchess of Somerset's Hostels Committee did comparable work on a smaller scale. They were helped by grants from the Local Government Board, first through the War Refugees Committee and later with direct payments. As donations fell, grants increased. In making grants, the War Refugees Committee stipulated that every practicable step should be taken to ensure that every refugee from the hostels who could work was in paid employment. Working refugees and those with private resources were expected to make a reasonable contribution towards their maintenance. Inspectors were satisfied that these homes and hostels were economically administered and that they 'were occupied by persons for whom no other form of assistance was appropriate'. Even at the Earl's Court Refuge, the authorities maintained the differences in how the different classes were treated.

Baron and Baroness Anatole Von Hügel, and some of their friends, set up the Hügel Homes in Cambridge. They took full responsibility for sixty people in five homes and gave temporary hospitality to forty others. They took great care to ensure they only housed people with similar political, religious and class backgrounds together. The organisation was disbanded in the summer of 1918, as they only had one family left, which was passed to the Borough Committee with the balance of funds.

Herbert Samuel was determined to maintain the voluntary nature of the War Refugees Committee's work, as far as possible, but did recognise that the Government had to step in with financial support. The Government did provide help, but wanted its role to be kept as quiet as possible so that the essential level of volunteer assistance would not diminish. Help generally consisted of *per capita* grants to local committees who were struggling to support their refugees. In April 1916 a committee, chaired by the Duke of Norfolk, was set up to review the situation. It considered the measures that had been adopted in Britain for the assistance and relief of refugees. The committee paid tribute to the work that had been done but felt the time had arrived for the Government to take on the main burden of financial help. In addition, it wanted there to be full governmental control of the War Refugees Committee and Sir Basil Peto became the unpaid Chief Commissioner.

Once it was clear that large numbers of Belgians were arriving in Britain, an appeal was put out to councils throughout the country asking them to set up local committees to organise hospitality for refugees. Over 2,000 local committees were set up with at least 303 refugee committees in Northamptonshire alone. Communities that took in Belgians were also able to congratulate themselves on their attitudes and efforts.

Scots were eager to show they could do as well as the English in opening their doors to refugees. All over the place, competition with neighbouring communities was an important factor in the scale of efforts. The Mayor of Alresford, in Hampshire, made a speech encouraging people to give by insisting that people in a community a few miles away had been more generous and that they had to catch up – the honour of the village was at stake. Most committees had men in the key posts of chairman, treasurer and secretary but they were supported by eager and efficient groups of women who prepared the accommodation, getting houses cleaned, decorated and furnished in a remarkably short time. They also arranged with local tradespeople to supply specific foodstuffs and fuel to the refugees at reduced prices.

Once they had settled in some of the refugees chafed at the restrictions placed on where they could shop, and even what they could buy, but after the first flush of enthusiasm the level of donations dropped and many committees struggled to maintain the level of support that the refugees had come to expect. Some refugees were extravagant in the level of maintenance they required but their wishes were met more often than not. One family, who were living in a large, well-furnished house, demanded a piano. It was provided.

A large group of Flemish refugees, from the poorest parts of Antwerp and Ostend, were crowded into awful conditions in Fulham. The War Refugees Committee investigated the situation and was so shocked that it opened a branch in Fulham, under the leadership of Miss Newton who was very experienced at working with refugees. Some families received cash grants and others were placed in furnished flats. Prizes for the best kept houses and flats were presented at an award ceremony and standards steadily improved.

Help was not only arranged by local authorities and a number of professional groups undertook to help their Belgian refugee counterparts. Such funds included the Belgian Doctors' and Pharmacists'èè Relief Fund, the Belgian Journalists' Emergency Fund and the Belgian Lawyers' Aid Fund.

***

Cambridge had three separate committees. The Borough of Cambridge initially offered to take 100 refugees. In total, they cared for 262, with three births and one death. They refused to take any Belgian men of military age unless they had been discharged from military service. The men were all inspected on arrival to see whether they should be fighting. The committee provided courses in intensive horticulture on ground that had been lent by Girton College. The teacher was Belgian.

The Belgian Hospitality Committee in Cambridge acted with great understanding and imagination and got two of its members, Margaret

Clapham and Ethel B. Clarke, to prepare a guidance booklet to help the refugees settle into their new homes. It was called *Le Mènage Belge en Angleterre* and the text was in English, French and Flemish. The introduction explained that the booklet was designed to help the Belgians living in England find the best bargains when shopping, explained essential matters for their wellbeing and how to conform to the traditions and tastes of England. There were translations of weights and measures, hints for housekeepers and recipes that, the authors insisted, took increasing food costs and the shortage of saucepans into consideration. There were simple recipes for dishes some of whose names, such as Toad in the Hole or Cottage Pie, must have bewildered the Belgians. Some of the recipes were designed for using left over food. The writers explained which cuts of meat were best for specific dishes, assured the Belgians that Colonial meat was as good as British, and listed the cheapest types of fish. Translations of household goods, right down to hearthstone and black lead for stoves were given, beside guidance on where to buy a range of essentials including muffs, shoelaces, drapery, kitchen utensils, and sanitary towels. It is a shame that a comparable booklet was not available in every community.

There was also a County of Cambridge Committee that placed 338 refugees in forty-two villages. The committee paid for the maintenance of those who were housed in Caxton Workhouse and the villagers paid for the rest. For the last two years of the war, grants from the War Refugees Committee were essential for the continued support of these refugees. A small colony was formed at Littleport. Most of the members were peasants and, before long, they had become self-supporting.

The Vice Chancellor of the University rather rashly offered hospitality to the entire University of Louvain and set up a sub-committee to make sure enough accommodation was available and made an appeal for funds. They were also worried about Liège University but decided to concentrate on Louvain first. Understandably, they had trouble contacting the Rector of Louvain University. When they were eventually able to transmit their offer, the rector replied that conditions made it impossible to transfer the entire university. Cambridge then decided to invite professors and students from the four Belgian universities of Louvain, Liège, Ghent and Brussels to come to study in Cambridge. A few professors from Louvain arrived and others followed as word of Cambridge's support spread. Financial help came in from former students. It proved impossible to arrange a course of lectures that would be officially recognised by any single university so it was decided to have lectures that combined, as far as possible, instruction on the lines of Belgian universities with the individual requirements of students.

Attendance was free of charge. Lectures were offered in philosophy, letters, law, commerce, medicine, natural sciences, engineering and agriculture. Each faculty had several professors, one of whom acted as secretary. Engineering was most popular. English lessons were also provided. Twenty-seven Belgian students who were declared fit to fight by a local doctor soon left the town.

When they arrived in Cambridge each student was met at the station by an undergraduate and taken to the committee room to have his name, age, university, and faculty recorded. Complete hospitality was offered to those who needed it. Some were housed in accommodation left by British students who had joined the forces. Emmanuel and Christ's College offered, and partly paid for, a few sets of lodgings, and Kings and St Catherine's took two or three students each, for a very small payment. Three women from the University of Liège were given full hospitality at Girton. Efforts were made to lodge friends together. There were great difficulties between landladies and students due to the lack of a shared language, differences in customs and taste in food but, with goodwill on both sides and help from the university, the problems were overcome. Each student was given weekly 'pocket money' by the university. Housing Belgian professors, their families and their servants in suitable conditions was more challenging and expensive for the hosts. Records show that one student and one maid, both suffering from incurable diseases, were sent back to friends in Belgium, which seems rather harsh.

A private house was opened as Le Vestaire Belge, where volunteers collected and distributed clothes. Later, when they ran short of clothes, they appealed to East Coast towns in prohibited areas (who did not have refugees) and to American universities for help. The response, especially from America, was very generous and they had to take over a room in the Archaeological Museum as a sorting depot and recruit six extra helpers. Garments that were not considered suitable for the Belgians in Cambridge were sent to The Serbian Relief Fund, another society for the help of Serbians, The French Wounded Emergency Fund, Italian Alpine Troops, and the Belgian Hospital at Chartreuse de Neuville in the Pas de Calais. There was clearly a perceived hierarchy of worthiness among refugee organisations.

At the end of the academic year, some professors left to take offers of work from other universities, some students decided to give up their studies and get jobs and a few enlisted in the Belgian Army. The offer of hospitality stayed but the number of refugees dropped significantly. However, 220 students and forty families had been helped.

* * *

On one occasion, twenty-two Dutch fishing boats arrived in Lowestoft laden with Belgian refugees. When the refugees had all been taken ashore, officials found that they had left thirty-eight dogs, cats and rabbits behind on the boats. The RSPCA had to be called to take care of the animals.

As soon as the first appeals for help were made, groups of women in Manchester started making clothes for refugees. In late August 1914 the Consul General in London asked the Belgian consul in Manchester if the town could take some refugees. A local committee was immediately set up. When the first group of forty-four refugees, mostly from the Aerschott area, arrived in September, thousands of Mancunians lined the route from the station to the town hall. The refugees were greeted by the mayor, then registered, given refreshments and seen by a doctor before being sent to the Tame Street Refuge in Ancoats for their first night. They went to their individual billets the following morning. From then until the middle of October, new groups arrived every five days. By early November, there were 1,400 refugees in Manchester. Apart from providing tens of thousands of garments, the committee also gave wool to 300 Belgian women to knit mufflers and socks for Belgian soldiers. Clothes were not issued until the organisers had checked that they were really needed. A Visiting Committee of ladies was set up and they visited the refugees regularly to identify any problems and try to resolve them. Many of the refugees quickly found work, impressing their hosts with their adaptability. The committee provided classes for refugees who wanted to learn English, only to find that many of those who would have liked to attend could not do so because of the long hours they worked.

Once the people of Hove had agreed to look after some refugees, they expected to be sent a sizable group of women and children. The refugees were to go to a temporary hostel in nearby Portslade before being dispersed to individual hosts. The first group arrived on 3 September 1914 and consisted, to the disappointment of the organisers, of three women, two men and only one child, all Russian Jews from Antwerp. A larger group arrived the following day but instead of being just women and children, consisted of families, which later swelled as further relatives arrived. A family could consist of ten people, who insisted that they should not be separated. Within a few weeks, 230 people in sixty-nine family groups had passed through the hostel. They were followed by a number of wounded Belgian soldiers who were treated in local hospitals. For a while all went well but, over time, individual families felt the strain of providing extended hospitality and the committee gradually took on the full responsibility. Hove Council played its part by remitting the rates and the local gas company took a third off its usual price when the customers were refugees. One of the volunteers in Hove who was particularly active in her support of the Belgian refugees was Miss Grimwood. In a report in 1916, when desperate appeals were being made for help for the Serbians, she wrote that although there might be other countries whose sufferings appealed to the British people more than those of Belgium, their claim for help could never be as great. The Hove Committee ran a clothing depot at 4 Adelaide Crescent, set up a school for Belgian children and organised English classes for adults. The committee ran two hostels and three clubs. Over the course of the war, they spent nearly £14,000 supporting their refugees, about half of which was raised locally, with the remainder coming from the War Refugees Committee. Early refugees included a group of nuns from Malines who ran a school for refugee children until, one by one, they were called back to their Mother House in Belgium.

During the war there was a craze for collecting soldiers' buttons. In Croydon, one of the refugees apparently made a nice speech about how he had lost everything except his uniform. He then presented one of the volunteers, Mrs Goodsir, with two buttons from his tunic as a symbol of his gratitude for how he had been treated in Croydon. She had them gilded and made into a brooch. She was very proud of this brooch, until she found that the Belgian had cut the buttons off the tunic of one of his compatriots who was very ill in hospital.

Even small towns like Sedbergh, near Kendal, were keen to welcome refugees to their community, though one Belgian couple found the area far too quiet for their taste and asked to be sent back to London. The local committee was keen from the outset that the refugees should get jobs. One man quickly found work in Mr Edmondson's bakery. However, one young couple would not accept any of the jobs they were offered. The man had been a diamond cutter in Antwerp and was not willing to adapt to another trade. The committee set £15 aside to be given to the refugees when they were repatriated.

The Ilford Belgian Refugee Committee found that offers of hospitality were hard to come by. They had plenty of offers to take children but it was families who needed accommodation. Luckily, Valentine's Mansion was made available to them at a cost of £40, including the electricity supply. The first group of refugees arrived on 10 November 1914 and consisted of nine men, eight women and four children, who were said to be of a class similar to the Ilford people. Refugees normally arrived in the early hours of the morning and were met at the mansion with food and drink, but no speeches (apart from the first group). Valentine's Mansion was run by a volunteer housekeeper, Mrs Sarah Roper, who had formerly been the Matron of Christ's Hospital. She was very popular with the refugees. It was not only the refugees' immediate physical needs that were catered for. On four evenings a week friends were allowed to visit to play games and sing. However, the lack of privacy in the mansion was an ordeal for many of the residents, as must have been the Saturday afternoons when members of the Ilford Belgian Refugee Committee could visit to inspect the mansion and, undoubtedly, the refugees. Other visitors had to get a ticket from a member of the committee. The local Roman Catholic Church offered confession in both French and Flemish. Many of the women got jobs in shops in central London and the men in munitions factories. Local postal workers offered support to refugee postal workers, each of whom had a state pension of about 100 francs a month. This group was gradually dispersed around Britain. On 22 March 1918, the council announced that it wanted the mansion back and the remaining refugees had to move elsewhere. Valentine's Mansion then became a convalescent home for wounded soldiers. A few of the refugees remained in Ilford after the end of the war.

Refugees sent to the Derbyshire town of Matlock Bath came in for a nasty shock. They were just sitting down to breakfast on their first morning in town when there was a series of blasts. They were so traumatised by their recent experiences in Belgium that each of them dived under the breakfast table to take cover. The blasts were a regular event at the local quarry but must have been a continuing ordeal for some of the refugees.

In 1917 the Local Government Board wrote to the secretaries of local refugee committees, asking them to try to restrict the amount that refugees travelled by train. This was both to reduce demand on the network and to ensure that they should not leave their locality unless they had the means to provide for themselves at their destination. New regulations also stated that refugees earning more than £130 would have to pay income tax. However, the Government recognised the problem caused by the German tax on absentee Belgians and said that this tax could be deducted from the income tax any Belgian was liable to pay in Britain.

Brandreth House, in Sheffield, was a substantial property that was carefully prepared to house refugees. There was disappointment when the owner, Mr Bramley, had to report to the committee that two families who had been earmarked for Brandreth House had refused to leave Folkestone. However, someone heard of a party of twelve Belgians in need of accommodation and they were invited to go to Sheffield. The group consisted of a couple with their two sons, the gentleman's uncle and sister-in-law, two ladies and five other boys. It perhaps illustrates the grandeur of Brandreth House that among the supplies that were arranged was coke dust for the carriage drive. Before long, there were problems when the committee felt that the allowances given to the Belgians must be too high as they had erected chestnut fencing around the garden to increase their privacy. The ladies of the party frequently issued demands for new kitchen equipment, for the Chesterfield to be reupholstered, for a piano and, regularly, for more blankets. The committee made every effort to meet these demands. The Belgians also wanted a charwoman but none of the Belgians in the area was willing to work for them. Further problems arose when the committee asked them to agree that another family could move in and the initial group threatened to leave if they were forced to share.

When homes were needed for refugees in York nine families were billeted in houses in the village at New Earswick that Joseph Rowntree had built for workers at his chocolate factory. The refugees were not charged any rent and the houses were furnished for them. The firm set up a fund to help support the families.

The people of Rhyl had been planning the reception of their first refugees for days. A house had been set up as a home and was besieged with enquirers wanting to learn when the refugees would arrive. At the appointed time at least 200 people gathered at the railway station with thousands more along the High Street. All the elementary schoolchildren were there with banners and flags and had even started afternoon school early so they could be free to attend. Unfortunately, the refugees were delayed and arrived rather late from Liverpool. The group of twenty-two, from Aerschot, was given a warm welcome and taken to the Home in a charabanc decorated with Belgian flags. Welcome Home had been written on the glass in front of the driver. Each of the children was given a bag of sweets tied with red, white and blue ribbons. At the top of the High Street, the newly formed North Wales 'Pals' Brigade, who were training in Rhyl, had lined up at attention. The party was assembled on the steps of the home for a photograph. The chairman of the local committee, Cllr F. Phillips, was too choked with emotion to deliver his speech so he just gave three cheers for the Belgians.

In September 1914 the first group of Belgian refugees was taken to Letchworth. They were all Flemish speaking and unable to understand either French or English. Luckily, help was to hand in the form of the local Catholic priest, Dr Adrian Fortescue, who spoke some Flemish and a local boy scout, Frans Bogaert, who had been born in Antwerp. The refugees were given a warm welcome, not a word of which they understood. They were given coffee, cakes and fresh clothes at the Spirella factory before being taken to their billets. The reception was arranged by the Spirella Needlework Guild. The refugees soon settled in but there was some resentment over the rumour that they were taking jobs in local factories at the expense of Letchworth's unemployed men. Jacques Kryn was a diamond merchant. His brother

Georges, and Raoul Lahy who arrived with them, were engineers. After they reached Letchworth in 1914 they set up a munitions factory, later building parts of tanks, bridges and other military equipment as well. Almost all of the workers were Belgians. By the end of August 1916 Belgians made up a quarter of the town's population. The Belgians were given a warm welcome, notwithstanding issues caused by a few of them cycling on the wrong side of the road, or getting drunk from time to time. A more serious issue arose when many of the Belgians failed to adhere to the blackout regulations that were imposed in late 1915 due to the Zeppelin raids; a large number were fined for breaking the regulations, some of them several times Two thousand refugees were too many for the town to house. Some of them were crammed in, two or three families at a time, into small cottages. Others had to live in the empty Hayes Reynolds factory and in shops. Hitchin Rural District Council eventually got a loan from the Local Government Board to build 100 houses. The authorities had to change their plans over where to build the first group of houses when local people complained that having the Belgians there would reduce the value of their own houses. The area came to be known as Little Belgium. Some of the Letchworth shopkeepers tried to employ French-speaking shop assistants, or even to learn some French and cafes printed bilingual menus. This was well-intentioned but it is not clear how many of the refugees were French-speaking. After the war ended a few of the Belgians remained in Letchworth. Kryn & Lahy went into voluntary liquidation in 1927 but was saved when it was bought by George Cohen Sons & Co. Ltd. Munitions were produced there during the Second World War.

In Hull, as elsewhere, some refugees were taken into private homes. They were generally treated as guests and included in their hosts' social lives. There was anger when the whole East Coast was made into a restricted area, meaning that refugees could no longer be sent there. Groups whose energy and commitment had been stimulated by the early arrivals did not let their efforts go to waste and continued to raise money, which they sent to committees further inland. Hull, for example, took responsibility for refugees in York, Knaresborough, Ilkley and Harrogate in Yorkshire as well as some in Cumbria and Kent.

Refugees in Rushton, in Northamptonshire, included a wounded soldier who had been a slipper-maker before the war. He was amused to discover that when he arrived in Britain he had been registered as a builder. When refugees arrived in Rushton they were taken to their new home and given a meal of hot Bovril, bread, butter and cakes. From then on, their meals were to be bread and butter with café au lait for breakfast and supper and soup, meat and vegetables for dinner.

Blackburn's Belgian Relief Sub-Committee was formed in September 1914, in conjunction with the Blackburn War Relief Committee but local people had already sent more than £1,700 to the National Belgian Fund. Refugees were housed in vacant cottages and terraced houses and up to eighty-seven were cared for at a time. The committee was pleased to accept Mrs Robinson's donation of Ivy Bank, a large house on West Park Road, which was used to house refugees when they first arrived in Blackburn until they could be distributed to other houses. As well as being used as a central distribution centre, it was used as a hostel to house Belgian soldiers on leave. One other notable figure was Mr Joseph Dugdale, of Claremont, who offered the use of Oxendale Hall, Osbaldeston, to the committee. Oxendale Hall was furnished throughout and Mr Dugdale offered to cover the maintenance costs. Several local churches allowed their parish rooms to be used to house groups of refugees. Surprisingly, the refugees who arrived in Blackburn included one couple, Mr and Mrs Piens from Brussels who already knew a local resident. They had entertained Mr G. A. Yates a few years earlier, when he had visited Brussels on business. Over time, many of the refugees got jobs, often in local munitions works, and became self-sufficient. There was therefore less call for support from the local committee. Traders in Blackburn were also willing to help the Belgian Refugees and supplied them with food and other necessary goods at reduced prices. A sub-committee was set up to support Belgian POWs; twelve of them were adopted by private individuals on the recommendation of the London Committee. It was intended that food parcels and other such necessities would be sent to the Belgian POWs on a fortnightly basis; this fund ceased in 1917 owing to new regulations issued by the London Committee. The Blackburn Committee frequently received offers of accommodation and funding from the public in the opening years of the war. In July 1915 the children of Audley Range Council School raised 18s for the local Belgian refugees. Mr Oliver also made a donation of a £140 towards the Belgian Fund, having raised the money through two performances by the Amateur Dramatics Company. Blackburn Rovers Football Club gave a donation of £150. The committee also received donations of clothing and furniture. Many of the Belgian children attended the local schools while six Belgian girls were educated at Notre Dame Convent, as a gift from the Sisters, and three boys received free education at Blackburn Grammar School. A Fund for the Repatriation of Belgian Refugees was also set up in Blackburn. Its aim was to help refugees with gifts of money or goods to ease their return to Belgium. All refugees leaving Blackburn to go home were also given warm clothing and boots. The money needed to pay for these gifts was raised by three ladies: Mrs Henry, Mrs Thom and Miss

Dugdale, in 1916. The Repatriation Fund ran until March 1919, when the last of the Belgian refuges left Blackburn.

Trouble arose in Fulham in London in 1916. Local people's sympathy for the refugees had worn a bit thin and tension grew when British men were being conscripted to fight a war on the Continent while some Belgian men were content to earn a good wage in Britain. Rumours began to circulate that Belgians were taking jobs left by British men who had been called up. On Sunday 21 May there was an argument in the street. The trouble escalated when a crowd gathered, throwing insults, stones, and bottles at anyone thought to be Belgian. The police had to be called to restore calm. For a while, there was no further trouble but there was another clash in September. A rumour spread that there were Germans inside a club for Belgians and an angry crowd gathered outside. Police were again called on to disperse the crowd.

One group of women in Chart Sutton, in Kent, sent off a generous parcel of clothes to the Commission for Relief in Belgium in December 1914. However, they asked that the clothes should be forwarded to Belgians who had stayed in Belgium or to refugees in Holland as they felt that those in England were being well cared for. The clothes had been made by the Ladies' Work Party, the Girls Guild of Help and the girls of the local National School. The letter they received from J. W. Dickson thanking them for their generosity emphasised the needs of Belgians in the camps in Holland. It went on to add that a recent government embargo had stopped them sending any second-hand clothes to Belgium, so they would forward the parcel to refugees in the Dutch camps.

* * *

Scotland took more than 18,000 refugees. Glasgow alone housed over 8,000. The Glasgow Corporation Belgian Refugees Committee, under the City Assessor Alexander Walker, acted as the central authority for receiving and distributing refugees throughout Scotland. He was fully occupied with this work for several years. The task was complicated by the fact that much of Scotland was a prohibited area. The committee raised more than £191,000 for the refugees, and local committees in the rest of Scotland raised another £170,000. The Local Government Board repaid Glasgow for transporting refugees and for telephone, telegraph, and postal expenses and contributed to the cost of fundraising meetings. It also bore the cost of supporting the wives of Belgian soldiers resident in Scotland, maintaining the sick and insane in institutions and the treatment of consumptives in sanatoria. Many people in Glasgow were keen to help in whatever way they could. The Glasgow Committee quickly rented or borrowed 400 small houses. Many refugees were also housed in hostels and old mansion houses. Many of the houses were made available rent free. The only men of military age were those who were exempt from military service. The cost of supporting the refugees was about £1,000 a week and from the outset the committee was determined that all able-bodied refugees should work. Many got jobs in munitions factories, then paid around half the costs of their maintenance. Some of the men got work in the shipyards and soon learnt to speak broad Glaswegian. A number of workshops were opened where the men could make furniture to use while they were in Scotland and to take back to Belgium in due course. There were also workrooms linked to a clothing store for refugees. Reports make it clear that support was at a basic level with no luxuries and the bare minimum of necessities. The City of Glasgow spent more than £75,000 caring for the refugees. There was a series of homes with resident matrons some of whom were paid and others were volunteers. There were standard menus for the refugees in these hostels. The food was simple and dull, and bread and butter loomed large at every meal. Families placed in tenements were at least able to choose and prepare their own food.

One home was run by two upper-class friends called Henrietta and Diana. They had never done anything like this before, indeed, Diana wrote that she had always avoided any practical work. One of her first tasks, and one which really daunted her, was getting the home ready to receive sixty refugees. Luckily, she was introduced to the head of a big store in the city who gave her a cup of tea before introducing her to his department heads, who spent two days helping her to choose furniture, bedding, cooking utensils, crockery and cutlery, all of which were supplied at pre-war prices. The home was fitted out in an attractive manner with white linoleum on the floors with red, white or blue mats at each bedside and in front of the dressing table. Each bed had a white quilt and a scarlet eiderdown. There were movable chintz screens or a curtain running down the rooms for privacy, stained-wood wardrobes made by Belgian carpenters, marble-topped washing stands, rush chairs and white casement curtains. There was also a copy of the House Rules on the wall of each room covering issues such as punctuality at meals, cleanliness in the bathrooms, no smoking in the bedrooms and being back in the hostel by 10 p.m. There was a bathroom on each floor where a rota, listing the time for each person's bath was pinned up. Diana regretted the need for being so proscriptive but felt that with so many people it was the only way to manage. The refugees were responsible for cleaning their own rooms and took pride in it, even though many of them initially declared that they had never touched a duster. Cleaning also helped fill the empty days. Diana and Henrietta were helped by a Belgian chef, who had been a steward on a ship, and his wife Victorine. Their next refugee arrived unannounced, moaned constantly about the rooms and was described as being both melancholy and slightly sarcastic. In time, she proved to have a talent for making fine lingerie and boudoir caps, which were sold through the smartest shops. The chef recommended they should employ a former police officer and landowner called Emile. His main duty, for which he was utterly unsuited, was to wash the two large stone staircases. When they asked Emile to clean the taps in the top floor bathroom, he took the taps off, causing a flood. He got more and more demanding and unreasonable and after he quarrelled with the chef, Diana asked him to leave. He did, stealing a blanket. Diana later heard that his wife was removed from him after he was seen pulling her around by her hair.

Refugees arrived in Glasgow on Thursday mornings. Diana reported that some seemed remarkably ignorant of geography. Other refugees had told them that the British would not keep them and would send them on to Canada or India. They believed that if they started their journey on a Wednesday their destination was Canada and if they started on a Saturday they would be sent to India. Many of the refugees were struck by the seeming abundance of food. Whenever the refugee trains stopped at a station, ladies handed in food, chocolate and money to the children. On reaching Glasgow, the refugees were all sent to the Christian Institute and given a solid breakfast, during which they were inspected by any matron who had vacancies in her house.

Diana found it was very difficult to tell someone's character while they were eating poached eggs. She was disconcerted by their habit of balancing their eggs on a knife. She always hoped to find people who would be amiable, clean and willing to do more than sit around in the hostel all day. She reported a belief among the refugees that they would get a better billet if they arrived well dressed, only for them to fall foul of the eggy breakfast. She was deterred by the sight of refugees dressed in sable and wearing diamond brooches and was struck by the fact that some the refugees only had a bundle of goods wrapped in a shawl while others had a number of trunks.

Diana was heartened by the support they received from various churches but felt that the Roman Catholic Church was the least forthcoming and felt that this was damaging the reputation of the Church among the Belgians who were Catholics. A surprising reluctance by the Catholic Church to get involved with the refugees was widespread, although in some areas it did make a significant contribution, particularly in the fields of education and health.

While very sympathetic with the situation the refugees found themselves in, Diana was far from impressed by some of them. One refugee was apparently unhappy when he was not given as much money as he demanded and knocked over three clerks and a heavy desk in the

Refugee Committee's office before being removed by the police. He was recommended for military service in the hope that his energy would be invaluable against the Germans. Another claimed that he had no money to support his family though he was known to be earning big wages. He laid his six children out with their pillows on the pavement outside the office, saying that they had nowhere else to sleep.

After a while, a Scottish laundress was hired to do the laundry, replacing a Belgian who had charged more for fewer hours work. She washed five garments a week for each refugee as well as the household linen. Once a week the Belgian women had the washhouse to themselves, so that they could do the rest of their laundry.

Diana sometimes felt overwhelmed by the weight of the refugees' anxieties, backbiting, lack of consideration and the hopelessness of their situation. However, on the whole she was very aware how hard the loss of independence was for the refugees and was very aware of the need to give them sympathetic comprehension rather than sentimental sympathy.

***

Hospitality was offered by many communities in Ireland. Dublin had a very strong committee and part of the Dunshaughlin Institution was converted into a central hostel. The Dublin Committee paid not only for the institution to be fitted out but also its ongoing maintenance and for the transport of refugees. Unfortunately, it was difficult to persuade refugees to go to Ireland. Having crossed the Channel and reached a safe haven in mainland Britain, they were loath to set sail again to cross the Irish Sea.

It is inevitable that some kinds of help are more welcome than others. In 1915 people around Lake Ellesmere in New Zealand were fed up with the large numbers of black swans on the lake, which were deterring the more desirable, and palatable, duck population. Swans were not eaten widely. Some local people suggested that the eggs should be collected for sale in Australia, with the money being sent to Britain for the support of Belgian refugees. They believed they could make £2,000 a year by selling 2,000,000 black swan eggs to Australia. However, the local Acclimatisation Society claimed exclusive rights to swan eggs. Thwarted in their desire to collect and sell eggs, local people decided to round up and kill the swans instead. More than 200 guns went out in fourteen motorboats and, over two days, they killed 1,400 swans. A local freezing works froze the birds, fully feathered, which were then despatched to the Belgian Refugees Food Committee in London, with a recipe. One local doctor said that there was very little nutrition in a swan and they should send sheep instead. It is not clear whether the authorities in London had advance warning of the frozen cargo making its way across the world but it is easy to believe that they were somewhat nonplussed by this example of colonial generosity. The Port of London Authority kept the swans in a cold store until they could be used. *The Akaroa Mail and Banks Peninsula Advertiser* published a letter from an official in London in February 1916. The writer said that he was sure that the swans would be good to eat and that they planned to use a few then and save the rest for Christmas. He thanked the New Zealanders for their unique gift and added that he had had the recipe translated into French and Flemish. A subsequent letter from the Belgian Minister in London reported that consignments of swans had gone to hospitals behind the lines in Belgium, to Ireland, to King Albert of Belgium's five hospitals for Belgian soldiers, and to the mayors of Hackney and Poplar in London. He said that not all of them had yet been eaten, but that the down and feathers had all been used. Amazingly, there is a letter about one of these swans from Lady Dorothie Feilding, who was nursing in Belgium. On 28 January 1916 she wrote to her mother that they had been given a black swan to eat and that the cook said it would not fit in the oven. Two days later, she wrote that the swan was still going strong and had reached the soup stage. They were decidedly sick of it. She added that cooking the swan released a curiously penetrating smell that attached itself to anything they touched.

Large donations of money for caring for the Belgians came in from places as far away as Australia, New Zealand, Trinidad, the Malay States, Nigeria and the Gold Coast. The Canadians sent large amounts of food including consignments of 1,000,000 bags of flour, followed by another 250,000 from the Province of Ontario, 4,000,000 pounds of cheese from Quebec, 25,000 cases of tinned salmon from British Columbia, and 100,000 bushels of potatoes from New Brunswick. Everything, apart from a few bags of potatoes that had got wet, arrived in good condition. Various ports around Britain stored the food for free until it could be dispersed. The flour was sent to bakeries, which made bread that was then given to the Belgians.

Provision of education varied around the country. In some places, Belgian nuns or teachers ran the schools for the refugees. In others, local elementary schools absorbed the refugees. Secondary education was more of a problem and depended on free or subsidised places being made available.

***

A significant number of refugees had mental or physical health issues. Their care was managed by the War Refugees Committee, the Local Government Board, the Metropolitan Asylums Board and the Boards of Guardians throughout the country. The War Refugees Committee quickly set up a dispensary in London to provide medicines and outpatient treatment. They soon realised that this was inadequate and set up another, small, hospital. The Metropolitan Asylums Board made the Sheffield Street institution available and also fitted it out and made it available to the War Refugees Committee. It was mainly an outpatient hospital but also had forty in-patient beds and a system for referring patients elsewhere as necessary. Refugees who needed in-patient treatment were generally dealt with by infirmaries belonging to the Board of Guardians and the Local Government Board paid the costs, if asked to do so.

Patients with tuberculosis, then a common disease known as consumption or TB, were examined then and there, then sent on to sanatoria. In the provinces, cases of TB were reported to the headquarters in London and then arrangements were made for the patients to be sent to sanatoria. Several cases were sent to the Royal Sea Bathing Hospital in Margate. If the family could not pay for the care, the Local Government Board covered the costs. Placing chronic consumptives in a healthy rural setting where they could live with their families after they left the sanatoria was difficult. In 1917 Mrs Gilbert Samuel set up a Colony for Consumptives, on behalf of the Local Government Board, at Gunnislake in Cornwall. To start the colony the Devon and Cornwall Committee acquired and furnished four cottages overlooking Plymouth Sound and the local committee agreed to support the refugees. By November, they needed more space and took on two additional cottages. They needed even more spaces but empty cottages were not available. In May 1918 the colony housed thirty-two people from six families. The men all worked hard creating gardens and two had also taken on allotments. They had been given tools and a low-interest loan to buy manure and seeds. They also had a panel of experts from the Royal Horticultural Society available to offer advice and support. The children all went to the local council school.

Refugees who were judged to be insane were received in county asylums unless special arrangements had been made. The Local Government Board covered the costs. Some Flemish-speaking refugees, who were considered insane, had been placed in institutions without any Flemish-speaking staff so the Belgian Official Committee grouped Belgian 'lunatics' in asylums where Flemish-speaking attendants could be provided. Most were placed in the Colney Hatch Asylum in London. At a later date, the London Asylums Committee suggested that inmates paid for by the Local Government Board should be reclassified as private, not poor-law, patients. The Local Government Board agreed and this privilege was later extended to patients in the provinces too.

Maternity cases and dental care were dealt with by the Health Department of the War Refugees Committee. It also provided grants for children in homes at the seaside and grants for milk, eggs and extra nourishment in cases of sickness. Medical accessories such as spectacles, trusses, bandages, etc., were also paid for. The Local Government Board made substantial grants towards funeral costs for Belgian patients who died in this country.

* * *

The issue of Belgians taking jobs that could have been given to British workers was thorny but it quickly became clear that for the good of the refugees' physical and mental wellbeing, they needed to work. A report into the employment of refugees was published in December 1914. It divided the refugees into three main groups: workers such as miners, agricultural workers and textile workers, who were qualified to fill vacancies in industries where there was a shortage of British workers; workers both qualified for and in need of work in areas where there were no vacancies such as cabinetmakers and jewellers; and thirdly other special groups, mainly professional workers including musicians, teachers and clerks. The report advised that the first group should find work, through the Labour Exchanges, and that an increasing number from the second group should retrain if necessary then take the same kind of jobs as the first group. People who had to move to take work in munitions factories were given help finding accommodation and 65,000 vacancies were filled by Labour Exchanges. It was widely acknowledged that the third group of workers were going to be very hard to place and that a considerable number of them were unwilling to adapt to the available positions. The Committee for the Employment of the Professional Classes spent a great deal of time and effort trying to arrange employment but could only report a limited success.

Many refugees in Kent found work in hop fields and orchards. It was soon seen as an advantage for shopkeepers to be able to advertise that they had French-speaking staff and numerous French-speaking refugees were employed as shop assistants. The committee in Folkestone, as elsewhere, was very careful to ensure that refugees were paid at the same rate as British workers.

The Bradford Committee was concerned when only seventeen of their 164 employable refugees found work, partly because the local woollen mills were not allowed to employ refugees. They therefore set up a number of workshops where refugees could be trained in new trades. Refugees attending the workshops could travel free on the trams and received 1s a week while they were being trained in skills such as woodworking, dressmaking and millinery and were thereafter paid for the work they did in the workshops. Fifty per cent of their earnings were deducted for their maintenance. They were given fifteen per cent of the remainder as pocket money. The residue was set aside to be returned to them when they were able to go back to Belgium. The council lent the project a large building in the city centre and it also housed a well-attended Belgian Institute. The first thing each woodworking student made was a box to hold their belongings when they returned to Belgium. The organisers hoped to get enough boxes for all their refugees. Training and working together helped to break down class barriers among the refugees. The Bradford workshops were widely admired and emulated on a smaller scale by other areas. However, when Kent County Council came under pressure to set up training workshops they rejected the proposal as totally unsuitable for a rural area.

The Croydon Committee was more receptive to the idea. A workshop was opened in premises belonging to the Corporation in High Street. A number of local builders lent carpenters' benches. Materials and tools were provided by the Belgian Government and the refugees were soon turning out good-quality furniture. Belgian women were employed in workshops run by Queen Mary's Needlework Guild.

For social, as well as economic reasons, it was increasingly important for refugees to find work. The cost of living rose dramatically during the war and it was more and more difficult for committees to raise enough money to support their refugees. At one point, it cost 18s a week to rent a room in Coventry and this was beyond the means of the committee. They needed a contribution from the refugees. Language was an inevitable barrier in some industries and the Miners' Union reasonably refused to allow any refugees to work underground unless they spoke good English. About 600 Belgian miners were employed in surface jobs. Many ships from the Belgian fishing fleet went to Milford Haven where they did well while British trawlers were out on patrol work for the military authorities.

Detailed records show that refugees in Glasgow came from an amazing number of trades and professions, from professional cyclists to musicians, teachers, lawyers, nuns, miners, carriage painters, mechanics, dressmakers, diamond workers, servants, judges and a troop of acrobats. Many could not be found equivalent jobs in Britain. However, sixty lawyers found work of some kind, one university professor in Blackpool found work in a tram depot, while it was reported that when one of the refugees in Blackpool was encouraged to take an unskilled job in the chemical industry at 30s a week, he refused, stating that he did not have to work as he was the King of England's guest! A number of diamond cutters were employed doing similar work in London.

The Belgian-owned and run Kryn & Lahy factory in Letchworth and the Pelabon Works in Richmond were employing more than 3,000 men and 675 women by the end of 1916, relieving the need for local people to support the refugees. However, the largest Belgian works of all were set up at Birtley in County Durham as part of Lloyd George's programme of national projectile factories that, in an early example of a public-private partnership, were to be funded and supervised by the government but built and managed by private companies. The factory, which opened in 1916, made shells and came to employ 4,000 workers. This self-contained Belgian community was named Elizabethville, after the Belgian Queen. Early living conditions were poor and the workers chafed under the behaviour of the Belgian authorities who ran the town. By the end of the war, Elizabethville was a thriving community. Its residents were no longer dependent on local funding and it had its own shops, recreation halls, school and even a Scout group.

In 1917 an anonymous writer produced a booklet called *The Condition of the Belgian Workmen now Refugees in England*. Available in both Britain and America it was published in response to an article, by a Swiss writer, called *The Enslavement of Belgians by England*. That article accused the British Government of systematically removing Belgians from France and Holland so that they could be forced to work like coolies in munitions factories; the author claimed their only escape was to join the Belgian Army and many had chosen to face death rather than to continue in forced labour. To refute these claims, the writer of the booklet said the Belgian Department of Records had gathered information that showed no Belgian was forced to work in Britain, that they could get the same help from Labour Exchanges that was available to British people, and that employers had to get a permit to employ Belgian workers. He went on to say that all workers were subject to the same restrictions when changing jobs, to avoid sabotage and wastage, Belgian and British workers were paid the same and that a skilled workman could earn up to £5 a week. He pointed out that many Belgians were employed by Belgian employers. To counter the claim that Belgians were housed in concentration camps, he described the conditions at Earl's Court and elsewhere and the care that was given to the elderly and sick, as well as referring to the committees of charitable people devoting their energy to the welfare of the refugees. About a third of the Belgians who were considered employable eventually found work.

***

The *Eastbourne Gazette* of 30 August 1916 reported the court appearance of a Belgian, Alphonse Edmund Weeze, who had been charged with being in Eastbourne, a prohibited area, without the permission of the Chief Constable. In court, the Chief Constable stated that Weeze had earlier lived in Eastbourne, and had twice been convicted of drunkenness, after which he had been sent back to the War Refugees Committee in London as an 'undesirable'. Weeze had written to the Chief Constable apologising and asking to be allowed back to Eastbourne. When he got no reply, he turned up at the Chief Constable's office and was promptly arrested. Weeze was fined £1 but lacking the means to pay was taken into custody.

Hospitable British feathers were ruffled when some refugees behaved as though support was their right and not a generous gift. They believed they were owed a good level of support because of what had happened in Belgium in 1914 and seemed unable to see how much other people were also suffering as the war dragged on. The Crediton Committee complained how this attitude meant that many of the refugees would neither work nor look for work. A number also refused to contribute to their maintenance costs. An extreme situation arose in June 1915 when the local committee's decision that Belgian refugees who were employed should contribute fifty per cent of their wages towards their keep induced the refugees to go on strike. It is clear that this attitude was not restricted to Crediton and led many committee members to become disillusioned. There was a feeling that some of the refugees were actually trying to profit from their position, with no consideration for how hard it was for their hosts to go on supporting them.

As the war progressed and vast numbers of new and old charities appealed for financial support and volunteer workers, the Belgians were no longer 'flavour of the month'. A serious blow to many people's enthusiasm for supporting Belgians was the refusal of many young Belgian men to enlist in the Belgian Army. There was no way of compelling them to join up and some were open in their determination to stay in Britain. Not only was it safer but they were earning more than they had in pre-war Belgium or would earn in the Belgian Army.

Numerous short propaganda plays were written and performed during the war, covering a range of subjects from the importance of the blackout to the need to spot spies. Some featured the issue of the Belgian refugees, encouraging British people to support them. In *Listing for a Sojer*, by J. J. Wild, a man is keen to enlist, against his wife's wishes, but when he is found to be unfit for military service he and his wife take in some refugee children so that they are still 'doing their bit' for the war effort. Other plays featured Belgians recounting the horrors they had undergone to spur reluctant British men to enlist. Bridging the genres *Spy and Sire* by A. P. Harker and F. R. Pryor featured a Scottish cook trying to entrap a Belgian refugee who turned out to be a spy. Conversely, *Marie Sees it Through* by R. Hope-Lumley had as its heroine a Belgian refugee who prevented a spy from stealing the secret formula he was after.

Among the refugees were about 15,000 Russian Jews who had worked in the diamond industry in Antwerp. The Jewish community in Britain took responsibility for looking after this group and around 6,000 were fully maintained by the Jews in London. Temporary accommodation was provided by the Jewish Committee in Leman Street, Whitechapel, and later by the Jewish War Refugees Committee. In the early stages of the exodus the Local Government Board lent them the Poland Street Refuge. The Local Government Board met the costs of preparing the refuge for its new occupants. The Poland Street Refuge was not big enough and so the Clergy Mutual Assurance Company lent them the Manchester Hotel, to be used as another refuge, free of charge. In time the Local Government Board gave up the Manchester Hotel and rented thirty-nine houses in North London. Up to the end of February 1915, the Jewish Committee carried the full cost of caring for these refugees but a drop in funds meant they then had to take a grant from the Local Government Board. As a condition of its grant, the Local Government Board stipulated that all employable refugees had to work and that part of their wages should go towards reducing the grant. The board was not as tough on any other group of refugees.

Shortly after war started, the Belgian Government issued a strong appeal to all unmarried Belgians of military age to enlist for the duration of the war. They also asked officers and men of the Belgian Army who had retired, but who were under forty-five, to contact the Belgian Military Attaché so that they could go and fight. There were recruiting officials at Earl's Court and Alexandra Palace. The Local Government Board helped the Belgian authorities by arranging facilities for meetings at which Belgian officers could appeal to their compatriots to join them. The Local Government Board also asked local committees to send in detailed lists of all male refugees of military age. The Belgian efforts to recruit more fighting men increased from March 1915, after which all men aged eighteen to twenty-five were required to appear before a board for enlistment or exemption from military service. Exemptions were granted to men who had married before 15 November 1914, were physically unfit to serve, or who had been discharged from further service. Men working in munitions factories were also exempt. The upper age was later raised to forty. There was no way of enforcing these regulations and appeals and many of the Belgian men steadfastly ignored them. While British men were fighting and dying in Belgium in their thousands, this attitude was very hard for British people to swallow.

***

As early as 1916, the British government asked the Local Government Board to start planning for the day when the Belgian refugees could be repatriated. A joint British and Belgian committee was set up to consider the issue. This early planning was vital when the day came for repatriation to begin. In a generous move, the British Government offered to cover all the costs involved. Soon after the Armistice, the Local Government Board presented their plans to the British Government.

The British Government wanted priority to be given to repatriating working-class refugees and those not able to support themselves, as quickly as possible, to avoid the risk of labour problems in Britain. It was agreed that Britain would not compel any refugees to go back to Belgium but that if they refused the offer to pay for their repatriation, they would get no further support from the British Government unless they were ill. The authorities rejected the suggestion that refugees should be repatriated region by region but wanted to send batches of around 10,000 a week with all the sorting out to be done when they were back in Belgium. Hostels for receiving the refugees needed to be set up in Belgium. The Belgian Government gratefully accepted these proposals.

It was thought, at first, that the War Refugees Committee might need to take on additional staff and send them all over the country to plan the repatriation but many local committees offered to take on this role themselves. The Preston, Manchester, Liverpool, Birmingham, Shrewsbury, Oxford, Cardiff and Newport Committees dealt with refugees from the surrounding areas as well as those they had been caring for.

At the end of October 1918, when it was clear that the end of the war was coming, notices and large posters were distributed warning refugees not to leave the place where they were staying to try to go to London or ports in an attempt to get priority in repatriation and to wait for further information. The bureaucracy involved was cumbersome, not least because many of the refugees lacked passports or other Belgian paperwork. The Home Office and Intelligence Department agreed to waive the requirement for any Belgians leaving the country to have a permit. Instead, each refugee was given a large white Authorisation Card, which could be used in conjunction with an identity book in lieu of other paperwork. As well as allowing them to leave the country and enter Belgium, it allowed the refugees free transport on Belgian trains.

Detailed instructions were issued in French and Flemish to inform refugees what to do to be repatriated, about their luggage allowance and certain prohibitions, such as a ban on taking food or livestock. Each refugee was allowed 300 lbs (136 kg) of luggage, including bedding. Due to transport difficulties, they were not able to take furniture and were advised to dispose of this before leaving. After considerable discussion, they were relieved to be told that they could also take a certain amount of food with them. During the repatriation, emergency support had to be arranged for refugees who had been thrown out of work when the munitions works and factories where they had worked were closed. They were given the standard unemployment benefit of 7s a week if they complied with the necessary conditions.

Collecting and transporting luggage was a major headache until the Ministry of Munitions stepped in to help the Ministry of Shipping. It was also very difficult to get the refugees to take any notice of the weight restriction, as they naturally wanted to take as much as they could with them to help them rebuild their lives in the former battle zone. Some simply dumped the excess on station platforms. Repatriation progressed more slowly than any of the parties involved would have liked. The first group set off from Birtley at the end of November 1918 and were soon followed by groups from Scotland and Hull. Up to the middle of January 1919, Antwerp was the only Belgian port that was open and the only available ships were those that had brought POWs back to Britain. For the following four months, the Ministry also used four ocean-going liners. After May 1919, the offer of free transport was withdrawn.

The British Government spent about £3,000,000 on the Belgian refugees. It is harder to quantify the voluntary aid and help in kind that was provided all over Britain but in December 1917 the War Refugees Committee estimated the value of such help at in excess of £6,000,000.

2

Caring for the Sick
and Wounded on the
Home Front

In 1917 Thekla Bowser published a book called *The Story of British V.A.D. Work in the Great War.* She had served as a member of a Volunteer Aid Detachment (VAD) in France and her book had the full support of the British Red Cross. Linked to the book's publication she gave a lecture in Birmingham, which she started by saying that there were extraordinarily few people who knew anything about the Voluntary Aid Detachment scheme or how it had been started. If that was true in 1917, it is even more so today when, for many people, VAD is synonymous with female nurse in the war zone. This narrow vision does the thousands of members a real disservice.

Volunteer Aid Detachments were set up in 1909–10, at the instigation of the Government and were the brainchild of Sir Alfred Keogh, Director General of the Army Medical Service at the War Office. Their creation was delegated to the British Red Cross Society and the Order of St John of Jerusalem. In the same way that Territorial troops were only intended to be used if Britain was invaded, VAD members were only meant to work in this country and to supplement the work of the Territorial Medical Service. Like the Territorial Force, Volunteer Aid Detachments were organised on a county basis, and thousands of people all over the country were recruited. The term VAD quickly came to mean an individual member of a Volunteer Aid Detachment as well as the detachments themselves.

There were separate detachments for men and for women. They had different structures and each detachment had to be registered with the War Office, once it had reached at least seventy per cent of the required structure. The War Office then issued it with a number; odd numbers for men's detachments and even numbers for women's. As the war progressed, and more and more men enlisted in the armed forces or were called up, the majority of VADs were women. Although they were originally meant for home service, selected candidates were soon sent abroad. A small number of VADs were trained nurses who had had to give up their work when they married.

The Volunteer Aid Detachments were intended to give opportunities to civilians who wanted to offer their services to help with the sick and wounded. Members worked hard to develop their skills, training in First Aid and Home Nursing. Much of this training was provided by sympathetic matrons and sisters. VADs were also given training in administration, hygiene, sanitation, carpentry, storekeeping and improvisation.

As most of their work was actually done in emergency situations, this early understanding that they would need to be good at improvising contributed to their later success. In the event of war, they would have to be able to take on any duty the regular medical services did not have the resources to cover. All classes worked together. Among the required skills were the ability to prepare country carts and other vehicles to take stretcher cases and to convert premises, including houses and public buildings, into temporary hospitals. Many of the detachments went to camp and on training exercises in the years leading up to the outbreak of war. Mrs C. S. Peel quoted a schoolboy who had complained that he was constantly being bandaged and un-bandaged by girls who wanted to be VADs. Far from being impressed by their skills, he expressed his sympathy for any wounded soldier who was ever bandaged by them. When Red Cross detachments were mobilised their members wore a Red Cross armband and were protected under the Geneva Convention. Under the same Convention, their work was restricted to helping combatants and not civilians.

By 1911, 20,000 people had enrolled in 659 detachments. A small number served overseas during the Balkan War in 1912. By 1914, their numbers had soared so that there were 40,018 women and 17,696 men in 1,800 Red Cross Detachments. By the end of the war 126,000 people had served as VADs. The impressive fact that 364 of them had been decorated and a further 1,005 Mentioned in Despatches is a testimony to their courage and dedication. A number had also died during their service.

Although they kept their separate identities, the British Red Cross Society and the St John Ambulance Association formed a joint committee in October 1914. The VADs worked under this Joint Committee, which was run from the Duke of Devonshire's house in Piccadilly, London. Nearby premises were used for the workers who allocated medical staff and despatched supplies. Staff and volunteers were soon crammed into every available corner. In the early days of the war, VADs were mobilised to set up auxiliary hospitals and convalescent homes in their own districts. The scope of their work broadened significantly over time. Individual VADs were unpaid and had to cover many of their own expenses. This inevitably restricted membership to those who had a private income or who could afford to live without pay for the duration of their service.

Most VADs not only had to be able to support themselves but also to afford to buy and maintain their uniforms. The issue of uniform remained contentious and there was a separate department at Devonshire House devoted to dealing with uniform issues. Each female VAD had to have three dresses, sixteen aprons, a hat, an overcoat, eight caps, four white belts, six pairs of sleeves, and a mackintosh apron. This cost nearly £17. It was estimated that each VAD had annual expenses of nearly £13 for the care and replacement of her uniform. Each year they had to replace one dress, one cap, six aprons, two pairs of sleeves, two white belts, and six collars. This cost excluded shoe leather, which was a serious expense. Nursing members also had to buy equipment.

Later in the war a VAD cook in a military hospital had to start out with three overalls, fourteen aprons, eight collars, eight belts, eight pairs of sleeves, four caps, an overcoat, a gabardine cap, a pair of gloves, a patent leather belt, a coarse sacking apron and two badges, at a cost of nearly £7. Replacing bits of uniform throughout the year cost nearly £2.

Getting assigned to a hospital was complicated. The VAD initially handed her completed application form to her commandant with proof of her identity, a medical certificate from her own doctor and references. The references had to include one regarding her parents' nationality, a character reference from her head of school or college, which also covered her qualifications, a reference from a lady who had known the applicant for at least five years, and one from her matron, if she had any previous hospital experience. The commandant would countersign the application and send it to the county director, who would also countersign it before sending it to Devonshire House. The VAD was then sent an interview form with a list of matrons currently recruiting and their interviewing hours. After the VAD had been interviewed at the closest hospital that needed staff, the matron would send all the forms back to Devonshire House.

Rejected candidates were notified the result through their county director. Those who were accepted were told to get inoculated against typhoid and were sent a list of equipment to assemble while waiting to be allocated. Successful candidates were also given a leaflet on hospital etiquette, personal hygiene and other important issues. Red Cross VADs were admonished to wear their uniform smartly and without any personal adjustments. Uniforms had to be clean and un-rumpled, with the apron always shorter than the overall. When they lived outside the hospital where they worked, they were told that they must not travel to work in their clean aprons and sleeves. They were also told to carry a spare clean apron for emergencies. Before entering a ward they had to change into clean, comfortable shoes that laced lightly and had low rubber heels.

Personal hygiene was of paramount importance both to keep the VADs healthy and to hinder the spread of infection. They were therefore advised to keep their nails short and clean with no rough edges or torn cuticles, and to try to avoid getting any scratches on their hands. Any scratches had to be covered with gauze and collodion (a solution of nitrocellulose in alcohol and ether) before a VAD helped in the operating theatre or changed dressings. The importance of washing their hands before meals or after (but not before) doing dressings was stressed, as was the need to immerse their hands in disinfectant whenever possible. If, after all this, the skin on their hands roughened they were told to wear gloves at night. They were advised to gargle with carbolic or glyco-thymoline night and morning, with the evening gargle being most important. Combing their hair once a day with a small-toothed comb was also strongly recommended.

They were told they must not wear jewellery or make-up as it would bring discredit to the Red Cross, that they should eat regular meals, get fresh air and a good night's sleep and must stand to attention when anyone in authority spoke to them or entered the ward. Above all, they were told that VADs should be ready to do anything asked of them willingly, promptly, and without question, in order to help their country and build up the good name of the organisation. For some VADs this last admonishment was probably harder than keeping to all the hygiene and uniform regulations. Many young women who signed up must have been shaken by the range of tasks they were called upon to undertake, including close contact with men's bodies. In some hospitals VADs worked in the pharmacy helping keep everything well-stocked and in order. In contrast, many worked in kitchens doing dull jobs such as peeling potatoes. In one Lancashire hospital, this meant hand-peeling an incredible 186 lbs a day.

When assessing applications, the staff at Devonshire House noted all the applicant's useful qualifications so that they could make the best use of each VAD's skills. They also took an ongoing interest in the volunteers, trying to give them any help they needed and keeping careful records. If a VAD was not considered suitable for her posting, the matron or another woman officer under whom she had worked would send a written report to Devonshire House. If the VAD's work and character were considered satisfactory she would appear before a Selection Board and could then go on the waiting list for another appointment. Devonshire House staff were responsible for appointing all VADs to serve in military hospitals in England, Wales and overseas. Scotland and Ireland each had their own selection board.

Daisy Spickett joined her local Red Cross VAD in South Wales in 1910 and by the time the war started, she had gained useful experience helping in the aftermath of a colliery disaster. She longed to be a military nurse and served both in this country and on hospital ships. She described a VAD as someone who 'goes where she is told to go, does what she is told to do, and produces anything she is told to get by hook or by crook.' She felt VADs often had to deal with such large numbers of wounded that they had no time to think; this was particularly true when they worked overseas and she believed it helped them to cope. Like many other VADs, Daisy remarked on the impact the attitude of the sister they worked under had on a VAD's life. Sister and Nurse were titles reserved for the professional nurses and not to be applied to mere VADs. However, it must have been very hard not to react, or possibly to feel gratified, if a patient or doctor addressed you in that way. Doctors got confused and sometimes took to addressing everyone as Nurse or Sister, too busy to worry about the niceties of the hospital hierarchy. Some patients, realising the trouble it caused, would address a VAD as Sister out of simple devilry.

Before the war, trained nurses had struggled for professional status and recognition. This could, understandably lead to tension between them and the VADs who had only undertaken short courses before being appointed to a hospital. There were also stresses caused by the different classes from which the trained nurses and VADs came. Class tensions arose from many of the upper class VADs having to take orders from lower class, but more experienced, VADs; from trained nurses, and having to do the most menial tasks. Some of the trained nurses condemned the empathy with their patients, which characterised many of the VADs, as unprofessional. In reports and memoirs of the First World War, it is clear that VADs complained more about qualified nurses than vice versa. This probably reflects their own insecurity and lack of confidence in their role as well as a natural dislike of being asked to do the most menial tasks, resentment that the nurses were paid, as well as class prejudice. On the other hand, although such friendships were not encouraged, some VADs and sisters did get on very well, respecting and liking each other.

VAD Dorothy Feltham served in Dover, from where she wrote to her fiancé about how well she got on with one of the sisters she worked with and who treated her fairly. She also commented that they all found the need to adapt to the fads and fancies of each new sister very tiring.

Sister Edith Appleton was a member of Queen Alexandra's Imperial Military Nursing Service and was fascinated by the VADs, whom she clearly admired. She described them as splendid and divided them into groups she called Stalkers, Crawlers, Butterflyers and Pushers. In essence, the Stalkers were well-meaning girls who may have looked alarmed at some of the jobs assigned to them but who then did the work well and with a good attitude. The Crawlers were girls who behaved as though they believed they were unworthy to do anything. The Butterflyers tended to be irresponsible aristocratic girls who might crassly describe nursing badly injured patients as 'ripping'. The Pushers, on the other hand, were in many ways unremarkable but were reliable, versatile, and strong and once shown how to do something, never forgot.

The establishment of a Volunteer Aid Detachment in the community of Tyringham in Buckinghamshire may be taken as an example of how many were set up. In April 1915, two local women, Helen McFerran and Annie Wood, decided to set up a detachment, based in their cottage. Miss McFerran was the Lady Superintendent and Commandant, and Miss Wood the Quartermaster. Their surgeon was Dr C. Bailey, who had been a member of the St John Ambulance Brigade for twenty-one years. Members were trained by William Knight, who was Superintendent of the Olney Ambulance Division.

By February 1915, the War Office had to acknowledge that there were not enough trained nurses to staff all the military hospitals and asked the Joint Committee to provide members of women's VADs to ease the shortage. To be considered for work in a military hospital the VADs had to hold certificates in both First Aid and Home Nursing, be between twenty-one and forty-eight for home service and twenty-three and forty-two to serve overseas. After one month's probation they had to be ready to sign on for six months, or for the duration of the war, wear their detachment's uniform, be thoroughly recommended, work under fully trained nurses, keep to the Regulations and Standing Orders of the Queen Alexandra's Imperial Military Nursing Service and live in the quarters provided. Unlike other VADs, those working in military hospitals were paid £20 a year in addition to getting their accommodation, food, allowances and a grant towards the cost of their uniform.

While the majority of VADs were happy with their appointments, Katherine Furse, the VADs leader and later Commandant-in-Chief, said that the main complaints she received related to a lack of encouragement from trained nurses and uncertainty about their role, as an experienced VAD who had previously been given responsible work might be transferred to another hospital where she was only given menial tasks.

In an attempt to address this problem, capable VADs who had served for thirteen consecutive months wore a white bar. VADs with the bar were only meant to be given more responsible work. A number, so small that Katherine Furse described it as negligible, complained about their food or quarters. She did receive a small number of complaints from matrons in military hospitals about VADs' lack of discipline, unwillingness to accept criticism, and independence.

As the demand for military recruits grew ever more clamant, the authorities recognised that women VADs could play an extended role, releasing men for military service. A new type of General Service VADs began to replace members of the Royal Army Medical Corps (RAMC) who worked in various departments of military hospitals. The Joint Committee was responsible for recruiting and allocating members to work as cooks, waitresses, clerks, telephone operators, storekeepers, laundresses, drivers, mechanics, dispensers, laboratory assistants, and X-ray, dental and optical assistants. Although they were paid according to their grade, they were not provided with quarters or, as a rule, food. General Service Members either lived at home, or in hostels where they were supervised by a VAD commandant. The cost of their lodgings was deducted from their pay. A Chief Dispenser earned about £2 a week, while a trained, resident Head Cook was paid around £30 a year, including food. Telephone operators, storekeepers and X-ray attendants might earn £1 a week. About 20,000 General Service Members worked in military hospitals in Britain and, where more than sixty were employed in one hospital, a General Service Superintendent was appointed to help the matron supervise them. The number of women acting as General Service Members could have been expanded significantly if the authorities had been willing to review the terms and conditions under which all VADs served.

As the war dragged on, it became increasingly difficult to recruit VADs or to replace those who left. There was an ever-widening range of paid employment available to women for the first time and many women, who could no longer afford to volunteer, were drawn to these jobs. In the six months to November 1916, more than 2,000 VADs left. While most left at the end of their contract, 199 were deemed unsuitable, 450 had health problems and 604 left for personal reasons. If a VAD married, she had to leave the service. Dorothy Feltham was one of many who would have been asked to re-enlist at the end of her initial six-month contract but for the fact that she was about to marry her soldier fiancé. She remarked how stressful they all found it waiting to hear who would, or would not, be asked to renew their contract. Those who were asked to stay on then felt awkward when faced with those who had been told their contracts would not be renewed. Senior staff must have regretted the loss of women like Dorothy, whom they had trained and who had gained valuable experience. In many cases their husbands were away serving and did not need their wife at home to look after them, so insisting that they leave was not in anybody's interest. 'Personal reasons' also included wanting to work abroad, to change hospitals or needing to go and care for relatives. In some cases, a VAD was called home to support her parents after a brother had been killed or taken prisoner.

Some VADs found nursing patients with severe facial wounds even more traumatic than dealing with amputations and severe injuries fresh from the battlefield. Back in the comfortable surroundings of a British hospital, they had to steel themselves not to react when bandages were slowly peeled away from the remains of a face, knowing that what they were about to see would be shocking but also aware that if they let their feelings show it would be like another injury to the wounded man. They felt even sadder for these men that for the amputees, anticipating how hard it would be for them to leave the security of a hospital where they were with other similarly injured men and to rejoin the rest of society disfigured and a shock to everyone who saw them. Kathleen Scott, widow of polar explorer Robert Scott, was a sculptress who volunteered to work with disfigured men, taking plaster casts of their wrecked faces so that accurate masks could be made to conceal their injuries and help them cope in civilian life.

Volunteer Aid Detachments for men had been set up from the outset and were designed to be ready to go to work if Britain was invaded – but many members did not wait for an invasion to happen and joined the RAMC immediately the war started. Members who remained with their detachment helped set up and run hospitals and rest stations.

In Bristol, ninety-one male members of the Red Cross Society volunteered for permanent duties at the base hospital; 118 VAD officers and men joined them and they were all given uniforms from the society's stores. In Bristol, Brighton, and elsewhere, the men received the sick and wounded from ambulance trains and stretchered them to the ambulances before transporting them to hospital. Local people also lent cars to be used for transporting patients who could sit up. The Bristol Tramways & Carriage Company Ltd lent several motor landaulettes and also helped to pay for several ambulances to be fitted out.

Male VADs worked as orderlies under the RAMC at docks such as Southampton. Some helped with patients during the crossing from France while others were stretcher-bearers, carrying patients from the ships to ambulance trains or to the sheds where they could receive urgent care. In Southampton, VAD men who had full-time jobs during the week took over from the regular stretcher-bearers at weekends so that they could have at least a few free hours.

Clearing hospitals had a regular throughput of patients and so the orderlies had to do a great deal of heavy lifting. Male VADs often branched out, creating new jobs for themselves whenever they identified a fresh task that needed doing. At an auxiliary hospital at Great Malvern, one of the VADs taught carpentry to convalescent soldiers. The men made wooden toys in the style of the thousands that had been imported from Germany before the war. At a Birmingham hospital, patients helped out in the kitchen garden as soon as they were fit enough, thereby getting fitter themselves and helping to grow food for the hospital kitchens. As the war progressed many male VADs went on to join the medical branches of the Army and Navy, either voluntarily or through conscription. Their VAD work was often taken over by their female counterparts.

The first group of wounded soldiers arrived in Bristol on 2 September 1914. They had been injured at Mons and made the long journey to Bristol via Southampton. A steady stream of wounded men followed, including a group of Belgian soldiers from Antwerp.

When the Bristol Red Cross Committee heard that dead soldiers would be buried in communal graves they stepped in to pay for proper funerals for fourteen soldiers and five Belgians. They bought a plot in the Arnos Vale Cemetery that was suitable for fifty burials and which could be enlarged if necessary. This committee also recognised that medical help was not all that the wounded needed and made it clear, from the outset, that it would cover the cost of providing various 'extras' for military patients in local hospitals. The comforts they funded included eggs, fruit, cakes, jams, Bovril, extra milk for puddings, daily newspapers, tobacco and cigarettes, which were beyond the strict service diet. They also provided regular haircuts and shaves for the men, which did a great deal for morale and which cost the Red Cross up to £20 a month.

In 1917, anticipating a shortage of VADs, an appeal was made through the newspapers for more volunteers. Katherine Furse was reported as saying that there had been many occasions in 1916 when she could not provide the nurses she was asked for and that with a big push likely, another 5,000 recruits were needed urgently. There were openings for VADs for both home and foreign service. Roles included nursing, pantry work, driving, cooking, and superintending hostels. Nursing members employed in military hospitals were paid £10 a year with increments of 10s every six months after first six months, for those who agreed to serve for as long as needed. They also received a uniform allowance of £3 10s every six months after completing their initial one-months' probation and got further allowances for travel and board.

The Spectator urged more women to volunteer and asked mothers not to hold back girls who were willing to serve. The writer declared that VAD nurses were too good for him to write a paean of praise to them, and went on to give a fair picture of largely untrained and often young women whose ignorance was sometimes matched only by their willingness for self-sacrifice and their zeal. He acknowledged they had their faults and that they could be hard to manage, due to their high spirits, yet he felt anyone who had watched them work, when exhausted by hours of hard labour, wracked by the pain and suffering they had observed, utterly drained, and haunted by the agony of men who had been gassed or who were shell-shocked, would accord them the highest respect for their work. He appealed for another 20,000 volunteers and detailed a list of jobs that would have deterred many a parent from agreeing to their daughter's enrolment and would have frightened off all but the most dedicated volunteers.

In February 1917 the Government announced the formation of the Women's Auxiliary Army Corps (WAACS). Members were volunteers but unlike the VADs and many other groups, they were paid and their terms and conditions of service were different, as they were an official part of the British Army. Volunteers rushed to join, causing something of a draught for the VADs, with whose work they overlapped. The arrival of the WAACS brought simmering problems within the VAD organisation to the surface. There is no suggestion that the WAAC were unwilling to co-operate with VADs or vice versa.

As early as March 1917 Mrs Furse was urging the chairman of the Joint Committee, Sir Arthur Stanley, to clarify and formalise the relationship between the two organisations. He was unwilling to do so and blithely assumed that VADs would do all the hospital work. Mrs Furse was anxious that competition for recruits should be avoided and suggested joint procedures. She was also insistent that terms and conditions should be the same for both organisations and for VADs working in military and auxiliary Hospitals, again wanting to avoid competition and maximise efficiency.

A particularly thorny issue was how to manage the fact that General Service Members were doing the same jobs as WAACS who benefited from, among other things, recruitment through Labour Exchanges with free medicals, free travel to Selection Boards, free uniform, provision of depots for housing women while were they being vaccinated, inoculated and uniformed and who paid from their date of enrolment. Many categories of WAAC were directly equivalent to VAD General Service Members, throwing the contrast in their terms and conditions into stark relief. Mrs Furse wanted VADs to be treated the same way as WAACS.

In May Mr Pearson, a member of the Central Joint VAD Committee, remarked, from the lofty height of his paid position, that paying VADs working in auxiliary hospitals would be to 'kill the voluntary spirit of the organisation.'

Complaints about the organisation of the headquarters at Devonshire House focussed on the belief that the military authorities saw it as little more than an employment office and that staff had no power to ensure that VADs had proper working or welfare conditions. This led many VADs to feel let down by their leaders. They did not realise that their leaders did not have the authority to help them.

The lack of any grading or possibility of promotion was a cause of widespread dissatisfaction. Katharine Furse protested that even though they had done everything asked of them, and more, for more than three years, being a VAD was seen as a dead end. She said many hospitals lacked inspirational matrons and, as demand increased, were having to rely on the dregs of the nursing profession. Tension was caused by these women being put in charge of highly educated VADs and in some cases resorting to bullying. She further claimed the acrimonious spirit in some hospitals made VADs say that after the war they would never go near another hospital. She felt this was a waste of potential as they formed an obvious pool of prospective trainee professional nurses after the war. In fact, only 129 of the 120,000 VADs who were working at the end of the war went on to train as nurses through the VAD scholarship scheme.

The debate rumbled on for months with Mrs Furse making recommendations, which were blocked or ignored. However, the esteem in which Mrs Furse was held is demonstrated by the fact that in April 1917 she was made a Dame. The situation deteriorated to the point where she was accused of of putting obstacles in the way of links between WAACs and VADs and of having a destructive attitude.

Lord Derby intervened and suggested, as a compromise, that housing, discipline and leave should be the same for VADs and WAACs but that the VAD organisation should have the option of sanctioning supplementary comforts and further regulations as to conduct for their own organisation while WAACs would have shorter contracts. Some concessions were agreed in August but there were further strains when Dame Katharine believed the Joint Committee reneged on changes she thought had been agreed.

Dame Katharine eventually decided that she had no option but to resign and bring matters to a head. She felt she was not given the authority to do the job she had been appointed to and that although she was Commandant-in-Chief, her job was largely restricted to recruiting, appointing, and posting VADs. She did not have the authority to investigate complaints by or about her volunteers. She faced long, frustrating delays when she tried to bring any issues to the attention of the War Office and could not introduce the reforms she believed were essential if the service was to continue.

Before her resignation was announced, Rachel Crowdy, Principal Commandant of the VADs in France, wrote to her long-time colleague, saying it would be a national calamity if she felt she had to resign. Rachel Crowdy paid homage to her work and said she felt that all VADs would agree with her. Perceptively, she added that if Dame Katharine did resign she was sure the changes she had fought for would soon be introduced but that it would not compensate for her loss.

Dame Katharine was widely admired and her resignation drew extensive comment and support. The *Manchester Guardian* quoted Mrs Oliver Strachey, of the Women's Service Bureau, who had been in a position to watch Mrs Furse at work and said she was completely sound. Apparently Dame Katharine's only fault was to be too efficient, too progressive and too anxious for the development of the work. Dame Katharine issued a statement in which she said how much she had loved the VADs and that leaving them was one of the biggest sorrows of her life. Other resignations followed but Dame Katharine and the Devonshire House staff offered to stay to help their successors settle in. Their offer was rejected. Five senior staff, who had worked uninterruptedly under Dame Katharine for three years, were sent away at three days' notice and with no word of thanks from the Joint Committee. Dame Katharine promptly accepted the post as Director of the Women's Royal Naval Service.

There were thirty hospitals and convalescent homes for sick and wounded servicemen in Sussex alone, but only one of them was a military hospital and therefore able to take patients directly from the front. This hospital was in the asylum at Graylingwell, Chichester, from where all the mental patients had hurriedly been transferred. Nearly 30,000 patients were treated in Graylingwell of whom only 142 died. The staff carried out 615 operations in its three operating theatres. There were six auxiliary hospitals affiliated to Graylingwell, staffed largely by volunteers.

At the start of the war the Stobhill Hospital at Springburn, Glasgow, was requisitioned by the RAMC's Territorial Force, split, then renamed the 2nd and 3rd Scottish General Hospitals. A temporary station was set up in the grounds to enable ambulance trains to take patients close to the hospital. Members of the St Andrew's Ambulance Association transported them from the station to the hospital itself.

The first two trains of seriously wounded men arrived at the hospital in September 1914. Apparently, the fact that the hospital had its own station meant most local people were unaware how many wounded men were arriving, to the relief of the authorities who did not want people to know the scale of casualties the Army was suffering. When one local lady heard a train arriving she would rush down to see if she could help in any way. On one occasion the first patient carried off the train was her brother-in-law who had not been heard of for two years and who had been wounded at Gallipoli.

In the autumn of 1914 Hugh Fletcher lent the premises occupied by the New Thames Yacht Club in Gravesend to the British Red Cross Society for use as an auxiliary hospital. Organised and equipped by Kent 92 VAD, the Yacht Club VAD Hospital, Clifton, Marine Parade, Gravesend, opened in October 1914. The first patients to arrive were fifty-six wounded Belgian soldiers. Before long, more space was needed and the Rosherville Hotel was requisitioned. Not long afterwards, Knock Hall Lodge was taken into use as an annexe bringing the number of beds to 106. It was affiliated to the Chatham Military Hospital at Fort Pitt. The local community was typically generous and paid for the operating theatre. A Mr L. Cust gave X-ray equipment, for which they then had to install an electrical supply. This was funded by the Imperial Mills Paper Company. Local people took patients on river trips and also made gifts of food and equipment. During an air raid in June 1915, a bomb fell close to the south west corner of the hospital and destroyed most of the wards. There were no serious injuries, although the patients had to be moved elsewhere for a month while repairs were done.

On Friday 9 October 1914, an eager crowd filled the area around the railway station at Boscombe, near Bournemouth, to watch the first batch of wounded soldiers arrive. Members of the St John Ambulance Brigade were on hand to help the men from the ambulance train to the Boscombe Military Hospital. The hospital consisted of marquees set up in the grounds of the Royal Victoria and West Hampshire Hospital. The first tented wards were named after King George, Queen Mary and Lord Kitchener. A later addition was named after Queen Alexandra. The canvas sides were seen as an advantage as they could be raised to let in fresh air. The Mayor of Bournemouth's War Relief Fund made several grants to help pay for equipment, a final addition being a gymnasium for the wounded, known officially as the Mechanic Therapeutic Department, which opened in May 1918.

In the early autumn of 1914, it was as though everyone who owned a house of any size wanted to hand it over to the government for use as an auxiliary hospital. Not all the offers were completely altruistic as some owners clearly wanted to delegate the responsibility for their properties. Offers received by the War Office were passed over to the Red Cross for sorting. Red Cross officials had actually begun to identify buildings that would be suitable for use as auxiliary hospitals before the war. In addition to the buildings they had identified they quickly listed offers of 3,000 houses, some 700 of which were accepted by the War Office and turned into hospitals with 20,000 beds. By the end of the war, there were 1,500 auxiliary hospitals in Britain with 81,000 beds. Among the larger buildings that were taken into use as hospitals were a number of workhouses and a few mental hospitals including Napsbury in Hertfordshire.

Auxiliary hospitals were run by a VAD Commandant who was responsible for the organisation of the general work of the hospital and a Lady Superintendent, who was a fully trained nurse, responsible to the Medical Officer for managing the nurses and caring for the patients. Some hospitals used both trained nurses and VADs and some just VADs. No matter who was in charge, admission and discharge records had to be kept according to Army regulations.

In the first six months of the war, the British Red Cross Society supplied nurses to seventeen hospitals. In some instances, such as at Epping Bungalow Hospital, this was just one nurse; in others it was more. The Hospital for Indian Troops in Brighton took eighteen, Lady Onslow's Hospital at Clandon Park took six, while two were sent to the both the Margate Sea Bathing Hospital and to Levenshulme in Manchester. The largest group of twenty-one went to the huge Red Cross hutted hospital at Netley in Southampton.

Various large houses around Bournemouth were turned into auxiliary hospitals. Grata Quies in Poole housed wounded Belgian soldiers and was later taken over by the War Office for British soldiers. The Mont Dore Hotel was a hospital for Indian soldiers. The Poole division of the British Red Cross started a hospital at Crag Head, which initially served as a convalescent hospital for soldiers who had recovered enough to leave Netley Hospital on Southampton Water. Before long it was needed for acute cases, as there was a severe bed shortage in the area. It had fourteen wards on three floors, all served by lifts, which made a huge difference to moving patients around. It was staffed by a mixture of trained nurses, Red Cross probationers and VADs. Lady Malmesbury, vice president of the Bournemouth and Christchurch Division of the British Red Cross Society, opened a hospital, for non-commissioned officers and other ranks, in her house. Patients sent to Heron Court did not need much nursing beyond having their dressings changed.

The Bristol branch of the Red Cross was given the use of the King Edward VII Memorial Infirmary and the nurses' home as a general base hospital with 520 beds. It was ready to take Territorial troops, in case of invasion, as well as the sick and wounded from the British Expeditionary Force. The local organisation raised the money to run the hospital so it would not be a burden on the headquarters. The equipment alone cost over £3,600. Bristol also had a brand new Infirmary belonging to the Board of Guardians. It had been built to house the local sick poor but the Red Cross Committee managed to persuade the Board of Guardians to offer it to the War Office. It is not clear where the sick poor were treated during the war.

Even before the war, VADs in Birmingham had been busily training. The first VAD hospital in the city opened in the autumn of 1914. All the equipment and maintenance costs were met by local people. Because of the training they had already undertaken, VAD members were qualified to work as probationers, supervised by trained nurses. Non-nursing members ran an on-site laundry as well as undertaking other duties. In a typical piece of VAD energy and innovation, they managed to make another twenty-five beds available at a few hours' notice, partly by arranging mattresses on billiard tables. There are numerous similar stories of hospitals being created or extended and made ready for an influx of patients at only a few hours' notice.

Many auxiliary hospitals were funded by the owners of large houses and their friends. Two of the grandest must have been at Woburn Abbey, where the Duchess of Bedford opened a hospital with herself as matron, and in the long library at Blenheim Palace. The riding school at Syon House, on the western edge of London, was turned into a convalescent hospital by Helen Magdalen, Duchess of Northumberland, in June 1916. The duchess was, naturally, the commandant and the hospital was staffed by members of Middlesex 64 VAD, which was also involved in running the County of Middlesex Red Cross Hospital in Hanworth Park. The hospital at Syon was affiliated to Fulham Military Hospital and had just thirty-five beds.

The owner of Brownsea Island in Dorset, Mrs Van Raalte, imaginatively took in officers who were severely shell-shocked or who had had nervous breakdowns, allowing them time to make what recovery they could in the peace and quiet of the castle and its garden.

Even in wartime, officials managed to devote attention to matters that may seem less than crucial to most people. Regulations soon stated that the Red Cross flag could only be hoisted over a hospital with the consent of the military authorities. If the Red Cross flag was flown, the Union Jack had to be flown alongside or below it.

Another issue that drew close attention was that of uniform. Ladies who turned their own houses into hospitals often appointed themselves as commandant and were careful to choose a fetching uniform that made them stand out from the other staff. Some were even designed by the famous couturier, Worth. In some hospitals, the patients' clothes received special and sometimes eccentric attention. The junior officers being nursed on the first floor of Mrs Freddie Guest's hospital at

26 Park Lane, London, apparently wore blue silk pyjamas while the senior officers, on the floor above, were decked out in pink silk. The wards were decorated in the same colours. One patient recorded that the nurses were mostly pretty VADs from Mayfair, the posh area around the hospital.

Not all soldiers and seamen needing hospital care had been injured. Many were simply sick. A hospital for recruits based at the White City in London was set up in the Royal Pavilion. People in the surrounding area had already made a commitment to lend furniture and equipment if the need arose and VAD members set to collecting and recording all these loans and gifts. Anything not acquired in this way was bought with Red Cross funds. When they took over the Pavilion at 2 p.m., work was still being done on the drains, lighting, heating, and gas stoves. One ward was ready by 6 p.m. and by 10 the next morning, the hospital was fully equipped and able to receive its first patients. Apart from the matron and one trained nurse, all the staff were VADs.

Military and naval patients who were not bedridden all wore readily identifiable blue suits with white shirts and red ties. When they were outside the hospital grounds this allowed them to be identified as servicemen and protected them from the abuse many men in civilian clothes received from people who were quick to assume that they had not 'done their bit' in the war. The men often complained that these suits did not have a single pocket. Officers and other ranks were treated in separate hospitals.

Violet, Lady Beaumont, of Slindon House in West Sussex, worked for the Chichester Division of the British Red Cross Society as the Official Searcher. Her important role was no doubt replicated around the country and involved visiting hospitals on a regular basis to try to identify men who were recorded as missing or to speak to the men about their former colleagues and gather information about what had happened to them.

In October 1914 the Red Cross opened a hospital with 500 beds in twenty-five huts beside the vast old Royal Victoria Hospital at Netley on Southampton Water. By January 1915, the hutted hospital's staff had dealt with more than 1,000 admissions. Twenty-two huts had been endowed and eighty-four of the beds were maintained by private donations. Whenever possible orderlies were recruited from the counties that had endowed huts, to help make the patients feel at home. Women VADs from each county that had endowed a hut came to nurse there, two at a time.

From early on female VADs ran a small detention hospital in a wooden hut in Southampton docks where they cared for men who could not immediately be sent on to a hospital for treatment. The VADs did the cleaning, cooking, clerical work and also wrote handwritten notes of thanks to everyone who sent in gifts for the soldiers.

People of all classes were keen to do whatever they could to help. Girls from one mill in Manchester got up at 5 a.m. to clean the small local hospital before going to do their normal shift at work. In the evenings they went back to the hospital for another couple of hours to help serve the evening meal, make beds and generally tidy up. To deal with the jobs that needed to be done during the day, women who normally stayed at home with their children gave whatever hours they could to help. In reporting these efforts Thekla Bowser stressed that they were not women who had time to spare but women who were already fully employed, squeezing the extra work into their already busy days. She commented that many rich women could learn from these mill workers.

Just before 8 o'clock on the morning of 16 December 1914, the St John VAD hospital in the Masonic Hall in Hartlepool was bombarded by the Germans. It has the dubious distinction of being the only one to suffer in this way. Just as the VAD member on duty had ordered the patients, all of whom were convalescent, to get up, a piece of shrapnel came through the window and landed on the only empty bed. Throughout the day, the hospital dealt with a stream of patients who had been injured during the bombardment. Both men and women VAD members were available to help with air raid duties all over the country.

The war was a gaping maw of need, swallowing munitions and other goods as fast as all our factories could produce them. This pressure in already dangerous surroundings meant that inevitably there were accidents. In some factories a small area was set aside and staffed around the clock by members of the Ambulance Department. Team members had to be prepared to deal with anything from a minor burn to a major explosion. The two VAD nurses in one munitions factory dealt with 1,000 small incidents in their first seven weeks in the post.

As in other counties, the Territorial Force Association in Middlesex was responsible to the War Office for organising voluntary aid in the county. The Southgate branch took on the particular responsibility for selecting and providing equipment, fundraising and maintaining the auxiliary hospitals. They got a small grant from the War Office and raised most of the money needed to provide equipment for the thirteen hospitals and convalescent homes in the county and funded ambulances to transfer the wounded to hospital. There were more than thirty Volunteer Aid Detachments in Middlesex, with 1,500 members. Dr Woodcock trained the Men's Detachment and sixty of the men qualified to do stretcher and ambulance work. A number of the women trained to work in military hospitals. As both men and women who were approved to work in military hospitals had to sign up for at least six months, the local committee felt it was wrong that these volunteers would have to bear all their costs themselves, so set out to raise at least £200. With auxiliary hospitals up and running at Grovelands and Tottenhall, they started raising a 1,000 guineas so another hospital could be set up.

In 1909, the decision was taken that if there was ever a war, the new buildings at the University of Birmingham would be turned into a 500-bed hospital. Plans were drawn up and in 1914 these were carried out smoothly, creating the First Southern General Hospital. The first patients arrived on 1 September 1914. More and more of the university buildings were gradually 'conscripted'. By the spring of 1915 there were 1,000 beds. At its peak, the hospital could look after 130 officers and 2,357 other ranks. There were ultimately beds for 8,827 wounded and sick military personnel in the City of Birmingham, with large hospital supply depots in Birmingham and Worcester.

Statistics like this, replicated throughout Britain and overseas, lead to the realisation that the supply, laundry and maintenance of all the linens; sheets, pillowcases, towels, aprons, pyjamas, and other clothing was a quite incredible undertaking. Beyond the work done in the hospitals and their ancillary buildings there were the factories making all these items and the factory owners must have got rich on their profits. It would be nice to think that some of these manufacturers might have donated a quantity of linen to their local hospital but, as yet, very few references to any such generosity have been found.

The area around Birmingham Auxiliary Hospitals came under the general organisation of the First Southern General Hospital. Uffculme, the former home of Richard Cadbury, had been used for Belgian refugees during the first wave of arrivals and was then turned over to the Friends Ambulance Unit who made it into a 200-bed hospital. In 1918 it became the regional limb-fitting centre for soldiers from Warwickshire, Worcestershire, Northamptonshire, Leicestershire, and Oxfordshire. Highbury, the former home of Austen and Joseph Chamberlain, was turned into a VAD Hospital, funded in part by the employees of the Kynoch Munitions Works in Witton. Kynoch's Board was chaired by Arthur Chamberlain.

On a smaller scale Barnet, in Hertfordshire, had two hospitals. Members of the Herts 32 VAD turned St James's Hall in New Barnet, lent by the parish committee, into a twenty-bed hospital. By 1917 the number of beds had risen to twenty-two. It was affiliated to the larger hospital in High Barnet. In 1915 Pickering Lodge Mansion, next to the old Victorian Workhouse and partly built Infirmary, was taken over by the Army Council. They completed the building and used it as an acute hospital where more than 6,000 sick and wounded men were treated. In 1920 it was handed back to the local Guardians, who not only got a completed hospital to replace the incomplete shell that had been requisitioned but who were able to buy the hospital equipment from the War Office at ten per cent less than it had cost in 1915.

Converting buildings into hospitals had its own particular challenges. At the Whitworth Institute in Darley Dale, Derbyshire, the £100 spent on the conversion included the bill for laying a floor over the swimming pool.

Early 1915 the military authorities in Glasgow were expecting such a large influx of wounded that they knew they had not got the capacity to cope. The Red Cross decided to set up a new hospital in a district where there were no existing hospitals. As they could not find any suitable buildings, they eventually accepted the design by a Mr Skipper for a 700-bed hutted hospital. The chosen site was at Bellahouston Park and the huts, built of asbestos blocks, were quickly put up. The hospital had seven connected blocks with two wards of fifty beds. It opened in October 1915, by which time the public had donated £53,000. There were 157 auxiliary hospitals in Scotland.

Lord and Lady Plymouth, owners of St Fagans Castle near Cardiff, allowed a large detached banqueting hall to be used as a convalescent hospital. It had seventy beds, in cramped rows, each with a small bedside table. It was run by the Red Cross and staffed by VADs as well as professional staff. Some of the volunteers, such as Mary Ann Dodd, were also members of the castle staff. Mary was a housemaid at the castle. On the fortnightly rota she cooked, cleaned and did laundry for the hospital. She commented on the poor state of the soldiers' socks, in spite of the efforts of the legions of people who were knitting for them. St Fagans Castle had also been the base for the first Welsh Volunteer Aid Detachment, which had been set up in 1909.

The Red Cross Hospital at Willersley, near Matlock, was run by Mrs Arkwright and funded by her family, who steadfastly refused all offers of financial help from the Government. The hospital was staffed by Mrs Arkwright's friends and family, including her widowed daughter Mrs Bonham Carter. When the hospital closed in 1919, they were proud to report that only two patients had died, one in 1916 and the other in 1918. When the hospital staff were hit by the flu epidemic, Mrs Arkwright's friends rallied round to cook and clean and help in any way they could. A month after the hospital closed, many of the nurses went back to Willersley to help with a sale of work in aid of St Dunstan's Home for Blinded Soldiers that raised more than £100.

While there are numerous positive reports about the care and support people gave to sick and wounded men, being treated in their area, there were clearly some problems. In Belper, in Derbyshire, there were repeated problems caused by local people buying alcoholic drinks for the men. At the Petty Sessions, two women were found guilty of buying alcohol for men from Green Hall Red Cross VAD Hospital. One of the women was fined £1 and the other was imprisoned for a month.

The Kitchener Military Hospital for Imperial Troops was set up in the Elm Grove Workhouse in Brighton, now the Brighton General Hospital. Indian troops were also treated in the Indian-inspired splendour of the Royal Pavilion. Official policy prevented women nursing Imperial troops but a group of Lady Visitors was set up by Lady Seton, wife of the men's Commanding Officer. The Lady Visitors made sure that each ward in the Kitchener Hospital was visited regularly and supplied with carefully arranged flowers. The ladies all wore grey armbands embroidered with K.L.V for Kitchener Lady Volunteers. In 1917 and 1918 they collected enough money to buy a Christmas present worth 2s for each Imperial soldier. They also bought materials so the men could do fancy work to while away the time. After 1916 the Royal Pavilion was used as a hospital for treating amputees before they were fitted with their prosthetic limbs.

When a hospital for wounded Belgian Soldiers was set up in the Royal Exchange in Buxton, the public was allowed in to have a look around on one Sunday a month. This proved to be so popular a Sunday outing that staff had to put up barriers to help them control the crowds.

One of first auxiliary hospitals to open in a private home was in Mrs Florence Rudge's house, Evesham Manor. The hospital opened in September 1914 with Mrs Rudge as the commandant. She initially covered all the costs herself but later accepted the War Office allowance for each patient. By 1916, the hospital had 100 beds, having expanded into the Palm House and tents in the grounds. The demand for beds was so great in 1918 that she leased the nearby Chadbury House as a further extension of the hospital. When the hospital closed in 1919, she was proud to report that not one of the 3,612 men who had been treated there had died. While this is, undoubtedly, a tribute to the hospital staff it may also reflect the fact that seriously sick or wounded men were not sent there.

Auxiliary hospitals were often supported by local businesses and received food from local farmers. Women frequently provided accommodation for relatives visiting the sick and wounded, while many doctors often helped by working in the hospitals for a number of houses free of charge. Servicemen often enjoyed the relative informality of the hospitals but were less enthusiastic about being treated as a spectacle by local people when they were fit enough to go beyond the hospital grounds.

When men no longer needed an acute bed, they were moved on to a convalescent hospital. There were 21,399 beds for convalescent patients by February 1915. Many of these were in large private houses. Some were at least partially funded by the house's owner, while in other instances, the house alone had been offered to the Red Cross or St John, either furnished or unfurnished.

Prince Henry of Battenberg's Hospital for Officers was in 30 Hill Street, just off fashionable Berkeley Square, in London. It was owned by Jeanne, Lady Coats, who offered the house to Princess Henry of Battenberg as a convalescent hospital for officers. The princess's personal physician, Dr A. J. Rice-Oxley, took on the role of Medical Superintendent. Although it was small, with only sixteen beds, its society links meant it was particularly well-equipped and even had its own operating theatre and X-ray room.

Elizabeth Vaughan worked at the VAD Hospital in Braintree in Essex. She apparently reported that when one patient regained consciousness he was told that he had a mustard plaster on his chest, a vinegar-soaked bandage around his head and salt bags on his feet. The salt bags were to treat frostbite. He retorted that the nurse should fetch some pepper so that he would be a complete cruet.

Individuals and organisations sponsored a considerable number of hospital beds both here and abroad. Sponsoring a bed cost between £25 and £50 a year and the bed was usually marked with a plaque showing the donor's name. The children of Vickerstown School in Barrow in Furnes raised the money for a bed in Caen Military Hospital in France by holding a bazaar. While Edinburgh friends Alice and Alison had little trouble raising the money to sponsor a bed for one year, they had considerably more difficulty in subsequent years.

* * *

The London Ambulance Column was formed by a Mr and Mrs Dent, with approval from the Red Cross and the War Office. The column was run from a house provided by the Dents and was almost fully funded by them. They set up the column after the Battle of Ypres, when they realised there were no plans for how the wounded would be transferred from ambulance trains to hospitals. Wounded soldiers could end up spending hours waiting for transport. The first group of volunteers were staff from the Derry & Toms Department Store, who worked for the column at night after having completed a full shift in the shop during the day. Young Mr Toms led a group of bearers and the store donated all the linen the column needed. The team included fifty nurses as well as bearers and orderlies, and had a fleet of 140 ambulances. There were twenty-five phone operators to take calls from the Red Cross with details of when ambulance trains were due, always after the rush hour was over. The operators had to contact all the volunteers who then went to the appropriate station. Volunteers who did not have telephones were contacted by despatch riders.

Nursing members of the column were nicknamed 'Bluebottles' because of the thick navy blue woollen cloaks that they wore over their long white skirts. The Dents were determined to try to prepare their team for what they would see when dealing with wounded soldiers and sailors, so that they would be able to work quietly and unobtrusively without fainting or panicking. They were aware that if members of the team did not cope the column would be closed down by the Red Cross.

One volunteer was Claire Tisdall, whose diary in the Imperial War Museum gives a unique insight into the column's work. She was a fairly typical recruit, with a full-time job that she could not afford to leave. She was not satisfied with the thought that rolling bandages might be her only contribution to the war effort so night-time work with the column suited her. When a train arrived, each nurse was allocated a group of patients to get into the ambulance and accompany to hospital. They were given a quick summary of each patient's condition, which they had to remember and pass on to staff who met them at the hospital. Like her colleagues, Claire found working at Victoria Station was much easier than at Waterloo, where the wounded had to be carried up and down stairs on stretchers. The nurses and orderlies were generally exhausted and hungry. To give her patients some additional comfort Claire had a number of hot water bottles ready when the trains pulled in. She also learned to put any patient who was bleeding heavily on the bottom layer so that they would not bleed on the other patients. She felt that after July 1916 they were never free of the lingering small of gas. It clung to the men's clothing and mixed into an unspeakable cocktail with the ever-present smell of gangrene. Soon, every train that arrived carried some patients who had been gassed. Dealing with them shocked even experienced staff and Claire fainted the first time she went into a carriage full of men who had been gassed. She was carried out but quickly recovered and went back to get on with her work. Because the nurses had to be alert to any change in the breathing of their gassed patients, Claire preferred to travel on the floor between the men so that the sound of their laboured breaths was not drowned by the noise of the ambulance's engine.

Members of the public often brought flowers to give to the wounded men. The flowers often got in the way and there were times when the lingering gas turned them all black. As the Dents knew that the men wanted cigarettes, not flowers, they made sure there were always plenty at the stations. Claire always carried dry matches so that she could light cigarettes for the men. Almost every man wanted a cigarette, no matter how badly they had been injured. When men had severe facial injuries she had to learn how to put the cigarettes in their mouths without setting their gauze dressings alight.

Claire reported that later on trains sometimes had some unmarked, grey carriages at one end, which were not unlocked until all the sick and wounded men had been taken away. She discovered that mental patients were kept in the locked carriages and only removed once the station was empty. Members of the column never dealt with these men.

She felt that the public's attitude gradually changed and that the crowds of sympathetic onlookers were replaced by those who just went to get a look at the terribly wounded men. People even tried to undo the canvas flaps on the ambulances to peer at the men as they approached New End Hospital in Hampstead.

As the war progressed, the column's workload got heavier and heavier until, in 1917, many of them were given leave of absence by their employers and some even took to sleeping on camp beds at the Regents Park headquarters during the day. At one point Claire worked for seventeen nights in a row, had one night off, and then worked another twelve nights in succession. The drivers, nurses and orderlies were all utterly exhausted. They were not the only ones to suffer. Their founder, Mr Dent, had a nervous breakdown and had to stop his work for the column. By early 1918 they were all at breaking point and their employers' patience with their absences and exhaustion was wearing thin. The end of the war came none too soon for this group of volunteers who often felt as though they were struggling alone with their gargantuan, self-appointed role. After catching flu in 1919, Claire also had a nervous breakdown and carried mental scars from her war work for the rest of her life.

* * *

Transport was often done in private cars, lent by their owners. One car owner, with an imperfect grasp of reality asked that he should be given two days' notice whenever his car was needed. Apparently the section leader replied that he would be happy to give two days' notice providing the car owner could arrange for the Kaiser to give two days' notice of any planned attacks. Female VAD drivers, or chauffeuses, were also attached to the headquarters staff and to various hospitals and hostels. When VADs were transporting men from the stations to hospital, the heavy work of carrying the wounded on stretchers was done by the male VADs. Most convoys arrived at night and many of the VADs were on duty after having done a normal day in their full-time jobs.

In Birmingham most sick and wounded were transported by private volunteers until 1916, when members of the Motor Transport VAD took over the bulk of this work. They also provided a night-time car service so servicemen arriving on leave late at night could get home without having to wait hours for public transport to start up.

Volunteers soon devised standard procedures for dealing with the arrival of ambulance trains in their area. In Bournemouth, most trains arrived at Boscombe Station, although patients going to the Mont Dore or Gratia Quies hospitals sometimes went to the Central or West Stations. When news came in that trains would be arriving, volunteers were notified by telephone or messenger and assembled at the station. The walking wounded were taken off the trains first and then the men from the double tier of cots were lifted gently onto stretchers and taken to the ambulances. A doctor was always there to decide which hospital each man should be sent to.

Each volunteer knew what they had to do. While some unloaded the stretchers from the trains, others would be ready to load the ambulances and then drive to the various hospitals. On arrival they would help unload the ambulances and get the patients to their beds. When the trains were delayed, the volunteers played cards or dozed on the stretchers to while away the time. Boscombe Hospital provided cocoa, bread and cheese for volunteers who were called out at night. Many of the ambulances were funded by private individuals and by 1916 there were ten ambulances, five of which were converted tradesman's vans. Shortly after the start of the war, Miss Laura Starkey donated an ambulance, which she then drove. She also paid for its upkeep and later added another three to her fleet.

Mr W.W. Graham, the managing director of Elliott's charabanc firm in Bournemouth provided a small coach to help take the wounded to the hospitals. However, the coach was not really suitable for carrying stretchers so he had two of the firm's hire cars converted into ambulances, one of which was made into a mobile X-ray unit. The coach was used for carrying walking wounded. Several firms converted their trade vehicles into ambulances.

Bournemouth had a branch of the Women's Reserve Ambulance, also known as the Green Cross Corps. This was a volunteer organisation set up to help in hospitals and with other war work. The Bournemouth Battalion had forty-five members and three officers. From March 1916 they had a Sunbeam Motor Ambulance, which they used to transport patients from the various local stations to the appropriate hospitals. It could hold four patients on stretchers or eight sitting cases. They also drove patients to and from various entertainments. Apart from their driving duties, members of the Women's Reserve Ambulance also acted as ward orderlies, cleaned the recreation room at Boscombe Hospital, and served as canteen workers in WMCA huts. All their work was funded by donations and subscriptions.

In Scotland, the Red Cross took responsibility for transporting all patients from hospital ships to ambulance trains to hospitals. They often worked with the St Andrew's Ambulance Association, who lent both trained staff and ambulances. Private people throughout Scotland generously lent their cars to carry the walking wounded. Each cot case on the trains was allowed three blankets and one or more pillows. After a train had been unloaded and the cot cases distributed to the various hospitals, the team gathered up their equipment and returned to base, where they carefully folded and stored the blankets ready for the next time they were needed. Blankets and pillows regularly needed to be repaired. All blankets and pillows were periodically sent to the laundry.

It does not take much imagination to realise that the provision of bandages, dressings, pyjamas and other hospital necessities was a task of Sisyphean proportions. It soon became clear that it was one for which the military authorities were spectacularly ill-prepared. The work of volunteers and War Hospital Supply Depots prevented a catastrophic lack of essential hospital supplies both in Britain and overseas.

The first War Hospital Supply Depot was established in Kensington, in London, in January 1915 by four energetic people with a shared capital of £15. Initially based in two houses, it grew until it occupied eight houses. It soon had 6,000 volunteers on its list. An average of 1,200 volunteers a day produced in excess of 50,000 articles a week for 1,300 hospitals at home and abroad. The depot eventually opened twenty-one departments, each concentrating on a particular area of need. Products were made to a very high standard and a writer in *The Spectator* said they produced every type of hospital or surgical appliance that could be made by hand including crutches, swabs and sterilised dressings, bandages, sheets, pyjamas, shirts, bed-jackets, and hospital sandbags – then a new idea for keeping wounded limbs immobile. The volunteers even made beaded muslin covers to keep flies off food and drink. In just one week they made nearly 17,000 swabs and surgical bandages, 1,000 handkerchiefs, 100 dressing-gowns, 350 pairs of slippers, 800 splints and hundreds of other items. Demand was endless and varied. They tried to meet every demand but always needed more money for materials and more volunteers. *The Spectator* writer urged manufacturers and drapers to send as much linen, flannel, cotton and towelling as they could spare, timber merchants to supply as much suitable wood as they could manage, members of the public to donate as much as they could afford on a regular basis and to send their old sheets, linen, and white counterpanes to be recycled into hospital requisites. From the outset the founders were determined that the depot would be run on sound business lines. They estimated that for every £10 they spent on materials, they produced goods worth £100. Workers paid an administrative fee to the depot and every penny donated by members of the public was used to buy materials.

Hundreds of other depots were set up on the same lines and members of the Kensington team gave help and advice whenever they could. The other depots often grew out of Red Cross working parties that had been set up just after the war started. Staff often devised ingenious innovations to alleviate suffering among the wounded, some of which were taken up by the War Office and some were patented by their inventors. Each depot could have dozens of linked working parties in the surrounding area.

Staff at some depots decided to specialise in particular items. One lady at the Banff depot produced surgical slippers made almost wholly from cork and tweed remnants. In Bedford, they made fly veils, respirators and, although this seems a little odd, thousands of patch pockets for the 53rd Welsh Division. Rotherham staff developed and made a new type of peg-leg. The Cambridge volunteers made many items for combatants but also dealt with special requests from officers for anything from blankets to tins of milk, field glasses, periscopes, telescopes, spare telephone parts and, for the medical officer, a stove, a lamp, a portable steriliser for instruments, a large irrigating set and tube, four India rubber tourniquets and two stretcher carriers. The wives of professors at Sheffield University set up the Sheffield University War Hospital Supply Depot and members of the University's Faculty of Engineering formed a Surgical Appliance Branch. Workers in the Grimsby Depot were delighted to hear that friends of a wounded soldier, who had gone to visit him in France, found him wearing items they had made.

Historically, images of Flanders mud and trench warfare have dominated the popular picture of the First World War and yet many troops served abroad in hot, dusty countries and their needs also needed to be met. The Reading Depot started out making sandbags but later switched to surgical necessities and had fifty-nine working parties, including some in schools, all linked to the depot. They worked to make walking sticks more comfortable to use and also produced large quantities of mosquito nets and sunshields.

Although the Lowestoft Depot was the only one to suffer aerial bombardment, the volunteers never missed a day's work. Many depots set up arrangements so that some volunteers, who had full-time jobs, could work at home. They either collected materials from the depots or had them delivered to their homes. The finished items were either delivered to the depot or collected.

It is easy to imagine the women volunteers sewing, knitting or rolling bandages but there were also many male volunteers who set up workshops to make a different range of much-needed items. Carpenters, at workshops like the one in Battersea, London, made large quantities of splints, bed tables, crutches and foot rests.

Over time, some organisers had to work harder than ever to encourage enthusiasm among their volunteers. In spite of this, the group in Westerham in Kent more than doubled their output to 4,267 garments in 1916 and this rose again, to 8,349, in 1917. The number of volunteers in the workroom had increased from 260 to 328. Their output included more than 1,000 pairs of socks, mufflers, bed socks, handkerchiefs, mittens, gloves, hospital bags, anti-vermin vests, helmets, sunshields, nightshirts, pyjamas and sweaters.

Magnus Volk and his wife set up the Brighton Comforts for Soldiers War Work Depot in their drawing room, just four days after the outbreak of war. Because of their prompt start, they were the only working party in the area that was able to supply essential bandages and clothes to local hospitals. They later expanded their work to sending parcels to men on active service, POWs, hospitals in Belgium and various naval crews.

In Brighton, too, the firm of Miss E. Willmer, Builder and Decorator, arranged for carpentry employees to stay after work to make all kinds of splints with the firm donating the materials. The firm also took wounded men out for rides and to tea, and donated a New Zealand flag to a convalescent home for officers from the New Zealand Expeditionary Force in Lewes Crescent.

A forgotten, but once popular, competitive sport in England was bandage-rolling. Volunteer Aid Detachments, War Hospital Supply Depots and other groups competed against each other at local events across the country. In 1914 Muriel Shipman and her Red Cross Unit from Woodbridge came second in a first aid competition between various units from the Beccles and Great Yarmouth area. Another competition was held in the ballroom at the Rockside Hydro in Matlock when the judges included the matrons of various local hospitals. In 1918 the Ascot War Hospital Supply Depot won first prize, a silver cup, in a surgical dressing competition at their depot's fete. These events were presumably designed to attract fresh recruits as well as maintaining enthusiasm among existing volunteers.

Queen Mary's Needlework Guild set up its own Central Surgical Depot, with numerous branches, which provided more than 1,000,000 articles for allied hospitals and hospital ships. Its earliest specialist department was the Surgical Requisites Association in Chelsea. Some of its workers made a number of innovations that were taken up by other workrooms and they also set up a centre for helping volunteers from other branches learn how to make various items. Elinor Halle specialised in the imaginative use of papier mâché as a support. She was the first person to use papier mâché to make arm cradles and a light boot with a papier mâché back for men with dropped feet. This boot was so popular that centres for making them were set up in France, Italy and India, as well as in Britain. The technique of using a cupro-ammonium solution with cotton wool to replace paste in the final layer of papier mâché made it waterproof. This was invented by another volunteer, Miss Acheson, and could be used to make baths. This technique was also applied to splints. It was very important that splints should fit the injured limb as closely as possible to avoid the risk of causing chaffing and additional pain. Volunteers therefore visited military hospitals to take plaster casts of injured limbs, which they then used to make accurate splints.

HRH Princess Christian became president of the Belgravia Depot. Unlike most depots, its fifty-two branches were scattered throughout the country and included one as far away as Launceston in Cornwall. Workers devised a range of sought-after items such as the Belgravia Sling, the Roller Crutch, the Half Ring Crutch, the Maffei Finger Extension, a life-saving waistcoat and the Worsfold Stretcher. Each of these was taken up by the Director General of Voluntary Organisations for wider manufacture and distribution.

The ladies of Alderley Edge teamed up with the boys at the nearby School for the Deaf and Dumb to supply more than ninety hospitals with splints. The Girl Guides ran a laundry for the local Red Cross Hospital.

In July 1915 an article appeared in various Sussex newspapers announcing a proposal to start a Horsham branch of the Hove War Hospital Supply Depot. It was to have four main aims: to collect or buy materials for making war hospital requisites, including bandages and splints, to have a team of volunteers making the articles each day under expert guidance, to collect and receive gifts of all sorts of other requisites including antiseptics and clothes, and to distribute everything to various hospitals on the front. An urgent appeal was made for funds to get the depot up and running. With qualified generosity Councillor Charles Rowland offered the use of his property at 8 The Causeway, free of charge as long as it remained untenanted. The workroom was to be open for six hours every day except Saturday and an appeal for volunteers made it clear they could do whatever hours they could manage. Donations of equipment for the depot included a kettle, an oil stove, two clocks, tables, and two sewing machines. Within a month, 217 volunteers had come forward. In December they held an exhibition of the clothes they had made.

Like workers in other depots, the Horsham volunteers found demand for their products increased dramatically during the Battle of the Somme in July 1916. Grateful letters from soldiers and hospital staff gave a welcome boost to the volunteers' morale. Local papers regularly published reports of the various depots' achievements and fundraising efforts.

Various organisations set up depots in and around Aberdeen. The Aberdeen City Association had forty affiliated work parties including teachers and pupils in local schools and students at the university. They were given the target of attending the depot twice a week and knitting one garment or sewing two. The targets were set low, as most of the members had full-time jobs. The Aberdeen Ladies Needlework Guild had thirty-five groups, each of which had fifty-four members. They devoted themselves to providing patients at the 1st Scottish General Hospital with clothes and knitted comforts, and gave each man a gift when he left. They also produced all kinds of dressings, wooden articles such as crutches and bed cradles, papier mâché and vulcanite items, splints, leather boots for drop feet, and temporary artificial limbs. As if this was not enough they also mended vast numbers of garments for the patients, organised occupational health for bedridden men in the wards and for the more mobile men in huts, and sometimes sent consignments of goods to overseas hospitals through the Director General of Voluntary Organisations.

It is remarkable what detailed records depots kept of their output and there was clearly informal competition between neighbouring depots over which could make the largest number of items. The list of items made by the Horsham Depot is a good indication of the range of goods produced. Their output included sterilised dressings and amputation dressings; flat gauze swabs; operation towels; ligarette drains; gauze handkerchiefs; surgeons' operation gowns and caps; wool and gauze swabs; many-tailed, chest, amputation, head, and roller bandages; slings; shifts, pyjamas, bed jackets, socks, bed socks, and stockings; bed tables; splints; loose pads, heel pad packets; finger stalls, hand stalls; pneumonia jackets; knitted swabs; cup covers; slippers; treasure bags; surgeons' mackintosh aprons; and sphagnum moss bags. As time passed, and it got more difficult to raise enough to pay for materials, many volunteers bought them with their own money. Depots also made vast numbers of shrouds and literally millions of sandbags, but the shrouds rarely get a mention in the production statistics.

In 1915 The Central Work Rooms were set up to co-ordinate the activities of all working parties so that duplication of effort could be avoided. There were eventually almost 3,000 affiliated workrooms all over the world, from Cuba to Casablanca, Panama to Ecuador and Alexandria to Barcelona. The Central Workrooms opened their headquarters in part of the Royal Academy in Burlington House, London, in October 1915. As well as registering existing workrooms and co-ordinating their production, their remit was to open new workrooms. They also allocated work when there was an urgent need for a particular type of item, and helped train volunteers who then went on to train other workers. When each volunteer paid their registration fee, they were given a reference number and a blue linen Red Cross overall, marked with the same number. They provided their own white caps and sleeves. The hours put in by each volunteer were meticulously recorded. The working hours were 10 a.m. to 1 p.m., and 2 p.m. to 5 p.m. Workers travelling some distance were allowed half-an-hour's latitude in their arrival time. The only break in work was for two months after a bomb fell on another part of Burlington House in November 1917. As soon as they could get back into their rooms, they continued to work in spite of broken windows, roof and doors – and a complete lack of heating. Reflecting the war-time love of a uniform, the organisers quickly set a group of workers to replacing the 400 uniforms that had been lost. Workers were awarded certificates if they completed 300 hours' work within four months. After 600 hours, they could attach a red chevron to their overall sleeve, with further chevrons when other milestones were reached. Many of the workers attended the workrooms throughout the time they were open. Each workroom was allowed considerable autonomy in how they set about their task but to encourage uniformity, patterns and instruction books were provided. To harness the enthusiasm of women in full-time work, or who were not well enough to attend a workroom, they set up a separate department to manage home-workers. Most were given patterns and materials and then either delivered the finished articles or had them collected by other workers. Some materials were issued free or at cost price to registered work parties. Women who had time to spare, but who could not get to a workroom, not only paid a registration fee but bought their own materials. They were issued with printed labels for their parcels and lists of what items were needed most urgently. They were expected to make at least four garments a month or an equivalent in rolled bandages. One garment was assessed as being the same as twenty bandages.

The Garments Department of the Central Workrooms made various shirts for general patients, those with typhoid, and those who were helpless. In addition to the normal range of hospital garments they made pneumonia jackets, kitbags, surgeons' overalls, and operating gowns. They also made 1,000 special sleeping suits for patients in Mesopotamia where large numbers of sandflies, not deterred by normal pyjamas, were an added affliction. The special suits were fly-proof, having sleeves that covered the patients' hands, trouser ends that covered their feet, and a hood with a muslin veil. They must have provided a welcome protection but does beg the question of how the medical staff got access to their bodies to care for them and dress their wounds.

Workers soon realised that many of the existing patterns for hospital garments needed to be adapted to meet the needs of the patients and so that they could be made as simply as possible with the minimum materials. Outfitters, Messrs Hodgkinson, offered to help and produced new designs for a range of garments, which were then turned into paper patterns that were distributed, with instructions and a photograph of the finished garment. Pattern books for knitted garments were also issued. The patterns were regularly updated to deal with fluctuations in the supply and quality of materials. Leading surgeons helped with the design of various types of bandage. More than 41,000 paper patterns and books were sent out.

With a ready eye for an opportunity, the Knitting Department and the British Dogs' Wool Association collected combings from long-haired dogs such as Pekinese and Pomeranians. The wool was then sorted, sterilised, carded and hand spun. The yarn was used to make warm and light garments. The National Salvage Council was very interested in this scheme.

Rather than having a specific base, the women of the Bournemouth War Hospital Supply Depot initially met to work in each other's houses. In September 1915, a depot opened at 3 Bodorgan Road with 333 registered volunteers. This number had doubled within a year and went up to 975 in 1917. The depot was affiliated to the St Marylebone Central Surgical Branch of the Queen Mary's Needlework Guild. Members devoted their energies to making bandages, dressings, swabs, clothes, slippers, bed and hospital equipment, and wooden items such as crutches, bed tables, bed cradles, and splints. In February 1916, members were awarded a certificate of excellence for the quality of their work. About three-quarters of the items they made were sent to local hospitals, while the remainder were sent overseas. As with many depots, they had a surplus of items they had made when the Armistice came into effect. Depots often sent their surplus to returning refugees in France or Belgium but in the case of Bournemouth, they were sent to help fit out a hospital in Romania.

Mr W. Mould taught joinery and carpentry at the Municipal College in Bournemouth. He knew there were a number of men in the area who had good carpentry skills and who would be willing to use some of their spare time for making wooden articles needed by local hospitals. He therefore set up a dedicated carpentry depot where these men made a range of articles from wood that had either been donated or bought at a greatly reduced price. Much of the wood came from clean wooden boxes such as tea chests, which were carefully dismantled so that the timber could be reused. Local Scouts helped to collect the wood and later to pack the finished goods. The depot was set up at the Pokesdown Technical Institute. As demand increased, the depot extended its opening hours until it had fourteen volunteers each day and nine in the evenings. Over time, the skilled carpenters transferred to the forces or munitions work and were replaced by less-skilled amateurs. Their output was varied and imaginative. They supplied thousands of crutches to the Kensington War Hospital Supply Depot and their other products included lockable cupboards for storing drugs on the hospital wards, bed tables and rests, dressing trays, and writing boxes. The Hampshire Football Association Wounded Soldiers Fund added some additional comforts before sending the packed crates by rail to hospitals in this country and abroad. The articles the Carpentry Depot made were greatly appreciated and various matrons wrote letters of appreciation. One letter thanked the workers for having designed and made special bed tables for men who had lost an arm. The bed tables enabled them to read and write in comfort. Such imagination and creativity were priceless.

When the registration of war charities was introduced in 1915 a number of organisations in Kent were brought together as the Canterbury and District War Work Depot. The Archbishop of Canterbury's wife and the mayoress agreed to be patrons. The organisation sounds cumbersome as there were sixty-five members of the general committee, several sub-committees and an executive committee. The depot's stated aims were to carry on providing support for hospitals, as they had since 1914, to provide clothes and bedding to troops who were in hospital or who were POWs and to make sandbags to be used in the defence of the Kent coast. Many of the clothes were made by Canterbury schoolchildren. Whenever possible materials used in the workrooms were locally produced.

The depot's work did not end with the Armistice. Anticipating Sir Edward Ward's instructions, the executive committee met on 10 December 1918 and agreed to send surgical necessaries to France and Belgium for civilian use and to make garments for civilians 'in the desolated countries'. Even after the depot closed, the executive committee carried on until November 1919, disposing of its remaining assets to charities.

***

Sphagnum moss has been used as a dressing in some areas for thousands of years. It is ideal for use in field dressings, as it is very light and can absorb several times its own weight in water or blood. Once the sheer numbers of wounded men and the severity of many of their wounds were apparent, the British Army started to use sphagnum moss dressings.

Vast quantities of moss were gathered by co-ordinated bands of volunteers wherever it grew in the British Isles and also in some parts of the Empire, including Canada. Landowners readily gave permission for it to be collected from the boggy parts of their properties. They may have had a personal incentive for doing this, as the destructive heather beetle laid its eggs on the moss and they wanted the heather for their game birds. The largest amounts were collected in Scotland, Dartmoor and Ireland.

Gathering moss was tiring, back-breaking work and volunteers often had to walk some way to the peat bogs before they could start their work. Bad weather added to their difficulties. The moss was either collected by hand or by using a rake. Naturally, as it was highly absorbent and was collected from bogs, the moss needed to be squeezed out as much as possible to reduce its weight and volume, before it was put in sacks to be transported to processing depots. In Orkney, the lorries for transporting the moss to Kirkwall were provided by local businessmen.

In Devon, members of the Okehampton Bible Class were among the volunteers who collected 200 sacks of moss in only two months. Another Devon volunteer, Mr John Durant, devised a special rake to help him collect about 1,000 lbs of moss in the Yes Tor area. It was estimated that this involved him in walking about 800 miles.

The Prince of Wales funded a centre for processing sphagnum moss at Princetown on Dartmoor. It supplied hundreds of sacks of moss and 500 prepared dressings a week. When the moss had been collected it was spread out on an asphalt tennis court to dry. This stage of the process was often hindered by wet weather. When the moss had been dried, it was taken to a meticulously cleaned, dry house in Princetown where women, dressed in white overalls and caps, spread it above heating pipes until it was crisp and springy. At this stage, much of the moss was sent off to hospitals. Some was made into dressings on site, each of which took three hours' careful work. Any foreign particles had to be picked out before the moss was packed into flat muslin bags. The dressings were sterilised in a solution of mercuric chloride, mangled, and then dried until they reached the desired weight. The finished dressings were packed into packages of twelve. Bales of 100 dressings were wrapped in waterproof sheets, to keep them sterile, before being sent abroad. The Prince of Wales visited the workers in February 1918 and was really happy both with the work and with what his funding had achieved.

The Reverend Adam Forman managed his family's estate near Beattock in Dumfries and Galloway and mobilised local people to collect moss. He also devised a two-handled trolley for transporting the moss across the moor. In Ireland, one of the volunteers was VAD Mary Pakenham, who described how they hung a kind of two-ended sack around their necks, like a stole and then waded, barefoot, into the boggy pools to collect the moss. She described three kinds of moss. The best was brown and thick, next best was green and straggly and the worst, but sadly most common kind, was described as red and measly.

Wherever the moss gatherers worked, they had to contend with attacks from midges. In Aberdeenshire, Lady Semphill encouraged her tenants to get involved in collecting moss and they suffered badly from the midges, in spite of dousing themselves in citronella oil. Lady Semphill started a moss-gathering class on Saturday afternoons, weather permitting. The moss was placed in cricket nets and dried in the laundry loft. The class was so successful that another was opened on one evening a week. There were soon sixty volunteers, including children, some of whom attended both classes.

The Bridge of Allan Moss Depot only opened in 1918 but its members still managed to gather forty sacks of moss that were made into 4,222 dressings. So that nothing was wasted, the siftings were made into thirty-five cushions. The dressings were in four sizes, with the largest being 18 by 30 inches. They were sent to the Hon. Lady Monroe Hospital Supply Depot, London; The Scottish Women's Hospital Supply Depot, Edinburgh; The Sphagnum Moss Supply Depot, Edinburgh, and Stirling Royal Infirmary.

Volunteers were of all ages and, as demand increased, more and more groups and individuals got involved. Boy Scouts, Girl Guides, VADs and members of the Red Cross were all mobilised. Although the moss was all collected in rural areas, many of the dressings were assembled in towns and cities. One depot, in Battersea, London, made 88,000 dressings. The Edinburgh Depot, started by Lieutenant-Colonel Cathcart MAMC, had 104 workers and produced 2,204,220 dressings.

In 1916, the manufacture of sphagnum moss dressings came under the organisation of a committee appointed by the Director General of Voluntary Organisations. The committee's job was to ensure enough moss was gathered to keep up with the army hospitals' increasing demand for dressings. Gathering depots were provided with sacks and twine and production centres were given muslin for making the dressings. The Government provided transport and centres were set up in Edinburgh, Glasgow, Aberdeen and Perth. Sir John Cowan devised a mechanical cleaner, later used in most depots, that speeded up the production process. So much moss was collected that after the war had finished, the Disposal Board of the Ministry of Munitions announced it had a stock of 350 tons of moss for sale.

* * *

One short-lived but important voluntary organisation was the Soldiers' and Sailors' Dental Aid Fund. This was set up by Miss Bannister Fletcher and, when it was founded in December 1914, it was the only organisation concerned with providing much-needed dentures to servicemen. Once it was apparent how important this service was, it was taken over by the War Office in November 1915.

After time as a cowboy and as a real estate agent in the United States, Almeric Paget became a successful industrialist before returning to Britain and becoming Conservative Member of Parliament for

Cambridge in 1910. In 1914 he and his wife set up the Almeric Paget Massage Corps through which they provided fifty masseuses to the Government to work in military hospitals. Such was the need that a further fifty were soon recruited. The masseuse worked hard, seeing thirty to forty patients a day, with only a thirty-minute break for lunch and ten minutes for tea. The Pagets followed this by setting up an outpatient clinic in London to treat wounded officers and men. This clinic was fully funded by the Pagets but was established at the request of the War Office to relieve the pressure on military hospitals in London. About 200 patients a day were treated. Sir Alfred Keogh inspected the clinic in March 1915 and was so impressed that the Almeric Paget Massage Corps became the official body for all massage and electrical departments in convalescent hospitals and command units in the UK. It was given a grant to enable it to expand and set up its first outpost at the largest convalescent camp in the country: Summerdown in Eastbourne. The camp housed 3,500 patients, of whom 500 were massage cases. Lady Paget was nicknamed the Angel of Summerdown. In December 1916 the corps was renamed the Almeric Paget Military Massage Corps. After the war it became the Military Massage Service. In early 1917 the first members of the corps were sent to work overseas. During the war 3,388 people were employed by the corps.

Before the war, Grace Kimmins ran a home for disabled children at Chailey in East Sussex. She decided that she must also welcome both children who had been traumatised by air raids and wounded soldiers to Chailey, turning one of the buildings over to the care of amputees. She had a novel approach to helping wounded men adapt to the loss of a limb, pairing them with children who had been born without the equivalent limb. The child would be waiting to greet the patient when they came round from their surgery and the child would then mentor the adult, showing them how to adapt to the loss of a limb. They learned a trade together. As Grace Kimmins put it, the boy had a hero and the soldier had a friend, whom he was keen to impress. It was an imaginative and successful scheme. Princess Louise made an appeal in *The Times* for £5,000 to fund this 'Educative Convalescence'. Following the appeal, the centre was called the Princess Louise Special Surgical Military Hospital. We are used to hearing about air raids during the Second World War but it comes as a surprise to realise that large numbers of apparently uninjured children in London and other towns were deeply traumatised by air raids. After all, aeroplanes were quite new, so aerial bombardment came as a huge shock. Grace Kimmins was in the forefront of understanding that these children needed help. For every child who was killed or severely injured by bombing she understood that many others had suffered mental harm. She believed the damage would become permanent if the children did not receive immediate help. The children who went to Chailey were placed in a house, known as the St Nicholas Home for Raid-Shocked Children, near the main Chailey Heritage site. Between 1917 and 1920 almost 600 children were given sanctuary there. The work was largely funded through the efforts of the *Evening Standard*, though appeals for donations were also made in *Punch*.

3

Medical and Supporting Volunteers on the Western Front

Violetta Thurstan was a professional nurse who was born in Hastings and spoke fluent French and German. Before the war, she was a respected administrator and lecturer. In her record of the war years, *Field Hospital and Flying Column*, Violetta described London after the outbreak of war as a hive of ceaseless activity. Territorial soldiers were returning from their unfinished training, every South Coast train was crowded with Naval Reserve men who had been called up, everyone was buying kits, getting medical comforts, and living at the Army & Navy Stores. She said both trained and untrained nurses besieged the War Office, demanding to be sent to the front. They had unrealistic aims of what they could achieve and were determined not to miss out on the chance to do their bit before the war ended. After all, they expected it to be over in a few months so there was no time to be lost in getting involved. After a while, the atmosphere calmed as people settled to work or wait to be called on to help. Violetta was a very experienced nurse and was critical of some of her fellow nurses. She admired the VADs who could be seen as nursing probationers or fully trained ambulance workers who were also willing to turn their hands to working as auxiliaries, cooks, ward maids or cleaners. The people she objected to were those who had a few weeks or months training, started to call themselves 'Sister' and wheedled their way to the front. She felt strongly that a course of first aid classes did not give anyone the sense of discipline, knowledge of people and adaptability that thorough training and years of experience could inculcate. Presumably, as the war went on, even she would have admitted that there was simply no time for this level of training for the number of nurses that were desperately needed. She went on to work overseas and was awarded the Military Medal for Bravery in the Field in 1917.

Looking back over the decades, it is easy to imagine the frustration and even annoyance of the British authorities trying to cope in the early days of a war with their near neighbours while also having to deal with large numbers of determined, headstrong women who were determined to get out to France and Belgium. They discouraged voluntary offers of help, no doubt bolstered by an unrealistic confidence in the ability of the War Office and the Royal Army Medical Corps (RAMC) to make adequate provision for sick and wounded servicemen. However, they must surely have been conscious of the problems that could, and did, occur when British women who did travel to France and Belgium got into trouble with the German authorities. They had enough to do without sorting out these issues too; a flood of unorganised volunteers could have been a real liability. That these volunteers, once organised, turned out to be one of our greatest assets was sometimes a case of more by luck than judgement. In the early days of the war, regulations governing travel to the Continent were quite relaxed so even when the British authorities rebuffed offers from women doctors and nurses, the ardour of many of the volunteers was not dampened. Individuals and groups offered their services to the French, Belgian and Serbian authorities, who promptly accepted them. Many of these volunteers went on to make an important contribution.

Several aristocratic women raced out to France to set up hospitals. Lady Hadfield, the Duchess of Westminster, Lady Sarah Wilson, and Rachel, Countess of Dudley, all set up hospitals near British bases. A few months later, each hospital was taken over by either the Red Cross or the Army. Other units under the control of the British Red Cross included Sir Henry Norman's Hospital at Wimereux; the Liverpool Merchants' Hospitals at Paris Plage, Étaples and later Trouville; and the Baltic and Corn Exchange Hospital in Calais, later at Paris Plage and finally at Boulogne.

Within days of the outbreak of war, the Duchess of Sutherland had set off for France intending to join the French Red Cross. Undaunted by the strict regulations that stopped foreigners working as nurses in France, she went off to see the French Minister of War. Overwhelmed by her forceful persuasiveness he granted her a permit. She joined a group of French nurses setting off to work in Belgium but when the Belgian Red Cross suggested it would be helpful for groups of English nurses to go to help in Belgium, she switched her allegiance from the French to the Belgian Red Cross. Having sent a telegram to England asking for a surgeon and eight nurses, she set up the Millicent Sutherland Ambulance Unit and announced that from then on she would be called Sister Millicent. Her unit established their base in a convent in the border town of Namur and waited to be needed. Namur was shelled on 22 August and their first wounded patients soon arrived. Before long, they were followed by German troops who occupied the town. With all the hauteur and arrogance of an upper class British matron, Sister Millicent set off for the German headquarters and handed her visiting card in for the Commandant, General Von Bulow. No doubt nonplussed by her arrival he agreed to see her, said that he was sure that he had met her in Hamburg before the war and was persuaded to sign a paper to stop their stores being requisitioned by the German Army. The general may well have regretted ever letting her into his office when she repeatedly returned with demands and complaints, always ready to quote the Geneva Convention at him. The German soldiers remained courteous but their patience must have worn very thin. After all, Sister Millicent and her team were, in fact, their prisoners. They were eventually sent to The Hague and then returned to England. Sister Millicent was determined to go back to France and set about fundraising with her usual energy. However, the situation had changed and it was no longer possible for independent groups to go over to nurse the wounded. If she wanted to go on helping, she had to come under the British Red Cross and so, in 1915 they set up the Duchess of Sutherland's Red Cross Hospital near Calais. Sister Millicent was, of course, the commandant and the hospital carried on working to great effect until the end of the war.

One of the more eccentric groups was led by the Duchess of Westminster in Le Touquet. With a group of friends she set up a hospital in her villa. She was a beautiful woman who wore an elegant uniform and toured the wards followed by her wolfhound. It is not clear whether she and her friends actually did any nursing and they certainly enlisted the help of the British Red Cross to provide trained nurses to cope with the wounded arriving from Mons. One of the nurses reported that the ladies did the things that the nurses did not have time for, such as writing letters for the patients. They also took charge of the hospital administration. At whatever time of the day or night a new group of wounded arrived, the Duchess and her friends appeared in full evening dress, including diamond tiaras and went down to register the patients. They also set up a gramophone, which played while the patients were registered and sent to the appropriate ward. The bemused, bloody, muddy, and traumatised soldiers must have thought they were hallucinating when this pristine bevy of ladies, in every sense of the word, welcomed them. The Duchess believed that the least she could do was to try to raise the morale of the wounded soldiers. Such impossibly high standards could not last and demand for hospital beds was so great that they soon moved to a large casino in the nearby forest.

Mabel St Clair Stobart arrived in England from South Africa in 1907. She was shocked to find the campaign for female suffrage underway, but soon described herself as a feminist as she was instinctively convinced that women could achieve a great deal beyond their traditional sphere. She believed that women would only get the vote if they could prove how much they could help with defending Britain. She said that women did not feature in the plans for the defence of the country in the case of invasion, thus ignoring the First Aid Nursing Yeomanry (FANYs) and the VADs. When her attention was drawn to the FANYs, she dismissed them as impractical, romantic. The day after the war started, she set up the Women's National Service League with herself, naturally, as director and Lady Muir McKenzie as sub-director. Their aim was to provide a group of women who were qualified to give useful service here or abroad. Their foreign service division was to include trained medical staff, interpreters, and other staff necessary for setting up a war hospital. Members of the home division were to offer to do anything that needed doing. Their appeal for volunteers and donations was immediately successful and within a fortnight they had raised £1,200 for equipment. Lady Cowdray gave them X-ray apparatus and the residents of Hampstead Garden Suburb in London donated £200. Before long they had also recruited a number of women doctors, nurses and orderlies. Lady Cowdray approached Sir Frederick Treves, chairman of the British Red Cross Society, to offer the services of her organisation. He rejected her offer, stating his belief that there was no work suitable for women in the field of war. When she mentioned the work of the Women's Convoy Corps in Bulgaria he remarked that that had been exceptional. Through the intervention of her friends, Lord and Lady Esher, she made contact with the Belgian Red Cross and was invited to go to Brussels to set up a hospital for French and Belgian soldiers. Unfortunately, no sooner had Mrs Stobart and her group arrived in Brussels than the Germans occupied the city and she was taken prisoner and charged with spying. When a judge released her she took her group to Antwerp where they set to work caring for French and Belgian casualties in a large philharmonic hall. Many of the arrivals were hungry as well as injured and were quickly given Oxo drinks. Some of the men were so exhausted that they even fell asleep while their wounds were being dressed. One of her team members said that Mrs Stobart never seemed to rest at all. The Germans had shelled the reservoir their water came from so they had to struggle to collect all their water from a well. After a few weeks they had to leave the city and lay on top of a load of ammunition, smoking, as they were driven away. On 10 October they arrived back in England.

* * *

One writer, known only as 'A War Nurse' recorded her experiences in detail in a diary that was later published. In spite of being a qualified nurse she was initially rejected for foreign service by the Red Cross, St John Ambulance Brigade, the Military Nursing Reserve and various other bodies as they already had about 30,000 names on their lists. Then a doctor she knew called for ten nurses to go to Antwerp and she immediately volunteered. This time she was accepted and, as with soldiers, part of the preparation involved writing her will.

The unit was set up by Dr Beavis and Madame Sindici with Mr Souttar of the London Hospital as their chief surgeon. Some of the nurses apparently had so little faith in Madame Sindici's management skills that they each acquired a tube of morphine tablets to be swallowed in an emergency if they were taken prisoner by the Germans. A few of the volunteers dropped out even before they had set out, presumably because they were scared of what would be involved. The group who embarked for Belgium included, bizarrely, four lady farmers, a farm wagon, and a dray horse. They later ditched the wagon and horse but it is not altogether clear what happened to the lady farmers!

As with every unit, the leaders of this group had clearly sorted out the important things first: they had chosen a uniform for the nurses of violet cloaks worn over sky blue dresses. The doctors, chauffeurs, and unqualified staff wore khaki.

Arriving in Antwerp, they set up their hospital in a school that had previously been a royal palace. No sooner had they unpacked than the first deluge of Belgian and British wounded arrived, filling the wards, the landings, and even the nurses' bedrooms. Just a few weeks later they were told that Antwerp was about to fall to the Germans and that anyone who wanted to leave should take the last mail boat to Britain, which was sailing that night. This was followed by a message from the Germans giving civilians who wanted to leave twenty-four hours to do so before shelling would start. Only three members of the group left.

All the patients who could be moved were taken to a network of passages under the hospital. As the shelling continued staff decided they had to try to evacuate the most seriously wounded and one of the medical students persuaded the military headquarters to lend them three London Motor Omnibuses. Although this may sound bizarre, more than 1,000 London buses were used to transport troops to and from the battlefields. After the buses had left, packed with the most seriously wounded patients, the shelling intensified demolishing whole blocks of buildings at a go. Nothing daunted, their chief went and commandeered five more buses. They filled the buses, and five private cars, with patients and set off for Ghent. The patients were in such agony from the jolting on the fourteen-hour journey that the nurses got out their emergency tubes of morphine and doled out the tablets to the wounded. The journey was made even more harrowing by the crowds of pitiful refugees who filled the roads and by the fact that all the jolting added travel sickness to the patients' woes – and to those of the nurses who tried to look after them.

On a later trip to Ostend, the War Nurse and a friend heard a rumour that the group might be returning to England. They felt strongly that they had gone to Belgium to nurse Belgians and were determined to stay. The Belgian Red Cross provided them with two doctors, a father and son, and a group of Boy Scouts to run errands for them. They happily set to work caring for patients in their somewhat palatial surroundings but after only a few days a member of the Civil Guard arrived telling them all to flee. As they ran around the building, raising the alarm, the War Nurse and her colleagues were amazed to find refugees they had never seen before popping up from every nook and cranny. The medical staff were persuaded that it would have been madness to stay and be taken prisoner and so they sailed for Dover on a ship packed with sick and wounded soldiers.

Within a few days of getting back to London, the War Nurse and her colleagues were invited to rejoin Mr Souttar and a team led by the Duchess of Sutherland who had a hospital at St Malo-les-Bains, near Dunkirk. The new team was to be based at Furnes, which was about 15 miles east of Dunkirk, 20 miles north of Ypres and a couple of miles south of the resort of La Panne where Queen Elizabeth of Belgium lived during the war. Furnes housed the headquarters of the Belgian Army.

They were based in a Catholic College, still occupied by the principal and professors who soon became willing and capable hospital orderlies – scrubbing floors, cleaning grates and attending to the patients. One by one, these professors were called up and replaced by Belgians who had been repatriated through Holland and who, under the terms of the Geneva Convention, could not fight again.

The team of about thirty-five mucked in and the War Nurse recorded that, 'It is a great thing to feel you are fighting death and saving heroes, besides which we were a very happy crowd.' Happy they may have been but the War Nurse said that they were soon sick of bully beef. No matter how it was disguised, it was identifiable at the first taste. Wet black bread, rancid butter and rock-hard biscuits that resembled a bath tile were no more popular. She was impressed by how all classes within the group sat around the same dinner table to eat their unappetising meals.

They were immediately inundated with work as they had arrived during the Battle of the Yser. At one point, they had to evacuate the entire hospital to Poperinghe, but were able to go back to Furnes after only three days. As well as dealing with a horrific range of injuries, they soon had to cope with tetanus as well – as wounds often contained mud and impacted clothing as well as shrapnel. They even extracted a large brass time fuse from one soldier's shoulder wound. Luckily, they were soon able to get serum from England and give every patient, whose wounds covered a large area, an anti-tetanus injection. Their work was carried out against the endless, exhausting roar of artillery – day and night.

Most operations had to be done at night as it was safer for the wounded to be transported through the danger zone after dark. As a result, some operations had to be carried out by candlelight. One of the chauffeurs attached to the hospital was a clergyman who was also a good carpenter and engineer. He used his skills to turn sugar crates into furniture for the wards and shelves for the nurses.

The Munro Ambulance Corps was attached to this hospital. It was set up by Dr Hector Munro who worked at the Brunswick Square Medico-Psychoanalytic Clinic in London and who had also opened England's first nudist camp. It has been suggested that Munro was more supportive of greater rights for women than most of the women in his team. In spite of official attitudes, he had included five women in his initial group of ambulance drivers.

One of the drivers was Lady Dorothie Feilding, who many people credited with being the real leader of the group as Munro's intentions were far better than his organisational skills. She was twenty-five in 1914, spoke fluent French and, as daughter of the Earl of Denbigh, had society contacts that she later turned to the corps' advantage. She had done an intensive first aid and home nursing course at Lutterworth Hospital before joining up.

Other members of the team included the writer Sarah McNaughtan, Dr Jellett, a gynaecologist from Dublin, and writer May Sinclair, who had no relevant experience but who was meant to deal with the unit's administration and publicity. Lady Dorothie Feilding wrote to her parents that May Sinclair may have been brainy but that she was a 'perfect ass'. After a few weeks, May left the unit and returned to England. Elsie Knocker and Mairi Chisholm were friends who had both been ardent motorcyclists before the war. Elsie was a trained nurse and Mairi was the youngest member of the group by ten years. Additional members joined the team and before long, they had twenty ambulances.

Money was always tight and they received no official funding from the Belgian or French authorities, although the British Red Cross later allocated them two ambulances and £16 a week. The members of the corps paid their own expenses and Mairi even sold her beloved motorbike to raise money. On various occasions, Lady Dorothie wrote to her parents asking for help with her living expenses, and then spent part of what they provided on other people.

The corps had arrived in Belgium in late September 1914 and driven to Ghent where they worked for the Belgian Red Cross. They went out in their ambulances across the sodden water meadows, picking up the wounded from the battlefields. In the village of Nazareth they found nearly thirty Belgians who had been shot with dum-dum bullets at point blank range and whose heads had been smashed in. Elsie Knocker was struck by the fact that the only officer in the group had been killed by one clean shot through his heart.

Leaving Ghent shortly before the Germans arrived, they moved back to Ostend and then attached themselves to the field hospital at Furnes. When they had to leave Ghent, Lady Dorothie was exasperated by Munro's panic and by his insistence on stopping to pick up various women he knew. She described him as well-meaning and enthusiastic but said it was a joke to put him in charge of anything. She felt that he needed looking after. Lady Dorothie increasingly had to take responsibility for the unit and longed for a 'big strong man' to come and take charge. She felt that the situation improved when they joined the field hospital at Furnes, which was under the command of her friend Robert de Broqueville, whose father was the Belgian Minister of War. Her uncle, Everard Feilding, acted as the unit's treasurer.

The team occupied a house belonging to a Belgian doctor who had vanished, and which was near the hospital in Furnes. Up to eighteen people shared three beds and at times, it was so cold that Lady Dorothie and Helen Gleason clung together all night, fully dressed, trying to keep warm. One day they got back to the house to find there had been a break-in, but that nothing had been stolen. They were, understandably, taken aback when a French soldier appeared asking if he had left his revolver in their bed. They learned that a number of French soldiers had been sleeping in the house while the members of the corps were at work. With the privilege of her connections, Lady Dorothie was delighted when Prince Alexander of Teck, Queen Mary's brother, offered her the chance to have a hot bath.

The corps suffered a blow in March 1915 when the British Red Cross withdrew all the ambulances they had lent to the French and Belgians as they were needed for Kitchener's army. They tried desperately to raise money for replacements and planned to approach all the City Livery Companies for help. The *Daily Mail* published an enthusiastic report of their work and backed their appeal. Lady Dorothie's mother, the Countess of Denbigh, clearly stepped in to help, as Lady Dorothie wrote to her to say that her mother's 'tame millionaire' had paid for two ambulances to be sent out to them immediately. The Wire Ropemakers' Company also donated an ambulance.

In contrast to Mairi Chisholm and Elsie Knocker, Lady Dorothie never wanted to exaggerate her own contribution or achievements. She hated the journalists who pursued them, bemused by the unconventional roles these women were performing. She was also generous in her recognition of what other people did. She was unusual in praising the nursing work done by Belgian ladies and said that the organisation of the Belgian Red Cross was far superior to that of the British Red Cross. Her numerous letters to her parents are held in the Warwickshire County Record Office and a selection has been edited for publication by Andrew and Nicola Hallam. The letters are chatty, frank, and incredibly readable. She had an evocative way of writing such as when she described how an ammunition train had been shelled, reducing the train, men and horses to powder and jam.

For a while, she worked with a Belgian driver, as the women were not meant to drive their ambulances in the area closest to the front. He, however, was scared and whenever things got too exciting for him, she would let him get out, take over driving to collect the wounded and collect the anxious Belgian on her return journey.

In her first months in Belgium, Lady Dorothie enthused about their work in her letters home. She felt that it was 'jolly interesting' being so near the action and was thrilled to be being useful. Photographs taken when she first arrived in Belgium and two years later show what a toll her work took on her. In October 1914, she described war as 'an utterly incomprehensible horror'. However, she still believed that it was easier for her, being out in Belgium and actually seeing what went on, than for people like her mother, at home in England hearing everything second-hand. Her letters give an unusually realistic picture of how such intensive work made her tired, bad tempered and headachy, and how she longed for a little peace and quiet. Most available accounts of volunteers' experiences were written, edited and published after the war and give a less harrowing image of their experiences. Lady Dorothie's relationship with her family clearly gave her colossal support and enabled her to keep going through the worst times.

When the Germans tried to break through at Dixmude, Pervyse and Nieuport the corps was overwhelmed with wounded and for ten days handled around 1,000 a day. The glare from burning villages helped them to see at night, but also reminded Lady Dorothie of hell. She said it was only possible to keep going because they knew that if they had not been there, working as hard as they possibly could, the suffering would have been even greater. She remarked just how hard the French sailors – Marins – worked during this time.

For a while she was based at Dixmude, driving her motor ambulance between the town and the sea. She remarked that the French Marins, under her friend General Hély d'Oissel, had to rely on horse-drawn ambulances. She enjoyed going to dine with them and thought the Marins far superior to the French Infantry who, she claimed, treated them as though they were doing them a favour by letting them go and collect their wounded, when they had not got the courage to go and fetch them themselves.

In March 1915, allied representatives met at Boulogne to draw up new rules governing English civilians working the war zone. For a while, it looked as though the Munro Corps might have to close or come completely under the Red Cross, which would have meant moving to Boulogne or somewhere else that seemed tame to Lady Dorothie. Due to the enthusiastic support of the Belgians, they were given permission to continue their work.

By the spring of 1915, the strain was telling on Lady Dorothie. In April, she wrote to her father that she longed for the war to end and wished that she had been born in a previous generation; in the same month, she wrote to her mother that for all his shortcomings Munro had been a real pal to her and that without him she would never have had a chance to do a real job. The Second Battle of Ypres brought a seemingly endless stream of wounded and in May, she wrote that she was exhausted, peevish and thoroughly fed up with the war. In another letter she wrote that she had had enough. However, in the same letter she described her pleasure in a glorious sunrise over the flooded landscape at Reninghe where the church spire stuck out of the water. She had also set up a garden and asked her mother to send her plants for it. Her mother was clearly more and more concerned about Lady Dorothie's health and offered to pay her fare home for a rest. In spite of, or perhaps because of, her problems, Lady Dorothie found it hard to tear herself away. She eventually did go home for a break, during which she wrote letters to the papers trying to raise money for a new ambulance.

When she went back to Furnes she took her small terrier, Charles, with her and although he hated the shelling, especially from the Allies, he was clearly a real comfort to her. She said she hated going back, but would have hated just having to sit at home even more. It is clear that her colleague and friend, Dr Jellett, was worried about her health and he reported her lack of appetite and general poor health to her mother. Lady Dorothie wrote to her father, then serving in Egypt, that she almost thought that things were simpler for those who were simply blown up as she was not sure what would be left of the rest of them when the war ended. Although she came from a strongly Roman Catholic family, and kept her faith, she lost any belief in an afterlife. She said that when you saw the dead by the thousand, you did not think that humans were different to any other animal.

In April 1915, the *War Illustrated* reported that the canals around Dixmude were so clogged with bodies that when a shell landed human flesh rained down on the countryside. Dixmude was at the heart of the area where Dorothie took her ambulance to collect the wounded.

In August, Lady Dorothie again went home for a much-needed rest and Dr Jellet insisted on taking her to a doctor in London on the way to her parents' home. She worried that she was slacking and of little use as she was tired and full of aches and pains. This time she spent two weeks at home, after the family united to stop her going back sooner. The break made her feel much better.

She received the Croix de Guerre (bronze star) in 1915, after being mentioned in a 'Special Order of the Day' dated 31 December 1914 by the French Rear Admiral Pierre Ronarc'h Commander of the Fusiliers Marins. She only remembered to tell her mother about the medal in a postscript to a letter.

Lady Dorothie clearly suffered from terrible period pains and regularly had to have a day in bed when 'Tonks' (the family nickname for her period) arrived. She was in bed with period pains in November when Elsie Knocker and Mairi Chisholm turned up. Elsie was all excited and took Lady Dorothie's breath away by apologising for all the nasty things she had ever said to her. The reason for the apology became clear when Elsie announced she was engaged to a Belgian Lieutenant, Baron Harold de T'Serclaes de Rattendael. She wanted Lady Dorothie to tell her how to be a Catholic because of her future husband's religion! She later undertook formal instruction from a priest but her convenient failure to disclose that her first marriage had ended in divorce rather than bereavement is thought to have contributed to the failure of her new marriage.

In 1916, Dorothie was the first woman to be awarded the Military Medal, which had only been created in March that year. Dr Jellett had already been decorated for his work with the corps. In the letter of recommendation he sent to Prince Alexander of Teck, Commander Henry Crosby Halahan RN, Commanding the Royal Naval Siege Guns, said that when driving her ambulance '(She) was thus frequently exposed to risks which probably no other woman has undergone. She has always displayed a devotion to duty and contempt of danger which has been a source of admiration to all'. Her medal was presented to her by King George V at Windsor Castle on 1 September 1916. Sadly for Lady Dorothie, the award brought publicity and she started to receive anti-Catholic leaflets from the Protestant Tract Society of Ilford. She was also sent a press cutting about her award on which someone had written 'SHAME' in thick blue chalk and 'The Church of Rome always strives to remain in the public eye, regardless of the means employed'. This must have been very hurtful, especially for someone who shunned publicity.

Throughout her time in Belgium Lady Dorothie relished the parcels of chocolate, toffee, clothes and other comforts that her mother sent out. She was delighted to receive a pair of her favourite boots and her flea bag and sent a request for a new rubber bath (apparently superior to the canvas ones) when hers wore out. She regularly sent her mother lists of what they needed including hypodermic syringes, from Harrods, and Horlicks. The countess must have been very busy sending parcels as well as writing long chatty letters to them all, given that her husband and most of her large brood of children served in one place or another during the war.

Lady Dorothie was pleased at the arrival of a new recruit, 'Winkie Speight' and admitted to her family that she had sometimes been lonely. The company of an upbeat, independent woman of her own age was a delight. Winkie even set about learning Flemish from a nun. It made Lady Dorothie reflect that Winkie's attitude was much as hers had been when she set out in 1914. Strain began to tell on Dr Jellett who became increasingly cantankerous and talked of going home. In the warm weather, Lady Dorothie said she would have loved to go swimming but that the sea was so full of naked Tommies that there was no chance for the women to bathe.

January 1917 was so bitterly cold that although they thought they had completely drained each of the radiators, they froze overnight. Both the medical staff and soldiers preferred the frost to the mud they had endured for months. The canal froze when the temperature plummeted and they were able to go sliding. The floods also froze, as did the edge of the sea.

In April 1917, they were mildly gassed as the Germans advanced. Dr Jellett woke to the smell of gas and they all raced to get their gas masks on. They worked flat out all day and Lady Dorothie felt frustrated by how little they could do to help the gassed men, some of whom seemed reasonably alright for about twelve to twenty-four hours and then collapsed. She, herself, was left very tired by the amount she had inhaled and twenty-four hours later was shocked to find that she could only breathe in gasps that she likened to a frightened rabbit. She also felt faint off and on all day and eventually had to go to bed. Dr Jellett seemed unaffected but Winkie developed a really bad cough and Charles, the dog, wheezed for days.

Exhaustion and stress notwithstanding, she stayed with the Munro Ambulance Corps in Flanders until June 1917 when she went home to be married. Her husband was Captain Charles Joseph Henry O'Hara Moore of the Irish Guards, who she had known before the war. After the wedding Lady Dorothie wrote how much she appreciated feeling at peace. This is, in itself, a reflection of how traumatised she was by her experiences. Marriage did not stop her volunteering and, after the honeymoon, she went back to driving an ambulance, but around London rather than Belgium. She later became an active member of the British Legion.

* * *

Elsie Knocker was very much a maverick. She seemed to make a point of being unconventional and relished the attention this brought her. She was not designed to fit easily into any team. She and Mairi Chisholm had been volunteer despatch riders together in London before joining the Munro Ambulance Corps. Elsie was a trained nurse. They showed their independence, from the outset, by turning up in their own, unconventional, uniform of riding breeches, high lace-up leather boots, and khaki overcoats.

When the corps set out, Lady Dorothie was really pleased that Elsie Knocker was part of the team. She described Elsie as 'A1' and Mairi as 'a buxom colonial wench … capable'. She later revised her opinion. The dynamics within the corps were never easy and Elsie found the restrictions of being part of a team particularly frustrating. She was the sort of volunteer who needed a constant rush of adrenaline to keep motivated and active. After a few months, Elsie concluded that fewer of the wounded would die if they could be stabilised in a first aid post close to the front before being transported to hospital. She wanted to set up and run such a post. She clashed with Munro over this plan but he eventually agreed and in November 1914 she, Mairi Chisholm, Helen Gleason and Lady Dorothie went off to the remains of the village of Pervyse to set up their first aid post in the cellar of a wrecked house. Lady Dorothie was pleased to be working under Elsie Knocker as she was so much more capable than Hector Munro. She told her mother that she felt safer than before.

In her own memoir, Elsie Knocker glosses over the work done by Lady Dorothie and Helen at Pervyse although, to be fair, they were only there a relatively short time before returning to work with the Munro Corps in Furnes. By the spring of 1915, there was very little contact between Elsie and Mairi and the Munro Corps although Lady Dorothie seems to have had intermittent contact with Mairi, about whom she worried.

The post at Pervyse remained nominally part of the Munro Corps, although Elsie did all she could to prevent Munro having anything to do with it. Munro arranged for Elsie to go home for Christmas 1914 leaving Mairi, Lady Dorothie, and Dr Jellett to carry on in her absence. The group did what they could to celebrate Christmas and gave welcome presents of socks to the soldiers. Dr Jellett had been in charge in Elsie's absence and she would not accept his refusal to let her go back to Pervyse until the shelling had stopped. She and Mairi went anyway and a series of meetings between Elsie, Lady Dorothie and Munro was needed to smooth things over again.

In January 1915, the cellar post closed and they moved to a house, where they all lived. Conditions were extremely primitive and over that first, freezing, winter they had to use a shell hole as their toilet until Alphonse and Désiré, two Belgian soldiers who had been sleeping in the cellar, found a commode for them to use. They scavenged the deserted gardens for fruit and vegetables and frequently ate horses that had been killed in the fighting. They made cauldrons of soup and hot chocolate, which they served to any soldiers who came in, and also took drinks to those on the front line at considerable risk to themselves.

Elsie, in particular, was an excellent self-publicist and cultivated her 'celebrity' status, while always claiming that everything she did was in order to help the wounded. The publicity she achieved was possibly out of proportion to the numbers of soldiers she and Mairi were actually able to help in Pervyse. She and Mairi were nicknamed 'The Heroines of Pervyse' by newspapers back in England, which Elsie, in particular, relished. At Pervyse Elsie bizarrely kept a visitor's book, which she carefully preserved when she left.

Marie Curie and her daughter Irene visited Pervyse just after they had set up the first mobile X-ray unit. Their visit drew a lot of attention and put Elsie's nose out of joint as she liked to be the centre of attention. Elsie and Mairi were made Chevaliers de l'Ordre de Leopold and Elsie claimed that Lady Dorothie was only awarded the same honour because her family connections pulled strings. This reaction ignored Lady Dorothie's work at the heart of the Munro Corps.

In 1916, Elsie published a book called *The Cellar House at Pervyse*. It was designed to raise funds for Belgian soldiers. Having been involved in the work at Pervyse, Lady Dorothie was appalled by the book. While relieved not to have been mentioned by name, she felt there was enough about the Munro Corps in it for people to associate her with Elsie and that annoyed her. She felt the book was in the worst possible taste and that it made her sick to be a woman. She believed that the book unfortunately made Mairi look a fool and made the uncharitable comment that Elsie should have been drowned at birth! Lady Dorothie was not alone in her disproval and Peter Chalmers, who had been stationed in the area, apparently commented that there was too much about Mairi in it and not enough about the shells.

Money was always scarce and Elsie and Mairi had to make frequent fundraising trips to England. It became increasingly difficult to raise money as the war dragged on and on. There were more causes competing for money and the British public began to feel they had, perhaps, done enough for the Belgians and should concentrate on looking after their own. Souvenir hunting was rife on both sides of the conflict and both women were among those who collected all sorts of items from the war zone. Mairi also used to cut the buttons off the uniforms of dead German soldiers and auction them to raise money for their work in Pervyse. Elsie bought a German helmet from a French soldier in Dixmude. She also acquired, among other things, a pretty soup ladle and a salt cellar, both non-essentials. On one trip to England, they arrived at Waterloo Station dressed in filthy breeches, with Mairi carrying a German lance. It is no wonder that they attracted attention.

After one successful fundraising trip in 1915, they moved to the Villa Espagnole, a tiny cottage on the other side of Pervyse. It apparently smelt of death and broken drains and Mairi hated being left there while Elsie went to La Panne to collect their belongings. They soon decamped as they and their drivers were convinced the cottage was haunted.

After their first aid post had been hit by several shells they decided they needed a mobile hospital. Mairi raised money through an appeal in the *Nairnshire Telegraph*, playing on their link to the Munro Corps but adding that they had been seconded to the Belgian Army. They then enlisted the help of Mr Costa from Harrods, who was involved in building a hospital at La Panne. He arranged for the delivery and construction of a prefabricated log cabin with an external kitchen. Sadly, it was shelled shortly after it was finished and had to be repaired and moved closer to Steenkerke and further from the front. Because of the danger from shelling, they had a dugout next to the hut where they could shelter if necessary. The Belgian authorities started to give them rations for their patients but they had to depend on donations for food for the staff, and comforts such as cigarettes and books for the patients. They needed £30 a month for fuel, laundry, and spare parts for the ambulances. The British Red Cross paid £2 a month for Harrods to send them groceries.

Their move meant that once again the wounded had to travel further before getting help so Elsie and Mairi found another house in Pervyse, which Mr Costa and his team made stable and then the First Aid Post re-opened. The strain was showing on Elsie and when things did not go her way, she threw tantrums. On one occasion, she turned on faithful Mairi so badly that she fled to Helen Gleason in Furnes, even though Elsie forbade her to go. Elsie was clearly on the verge of a serious mental breakdown and Mairi accompanied her back to England for a rest. There is no mention of who looked after the Pervyse post in their absence. The trip exhausted Mairi, who told her aunt that she was worn out, as Elsie's illness had meant that she had to shoulder all responsibility for their work. Perhaps this was the same aunt, Lucy, who sent boxes of socks, scarves, and mittens and packets of Nestlé's Coffee to Pervyse.

Elsie continued to fight for independence from the Munro Corps, and yet to use their association when it was convenient. She stressed their link to show they had official approval of their work. In 1917, shortly before the Third Battle of Ypres, the British took over the Pervyse sector. Elsie was not pleased and clashed with Major Christian, who wanted the women to leave. A major row with the Commander of the Fourth Army, Sir Henry Rawlinson, followed – but he had to allow the women to stay as they had the backing of the Army Council.

In 1916 Mairi's father, Roderick, got permission to go and work with them. Things went well while the newly married Elsie was living in La Panne, but after she went back to Pervyse they clashed, fiercely and repeatedly. He frequently described Elsie as a mad, wounded genius and said that she loved the limelight. He also hated having to take orders from a woman and had never liked the influence Elsie had over Mairi. After six months he returned home.

In 1917 both women were awarded the Military Medal and the Order of St John of Jerusalem for their work in Pervyse.

In March 1918 an arsenic gas shell exploded close to them and gas poured into their post, killing one of their assistants and their dog. Elsie and Mairi were both evacuated to hospital in La Panne and then moved to London for further treatment. While Elsie was still recovering, Mairi went back to Pervyse only to be gassed again within a few weeks. She never fully recovered from the gas and neither of them was able to continue their work. Other women volunteered to take over but none was allowed to do so and the first aid post was closed.

* * *

Christmas in Furnes was celebrated in the greatest possible style. The War Nurse and her companions went to a big department store in Dunkirk to buy presents for their colleagues and for the children they had befriended at a local orphanage. They decorated the hospital with bunting, mistletoe and holly, and festooned three large Christmas trees with tinsel. They even set up a little shrine with statues of the Virgin Mary and baby Jesus surrounded by candles at one end of a large ward. The orphans, raised by nuns and singing beautifully, entertained the wounded. The War Nurse missed the distribution of presents as she had to snatch a few hours' sleep.

Later, when a group of them were playing hide and seek in the courtyard and being chased among the ambulances by chauffeurs from Munro's Ambulance Corps waving mistletoe, the town came under bombardment. In forty-five minutes that Christmas Day, more than 200 shells fell on Furnes.

The staff shared goodies they had been sent from home with the patients and then sat down to their own Christmas dinner, lubricated by wine the priest had brought up from his cellar and complete with crackers, silly hats and jokes. In the middle of the party the bell at the gate rang and wounded started to arrive, putting an abrupt end to the festivities. The famous Christmas ceasefire did not happen in the Furnes sector.

From Christmas the bombardment was incessant. After a couple of weeks, all the patients who could be moved were taken across the border into France. The wine cellars were turned into wards. One was even an operating theatre, lit by candles and oil lamps. No sooner had they moved the last patients to the cellars than a shell came through the roof and into an empty ward. The remaining patients were soon taken to Dunkirk.

The team started a new hospital at Hoogestadt, between Furnes and Ypres. It was closer to the front and, for their safety, they had tight restrictions on how far they could go from the hospital on the Belgian side. They were based in some former almshouses and the attic, where the twenty-six nurses, thirty orderlies and kitchen staff and half a dozen Flemish laundry maids slept, was up a spiral staircase with fifty steps. It was one vast room, which they divided into cubicles by tying bandages to the rafters and pinning sheets to them. They lived there for ten months surrounded by a waste of deep mud.

Over the winter their team shrank. They were less busy and some medical staff went back to Britain where they felt they would be more use. Some of the younger men joined the armed forces leaving only three doctors and nine nurses. In April 1915 the Second Battle of Ypres started.

To their horror, they found they were in the firing line and surrounded by allied guns that had been concealed in the outbuildings of the adjacent farm. For a fortnight wounded British, German, French, and Belgian soldiers poured in day and night. They were appalled by the suffering of the men, who had faced the first gas attack and who choked and suffocated in agony.

One operation after another was carried out with barely time for the blood from one operation to be wiped off the table onto the floor before the next patient was brought in. The War Nurse struggled to sterilize all the tools, by boiling them on a faulty petrol stove, before handing them to the surgeons as needed.

They were terribly under-staffed so the Belgian authorities sent them some military surgeons, led by a major – who took immediate charge, to the annoyance of the British doctors. The arrival of the Belgian surgeons gave the hospital a new, official, standing and they were able to expand and improve their facilities. It became, in effect, a base hospital and able to save more lives. Some prefabricated huts were sent out from England, each of which could be erected in one day by a team of twenty soldiers. Their X-ray unit benefitted from a visit by Marie Curie and her daughter. In case of further gas attacks they put respirators, soaked in hyposulphate, in mackintosh bags at the head of each bed. Each nurse also carried one in her pocket at all times.

The summer was quieter and the nurses were able to enjoy riding with the elegant and aristocratic members of the Belgian Cavalry who were based nearby. It gave them a wonderful feeling of release and freedom. Queen Elizabeth of Belgium visited the hospital several times, handing out chocolate, cigarettes, and flowers and chatting to the patients.

Up to this point they had been nursing ordinary soldiers but in the summer of 1915 the soldiers were moved into huts and the main building was occupied by the staff and a small group of wounded officers. The hospital was, by then, very well equipped and soldiers were provided to do the heavy work. It is clear that officers were treated very differently from the 'other ranks' with the War Nurse saying that they tried to give the men the comforts they would have had in a London hospital. In order to get these comforts, she wrote endless beseeching letters to the Red Cross and other organisations in Britain. In return goods arrived by the crate-load and the small eight-bed ward was made very attractive and comfortable. The staff dined with the officers and those who were well enough even went riding with the nurses on a few occasions.

The War Nurse was given the job of nursing the wounded general of the Premier Belgian Division. When the general complained that his bed was too hard, his friend, the King of Belgium, sent him his own bed and mattress. The Queen sent copious quantities of flowers and the eight officer patients were hurriedly, and to their fury, shifted to a hut and their ward was made into a nice living room. Madame Curie set up a bell for summoning staff and a telephone, linked to headquarters, beside the general's bed. He was badly injured with parts of his hip bones having been shot away and his lower back laid open to reveal his spine. A stream of important visitors came to visit him including General Joffre, who gave him the Legion of Honour and a 'Member of the British Royal Family' who gave him the Victoria Cross.

* * *

Although Violetta Thurstan was jealous that nurses who were less experienced than she was had managed to get out to the Continent, while she was stuck in England, she was soon asked to take a group of nurses out to Belgium to work with the Belgian Red Cross. Like all such departures, it was done with little notice and in a great rush and due to some bureaucratic hitch she had to go on to Brussels ahead of the main party.

Discovering that a German occupation was imminent, she sent a telegram to England to stop her nurses embarking. It never arrived and she soon discovered that twenty-six rather than sixteen nurses had, in fact, set off. Violetta had a look around Brussels and realized that people in England had no idea what war really meant or the impact it had on the whole population rather than just two opposing armies. It was as if the whole civilian population was trying to leave town to escape the German advance. The Belgian Red Cross sent her a message to say that the Germans were at the edge of the city and that she should ensure that all her nurses were at their appointed workplaces.

Undaunted by the arrival of the Germans, Violetta set about making her wards look as much like English ones as she could. However, she noted with regret that their patients were not British Tommies but eighty German soldiers with sore feet.

When the Belgian Red Cross asked for three nurses to go to Charleroi Violetta, Sister Grace and Sister Elsie were quick to volunteer. Violetta was appalled by the destruction of all the commercial and richer parts of the town, which she described as 'the Birmingham of Belgium'. Parts of the town were still burning when they arrived.

Their destination was a part-built hospital outside the town. French and German wounded arrived at the same time as the three nurses, who were sorely needed as the German doctor had left. The Belgian doctor only stayed a short while before going back to his civilian patients and the only nurses already there were girls who had just been to first aid lectures. The hospital was in chaos but they set to and coped in a way that was typical of the energy and creativity that characterised the majority of British medical workers. They were short of everything, apart from coffee, but had no means of heating water to make it.

The area around Charleroi was filled with Germans, who imposed increasingly onerous rules and regulations on the local population. They were not allowed to lock the door, or pull down the blinds or even let their dogs out of the house. All German soldiers had to be saluted and the local people were banned from wearing menacing looks, however they were to be defined. They were even forbidden to open any windows to prevent anybody firing out of them. This denied the patients essential ventilation. In spite of all the problems their status and condition brought, Violetta was happy in her work. She felt supported by the Belgian doctor and committee and was full of praise for her colleagues who were, especially at the outset, overworked and underfed while they got the hospital into good shape. The committee allowed her to keep the best of the Red Cross probationers and to refuse others, which made a big difference, allowing continuity and discipline. She was full of praise for the stoicism and good-natured attitude of her patients. French and German soldiers had to be nursed in the same wards and she felt that they all behaved well.

Shelling was incessant and in the early days she pictured swathes of men being felled by each blast. She later learned that comparatively few shells actually hurt people. They were constantly short of supplies and struggled to find anyone to do the hospital laundry, of which there was, naturally, a huge amount. They were also very short of food and subsisted largely on potatoes and lentils with occasional horsemeat. The catering problems were compounded by the fact that all the local watercourses were polluted with dead men and horses. Needless to say, they boiled all their drinking water.

In September, all the German patients were sent back to Germany. This lightened the atmosphere in the wards and also reduced the workload for Violetta and her team. The respite was short-lived, as they were then told that all the French patients were to be sent to Germany. They were horrified, as many of the men were too sick to travel. The hospital did not even have enough clothes for the patients and had to cobble something together. This highlighted one of the differences between untrained Red Cross nurses and their more experienced colleagues. The novices would cut anywhere to remove a wounded man's clothes while a trained nurse would try to cut beside a seam to make later repairing the garment easier. She commented on how poorly equipped the French soldiers were compared to their German counterparts.

Violetta got permission from both the Red Cross and the Germans to go to Brussels for a day or two to visit her nurses there. She was shocked by how much the city had changed and how grim life had become. Apparently, one of the things that upset the people most was the loss of all their valuable pigeons. She found that the nurses were bored and had little to do, as all their patients had been removed. There were more than a hundred British nurses in Brussels from the Order of St John, the British Red Cross and from privately organised groups. They were keen to get back to Britain where they could be more useful. There was a rumour that the Germans would rather have their wounded die than be nursed by English women. Dreadful stories of atrocities circulated, including one that English nurses put out the eyes of German patients.

When Violetta was due to return to Charleroi the Germans refused to let her leave Brussels. The medical staff were told that all private hospitals and ambulances in Brussels were to stop working and that the British were not to nurse any prisoners. Some members of the British Red Cross team were then accused of being spies and imprisoned for twenty-four hours. A large group of German Red Cross nurses arrived in Brussels, making Violetta wonder what the etiquette would be if she were to bump into any of the German nurses she had met at the last International Council of Nurses that had been held in Germany before the war.

After the Red Cross workers were released one of the doctors asked the Germans what was to happen to them, as they were no longer allowed to work as medical staff. To the surprise of the whole group, they were told they were going to be sent to Liège. As Liège was much closer to Germany and as they were not allowed to work, they felt that this sounded worryingly like imprisonment. The American Consul tried hard to persuade the commandant to change his mind but he refused. A few days later, they were told they were to be sent home after all.

While they were waiting Violetta decided to have a typhoid inoculation as she had not had time to get one before leaving London and the disease was widespread in Brussels. To her great annoyance, she reacted badly to the inoculation and had to go to bed with a high temperature and a badly inflamed arm. She was still ill in bed when the news came that every English doctor and nurse in Brussels was to leave for Holland under the care of the American Consul.

About twenty English doctors and around a hundred nurses were packed into third class railway carriages with two German soldiers with loaded rifles sitting by the window in each compartment. The soldiers were meant to keep the blinds down and to stop the medical staff looking out of the window. Luckily, the guards in Violetta's carriage seemed embarrassed by their job and kept the blinds up and the windows open. The train crawled along and by the evening they had only reached Louvain, where the soldiers seemed shocked at the burnt-out ruins of the once magnificent town.

As they travelled on through the night, Violetta realised they were heading for Germany rather than the Dutch border. When they crossed the border into Germany the next morning they were ordered onto the platform and their luggage was thrown after them. All their scissors and surgical equipment were confiscated. The two soldiers who had been in Violetta's compartment kindly grabbed their bags and took them back onto the train. The group re-boarded the train and learned that they were heading for Cologne.

They had a long stop at one station and to their relief bowls of a hot, thick soup were handed in. When the train eventually crawled into Cologne they were marched to a waiting room where they were given a meal and hot coffee and were able to buy rolls and fruit for the journey that lay ahead. The next leg of the journey, across Germany, was in a slightly more comfortable train and when they reached Munster they were delighted to be met by the women of the local Red Cross, who provided meals to all wounded soldiers and prisoners who passed through the town. These Red Cross members were surprised to have to deal with a group of English women but treated them well and even let them have a good wash at a standpipe.

Their treatment in Munster was in stark contrast to their earlier experiences. A large and hostile crowd had gathered at one station to watch them get out of the train. Although they were not allowed onto the platform itself they lined the railings outside, laughing, spitting, jeering at and insulting the English group. The doctors and nurses were careful not to react, afraid that the male members of the team would be taken away as POWs on the slightest pretext. Huddled in the waiting room they were served cold meat and bread by hostile German waiters. To their amazement a young German officer came up to them and asked if there was anything he could do for them as he had been treated very kindly on a trip to England before the war. He told the waiter off in no uncertain terms before plying them with chocolate and fruit.

They were stunned when they were allowed to enter Denmark and were free again after to being prisoners for two months. They were given an amazingly warm welcome in Copenhagen, where strangers sent them presents and invitations. The Danish Council of Nurses arranged a programme of visits to all the most important hospitals and tourist sights and they revelled in being able to write to their friends and families again and, quite simply, to relax.

* * *

Dr Louisa Garrett Anderson was the daughter of medical pioneer Dr Elizabeth Garrett Anderson and was keen to serve when the war started. With her friend and fellow suffragette Dr Flora Murray she realised that the British establishment would not be willing to accept their services. They therefore visited the French Embassy and, in shaky French, offered to provide a medical unit staffed and run by women. The official referred them to the French Red Cross. Their offer was snapped up and within weeks they had established the Women's Hospital Corps, raised £2,000 to cover their costs, recruited a team, agreed and acquired their uniforms and set off for Paris.

This was the first unit to have only women doctors in charge and they set up their hospital in the unfinished Claridges Hotel in Paris. They had a lot of work to do before they could open and with the help of some Belgian refugees, billeted on the seventh floor, the doctors and nurses set to erecting beds, cleaning the building and generally getting organised. Within a couple of days they were ready to take their first fifty allied wounded, delivered by an American ambulance unit.

In September they were inspected by an official from the War Office who was touring auxiliary hospitals. He fired out questions, hardly waiting for the answers until, to the relief of the staff, Madame de la Panouse, president of the French Red Cross, arrived. In response to his incredulity that British women appeared to be in charge in a French hospital, she informed him that it was her best hospital. His sidekick, a doctor said to be unconvinced as to the capabilities of women doctors, toured the wards. The patients he spoke to told him they were more than happy with the care they were receiving. The doctor came back the next day and asked if they would be able to expand their services or move closer to the front if asked to. He added that the British Army would not hesitate to use their services if the French Red Cross would agree.

The Claridges Hospital was a success and they soon opened as second one at Wimereux, on the Channel Coast. In January 1915, there was a change in policy and the War Office decreed that, whenever possible, casualties should be treated in Britain rather than in France or Belgium. The Surgeon General, Sir Alfred Keogh, asked Dr Murray and Dr Garrett Anderson to run a military hospital in London under the Royal Army

Medical Corps. This remarkable invitation put women in charge of a British military hospital for the first time. As the women made no secret of their militant suffragette views, their appointment was all the more remarkable. They opened the Endell Street Hospital in London and ran it, staffed only by women, from 1915 to the end of 1919. Sir Alfred Keogh later said that the staff at Endell Street were worth their weight not in gold but in diamonds.

* * *

At the start of the war, a fifty-year old Scottish doctor, Elsie Inglis, offered her services to the Women's Hospital Corps. When she heard that the team was complete she went to offer her services to the Royal Army Medical Corps (RAMC) at Edinburgh Castle. There her offer was met with the famously crass response: 'My good lady, go home and sit still!' Rebuffed but not deterred, she came up with the idea of the Scottish Women's Hospitals for Foreign Service (Scottish Women's Hospitals) and put her proposal for two hospitals staffed and run entirely by women to the executive of the Scottish Federation of Women's Suffrage Societies. They accepted her idea with enthusiasm, set up a Hospitals Committee and started fundraising.

When their proposed units were rejected by the British Red Cross, they offered their services to the Allies. The French and the Serbs were quick to accept their offer. Much of their initial funding came from suffrage societies but as word of their efforts spread funds came in from other sources as well. Before long, they had raised enough money for their first unit to set off for France and, soon after, a second unit was sent to Serbia. Preparing and despatching each unit cost £1,500. In late November Madame de la Panouse, started looking for suitable premises for the unit and, by the end of the month, had chosen the thirteenth century Cistercian Abbey of Royaumont, about 20 miles from Paris.

The Scottish Women's Hospitals team left Edinburgh on 2 December 1914 wearing the uniform the committee had chosen. It consisted of long skirts, sensible shoes, hip-length cloaks with velvet collars and tartan facings and broad brimmed hats. The choice of uniform proved controversial, as Dr Inglis complained that the fabric was shoddy, the sewing poor and that the collars did not fit. It was apparently lucky that they would not have to be seen in Paris so poorly dressed. The doctors bought their own blue uniforms to the fury of the uniform committee, who refused to pay for them until the hospital committee stepped in to mediate.

The team consisted of seven doctors, ten nurses, seven orderlies, two cooks, a clerk, an administrator, two maids and four chauffeurs. At the outset, two of the chauffeurs were men, as they were not sure the French would allow women to drive in the war zone. Later on all the chauffeurs were women.

The choice of leader for this first unit proved particularly successful. Miss Frances Ivens was a gifted administrator and surgeon and managed to build a good working relationship with the French authorities. Dr Inglis rarely visited Royaumont, turning her own attention to Serbia. There is, however, a film made when she visited the hospital in 1917. The nurses apparently had to fake various scenes. When Dr Ivens saw the film she said that it made her blood run cold and when it was shown at a post-war staff reunion, they all agreed that it was atrocious. It was, presumably, a piece of publicity that the hospital committee thought worthwhile.

When the group arrived at Royaumont the owner, Monsieur Goüm, let the team's clerk, Cicely Hamilton and the administrator, Mrs Owen, into his part of the Abbey but said that there was no more space and urged them not to bring the rest of the team. The two women were not deterred but were horrified at how filthy and neglected the buildings were. The stove had not been lit for ten years, all water had to be brought in by bucket, and the electricity supply was not connected. Cecily Hamilton, who had previously been an actress and playwright, kept the hospital's accounts meticulously and took them to Paris each month for inspection by the French Red Cross.

The cook, Dorothy Littlejohn, was an unlikely recruit for this unit as she was opposed to women doctors and women's suffrage. The team's equipment was delayed and Dorothy had a real struggle to cater for the group with what was available. She managed brilliantly, catering for twenty-five with only two small pans and some tiny French bowls, one kettle and the huge stove. The rooms were lit by candles. She borrowed cups from the village ironmonger and the team had to share one knife. Before long the electricity was connected. Even when the equipment arrived, there were shortcomings and for some time X-ray films had to be developed in a fish kettle and the team had to share two canvas baths. They employed two old women for the mammoth task of washing the clothes and linen in the nearby river. The drains remained a problem and Dr Berry had to clean them out herself. Furniture was made from recycling crates. Fuel for the anthracite stoves remained a major problem and had to be brought from England.

In spite of all their hard work, Royaumont failed the first French Red Cross inspection on 24 December. They were told that there had been too much haste and not enough planning. Miss Ivens accepted some of the criticisms but the group's morale inevitably slumped. Nothing daunted, Miss Ivens and Cicely Hamilton quickly arranged a good Christmas celebration for the team and, once the festivities were over, they all set to with renewed energy to bring the hospital up to the required standard. They passed the re-inspection on 7 January, and their sterilisers drew particular praise. Their X-ray facilities were the only ones in the area. On 10 January they received formal permission to start receiving patients.

Their patients had to be collected from the railhead, 8 miles away at Creil, which meant they suffered severe jolting as they travelled along the atrocious roads. Most of them arrived at the hospital in the middle of the night. The female chauffeurs had to be at least twenty-four years old and from a background rich enough for them to have had driving experience. Some had owned their own car. However, the War Office refused to give women passes to drive their own vehicles in the war zone. They were allowed to ride in them but men had to drive. Once they reached France they ignored the rules. The women chauffeurs were quite independent, had their own quarters in the stables and did not mix much with the medical team. The chauffeurs also did most of the vehicle maintenance. The military authorities insisted they had khaki overcoats and they later needed heavy rubber boots and goatskin overcoats as well. When they were driving under bombardment in 1918, they were issued with steel hats.

Few of the medical staff spoke French, although, ironically, many of the orderlies came from privileged backgrounds and knew some French. Dorothy Littlejohn could get by, Cecily Hamilton spoke good French and Miss Ivens became fluent over time. Some of the medical team knew more German than French having trained in Germany.

Royaumont opened in January 1915 as the Hôpital Auxiliaire 301 (H A 301), taking casualties from the Rheims, Soissons and Noyon Sector. The team earned the deep respect of the French authorities but they were eagerly watched for a while as the French were not used to dealing with female medical staff. The French Army's contribution was paying two francs per patient per day and also providing petrol, tyres, and other necessities for the vehicles and the equivalent of £1,000 for new beds, to be returned to them after the war. It was agreed that if there was any slack time the team could treat civilians. The French Army could not provide replacement clothing for the patients so no matter what condition garments were in, they had to be salvaged. They were all fumigated, washed and then mended by a local lady. Most local helpers were volunteers but a local factory owner, M Delacoste, lent two of his workers to the hospital each afternoon.

French bureaucracy lived up to its enduring reputation for complexity. Four forms had to be completed for each man arriving at the hospital, four for every man leaving and seventeen for a death. The forms had to be repeated for men who stayed longer than five days. Cecily Hamilton was in charge of meeting these requirements. The staff also kept detailed clinical notes for all their patients.

In May 1915, they opened a laboratory, run by Dr Elizabeth Butler, on the top floor. Dr Butler was fluent in French and German and been working on a cancer research project in Austria when the war started. The laboratory made a big difference. To reduce cross-infection, every new patient was inspected by a surgeon when they arrived and their wounds were swabbed for bacteriological examination. This enabled them to identify and segregate gas gangrene cases and incipient cases so patients could be operated on in order of severity.

Miss Ivens began to experiment with the effect of sunlight on wounds. Some patients were wheeled into the cloisters each day with only a piece of saline soaked gauze over their wounds. When they seemed to improve, patients were left in the cloisters day and night.

Their facilities were further enhanced when the London Society gave them an X-ray car fitted with all the most up-to-date equipment, including its own darkroom and water supply. It was designed to let them help patients in neighbouring hospitals where they did not have X-ray facilities. Marie Curie had advised them what equipment was needed. Before the car could leave London, the War Office commandeered its engine, and would only return it when Austin had delivered a set number of cars to the Army.

By the end of 1915, the hospital cost £1,000 a month in addition to the two francs per patient per day that was paid by the French Government. The committee, back in Edinburgh, was worried, as Dr Inglis had originally calculated that the running costs would be £500 a month and fundraising was getting harder. The committee also questioned the use of seventy-two pairs of rubber gloves a month and asked if a staff of ninety was essential. They sent out an inspector to identify potential savings but she reported that there was no extravagance at all.

The summer campaign produced enormous numbers of wounded in 1916. When the hall porter heard cars approaching, she sounded a horn and, apart from one orderly per ward, all the staff then rushed to the entrance hall to receive the wounded. Each patient was registered and bathed in a seemingly endless stream. All the staff had to be fit, the orderlies in particular, as they had to carry patients on stretchers up seventy-one steps to the wards on the second floor. In early January, 180 men arrived in one day. They were not wounded, but exhausted and hungry having been on the road for days. The French Army did not have canteens or rest centres for their troops and the ordinary 'poilu' was paid so badly that they could not support themselves when they were on leave. At Royaumont, they were given hot food and the staff spread straw on the refectory floor so that they had somewhere to sleep. When they had rested, they got up and gave a concert to the staff and patients as a way of expressing their thanks.

By January 1916 there were 250 beds. Each month two Sisters went to help direct a new surgical ward at Creil Hospital. Their first casualty came when Sister Gray died after an appendectomy. She was buried, with full military honours, in the local churchyard. Louisa Aldrich Blake, the first woman Master of Surgery was so keen to help that she spent her holidays in 1915 and 1916 at Royaumont doing anything from making toast to surgery. She was much loved and admired by the other members of staff. Three of Dr Inglis's nieces served at Royaumont; Florence as a doctor, Etta as an auxiliary nurse and Violet as an orderly.

In May, they were warned that they needed to increase their capacity to 400. By July, the front was only 25 miles away and the shelling could be heard from the hospital. Each of the ambulance drivers transported more than a hundred cases in twenty-four hours. The X-ray staff and operating theatres worked non-stop. Ninety per cent of the new patients had gas gangrene and the stench was appalling. The surgeons were working so fast that they grabbed the X-rays before they had even been rinsed. They were worried that the X-ray machines might fail and there were problems sterilising equipment quickly enough. Miss Ivens reported that 1915 had been child's play in comparison with what was being thrown at them in 1916.

In the summer the charge of extravagance was again made, anonymously. Miss Ivens reported to the committee that they had treated 1,693 soldiers and 138 civilians of whom only seventeen had died. They had carried out 1,898 operations. Nothing more was said about their supposed extravagance but fundraising was clearly a major concern for the committee. In 1917 there was another confrontation with the committee, this time because their one male chauffeur was paid £60 a year while the women were unpaid and had to provide their own uniforms. The staff needed improved food and better bathing facilities and in the end, the committee sent them some tin baths.

The French authorities finally realised they had to do something to improve conditions for the ordinary soldier and started to open canteens. The Scottish Women's Hospitals agreed to open two, at Creil and Crèpy, and the local authority asked Miss Ivens to open one in Soissons, where not one building was left intact and where the few civilians who had returned had no way of getting food. Miss Ivens agreed to help but commented that it was remarkable that French women did nothing to help their compatriots. In July, the committee supplied a mobile kitchen and opened a canteen in an abandoned schoolhouse. They planted salad in the garden, raided abandoned gardens for fruit and vegetables and served nearly 800 free meals a day. They also set up a small tin bath and some soap beside the pump and provided papers, magazines and writing materials. In seven weeks they provided 1,681 meals. The need for their services then abated and the canteen closed.

At the request of the French authorities they also set up an advanced casualty clearing station at Villers Cotterets. It was working by October 1917 and its aim was to give early operative treatment to patients and reduce the delays that increased mortality from gas gangrene. It was set up in a deserted wooden hutted evacuation centre by the station, on the edge of fields and screened by a forest. It was 40 miles from Royaumont. The huts were named after Allied countries. The team prepared 211 beds and there was space for an additional sixty. Some of the heavier work was done by German prisoners and by soldiers who were unfit for further military service. The walls were whitewashed and the beds had the usual Scottish Women's Hospitals red covers. The X-ray hut was described as superb, but the toilets were disgusting. Miss Winstanley was made Matron in Charge.

In order to relax, the team used more energy. They played hockey, no doubt encouraged by one orderly who had been an international player. They also put on concerts and held ceremonies on every possible occasion to boost morale. They put plaques on individually sponsored beds. The Canada Ward was funded by money raised in Canada. Some of the Senegalese soldiers were only sixteen and played hunt the slipper, musical chairs and bobbing for apples with members of staff.

They had a stroke of luck when renowned chef, Michelet, arrived with a minor wound. He had been chef to a Parisian millionaire and started to help in the Royaumont kitchen, spending more and more time there. He was even willing to peel vegetables. Miss Ivens eventually managed to get him seconded to them for the duration of the war. Royaumont became one of the best-fed hospitals in France. He did all the catering and marketing and reduced the need for French kitchen help. He was devoted to Royaumont but like many chefs, he was not easy to work under.

There was a lull in 1917, when the Front moved away again. Some of the staff wanted to respond to British appeals for doctors and VADs but Miss Ivens insisted that they continued to work with the French as her intuition told her that the action would soon return to their area. It did. The winter of 1917–18 was so cold that there was two degrees of frost inside the staff cubicles. Their hair froze to the pillows and their boots to the floor. Even the water in their stoneware hot water bottles froze. Snow lay on the ground for three months.

In February 1918 they started to prepare for a German advance and in March, all doctors who were on leave were recalled. In May the Germans reached Soissons and then Villers Cotterets during the climax of the Second Battle of the Marne. The facility at Villers Cotterets had to be evacuated under fire and at very short notice. It was destroyed. On their way back to Royaumont they were joined, to their disgust, by nurses from another hospital, reputedly wearing high heeled shoes, heavy make-up and Red Crosses and who had no intention of doing any hard work. A week later, the team was able to go back to Villers Cotterets to salvage what they could and Edith Storey apologised to the committee that they could not save everything. French people had looted the site before they got back. In the following weeks, many of the team felt they were strained beyond their limits and the chauffeurs were constantly under fire driving to Senlis to get the wounded.

It is a reflection of the horrendous situation they were in that the Army had to ask Miss Ivens to increase the number of beds to 600. The Abbey's owner and the French Red Cross were opposed to the idea but the Army insisted. With the increase in the number of patients the X-ray and theatre staff worked in teams with eight hours on duty and six hours off. Radiographer Marian Butler worked such long hours that she got X-ray burns. Miss V. Collum, who had started as an orderly in the clothing department but ended up as a radiographer, was so over exposed to X-rays that she was told she must take no more for ten years. The equipment performed well but did not give enough protection to staff. Three operating theatres were in action all day, and two at night. The committee became increasingly worried at the cost of dressings and urged the team to make a greater use of sphagnum moss rather than cotton.

Royaumont began to suffer from staff shortages. Several of the long-standing staff could no longer cope and had to leave. Others were close to breakdown. Eventually, when it became clear the chauffeurs could get well-paid work elsewhere, the committee agreed to pay them the equivalent of £12 a year, but only for three months, after which fresh volunteers had to be found. Miss Ivens fought this idiotic decision but lost.

Miss Ivens believed strongly in the hospital hierarchy and insisted doctors should only work as doctors and that they should be paid the same as a male doctor would be. She told the committee that she did better with educated staff as they did not miss town life as much as the less educated who were also less able to cope with boredom in the quieter times. However, she also said the orderlies were the mainstay of the hospital. They had to support themselves financially and she believed that if they were good enough, they should be promoted to auxiliary nurse and entitled to a salary. In all, 184 nurses served at Royaumont. Almost all of them completed their six-month contracts and thirty-seven of them extended their contracts. Only eighteen did not complete their initial six months, and for eleven of them that was because the war had ended. Three nurses were dismissed; one for insubordination, one for bad behaviour and one for an unspecified reason.

Royaumont was the largest continuously operating voluntary hospital in France by the end of the war. It ran from January 1915 to March 1919 and their mortality rates were better than those of army-run equivalents. Recognition of its standards came when the Pasteur Institute in Paris chose it as one of the few centres to carry out pilot studies of anti-gas gangrene serum. There were 10,861 patients treated at Royaumont and Villers Cotterets of whom 1,537 were civilian outpatients. The military patients were French and French Colonial with a few British and Americans, and German Prisoners of War. The death rate among injured servicemen was 2.8 per cent and among their civilian patients 4.37 per cent.

The staff at Royaumont celebrated the Armistice in style with concerts, food, and a bonfire where they burned an effigy of the Kaiser. Some of the team decided to stay in France to help the returning population and the committee gave Miss Ivens £100 for relief work. Other members of the team went to join the Scottish Women's Hospitals units that were still working in Serbia. Many of the women who had worked at Royaumont and Villers Cotterets had problems adapting to civilian life and Dr Elizabeth Courtauld, the oldest doctor on the team, helped them in many ways. She gave a loan to V. Collum to help her start on a literary and archaeological career. When the loan was repaid it was used to help other Royaumont veterans. Staff had a remarkable team spirit and The Royaumont Association, set up by members of the group after the war, only closed in 1973.

Miss Ivens had hoped that Royaumont could continue as a gift to France and be used as a home for limbless veterans or as a tuberculosis hospital but Monsieur Goüm, the owner, insisted that all traces of the hospital be removed. In the end, twenty railway waggons full of equipment, including 400 beds, were donated to the Hôpital Sauveur in Lille, which had been badly damaged. Miss Ivens and two other members of staff served at Royaumont throughout the time it was open. When the Scottish Women's Hospitals organisation was disbanded in 1922, their remaining funds were used to build the Elsie Inglis Memorial Maternity Hospital in Edinburgh.

* * *

The women who have come to symbolise nurses during the First World War are the VADs. Their stories have featured in numerous books and famous individuals, such as Vera Britten, have written widely read accounts of their experiences. Aspects of their work have been covered in the chapter about medical work in Great Britain and, although the nursing work they did overseas was vital, their experiences were not so different to those of nurses with other organisations. It is therefore worth highlighting the scope of the work they did beyond nursing to support the medical teams. Their leaders always wanted VADs to be versatile, innovative and willing to try their hand at anything. They did their best and their adaptability and willingness both at home and abroad led writer Mrs C. S. Peel to write in 1926 that 'the VADs never failed; they gave their ungrudging help in every direction under any conditions.'

The first twelve groups of VADs were in France by September 1914. This number had doubled by the end of the year and two other groups had been sent to Serbia and one to Montenegro. By 1918 there were 8,000 VADs serving overseas.

The first group of VADs to go abroad was led by VAD Commandant, Katherine Furse, and did not simply nurse but set up the first rest station in railway carriages at the Central Station in Boulogne. Within their first twenty-four hours they had provided hot drinks to 1,000 soldiers wounded at Ypres. This unit was said to have set the standards that all other units in France should aspire to. It was demobilised on 25 June 1919, by which time they had cared for 400,000 people, changed 16,000 dressings and provided food for repatriated Prisoners of War, refugees and civilians.

After a while, Katherine Furse noticed that the railway lines were in a disgusting state because the ambulance and troop trains often stood in the station for extended periods during which the toilets drained straight onto the tracks. She submitted a strongly worded report to the military authorities after which Sanitary Squads were appointed to clean the stations at all French bases. Sometime later rest station staff offered to clean and disinfect the stretchers, which had become really dirty. Their offer was refused but within three days soldiers had been detailed to clean the stretchers.

The war swallowed up so many men that it was not long before VADs were asked to act as orderlies in various hospitals, releasing the male orderlies for military service. These hospital VADs did so well that before long all Red Cross Hospitals were using VADs in some capacity. Katherine Furse was recalled to England in January 1915, to set up the new central headquarters of the VAD, and was replaced by her second in command, Rachel Crowdy.

In January 1915, the military authorities decided that women should not be allowed to drive. One of the VAD drivers had driven more than1,500 stretcher cases but had to stop driving. In 1916 this ruling was reversed and women took over an ambulance convoy at Le Tréport, releasing men for military service. They did so well that six further VAD motor units were set up. They drove ambulances along the lines of communication and filled in gaps, helping the sick and wounded wherever they could be of use. During one rush, the staff based in Étretat drove up to 130 miles a day, doing three journeys to Le Havre and back. They had comfortable billets in a house with a garden, and the other VADs in the house ensured that hot food was available for the drivers whenever they needed it. In Le Tréport, the drivers were housed in a large barrack-like room divided into cubicles. When not busy driving, they turned their hands to whatever odd jobs needed doing in the hospitals.

In a workroom at the Abbeville Depot, French women were employed under the supervision of VADs to sort, test and remake smoke and gas helmets before they were reissued for use at the front. They processed hundreds of thousands of helmets, often under considerable pressure. Similar depots were set up at Calais and Le Havre.

Military uniforms and equipment were always valuable and in short supply and we rarely consider what happened to those that belonged to soldiers who were killed. VADs were asked to supervise special Salvage Shops at Le Havre, set up to sort and clean clothing and boots from dead soldiers. However, this was not deemed appropriate work for Red Cross workers who, under their founding documents could only do work to help the sick and wounded. As the war progressed, requests were frequently made for VADs to do work that did not come within the remit of Red Cross workers.

They took on the vital task of setting up a department to trace the owners of the countless letters and parcels that were returned marked 'Wounded and gone to the Base' or 'Present location not known'. The VADs collected the post from the Army Post Office, or from the Red Cross Missing and Wounded Enquiry Department. They then searched the registers of all the hospitals, convalescent camps, and base detail camps to see if the men were or had been there. This was laborious work but they successfully traced the owners of eighty per cent of the lost letters and parcels. Their persistence was critical, as post was immensely valuable to servicemen.

Their work showed that the Army's non-alphabetical Admission and Discharge Books left much to be desired. They therefore contacted one hospital and offered to put these books onto a card index system and to devise a card that could be used for each new case admitted. Their offer was accepted and they identified 30,000 back cases, which they indexed. Their system was later adopted throughout the hospitals in France. VADs in British hospitals used a similar scheme.

Over time, VADs started to do secretarial and filing work in various Red Cross offices. The commissioners were the first to use them followed by the Medical, Transport, Missing and Wounded Enquiry Office and the Canadians. In 1916, a VAD commandant and five VADs took over the

British Red Cross Society Post Office and it was thereafter run by women until it was closed after the end of the war.

It is not widely appreciated that by 1916 VADs were being used to do confidential work for the military authorities in Calais, Abbeville and elsewhere. Their keenness and attention to accuracy was highly praised but the details of what they actually did has remained secret.

By 1917 the need to release men from work, so that they could fight, was more urgent than ever before. This led the military authorities to invite members of the VAD General Service Section to take on an increasing range of duties in France, working in military hospitals. In some areas, including discipline and transfers, the staff were under the control of a VAD Department. They were, however, working in military establishments. The Army provided their billets and the Red Cross did what it could to provide equipment and comforts. Many of the VADs worked as cooks, clerks, dispensers, typists and telephone operators but some took on the relatively new role of X-ray assistant.

The situation changed in 1917 with the arrival of the women of Women's Army Auxiliary Corps (WAACS), which became the Queen Mary's Army Auxiliary Corps in 1918. They were paid for their work, which was one of the reasons why joint working was contentious. More fundamental, however, were the differences in the basic principles underlying the two organisations. The WAACS advertised that they were going to France to replace the Tommies and could associate on an equal footing with the rank and file of the British Army. This was not the way in which VADs had ever operated and it was not clear where they would fit in the hierarchy when their General Service Members worked in military hospitals. The military authorities announced that the VADs in these areas would work for the same pay and under the same regulations and conditions as the WAACS. Many of the VADs were experienced and capable and understandably took umbrage at how they felt they were treated by the WAACS. VADs reported that it was as if their presence brought disgrace on their organisation. Working relationships between the two organisations were not easy.

The village of Étaples was swamped by the extent of the British hospitals that opened there. At its greatest extent it could treat 100,000 patients. Many of the nursing staff were VADs. During the night of 19–20 May 1918 the hospitals were bombed causing a number of deaths and injuries among staff and patients. One nurse was killed, a number, including VADs, were injured and VAD Miss W A Brampton was left shell-shocked. During further raids in June, staff casualties included a VAD who suffered a severe head wound. A number of VADs were awarded the Military Medal for their bravery at Étaples. Another group was recognised for their bravery in removing wounded soldiers from the area around an exploding ammunition dump. By the end of the war the military authorities were in no doubt about how valuable the VADs' work had been and one senior official remarked that they had saved the situation. We know that 245 VADs were killed while serving and that others were wounded or had to leave through ill health. We do not have any records to show how many VADs and other women serving overseas suffered from post-traumatic stress disorder, either immediately or some years after their service ended.

After the Armistice the British Red Cross Society decided to close all VAD units quickly, as it did not feel it could work on a peace footing with the Armies of Occupation and Settlement. The Red Cross Hospitals were the first to be demobilised. Convalescent camps were changed into staging camps. Recreation huts were handed over to the Army. Once the nursing staff had gone home, their clubs and convalescent homes were no longer needed and hostels, where relatives of the wounded had been looked after, closed and their staff also went home.

***

The First Aid Nursing Yeomanry (FANY) was created in 1909 and recruited 100 members that year. However, by January 1910, there were only seven or eight active members. Mrs McDougall rescued and re-organised the FANY. She wanted members to be able to provide mounted detachments to help the RAMC in wartime. The training in side-saddle riding, stretcher drill and bandaging was amended with compulsory riding astride and weekly drills, which alternated between horsemanship and stretcher work. The early uniform of scarlet tunics and navy blue skirts, both faced with white braid, was replaced with much more serviceable khaki tunics and skirts. Young women wanting to join the FANY had to be at least twenty-three years old. If they passed the selection interview they could join, on four months' probation. Only after they had successfully completed this period were they able to join a FANY unit. They were all volunteers and for every six months they were on active service they could take two weeks' leave.

FANYs were not like many of the other groups who set off to help the allied forces on the Continent. They were not simply nurses, or orderlies, or drivers or support staff. They did not come under the auspices of the Red Cross or any of the other established organisations. These differences led Surgeon-General Woodhouse, at Calais, say that they were 'neither fish, flesh nor fowl, but (you're) a damned good red herring'. They always wanted to be on equal footing with servicemen and seemed to think of themselves as part of the Services who happened to be women and who had a point to make about women's capabilities. They apparently 'only' saluted an officer once, in the morning. While they were not forbidden all social contact with men, as members of some groups were, they could not go out to dinner with a male friend unless another FANY went too.

Much of their training was supervised by members of the RAMC and trained nurses. Members were expected to get certificates in first aid and home nursing and gain practical experience in a hospital or infirmary. Their riding drill was supervised by the riding master of the cavalry regiment based at Hounslow. They attended strenuous residential training camps where their day started at 5.30 a.m. and activities lasted until dinner at 8 p.m. They were expected to provide, feed, and care for their own horses, which seriously restricted the people who could afford to become FANYs. In 1912 Colonel Ricardo, C.V.O., became commanding officer, with Mrs McDougall as secretary and a Miss Franklin as treasurer.

Once the war started they offered their services to the British authorities, who rejected them, and then to the Belgians, who accepted. Mrs McDougall led a FANY unit to Calais in October 1914. The Belgians allocated them to two old schools full of wounded, which they developed into the Lamarck Military Hospital, nursing both wounded and typhoid cases. Up to October 1916, when the hospital was closed by the Inspector General, they nursed more than 4,000 Belgian soldiers. After the hospital closed, two of the FANYs were asked to help open and run a new Young Men's Christian Association (YMCA) hut at St Pierre Brouck. Other staff from the Lamarck Hospital worked in canteens around Calais.

Always on the look-out for further opportunities, their diligence was acknowledged in 1915 when the FANY became a unit of the Anglo-French Hospitals Committee of the British Red Cross. However, on several occasions they undertook new roles only to have to give them up when they were judged too dangerous or otherwise unsuitable. They set up various groups to entertain the troops; the 'Fanytastiks' in Calais and the 'Kippers' in St Omer.

One of their more successful innovations was 'James'. They recognised how rarely soldiers had a chance to bathe and how much a bath would be appreciated so they took a mobile bath unit, known as 'James', close to the front line. 'James' contained ten collapsible baths, filled with water heated by the vehicle's engine, enabling forty men an hour to have a bath. The mobile bath unit was also used to disinfect the men's clothes.

Although they had initially trained as a mounted unit, a number of FANYs learned to drive and service motor vehicles. They regularly contacted the British authorities to offer to drive ambulances and finally, in 1916, a team, led by Miss Franklin, was allowed to transport sick and wounded Belgian soldiers around Calais. The Army provided rations for the drivers. They went out to collect wounded men during raids and also helped transport the French wounded from the ambulance trains to hospital. This work was extended to several other bases. In May 1918, sixteen FANY drivers were awarded the Military Medal for their bravery in one night. They were attached to the Belgian Transport Corps after the Lamarck hospital closed.

In 1917, the French authorities accepted their offer to do similar work in the Amiens area. Unfortunately, the French had not thought to ask the British General Headquarters for permission to send British subjects into this area. Permission was refused and the British insisted that the FANYs should be transferred to a different area. They later provided a motor ambulance unit attached to the clearing hospital at Épernay.

* * *

Motor ambulances were in short supply throughout the war. In October 1914 the Automobile Association appealed to its members for touring cars that could be converted into ambulances. About 250 cars were offered, though not all of them were suitable, and about £6,000 was donated by members who did not have suitable cars to donate. More than 200 cars were collected from all over the country by the AA's engineering department, then converted, overhauled, and shipped to France. The first fifty were inspected by the king at Buckingham Palace before being despatched.

The British Ambulance Committee was an independent body formed to provide convoys of motor ambulances to carry French wounded. Its members raised in excess of £300,000 and had sent five convoys by the middle of 1915.

Dennis Bayley and his helpers lobbied major industrial firms, asking them for a voluntary levy on output or wages to support transport for the wounded. Coal mine owners in Nottinghamshire and Derbyshire responded generously. The Dennis Bayley Fund raised £500,000 and provided ambulance convoys to work on the French and Italian Fronts. The Fund was taken over by the British Red Cross Society and the Order of St John, which also administered gifts from Lloyds of London and the British Farmers' Red Cross Fund.

Many members of the Society of Friends (Quakers) wanted to reduce the suffering caused by the war. It is completely against the Quakers' principles to fight but many of them volunteered to help with the wounded and the Friends Ambulance Unit (FAU) was formed. Its members' aim was to give first aid to the sick and wounded. They worked under the banner of the Red Cross and the terms of the Geneva Conventions and wore the Red Cross uniform. With characteristic thoroughness, the Quakers set about preparing the recruits for what they were going to face. As the FAU was set up as a Voluntary Aid Detachment, its members had to get their Red Cross or St John's First Aid Certificates and, if possible a Male Nursing Certificate as well. They were also advised to try to get hold of, and study, copies of James Cantlie's *British Red Cross Manuals on First Aid, Nursing, and Training*.

Time was short and the organisers realised that recruits might struggle to reach the required standard to pass their exams and that if they failed, the FAU would not be allocated any work. They therefore set up a training camp with a full-time instructor at their property at Jordans in Buckinghamshire. Unlike many people who confidently believed that the war would only last a few months, the Quakers took a more realistic attitude. They were not sure how many of their recruits would be called on in the short term but thought that demand could increase significantly over time.

Although most of the members were Quakers, the FAU was not exclusive and volunteers included a number of people who simply wanted to help heal the wounds of war. Members of the FAU were first used by the French Army and not only ran ambulances but also worked in hospitals and casualty clearing stations.

In accepting the Quakers' offer to provide volunteers to give medical help to the non-combatant population, the French Authorities commented on the similar work that the Quakers had done in 1871 during the Franco-Prussian War.

Supplied with eight new Morris ambulances, the first group of forty-three volunteers set off to cross the Channel on SS *Invicta* on 30 October 1914. They had not travelled far when they found the crew of the cruiser *Hermes* struggling in the water after their ship had been torpedoed. Working with the *Invicta*'s crew, they gathered up as many of the survivors as they could and took them back to Dover before setting off across the Channel once more.

They arrived to find Dunkirk in chaos, with wounded French and Belgian soldiers pouring into the town. Without waiting to be allocated to any particular area the FAU volunteers simply set to work. This was a real baptism of fire. Two huge goods sheds were said to have been paved with the dead and with dying men, screaming in pain and terribly thirsty. The sheds were filled with the stench of suppurating, rotting and neglected wounds. Within their first couple of months the FAU transported more than 10,000 wounded. The pace of work eventually slowed and they could look around to see what other help was needed.

They used the lull that followed this period of frenetic work to plan how they could make the best use of their resources when the next large influx of wounded soldiers started to arrive. This involved seemingly endless and exhausting negotiations with the French authorities but they eventually managed to put a scheme in place that would allow them to work efficiently, bridging the gap between aid posts and clearing stations. Having officially approved tasks to carry out meant they could relax and stop worrying that they would be told to stop what they were doing.

Olaf Stapleton was a FAU volunteer who worked in a team of forty-five running a convoy of ambulances, a mobile workshop, a soup kitchen, a lorry and a car. The winter of 1916–17 was so cold that when they slept in their vehicles their wine, bread, boots and ink all froze. He felt that many of the soldiers regarded them as 'amiable and efficient cranks' and that their popularity was enhanced by the fact that few of them ever drank their full ration of wine or touched their rum ration.

The convoy spent a long time working in the Champagne area and around Rheims. Olaf reported, in a very matter of fact way, that the entire unit had been infected with trench fever after suffering a plague of flies. Their numbers were halved, as a number of the team were too sick to continue and the remainder were perpetually exhausted and suffering from diarrhoea. He also reported that they had suffered during a gas attack and said how difficult it was to drive while wearing a gas mask. One of their team was killed.

Behind all the Quakers' work was the belief that they should do what was needed, and what was not being done, whether or not they had expected to do it, whether or not it suited their plans, and whether or not they wanted to undertake that particular work at that particular moment. They set about this with considerable imagination and understanding. They realised that civilians in France and Belgium were not getting the medical care they needed, partly because so many doctors had been called up by the army. They therefore set up large hospitals in Ypres and Poperinghe where they could treat sick or wounded civilians and carry out inoculations. When they realised there was the imminent danger of a typhoid epidemic, they opened the Queen Alexandra Hospital to take typhoid patients.

When they approached the British authorities with an offer of help, it was rejected. Although initially upset by the rebuff, they later reflected that it had never been likely that the British Army would accept a proposal to work in the battle zone from a volunteer organisation. When the next emergency came, as it inevitably did, they were not asked for their help but it was made subtly and diplomatically clear that their assistance, if offered, would not be refused! On the second day of the Second Battle of Ypres they managed to set up a casualty clearing station in Poperinghe and tried, without success, to run a linked motor ambulance. They also ran an aid post at the Sacré Coeur and another in a little estaminet just outside Ypres.

Once the battle was over, and with the German advance, the hospitals had to close but the Quakers were able to carry on with their ambulance and inoculation work. When making a speech to their headquarters in 1915 one senior member of the FAU remarked that they had not expected the Germans to shell them out of everywhere they stopped and that since the battle began they had been bombarded out of Sacré Coeur, Poperinghe A, B, D and E, out of Ypres and into Vlamertinghe, and then back to Ypres. They clearly lived a peripatetic life.

The speaker was keen to stress that this willingness to move from one place to another, every time they were bombed out or needed in a new location, was one of the essential features of a voluntary unit. The more the places that were shelled, the more they had to relocate their efforts. He forecast an increase in their ambulance work and reported that the British Red Cross was going to withdraw the more than fifty ambulances it had lent to the French. He felt that although, as the authorities kept reminding them, the unit was not indispensable, they would not be short of work as long as they maintained their standards of efficiency, intelligence and devotion. The Quakers also manned four hospital trains and two hospital ships and the initial team of forty-three volunteers grew into thousands.

In January 1916 the first Military Service Act was passed and allowed exemption from military service for men whose conscience would not let them fight. Some people nicknamed the clause that safeguarded conscientious objectors from the death penalty the 'Slackers Charter'. In the same year, the Quakers drew up a manifesto at their Annual Meeting in which they reaffirmed their complete opposition to military service. Twenty of the Friends died during their work in France and Corder Catchpole, Adjutant of the FAU, was awarded the Mons Ribbon for valour.

4

In the Balkans and Beyond

In June 1914 Gavrilo Princip killed Archduke Franz Ferdinand and his wife in Sarajevo, Serbia. The Archduke was the heir to the Austro-Hungarian Empire. Princip was a Serbian nationalist who wanted the southern Slav areas of the Austro-Hungarian Empire to be able to join together to form Yugoslavia, which means 'land of the south Slavs'. Having taken the time to secure Germany's unconditional support, Austria-Hungary declared war on Serbia on 28 July. This prompted the mobilisation of Serbia's powerful ally Russia, along its border with the Austro-Hungarian Empire, and was the start of the hostilities that became the First World War. The first bombardment of the Serbian capital, Belgrade, by Austro-Hungarian troops took place that night.

The Austrians invaded north-west Serbia two weeks later but were met by strong resistance that culminated in the five-day battle of Jadar, after which the Austrians were driven out of Serbia. The Austrians attacked again in September, gaining several footholds, and in November advanced, pushing the Serbs back to the east and south. By the end of the month the invaders held a line across northern Serbia from Chachak to Belgrade, and seemed to think they had won. The Serbs, almost out of ammunition, got fresh supplies from France in the nick of time and rallied again, driving the Austrians out of Serbia. This left 60–70,000 Austrian prisoners in Serbian hands.

There was then a lull in hostilities until the early autumn of 1915. During this period some of the medical volunteers went home as they felt they could be more use on the Western Front. Teams that stayed focused on dealing with epidemics of typhus, typhoid, diphtheria and other diseases, some of which were said to have started among the Austrian prisoners.

Serbia was attacked by German, Austro-Hungarian and Bulgarian troops in October 1915. The Bulgarians blocked off the route to the south. After struggling to release troops from the Western Front, the French and British finally sent a small expeditionary force to help Serbia but it was too little and too late, and the Serbian army was faced with surrender or retreat. In horrendous winter weather the army, and hoards of civilians, retreated south and west over the Montenegrin Mountains into Albania. Huge numbers died of wounds, cold or starvation along the way. The enemy was often close behind them and the Albanians harried them as they struggled to reach the coast. An estimated 240,000 people died during the retreat but around 155,000 soldiers and civilians did reach the Adriatic coast from where they were transported to Corsica, Corfu and Malta as refugees. Members of several medical units were caught up in the retreat, as they had refused to be evacuated when they had the chance.

Accounts of medical work during the First World War have tended to concentrate on events in France and Belgium and it is easy to overlook the scale of British volunteer involvement in other theatres of war, notably in the Balkans and Russia. By and large, the volunteers in Eastern Europe were a more intrepid and independent group than those working in Western Europe. Some, indeed, had been turned down by established organisations for not being 'team players' or, for lacking relevant experience. Their adventurous and pioneering spirit was essential in helping them deal with the exceptional challenges they faced.

As the situation in Serbia worsened, the authorities were overwhelmed by the numbers of wounded and sick. With the onset of winter in 1914 and the spread of typhus, Mabel Grouitch, the American-born wife of the Serbian Foreign Secretary Slavko Grouitch headed an appeal to the international community for help. She established the Serbian Relief Fund in London, holding meetings to raise funds and publicise the plight of the Serbians. Over time the fund helped to maintain five medical units in Serbia.

Among those to respond to her appeal were James and May Berry. Both worked at the Royal Free Hospital in London where James was a surgeon and his wife May was an anaesthetist. They wanted to work for the war effort but at that stage the military authorities were unwilling to use women doctors and James Berry was rejected for service in the RAMC because he had a club foot and other medical problems. The Berrys were in the unusual position of having travelled in the Balkans, speaking a little Serbian and knowing Mme Grouitch.

They suggested going to Serbia to work in the hospital of a Serbian friend. Mme Grouitch vetoed this idea, as she felt that Serbian and British ways of doing things were too different for this to work. She wanted the Berrys to put together their own unit and take it to Serbia. She believed they would simply have to ask their friends for money for drugs and equipment, select a few of the volunteers who were clamouring to go, get an invitation from the Serbian Government and set off. It seems that all too many units working abroad more or less followed this pattern but the Berrys had a different and more methodical approach, which stood them in good stead in Serbia.

Before raising a penny or recruiting any staff they consulted people already involved in running hospitals in France and elsewhere. They then spent three weeks learning how to run a charity appeal, recruited staff and obtained a leave of absence from the Royal Free Hospital. The Admiralty agreed to provide them with free transport to Serbia. They wanted to be called the Royal Free Unit but the hospital authorities refused to allow this. It was officially known as the Anglo-Serbian Mission but generally called the Berry Unit or the Royal Free Unit.

They sent out a personal letter and appeal to their friends and acquaintances setting out precisely what help they were seeking. They were inundated by people wanting to join the unit. However, they had decided that they would only take people who they knew personally, or who had been recommended to them,by people they knew, for their particular skills or experience. Helped by the Matron of the Royal Free, they put their team together, even poaching staff from other hospitals. Their Sister-in-Charge, Miss Irvine Robertson, had nursed in Serbia during the recent Balkan war and spoke a little Serbian. She had to be prised away from a military hospital. Nurses Bartlett and Gore had already nursed in Belgium, where they had briefly been held prisoner. They also took a couple of medical students and a group of VADs as orderlies. James Berry felt that the VADs' adaptability, enthusiasm and knowledge of French or German more than compensated for their lack of experience. He was delighted when one of them took her sewing machine with her, and used it to great effect. Jan Gordon, husband of one of the VADs, joined the unit in the important role of engineer. The cook, Miss Creighton, was a Cambridge graduate who was selected for her qualifications and experience as a cookery teacher. The fact that her father was an Anglican bishop was apparently a bonus that went down well with the Serbians.

One piece of advice they heeded was the recommendation to take large supplies of Maconochie's rations, tins of vegetable and meat stew, widely distributed to soldiers. Its virtues were more apparent to the makers than the consumers and many soldiers hated both the stew and the general flatulence it produced. The Berry Unit took so many tins that they were able to leave a large number behind as a gift for the Serbians when they came home. Money and supplies poured in and a mountain of parcels arrived at the Royal Free, where they were unwrapped, listed, sorted, and repacked by hospital staff in their off-duty hours.

After earlier service in Belgium and France, Mabel St Clair Stobart took a unit to Serbia in April 1915 to set up a hospital for the Serbian Relief Fund at Kragujevac. She later set up a number of roadside dispensaries to help the civilian population. As well as medical staff, her team included the unusually high number of four trained cooks, a dispenser, an English Chaplain, Percy Dearmer, and fourteen orderlies, some of whom doubled as chauffeurs. They also took an additional member of staff, a sanitary inspector, who was a vital addition to teams working in Serbia. Monica Stanley was appointed to take charge of food supplies and catering, taking a three month leave of absence from her job that was later extended to six months because her employers recognised the importance of her work in Serbia.

One of the more unlikely volunteers was Mabel Dearmer, a successful writer and illustrator, with no obvious qualifications for being an aid worker. Her husband, Percy, decided to go out to Serbia as Chaplain to the British Medical Units and she seems to have taken little interest in this decision until attending a farewell service for the Stobart Unit, with whom Percy was to travel. After the service, she went up to Mrs Stobart and asked if she could go too. Mrs Stobart scrutinised her carefully and asked what she could do. Mabel replied that she had no skills but was a sensible woman who could learn quickly and that she was ready to leave all her silks and jewellery behind and accept the unit's discipline. Surprisingly Mrs Stobart agreed that she could join the team. What Mabel had not admitted, was that she had a chronically inflamed knee that would cause her problems throughout her service. Once they reached Serbia, Mabel was put in charge of the unit's linen. She carried out her duties very successfully and enjoyed her work, in spite of her knee and how rarely she saw her husband.

Under the auspices of the Serbian Relief Fund Leila, Lady Paget (wife of Sir Ralph Paget who was the British representative in Belgrade), set up a typhoid hospital in Skopje; Cornelia, Lady Wimborn, ran another unit. There were also two British Farmers' Ambulance Units, one of which was to deal with the wounded and the other with infectious cases. They got their name because most of their funding came from British farmers.

Rear Admiral Ernest Troubridge was sent to Serbia with a small international force and was attached to Crown Prince Alexander of Serbia. When the British military authorities refused to send the hospital unit he had asked for, claiming that the naval surgeon they had already provided was adequate for the 400 men under Troubridge's command, he turned to his wife for help. Within weeks, she had raised enough money to fund a team and had arranged for it to be affiliated to the Red Cross. They were among those who sailed for Serbia on the *SS Saidieh* in March 2015.

In October 1916, the Joint War Committee assembled a team to go and set up a canteen for the Serbian Relief Fund at its Hospital Unit No. 6 in Kragujevac. The team was led by a Mrs Massey. Some of the staff appointments were not a success. One of the canteen workers, Mrs Rome, soon gave up and went home. One of the chauffeurs, Captain Butcher, was elderly, and, according to canteen worker Lucy Creighton, so completely unable to cope with his duties that he was soon made storekeeper instead. Another chauffeur, Ian Hamilton, was so bad he was made assistant storekeeper. Former VAD Miss Stirling, and Jennifer Davies, who had been a private chauffeur before the war, were apparently much better drivers. Other bad appointments included a Mr Easton who lasted three months before joining the US Army and Miss Snow Clifton who was too nervy to cope and had to go home. The entries in Lucie Creighton's diary are very critical of some of her colleagues. This may reflect how difficult it had become to recruit suitable candidates for overseas work. It may also reflect Lucie's general attitude.

In 1916 Ellie Rendel was a final year medical student when seeing pictures of the war made her decide to volunteer to serve with the Scottish Women's Hospitals in Russia for six months. She was snapped up, somewhat to her surprise, and this may again reflect the fact that numbers of experienced volunteers were diminishing as the war stretched on. The Russian Government had asked for four British medical units and the Scottish Women's Hospitals were to provide two while the Red Cross and The Order of St John sent the others. The unit members and their leader, Dr Elsie Inglis, gathered in Liverpool and spent a stressful afternoon at Samuels, the outfitters, waiting for their uniforms to be finished. The shop staff got increasingly stressed as the afternoon wore on and Dr Inglis got more and more impatient. After Ellie's father had a word with the manager, her uniform was completed at 9 p.m., but left a great deal to be desired and the skirt was two foot rather than the regulation 10 inches above the ground. Ellie had stuck meticulously to the specified luggage limit and was upset to find everyone else had ignored it and had been able to pack warm dressing gowns and other comforts.

The unit was in two parts. The motor transport section was led by Mrs Haverfield and Ellie described the members as being both smart and conceited, adding that Mrs Haverfield was a real stickler for discipline. The hospital section was led by Dr Inglis. To the annoyance of some unit members, they had to stand to attention at roll call and address Dr Inglis as Ma'am. Ellie described the nurses as 'the oddest collection of old Dugouts' and said that most of them were private nurses who had not been near a hospital for years. On the other hand, she described the orderlies as being active, intelligent and educated.

The British Society of Friends (the Quakers) decided that the most effective way for them to help would be by working with the Serbian Relief Fund. They provided the labour and the fund financed their work. They set up a relief camp in Kragujevac, to care for civilian refugees who were heading south. They could take up to 700 people and the camp was an important staging post on the refugees' journey to Corsica, where the French Government had offered to receive them. The Quakers often provided food for the refugees on their onward voyage. They later extended their work to caring for some of the refugees in Corfu.

Getting to their destination in Serbia was a challenge for every unit and the journey was slow, complicated and dangerous. Some groups sailed to Marseilles and then boarded ships for the next stage to Salonika and then travelled overland to Kragujevac. Their tons of equipment were sometimes sent separately. The Admiralty helped with transport for officially sanctioned units. This included providing a ship called the *SS Saidieh*, in March 1915, to transport 150 members from a number of medical units. Passengers included Mrs Stobart's Imperial Service League Unit with some of the Berry Unit, Mr Wynch's Unit (otherwise known as the First British Farmers' Unit), Dr Bevis' Unit, a Russian unit and Admiral Troubridge's Unit.

Monica Stanley said that the *Saidieh* was an awful, dirty tub and that most of the passengers were sick. She moaned that there were no stewardesses, simply black African stewards. Due to the danger of attack from U-boats, they were told to sleep in their clothes for the first few nights and were given tickets for the lifeboats. They whiled away the voyage (once they had got their sea legs) playing bridge, writing letters, doing exercises and learning Serbian, which Monica found very dull.

On another Admiralty ship, the *SS Dilwara*, members of the Berry Unit who were not being seasick worked hard in James Berry's daily Serbian classes and quickly nicknamed him 'The Professor'. They made the most of a two-day break in Malta to do some sightseeing before embarking on the *SS Caledonian* for the next leg of their journey. Although the first night was balmy, a severe storm blew up and they had to turn into calmer seas until the storm had passed.

Travelling with the Scottish Women's Hospitals' American Unit, Ishobel Ross had a more enjoyable voyage than many. After a frustrating wait of two weeks in Southampton, she boarded the *SS Dunluce Castle* on 2 August 1916. The *SS Dunluce Castle* was a hospital ship with a battalion of RAMC men and doctors on board. The Scottish Women's Hospitals group had physical drill each day, followed by several hours' tuition in French and Serbian. They also had periodic lifeboat drills, lots of deck games and lectures on subjects such as Diseases Spread by Water. Ishobel thoroughly enjoyed the journey and the glimpses of various countries they passed, recording that the Greek islands made her homesick for her native Skye.

The Scottish Women's Hospitals Unit heading from Liverpool to Russia on *HMS Huntspill* set out with a destroyer escort and had to zig zag constantly and detour via Ireland and Iceland to try to avoid U-boats. Ellie Rendel had a comfortable cabin to herself and the journey was spent in drills, roll calls, boat practices, concerts, fancy dress parties and Russian and Serbian classes. Their uniforms were already coming apart at the seams and the fabric was horribly thin. The food on board was unappetising so she was very glad she had packed plenty of chocolate. They docked at Archangel, which Ellie disliked intensely, and heard they were to go on to Odessa via Moscow. She hoped to buy some furs in Odessa and asked her family to send her cigarettes and chocolate. Travelling by train, she wrote to her mother that they had had a marvellous send off from Archangel with dancing, singing and a Russian band playing on the platform until 1 a.m. The train did not meet with her approval. It lacked a dining room, was dirty, and lit only by tallow candles. It was so slow that the journey was due to last at least twelve days. The only food they had was bread, cheese and jam, and a bit of her chocolate. They were cramped and uncomfortable and lacked blankets and pillows. They got off the train to stretch their legs at every stop. Their discomfort was increased by a legion of bugs and they had no insect repellent with them. Ellie got badly bitten. To her annoyance, their carriage was deemed too heavy for the locomotive and they had to change to an even smaller, dirtier, and less comfortable one. Writing from the train a week later, she reported that they had been unable to wash since leaving the boat.

They finally reached Odessa and were met by forty carriages in which they were driven, at a gallop, to a large open-air nursing home for nerve cases. They were treated well and met local English residents who invited them to tea. Everyone warned them how cold it would get later in the year and they were told they would be issued with leather coats. Not trusting this promise Ellie bought herself a fur coat. Their uniforms grew increasingly bedraggled. After just a few days in Odessa, they were back on a train, heading south, Ellie wishing she had thought to bring a map.

Ellie's diary shows that the Scottish Women's Hospitals tried to keep families informed about the whereabouts and safety of their staff. At the end of September, her parents were informed that the unit had arrived near the front. As they set sail down the river, she wrote her last will and testament and enclosed it in a letter to her mother.

Sir Ralph Paget was meant to co-ordinate the work of the various British units and certainly visited them periodically, doing what he could to ease any difficulties. However, it must have been very difficult to deal with the various organisations and spirited individuals, each of whom felt they had a particular mission in Serbia and would let nothing, and nobody, get in their way. The proliferation of organisations must have made it difficult for the British public to understand who the various units were and made fundraising a competitive, rather than a collaborative, effort.

Sir Thomas Lipton, founder of the Lipton's tea empire, was a noted philanthropist and ardent sailor. During the war, he used his steam yacht, the *Erin*, to transport members of various hospital units and their equipment from Southampton to Salonika. On one trip, the *Erin* carried several motor ambulances and tons of clothing, equipment and food. Medical personnel, on their way to Serbia, joined the yacht in Marseilles. When the typhoid epidemic was at its height Sir Thomas toured much of Serbia, visiting villages and hospitals and many of the British medical units. In 1916, he handed the *Erin* over to the Admiralty. She was sunk while going to the aid of a torpedoed cruiser.

Salonika was the gateway to Serbia, a busy hub where troops, as well as aid workers and supplies, poured in and out. Newly arrived units waited for their luggage, or to be told where they were to work. While waiting, some of the volunteers helped at soup kitchens and hospitals in and around the town, while others bought extra supplies or did some sightseeing and visited members of other units. Mrs Stobart's unit had wired ahead from Gibraltar to book rooms in the Hotel Olympus. On arrival they found there were not enough rooms for them all so they all ate together in the hotel and then some members of the group had to go back to sleep aboard the *Saidieh*.

Kathleen Courtney set out from England in December 1915, with members of the Friends' War Victims Relief Committee. She found the Hospital Ship, *HMHS Salta*, which transported them, very uncomfortable. She and her colleagues had to sleep in the wards, while the Medical Officers had airy cabins with bathrooms. She longed for a cool hotel room all of her own, with windows that opened. When the wards grew too hot to bear they got an orderly to carry their mattresses up on deck. The fact that the English nurses were not allowed to join them was just one of the ways in which she felt they were treated very badly. She believed the nurses would end up working ten times harder than the doctors but that they were expected to put up with terrible conditions. She said that the nurses were a wonderful, highly experienced group but that they were treated like children. They were paid so little that most of them had to have private means to be able to do war work and that they had to provide their own uniforms. She added that about ten of the 175 nurses on board behaved very badly, though she did not go into details.

Members of various units were quick to take advantage of the opportunity for a little sightseeing offered by calling at various ports on their laborious journey to and from Serbia. Due to transport difficulties, Kathleen Courtney and her group had to spend a number of days in Alexandria. They got so frustrated at the delay that they applied to the Admiralty for expenses while they were marooned there. Sightseeing helped to pass the time and they fitted in a day in Cairo visiting the pyramids and the Sphinx. Kathleen wrote home that Alexandria was like something out of the Earl's Court Exhibition but that, apart from the Sphinx, Cairo had lived up to expectations. She felt that the Sphinx was disappointingly small.

Monica Stanley was entranced by the scenery and the colourful people she met. On the train journey from Salonika to Kragujevac she was stunned by the sight of vultures and eagles, herons nesting on houses, blossoms, vineyards and fields of maize against a snowy mountain backdrop with women and oxen working in the fields. At one station, they were greeted by eight peacocks and two white guinea fowl strutting along the platform. At the same time, she was shocked by the seemingly endless cemeteries for Turks, Serbs and Bulgars. They were later taken to see the graves where a large number of women and children, killed in a Bulgarian raid, had been buried, and were shown photographs of the victims hanging from trees.

She was also enthusiastic about gathering souvenirs, which ranged from colourful dresses to hundred-year-old Turkish cannonballs and military bits and pieces. When Kragujevac was attacked by the Germans on 10 June 1915 the bombing came close to the hospital. Monica went out as soon as she could and excitedly gathered up fourteen pieces of shrapnel, a fuse and part of a propeller.

It took two and a half days to transport the Berry Unit's 390 bales and packing cases ashore in a lighter and to load them onto a train. Once this had been done, they were able to leave Salonika for Serbia on 9 February 1915. Unlike some other units they had equipped themselves with food and candles for their long journey, as they knew that the train would be unlit. At Guevgueli, on the Serbian border, they were met by some of the staff from the American Hospital who were nursing huge numbers of patients with typhus in awful conditions. Members of the Berry Unit were struck by how tired and depressed the Americans seemed. When Lady Paget met them at Skopje station, she warned them that typhus was spreading rapidly. When they reached Nish they were told they would be attached to the Reserve Military Hospital of Vrntse (now called Vrnjacka Banja). Like other foreign missions in Northern Serbia, they worked under the direct orders of the military authorities, whose headquarters were at Kragujevac. They were told that a very spacious building would be available for them in Vrntse. Keen to get there and to start work they set off on a further series of slow train journeys and at one point had to transfer both the personnel and all their luggage to a narrow gauge railway in the middle of the night at the unlit station at Krushevatz.

When they eventually reached Vrntse Station, 2 miles outside the town, there was nobody there to greet them and show them where to go. While the stationmaster rang around to find who was meant to be meeting them, the team repaired to a nearby café. After a long wait, they saw a collection of carriages approaching, carrying Colonel Sondermeyer, one of the heads of the Army Medical Department, and a group of officials. Leaving their luggage and stores at the station they all piled into the carriages and were driven into town.

The Girton and Newnham Unit of the Scottish Women's Hospital was a mobile tented unit named after donations from the alumni of Girton and Newnham Colleges in Cambridge. After serving in France, under Dr Louise McIlroy, the unit was asked to accompany the French Expeditionary Force to the Eastern Mediterranean. Their early base was an old silk factory at Guevgueli but when the Serbian Army began to retreat they were ordered back to Salonika.

Staff working for the Scottish Women's Hospitals always kept detailed records of treatments and operations they carried out. The summer of 1916 was terribly hot and the unit working at Kalamaria in Salonika, quickly expanded to have 300 beds. Even this was not enough and over a two-month period they dealt with 1,000 cases, most of whom had dysentery and malaria. So many of staff got ill that there were times when the remaining staff struggled to go on providing a service. The deaths of two team members had a bad effect on morale. In the autumn, the hospital began to fill with wounded men as the fighting spread. Staff had to deal with complex, multiple, contaminated wounds, more like those the teams in France and Belgium were used to treating. The Scottish Women's Hospitals drivers helped bring patients in from the front line to the hospital and the organisation's commissioner, Dr Blair, marvelled at the driving, skill, and courage of their 'girl chauffeurs'.

The Berry Unit found that Vrntse was a fashionable spa town, with a large hilly park and numerous boarding houses. They were told that some of the team were to be based in the Villa Agnes, one of the better boarding houses, until permanent accommodation could be found. The rest of the party were to sleep in the Drzhavna Kafana, a large restaurant, which had been used as a hospital, but was then empty. Although they were shown a number of empty villas, and were told they could use whichever of them they liked as hospitals and staff accommodation, they were bewildered, and asked what had happened to the large building they had been promised.

Someone mentioned there was a dilapidated hydropathic establishment outside the town. That afternoon they went off to have a look at it and decided that, although it was far from an ideal choice for a surgical hospital, the Terapia was better than anything else they had been offered. It was to be their main hospital with the disused village school on a nearby hill as a secondary one. The team also lived in the Terapia. It was an imposing building, overlooking a marsh, on the lower slopes of the Gotch Mountains.

They started to unpack and to create their hospital with the help of three Austrian prisoners acting as orderlies and engineers. One of the bathing rooms was converted into an operating theatre, with the room next door used for sterilising and storing instruments. On the rare occasions that they were visited by a chaplain, this room also served as a chapel. Another of the spa rooms was used as a receiving room, where all new patients were washed. Other rooms were set aside for radiography, a dispensary, a path lab and a room for fumigating clothes. The enormous dining room, which had windows down either side, was turned into the main ward. A carpenter's workshop was set up on the second floor.

Getting the Terapia ready to open as a hospital was hard work. They scoured the big dining hall with disinfectant, sewed mattresses and stuffed pillows, erected beds and whitewashed the operating theatre and storerooms. The empty packing cases were made into furniture. James Berry was not above doing manual work if necessary, to the amazement of local people. When the Crown Prince arrived unexpectedly, he found Berry, covered in mud, draining the marsh in front of the Terapia. Nothing daunted, the Prince settled happily in the kitchen for a cup of tea.

The location of the Terapia and its facilities made it the envy of all visitors from other units. Having been a large spa, it had a steam laundry in the basement, central heating, boilers for baths and an electric light plant in the basement. They all needed careful attention and maintenance by the Austrian engineers but allowed the team to work in relatively good conditions.

A hospital needs a good water supply and the Berry Unit was exceptionally lucky. A clean water supply had been brought into the town from the mountains a few years earlier. The team made checking the water channels and testing the quality of the water a priority but until it had been declared pure they boiled all drinking water. The closest water fountain was about 400 yards from the Terapia near the place where a British Red Cross unit was soon to set up their base. After two months of carrying all their water from this fountain, they persuaded the Serbs to extend the water supply to the Terapia and other hospital buildings, with the Austrian POWs doing the labouring.

All the British units made strenuous efforts to keep their hospitals and patients as clean and vermin free as possible. The Berry Unit took this one step further, and burned or buried all the manure and decaying vegetable material lying in the hospital grounds and on the nearby roads, as these would otherwise have provided a breeding ground for pests. They felt that this was one of the main reasons their hospitals were relatively pest free. They were also aware how important it was to disinfect all clothing, bedding and mattresses. For a while they fumigated them with burning sulphur in a sealed room in the basement, shaking out hundreds of dead lice at the end of twenty-four hours of treatment. This worked well, as long as the process was followed meticulously, but did not kill nits. Socks and underwear gave a particularly rich crop of vermin. In time staff preferred to boil everything that could be boiled and had large galvanised tanks made locally and then mounted on brick furnaces. They eventually brought out a Thresh Steam Disinfector from England.

The unit members believed good ventilation was important. They also realised that many people disagreed, and would close windows given half a chance. They therefore fixed one window in the main ward partly open and removed the glass from some of the upper windows on both sides of the main ward. This kept the ward smelling fresh even when it was crowded. However, when the weather was particularly severe, it was difficult to place all the beds so that the patients would not be snowed on. Although they had been warned that Serbs would not accept the open windows, and would refuse to stay, they found that the patients accepted the British insistence on good ventilation, even in very cold weather.

No sooner was the Terapia ready to receive patients that James Berry was called to Nish for a meeting of representatives from all the British units in Serbia. Everyone had similar tales to recount of epidemics, overcrowded and understaffed hospitals, and shortages of medical staff, disinfectant, drugs, and linens. Some of the units that had been in Serbia the longest were running very short of money and everyone agreed they lacked the resources to deal with the situation. They drew up a joint memorandum to the Serbian Relief Fund and the British Red Cross Society in London, reporting their concerns. James Berry believed this memorandum resulted in better fundraising and more supplies.

Captain Bennett, who was in charge of the Red Cross Unit, was not a doctor. He and his team arrived in mid- February. On 1 March medical staff from both missions and Captain Bennet met at the Terapia to discuss the best way to collaborate. They decided to adapt one of the hot springs for washing patients and to transform the nearby Drzhavna Kafana into a clearing hospital. As far as possible, every patient who arrived in town would be bathed, and spend a few days in the clearing hospital before being passed on to one of the main hospitals. Patients who did develop typhus were kept in separate buildings. They also decided to run the baths and Drzhavna jointly with staff taken from both teams.

The Stobart Unit made their way to Uskub, where they were met by Sir Ralph Paget at the station and provided with an unappetising meal of soup floating with grease, an omelette that was like a piece of leather and sour black bread. The next day they were sent on to their final destination of Kragujevac. The journey had been an ordeal and they were relieved to arrive. Tired as they were, they were whisked off to the dining club for officers in the Prince's Palace, and served a meal that started with Russian caviar and lasted until 10 pm. They slept on the train as it was too late to pitch their tents.

The next morning, Mrs Stobart and a group of officers picked out a hilltop site that had previously been a racetrack and sports ground as the place to set up the hospital. They worked hard all day setting up their camp. When the evening came, with another invitation to join the officers for dinner, they were too busy to accept. Nothing daunted, the officers sent dinner to them; fried fish, beef stew, a whole roasted lamb, and salad. The days were hot, and the nights cold, and Monica Stanley was delighted by the nocturnal calls of owls, nightingales, cuckoo, and bullfrogs.

The hilltop site brought many problems and was later admitted, by some, to have been a bad choice. The campsite became a slippery quagmire as soon as it rained and a trench had to be dug through the kitchen to drain some of the water. Staff worked raised up on duckboards supported by bricks. The most serious problems arose from the fact that the site had previously housed a large group of refugees with all their animals and associated rubbish and dung, making it a breeding ground for many kinds of bug and vermin. When the water in the various ponds around the camp became stagnant, the team's sanitary inspector treated it with chloride of lime. This may have purified the water but it did nothing for the wildlife and thirteen ducks from a nearby farm ran into the camp kitchen gasping, having drunk from the pond. They spent several hours drinking all the fresh water that was offered to them until they felt better. It was not a healthy spot to choose for a fever hospital and this may have accounted for how many of the team became sick in the months after their arrival.

Rear Admiral Troubridge acquired a large secondary school, the Third Belgrade Gymnasium, for use as The British Eastern Auxiliary Hospital. To the delight of the team's doctors, it was in good condition, with modern bathrooms and lavatories. However, since the pupils had left, it had been used as an Austrian barracks and the whole building needed cleaning. As it was designed for the care of men from the small international force, it was under-used and after a month there was not a single British patient, although many Serbs had been treated as outpatients. It was over-staffed, which led to boredom and frustration among the team, as they wanted to feel they were making a worthwhile contribution to the war effort. The surgeon in charge, Sir Alexander Ogston, wanted to close the hospital but Troubridge disagreed, believing his men might yet need it. Some of the staff, including Ogston, went home after a few months and went on to serve elsewhere.

When the Girton and Newnham Unit left Salonika for Ostrovo, they travelled in a convoy of thirty-seven motor vehicles, each twelve yards behind the one in front. As they went inland, the views got more and more beautiful with Mount Olympus in the distance, while the road got worse and worse. There was a deep precipice to one side. Disaster struck the column when the brakes on Mrs Shotton's car failed and it raced backwards over the edge, happily getting stuck in some trees. Mrs Shotton had to be taken to hospital and the driver was badly cut. Other cars got bogged down in the mud and had to be pushed out. Travel in Serbia was rarely straightforward.

Their arrival was delayed as Ostrovo was being shelled. The part of the unit that had been sent ahead had not managed to get the camp ready so there was no food waiting for the travellers on their arrival. As many as possible packed into the few tents that had been erected and the remainder had to sleep by the roadside. After a few days, Ishobel Ross and her pals Adam, Woody and Ethel (the only one to be called by her first name) were able to settle into their shared tent. It was bitterly cold at night and, as they were only 8 miles from the front, the sound of the bombardment was deafening. Ishobel was horrified to think that each boom could mean lost lives and was relieved when she later discovered just how many shells exploded without causing any injury or loss of live. Mosquitoes, spreading malaria, were a real problem and the Serbs made the team a covered kitchen with mesh sides, which helped to give some protection. Ishobel worked hard at her Serbian and was delighted when she could have short conversations with local people and patients. The part of her job she liked least was the daily chore of hacking up raw meat with a hatchet.

If keeping the hospitals and canteens on the western front supplied was a challenge, the administrators of the disparate groups working in Serbia must have had a far more difficult task. Several units tried to take every piece of equipment they could possibly need with them but inevitably had to count on buying most of their food locally. While this was reasonably easy while their supplies of money held out, it grew increasingly difficult. When the Stobart Unit arrived in Kragujevac, Monica Stanley found that the shops were quite good. She reported finding a surprising range of western goods, including Singer Sewing Machines, Sunlight Soap,

Colman's Mustard, Peak Frean's Biscuits, and Peter's Milk Chocolate. Rice, prunes, and haricot beans were plentiful. When any of the units needed more hospital equipment it had to be sent out from England.

The Serbian Relief Fund gave the Berry Unit £1,000 and advice on selecting their stores. Once the unit had the official sanction of the British Red Cross, they were able to call on the Society for ongoing help with supplies including blankets and disinfectants. To the relief of the Berrys, the Red Cross stores department also packed and despatched their supplies. In his account of their work, James Berry paid tribute to the help they received from various war hospital supply depots, and in particular those in Kensington and Marylebone, for all they provided. He made the point that they were well supplied with clothes and hospital necessities as long as the route from England remained open. They were also sent supplies and money from the Dominions, and from Baltimore and Minnesota in the USA. Before they left England they set up a small committee whose main job was to continue fundraising to support the unit.

The Berry Unit worked on the assumption that they would find nothing at their destination. So, as well as all the usual hospital supplies and equipment, they took beds, folding tables and chairs for the staff. The care they took in selecting their equipment is shown in their choice of hospital beds, which could be converted into stretchers. In practice, they were a bit low for the nurses and apparently prone to collapsing when moved by anyone inexperienced in their use but, all in all, they were considered a success. James Berry wrote that he felt they were ready to set up a fifty-bed hospital on a desert island or in the poorest part of Serbia. They hoped to be able to buy bread and meat locally.

James felt it was partly all the supplies they brought with them that enabled the British units to make such a difference in impoverished Serbia. When they arrived, the Serbian Red Cross was almost bankrupt and its storerooms at Nish were empty. He claimed one of the things that made it impossible to treat typhus rationally was the shortage of underclothing. One of the Serb officials added, perhaps simplistically, that what they needed most during the epidemic was 1,000,000 shirts. The Serbian military authorities gave them three dinars a day per member of the unit and gave them the freedom to buy their own food. They did this carefully and were left with money to spare, which they spent on the hospital.

Monica Stanley also gave an insight into the volume and range of equipment a unit needed to take with them. The Stobart Unit took everything with them that they thought they would need to set up a field hospital. This included more than sixty tents, 300 beds, with bedding, bales of clothes for the wounded and civilians, kitchen requisites including four cooking stoves with ovens, several portable boilers for hot water, large tanks for cold water, laundry equipment, medical stores, food worth more than £300, X-ray equipment, all sanitary necessaries, motor ambulances and, one has to assume, tools and spares for them, although no unit mentions this. Issues to do with cars were rarely, if ever, mentioned. In Kragujevac, she added various other items including a 56 lb tin of honey, which cracked and leaked honey into other pieces of luggage. To add to their problems, the cork came out of a bottle of paraffin, which also leaked. The London store, Derry & Toms, gave the unit a couple of carts. Once in Serbia they acquired a pair of oxen, quickly named Derry and Toms, to pull them.

Monica appears to have relished her job of buying food for the hospital and staff in the local market. When the exchange rate was thirty-five dinars to the pound, ducks were around two dinars each, eggs were nine dinars for a hundred and it was easy to buy sheep at twenty dinars each, lambs at fifteen dinars, turkeys at six for fifty-seven dinars, beef, sausages, carrots, and peas. Sugar was scarce and they could not buy butter because of the risk of typhus. Milk had to be boiled and tasted and smelt horrid. Animals were eaten the day they were slaughtered and small lambs and pigs were often cooked whole. While many local people kept pigs as pets, she preferred a friendly sheep; she called it Sir Thomas, presumably after Sir Thomas Lipton, and after she had cleaned and disinfected it and tied a blue ribbon around its neck, it followed her around. Although she did not mind it lying on her bed, other members of staff were not so enamoured of Sir Thomas that they wanted to share their beds with him and the day came when he had to be killed. Monica duly cooked Sir Thomas and served him up. The team said it was the best meat they had eaten but Monica was so upset that she could not eat any meat for days.

Staff periodically came and went from all units as people came to the end of their contracts, were too ill to continue, or had simply had enough. Anyone going back to Britain seems to have been sent with a shopping list for the parent committee to try to fill. Items on the list ranged from pleas for money, to blankets and more staff. It is remarkable how quickly the items on the list were usually despatched, although the fundraising committees must have had many an anxious moment wondering if they could raise the necessary money.

In hot weather, staff battled heat and dust. In spring and autumn, mud was an almost universal problem and in winter, they froze and had to cope with deep snow. The hospital was also buffeted by powerful winds and assaulted by hailstones as big as marbles. Monica moaned that their uniform skirts were impracticably long for the conditions.

While she had complained about the conditions on the ship that carried them to Kragujevac, Monica was remarkably unmoved by the difficulties she encountered later. As well as the problems created by the climate, she had to cope with dogs and cats getting into the kitchen and stealing food. There were masses of crickets that she said lived in black holes all around the camp and which sang all night. She caught one and kept it as a pet in her kitchen. It is not clear how her colleagues greeted this arrival. She was also admirably calm about the large black spiders whose webs seemed to get everywhere.

Mabel Dearmer shared a tent with three other women at Kragujevac, and found her sleeping bag and three blankets very comfortable. However, when her husband was away visiting other units, she did enjoy being able to sleep in his tent and have a little privacy. She felt as if she never stopped working and had endlessly sore feet, in spite of changing her shoes three to four times a day. She also had constant problems from her inflamed knee. However, she enjoyed getting her linen tent in order, and her department soon expanded so that she had three tents. She was responsible for the linen for the entire hospital, and clothing for the patients and orderlies, and had to be able to pack up and be ready to leave in six hours if necessary. Her letters to friends showed just how happy she was and how sure she was that she had found her niche.

Running her kitchen at the Scottish Women's Hospitals unit at Ostrovo, Ishobel Ross liked her colleagues Miss Kerr, the cook, and Miss Jack, who was the administrator and in charge of stores. In September 1916 they were inundated with wounded and everyone had to work around the clock. Ishobel and her team were hard at work in their rush-built kitchen with a blue paper roof and no oven. It rained so much that the kitchen floor became a quagmire but this did not deter visitors who would call in for a welcoming cup of tea, and where prisoners, working on the local roads, could visit for some bread and a chance to get warm. By November, so many staff were ill that Ishobel had to leave her kitchen and start helping in the operating theatre.

Many of the units used Austrian POWs as orderlies. Indeed, there were times when they would have been unable to cope without them. On the whole, relations between the prisoners and their Serbian captors seem to have been good and, in fact, some of the captives were Serbian-speaking Austrians. Many seemed happy to be out of the conflict. Monica Stanley had five Austrian prisoners working for her at Kragujevac. To start with, they refused to work for the unit unless they were paid. She retorted that unless they worked they would not be fed, so they started working. The literature contains many references to how dirty the Austrian prisoners were and they were often accused of introducing typhus through the lice they carried in large numbers. Monica therefore made her orderlies bathe from time to time. They were also given new clothes.

Working with these orderlies had its challenges. One of them used to go off for three or four days at a time to get drunk. After a while, Monica felt she had to report him to the Serb in charge, and then had to watch while he had his ears boxed by the sergeant. Another time, an orderly was seen giving alcohol to two of the patients, who became drunk. He was sent away. All twenty-seven Austrian orderlies were then lined up and given a talking to and the man who had bought the whisky had his ears boxed by the major in charge before being put in solitary confinement for ten days.

Boxing the prisoners' ears seems a strange kind of punishment to be meted out by soldiers. It was, apparently, the lowest of three levels of punishment. The next involved ten days in solitary confinement on bread and water. The most severe level of punishment was execution by being shot.

The Serbian government supplied a considerable number of prisoners to the British units to act as orderlies. James and May Berry commented on how much of the heavy work in Serbia as a whole was being done by Austrian prisoners who rarely had a guard and who were treated as though they belonged by local people. There were about 300 POWs in Vrntse, but not a single Serbian soldier. James was delighted to find that two of the three Austrian prisoners who were on site in the Terapia when they arrived, were engineers and versatile workers.

There were some instances of friction when the Austrian orderlies gave instructions to the Serbian patients who were, in reality, their captors. However, most of the Austrians treated their patients with notable care and compassion. Most of the prisoners were happy to work with the British units and were better fed there than they would have been elsewhere. The Berrys were meticulous about paying their prisoners the small amount that was allowed under the Geneva Conventions. It was, essentially, pocket money, but important. The regard was mutual and when a group of nurses went home, the Austrian prisoners presented them with large bouquets of flowers and when May Berry came back from a brief trip to England, the prisoners set up a triumphal arch at each hospital to greet her.

No matter where voluntary and charity workers served, they felt cut off from their friends and families at home. It was much harder to go home on leave from Serbia than it was from France and Belgium, so any news from Britain, or about the progress of the war, was hugely important to the workers. There were none of the clubs and canteens that were provided in France and which staff there appreciated for the respite they provided. In Serbia, they were often working with a small group of other British people, who they might or might not like, for months on end, with little or no chance of a break. Letters were often delayed for weeks or even months and were eagerly anticipated. Monica Stanley was overjoyed to receive nineteen letters, three newspapers and a book after a month with no post at all. She sat up nearly all night reading them, greedily.

Most of the teams were more at risk from illness than from bombing while they were in the Balkans. In the early summer of 1915, Nurse Read, a theatre nurse, was the first to fall ill with a high fever. The following day Mrs Stobart and Dorothy Picton joined her in isolation, soon to be followed by Nurses Willis and Booth and Miss Johnson, the laundry manager. Soon, ten of the staff had been isolated. Most of them suffered from very high temperatures for around two weeks. It was not initially clear what was wrong with them, as the disease did not follow the usual course for typhus. The doctors hoped it was 'only' malaria and staff began to use mosquito nets, as a precaution. Before long, the diagnosis of typhus was confirmed. Complacent about the risks, Monica Stanley was proud of her good health and sanguine about the chance that she might catch typhus. A few days later she began to feel ill, but hid when they were all meant to have their temperature taken. She struggled on, feeling worse and worse and getting hot and weepy as her temperature rose. She finally had to give up her claim that she was simply suffering from gastritis and had to accept a diagnosis of typhus.

Several team members who fell ill had to be sent back to Britain to recuperate. Monica stayed in Serbia but took a long time to recover properly. So many members of the Stobart Unit fell ill that nurses from the British Farmers' Unit, the Berry Unit and one of the Scottish Women's Hospital Units were sent to help out. Monica was among a group of sick staff who were sent to the Berry Unit at Kragujevac. She was really impressed by their hospitals. No sooner did she think she had recovered than she relapsed, several times. Banned from working in the kitchen until she was fully recovered, she was set to doing the unit's accounts instead, while a Serbian took over her normal duties. When she relapsed yet again she, and two sick nurses, were sent to the British Fever Hospital in Belgrade. She was fed up with being on a milk diet, but enjoyed watching the Danube from the window until she was well enough to make short forays into the town. She was shocked by the amount of bomb damage she saw. She reported that one of the patients produced an egg each day for his breakfast and that they all wondered where he got them. It turned out that he was hiding a chicken in his bed.

She was due to be sent back to her unit in August, when cases of malaria started appearing in Belgrade, but she relapsed again and had to stay in Belgrade. A few days later shelling began and she was moved to a ward at the back of the hospital for safety. On 21 August she and Sister Barnes left Belgrade with their driver, going as fast as they could to avoid being shot by snipers in the hedges. They drove to Skopje, where they stayed with the Paget Unit for a few days. She thought Skopje was lovely but was delighted when she got back to Kragujevac. She later learned that thirty-five foreign workers had died, mostly of typhus and typhoid, and that these had included six Austrian prisoners, but only two British doctors. One American had killed himself while delirious.

In October she heard that all the English missions had been told to leave Serbia. She was keen to go, as she was due to resume her normal job in England three weeks later. All the same, she found leaving her kitchen staff hard

When Mabel Dearmer got typhoid they hoped that it would be mild because she had been inoculated, but she grew steadily sicker. Towards the end, she had five doctors treating her and, as double pneumonia set in, was given oxygen every twenty minutes. In spite of her own determination to recover, and the efforts of her colleagues, she died. She was buried in the local churchyard at the same time as Nurse Ferris, another typhoid victim. They had to be buried the day they died because of the hot weather. The funeral was led by Percy Dearmer and three Orthodox priests. Monica Stanley made a large cross of white wild flowers, Acacia and Clematis to go on top of the Union flag that was draped over the coffin. The Serbian Government sent elaborate wreaths. A military band played and the mourners included French, English and Serbian officials and representatives from various other British medical units. After the service, Percy Dearmer left Serbia.

During the typhus epidemic, staff in the Scottish Women's Hospitals units took every precaution to avoid being infected. Many of the staff cropped their hair and they all wore long, white, calico smocks and Turkish style trousers tucked into high boots or socks and bound at the wrists and ankles with naphthalene soaked bandages to stop the lice that spread the disease, getting in. They covered their heads with tight skull caps and face masks. Even so, a number did catch typhus and several died, including Louisa Jordan, Dr Elizabeth Ross, Madge Fraser and Augusta Minshull.

Malaria was also widespread, especially in summer. Several members of the Scottish Women's Hospitals staff were infected. Catherine Millar was sent home to recover but died from the infection, as did Olive Smith. Eleanor Soltau, who was in charge of their first Serbian Unit, had to be replaced by Elsie Inglis in April 1915, as she caught diphtheria while helping fight the typhus epidemic. She recovered, but had to be sent home to recuperate. When nursing the wounded, staff knew that they had to be very careful to try to avoid any scratches that might get infected. In spite of her care, Nurse Agnes Earl was nursing a man with a gangrenous limb when she got a scratch that became septic. She died two days later. When any of the British workers died local people attended the funeral in large numbers, deeply appreciative of the foreigners who had come to help them.

Disease was not the only danger these workers faced. The stress of their situation told on most of them and one of the drivers, Angela Bell, had a nervous breakdown and had to be sent home. During the retreat in the winter of 1915, driver Caroline Toughill was trying to overtake a lorry, on a narrow road near Rashka, when the edge of the road gave way and the car fell down a precipice. She was buried in a nearby village.

The Berry Unit suffered a near disaster in March 1915. One of the team saw blue smoke coming out between the tiles above the storerooms that housed the owner's belongings. When they investigated, they found a fire raging in the top floor rooms above the kitchen and dining room. Staff formed a human chain to the water supply in the basement armed with buckets, jugs, kettles and any other vessels they could find. As tiles rained down, some of the group wore tin basins on their heads for protection. As the floors quickly burned through, they started to salvage linens from the floor below and the nurses prepared the patients for evacuation. They managed to stop the fire spreading to the main ward. With their usual foresight, members of the Berry Unit had placed buckets of sand and of water throughout the building in case there was a fire. When the fire was out they all sat down to a large lunch of bacon, eggs and extra rations.

It was perhaps inevitable that some of the women who had the courage, energy and drive to volunteer to work overseas, were also going to be pig-headed individualists who achieved a great deal but who rubbed other people up the wrong way. Enthusiasm and ability were not always enough when working in difficult conditions and some clashes between even the most adaptable of colleagues were also inevitable. Some were true mavericks who would never have fitted in with any of the official aid units for long.

In September 1915 the Scottish Women's Hospitals Unit at Ostrovo had a visit from Flora Sandes, an English women in the uniform of a private in the Serbian Army, who talked to them about her experiences. Flora was an untrained nurse who went to Serbia to work with the Serbian Red Cross in November 1914, when she was thirty-eight. She had trained with the FANYs in England, but when she tried to enrol as a VAD for Foreign Service, she was turned down because of her lack of experience. When she and Emily Simmonds reached Valjevo they found men who had had no treatment and were filthy, bloody and swarming with lice. There were hardly any trained medical staff and at one point, they began carrying out operations themselves, as there were no doctors available. Both the women caught typhus, but survived. After the typhus epidemic had passed, Flora wanted to join an ambulance unit, but was turned down.

Back in England, she launched an appeal through the *Daily Mail* and raised £2,000 for Serbia in three weeks. She used the money to buy more than 100 tons of medical equipment and supplies, which the Red Cross agreed to transport to Serbia. In January 1915, Flora was back in Serbia and at the end of the year, she was caught up in the Great Retreat and was then accepted into the Serbian Army as a private.

Flora was an effective self-publicist and used this skill to help Serbia. In 1916, she wrote and published *An English Woman-Sergeant in the Serbian Army.* It was a real adventure story, with herself as the undoubted heroine. She recounted how she had been seriously wounded and rescued by her comrades, and how she performed amputations with a pair of blunt scissors after all the doctors had died of typhus. It is hard to tell how much she exaggerated. Sales of the book made more than £5,000, much of which was spent on buying aid for Serbia.

Katherine Harley was another difficult woman. She was also the sister of Field Marshal John French, which certainly meant she occasionally enjoyed preferential treatment. When she went to work for the Scottish Women's Hospitals Unit at Royaumont in France she tried to take over and clashed with the matron, Miss Ivens and the Chief Medical Officer. She then moved on to become the administrator for the Scottish Women's Hospitals' Girton and Newnham Unit at Troyes, but was again determined to do everything in her own inimitable way, causing distress and strain for some of her colleagues. Her next posting took her to Macedonia, still with the Girton and Newnham Unit, where she helped set up a hospital in a disused silk factory at Guevgueli. Unfortunately, she soon clashed so badly with the Chief Medical Officer, Dr Louise McIlroy, over who was actually in charge, that she had to resign and went back to Britain.

The committee of the Scottish Women's Hospitals were peculiarly keen to retain her skills, and quite possibly her connections, and she was asked to go back to Serbia to set up an independent transport column. Conflict followed her. She was soon accused of being wilful and insubordinate and of putting the team at risk by working at night very close to the battlefield, when she had been specifically banned from doing so. She was also criticised for not enforcing discipline and the unit's members gained a reputation for drinking, smoking in public, late nights and short hair, which caused gossip. When a team came out from Britain to investigate both the Girton and Newnham Unit and the transport column they were shocked by what they found and Harley was persuaded to resign.

Katherine and her daughter went off to Monastir, rented a house, and decided to help the local people, to the annoyance of Lucie Creighton and the British Red Cross team, who were already working in the town. Lucie said that neither the Scottish Women's Hospitals nor the Serbian

Relief Fund would work with Mrs Harley any more, and added that the British Red Cross would have sent her home if she had not been French's sister. A stormy meeting, attended by Lucie, the Prefect, the Mayor, and Mrs Harley, was called to discuss the problems Mrs Harley had caused in Serbia, including having turned people out of their home because she wanted to live there. She was getting rations from the Serbian Government but did not have the funds to run a feeding programme. On 17 March 1917 she was sitting in her window, drinking tea with her daughters, when she received a serious head wound from a Bulgarian shell and was taken to the French Hospital where she died. She was buried in Kragujevac.

Most of the people who wrote about their experiences were appreciative and affectionate in their comments about their colleagues, in spite of the frustrations that must have arisen from time to time. The acerbic Lucie Creighton described Mr R. C. Bosanquet, the Serbian Relief Fund's chief administrator in Serbia, as a man of 'bad health, a bad temper, no inspiration and a bad manner' concluding that he was unsuited to his job. She felt personal animosities between the Serbian Relief Fund and British Red Cross Society staff in Kragujevac resulted in a problematic lack of co-operation between the two organisations. She was also blunt in her comments about the French troops in Serbia, accusing them of treating the Serbs as a conquered race and of being prone to stealing livestock and produce. Her employers, the Serbian Relief Fund, came in for criticism for showing a lack of interest in her work and personal welfare.

Another Scottish Women's Hospitals recruit, Evelina Haverfield, was not an unmitigated asset. She was a militant suffragette who had nursed horses during the Boer War and who thought that war was a great opportunity for women to show what they were made of. She took herself to Serbia in 1915, at her own expense, and became the administrator in charge of logistics and transport at Kragujevac. In no time, she had clashed with Dr Lilian Chesney and was moved to a unit in Mladenovatz. She was taken prisoner by the Austrians in October 1915 and was repatriated, with Elsie Inglis and a small group of other charity workers, the following February. Wasting no time, she joined the Russian Unit as the head of the transport column and in October 1916 went to Romanian Bessarabia with the Inglis Unit. She was in charge of the volunteers' money and earlier that year had converted it all into Romanian currency. Unfortunately, the currency then became worthless, leaving the volunteers penniless. Many of them blamed her and were very angry, resenting her total lack of sympathy for their plight. She was also criticised for pushing the volunteers and drivers too hard in awful conditions, for being unbusinesslike and, under the surface charm, incompetent. It appears that she then had a nervous breakdown and went back to Britain, where she began raising money for Serbia with Flora Sandes. After the war, she went back to Serbia and set up a hospital for war orphans. She died of pneumonia in 1920 and was buried in Serbia.

Lilian Chesney, who had problems with Evelina Haverfield was, herself, criticised for being unconventional and for having favourites. She was a martinet and prone to rubbing people up the wrong way at the hospital she led in Kragujevac. Her assistant, Ellie Rendel, was among her favourites, and enjoyed working with her, but commented that she was very rude to people she did not like. Her unconventional ways included doing her hospital rounds accompanied by two pet geese and a pig.

Elsie Inglis, founder of the Scottish Women's Hospitals, came into increasing conflict with the organisation in Britain. She worked in Serbia in 1915 and 1916 and then returned to Britain, keen to set up a new unit to go to Mesopotamia. She was angry and frustrated when the British authorities would not give their permission for the unit to be formed. She kept pressing the Scottish Women's Hospitals Committee in Edinburgh to extend their work, but members felt that the organisation was already overstretched and another unit could simply not be afforded. The difficulties reached such a pitch in June 1916 that she resigned. She was persuaded that a complete split would be very damaging for the organisation and the London committee agreed to raise the £9,000 needed to fund a new unit, named after Dr Inglis. The Inglis Unit went to Megidia in Romania to work with Serbs fighting within the Russian Army and stayed in Romania until September 1917, in spite of the inevitable difficulties caused by the Russian Revolution. She then rejoined the Serbs in Bessarabia.

It was not only the organisation in Britain that found Dr Inglis increasingly difficult to work with. Diaries kept by a number of her colleagues during 1917 show that she was growing short-tempered and rude and even more autocratic than usual. Some people attributed this to the dysentery that they all suffered from periodically. The reality was far more serious and at the end of September she collapsed, unable to operate any more. She was suffering from cancer and had known about it before she left England. Only her indomitable spirit and determination had carried her so far but in insisting on leading this unit she was, perhaps, putting her wishes above the needs of the organisation. When the unit finally left for Britain, she sent a telegram saying 'Everything satisfactory and all well except me.' She did not tell anyone what was wrong and when the boat docked in Newcastle, she spent twenty minutes saying goodbye to her team and wearing all her medals. She spent the next day with her sisters at a local hotel and died that night.

Various units suffered from a fairly high staff turnover. Some people found the conditions too gruelling, some got sick and had to return home and others got frustrated with nursing the sick. They felt that they had signed up to nurse wounded soldiers and not to battle typhus and other diseases or devote much of their energy to helping civilians. It seems some of the women who had served in France and Belgium in the early days of the war may have become dependent on the adrenaline their work had stimulated and, becoming accustomed to conditions there, had headed to Serbia looking for an even greater challenge. They certainly found some of their work in Serbia frustrating and angled to get closer to the front.

Elsie Inglis and Dr Hutchinson were running a hospital in Krushevatz when the country was invaded and everyone in the hospital, including the staff of thirty-two, was taken prisoner. One part of the hospital was soon taken over by the Germans, but Elsie continued to run the Czar Lazar Hospital with Dr Holloway. So many patients arrived that they had to tie pairs of beds together so that two beds could take three patients. Having arranged to take 400 patients, they soon had 1,200, with men on every shelf and in every outhouse. They were terribly short of food and subsisted on beans, bread and weak tea. Not long after the invasion, the team was sent to Southern Hungary, where they were treated as common prisoners but made such a nuisance of themselves that, after just six weeks, the Austrians sent them home.

James Berry recounted how they became POWs on 9 November 1915. Austrian troops went into Vrntse without any disturbance and the next day the hospital was formally taken over by a Hungarian lieutenant. Having completed the formalities he left a sentry at the gate and departed. Like many of the troops they were to encounter, the guard was an Austrian Serb who was very friendly to the staff, patients and former prisoners, who were in far better condition that the newly arrived invaders. The guard was removed the next day and they were free to come and go as they liked. Austro-Hungarian generals, colonels, a count and a prince came to visit and Colonel Dr Pick, who was in charge of all medical arrangements, was quick to confirm that he did not want to interfere with their management of the hospitals that were under his, nominal, supervision.

The hospital in the school quickly filled up with Hungarian troops suffering from frostbite. The Terapia and Drzhavna were filled to overflowing with Serbian wounded, but those with slight wounds soon had to move out to make space for more troops with frostbite. Berry was struck by how quiet and docile these men were and how much they appreciated even the slightest kindness. They often found that little provision had been made for feeding patients the day they arrived, and so staff spared whatever food they could for them.

Somewhat bizarrely the Austrian orderlies, who had been sent to work with the Berry Unit as prisoners, carried on working there for the first three weeks after the British workers had themselves been taken prisoner. Berry was sad to see the orderlies leave, as he was worried about their future. They were replaced by Hungarian soldiers. The Heads of Mission were in full charge of these men, including their punishment if they misbehaved. The soldiers accepted this, being happy to be away from the fighting. In time the Hungarians were replaced by Romanians. The British team met no antagonism for being members of the enemy but found it hard to keep motivated. James felt that they had failed in their work. However, the team members adapted and some took on tasks they had not ever expected to perform. The laundry staff had left, so the sister-in-charge, Sister Davies, took over the laundry herself, with various local assistants. Other Sisters took on the housekeeping tasks that had previously been carried out by the Austrian orderlies. Elsie Inglis's niece, Dr Inglis, who had been second in command, was no longer needed as a doctor so took over the cooking duties and Dr McLaren turned her energies to washing-up. Almost everyone helped in the kitchen in one way or another.

Food was by no means plentiful. The Austrians provided a daily ration of one-fifth to one-half of a loaf of black bread per person and meat, which usually consisted of almost bare ribs from some ancient cow or ox, with helpings of various organs known jointly as 'lights'. These rations were periodically supplemented with some haricot beans or a little coffee or little screwed up paper packets of tea, sugar, herbs or vegetables. Undaunted, the staff mixed whatever was available with their own stores of Heinz's beans and Maconochie rations.

Before the Austrian invasion, the team had set up their own stock of animals, to be eaten when times grew hard. They had sheep, a goat, a couple of calves, and various poultry. After the invasion they were so worried that someone might steal their livestock that they put the birds in one bathroom and the other animals in a small room beside the kitchen. Finding food for the animals was difficult, especially in snowy weather and they resorted to feeding them Benger's food, a powdered supplement, which had been sent out in large quantities. The Benger's food was also used for making sauces, puddings, pastry and cakes.

The Foreign Office had instructed Lord Paget to arrange the safe evacuation of all aid workers and their equipment but when he met hospital heads at Vrntse, he found most of the Scottish Women's Hospital staff had other ideas. Drs Inglis, Hutchison, Chesney and Holloway and Mrs Haverfield were among those who were determined to stay and carry on helping the Serbs as much as they could. They soon learned just how hard it was to be linked to a retreating army.

When the Bulgarian Army invaded Serbia in October 1915, Mabel Stobart was leading her field hospital, on horseback, near Pirot, close to the Bulgarian border. As the Serbian Army fell back, they kept moving to wherever it was most needed. Before long, it was apparent that the army was in full retreat and that the civilian population was leaving with it. The unit was ordered to go to Uvidno, where they had problems finding any land, in a vast quagmire that was dry enough for them to set up a hospital. They heard that both the Germans and the Bulgarians were advancing steadily. Orders to move were always delivered in a white envelope and before long a message had arrived telling them to move to Palanka. From there they were sent on again, generally moving south. When the roads got particularly bad, they had to carry the wounded to lighten the load. Mrs Stobart continued to enjoy herself, relishing each new challenge.

Army commanders advised them to push on through a gorge as fast as possible, as the enemy was approaching from several directions. They were desperate to get through before the Bulgarians from Nish could cut off the southern end of the gorge. The muddy road was clogged with a chaos of vehicles, refugees, and soldiers. When wagons got stuck in the deep mud, refugees threw their precious belongings into the roaring river to reduce the load and help the wagon get moving again. An angry backlog built up behind them. As they went on the rain turned to snow. Staff were exhausted and depressed as they struggled on across the Kosovo Plain, past heaps of bodies from the recent battle, to Pristina.

When they got there, they were joined by the unit from Kragujevac, which had been ordered to leave by the Austrians. As the Serbian Army was no longer fighting and did not, therefore, need their services, they were advised that all British units should head to Scutari, on the Albanian coast. Mrs Stobart refused to leave and insisted she would stay with the Serbs until the retreat had finished. In late November, she and her team set off for Petch, on the border with Montenegro, Serbia's only Balkan ally. When they reached Petch, some members of her team decided to join the unit from Kragujevac, also in town, and go home.

On 3 December, Mrs Stobart and her group set off into the Black Mountains of Montenegro, with most of their equipment loaded into bullock carts, which could only travel at 2 miles an hour. They travelled day and night. One of the team members, Miss M. I. Tatham, described how the weather soon turned inexorably wet, making progress for them, and for the endless column of exhausted refugees, even harder as the clinging mud deepened day by day. However, the rain was soon known as 'the little friend of Serbia' as it held up the Austrian advance, allowing much of the Serbian Army to reach safety. Every now and then they stopped, long enough to set up a temporary dressing station and dress wounds for as many of the weary men marching by as they could. They moved on as soon as the sound of guns and the advancing enemy got too close again.

As they approached the town of Rashka, one of their team was accidentally shot through the lungs by a farmer who was trying to stop some refugees stealing his horses. The poor girl was carried back 8 miles, to a Serbian dressing station and left there with two doctors and a nurse, who were taken prisoner two days later. However, the Austrians treated them well and, when the girl had recovered enough, they were sent home to England through Vienna and Switzerland.

When they were only two days' walk from Monastir, it fell to the Bulgarians, leaving the group no alternative to crossing the mountains and heading for the coast. They had been warned that women would be incapable of making the journey in the harsh winter weather and, indeed, the Serbian women stopped rather than attempt the crossing. Up to that point, the roads had been muddy and packed with other travellers. The route into the mountains was so narrow that they had to abandon their wagons and load as much as possible onto pack mules and donkeys. They were travelling through one of the worst blizzards for decades, on paths barely 2 foot wide, with a sheer drop of 1,000 feet on one side. Whenever one of the mules fell and died of cold and exhaustion, they froze where they fell. Everyone else had to climb over them. By the time they could see the coast, every pack animal had died and they were left with only what they could carry themselves. Gertrude Holland remarked that they kept passing dead ponies and donkeys which had had lumps hacked off them by people who were desperate for food. She also noticed that they passed dead soldiers who had been stripped of their uniforms and boots and left naked in the snow by people who had desperate need of clothes. Gertrude froze into her stirrups and saddle on Mount Velica and had to be taken off and thawed out.

There was no respite as they dropped towards the coast. The snow turned to rain and all their energy was focussed on getting through the deepening mud. They had word that an Italian ship would meet them at San Giovanni di Medua (modern Shëngjin), on the Adriatic coast. They struggled to get there in time for the rendezvous, only to find their ship had been torpedoed and that they had to wait three days for a replacement. Ships carrying food for the refugees were also torpedoed. While they waited, they could see the nightly fires of the Serbian soldiers in the surrounding hills, and the Austrian planes bombing them.

When a ship did get through, it evacuated all the Red Cross personnel and as many refugees as could be crammed on board. The soldiers and men of military age had to march on down the coast to other ports. The ship travelled across the Adriatic overnight to Brindisi. It was under fire and zigzagging until they approached the Italian Coast and British gunboats appeared out of the mist to protect them.

Units from both the Scottish Women's Hospitals and the Serbian Relief Fund looked after Serbian refugees in Corfu, Corsica, Bizerta in Tunisia and Sallanches, in the Alps. When a party from the Scottish Women's Hospitals, led by Dr Mary Blair, set off for Serbia in August 1915 they were invited to go to Corsica instead, to provide medical care for Serbian refugees. They ran a hospital in Corsica until April 1919, treating more than 17,000 patients. Some of their patients were Serbian soldiers, who later went to form the Second Serbian Army.

When Kathleen Courtney and her fellow Quakers reached Salonika harbour, they found that the refugees were being gathered into a camp, before being sent to Corsica in batches. The camp was being run by a Mr Jones from the Friends' Committee, and he was very pleased to hand everything over to Kathleen and her group, as he was about to set off for Corsica with the refugees. Russian, Serbian and British workers were all busy in the camp, but there seemed to be nobody in overall charge. The refugees lived in crowded tents, crammed with all the belongings they had salvaged from their previous lives. Water, for bathing and laundry, was heated in huge vats and each tent had a stove for heating and cooking. Kathleen was kept busy, looking after half the tents, ensuring the right people had beds, issuing tickets for clothes and helping refugees get passports and the other paperwork they needed before they could go to Corsica.

In the middle of January, Kathleen was sent to Corsica, not clear what her actual role would be, but aware that the authorities expected 1,700 refugees a day to arrive at Bastia. When she arrived, she found that one of the Quakers was in charge of two boats in the harbour. He wanted to unload the 1,600 passengers in Bastia, but was told they had to go on to Marseilles, to be quarantined. He was desperately trying to buy provisions. Neither of the ships had enough food on board. Such cooking as there was, was done by Emily Simmonds, a Red Cross nurse who had previously worked with Flora Sandes in Serbia. She was filthy, exhausted and longing to reach Marseilles and have a bath.

Kathleen and her three colleagues got to work finding a house where they could set up a hospital. They also rented and furnished houses where Serbian women and children could live, handed out clothes and arranged where the refugees could bathe and do their laundry. Some weeks later, she appealed to the authorities in Ajaccio for help and managed to get two medically trained staff to help run the hospital. She believed that it was a mistake to accept the French offer to allow Serbian refugees to go to Corsica, as there were too few resources there for them to be cared for properly.

The Inglis Unit finally reached its destination at Medjidia, in Romania in early October. Ellie Rendel wrote home to say how much she was enjoying herself, even though the town was being bombed on a daily basis. They were based in a large hilltop barracks, which she thought made an ideal target for shells. It was, predictably, filthy and had to be cleaned and whitewashed from top to bottom by the team and a group of Turkish prisoners. Conditions were basic, and they slept on tightly packed camp beds, each under three army blankets, a rug and a sheepskin. There was little heating and all water had to be brought from a pump. Wounded Russians began to arrive before they were ready to receive them, filthy but with good first aid dressings on their wounds. A visiting Russian general handed out medals and crosses to the patients. Each one who was expected to die was given a cross.

After a while, the staff moved into tents, which were colder but more comfortable. Food, particularly milks, eggs, fruit and vegetables were in short supply. Dr Chesney was not satisfied with what they were doing, and before long it was decided that she should take a team of twelve, including Ellie, and set up a field hospital closer to the firing line. Ellie was delighted when she was appointed Dr Chesney's sssistant and her salary was raised to £100 a year, which she considered very generous. She was gratified that Dr Chesney always introduced her as Dr Rendel, even though she had not qualified as a doctor. The team had to be ready to pack up and move at two hours' notice and were to wear breeches, unless any officers came to tea, when they were to change into skirts.

Communication with Britain was difficult. In late October, Ellie's parents were informed that the organisation was feeling anxious about the Inglis and Haverfield Units and would be in touch as soon as they had any news. Although she wrote to her parents regularly, her letters were slow to reach them. In mid-November, her parents were told that word had been received from Miss Henderson, the administrator of the Inglis Unit, that all was well.

They were forced to retreat with the army on several occasions. Near Constanza, they camped with a Serbian hospital unit and could see the town burning in the distance. They joined a stream of refugees heading for Russia and hoping to cross the Danube at Kramagat. They were shocked to see large numbers of Romanian troops running away in disarray, flogging their horses in their haste. They knew that all the wounded men who had been left behind would be killed, as the Bulgarians did not take prisoners.

Finding they could not get over the Danube as planned, and in danger of being attacked by the Bulgarians, they headed for Iskakrcha, hoping to cross there. By this point, their rations consisted of ship's biscuits and bully beef. They crossed into Russia on 27 October. Cold and wet, they were relieved to be able to pitch camp and wash for the first time in nine days. Before long, they were on the move again and reached Ismail on 3 November. Ellie was keen to get back to the front, but thought that this was unlikely to happen. She wrote to her mother that, having done a retreat, she was anxious to do a victorious advance.

By December she had run out of reading material, and out of conversation with her colleagues. As they had packed up and were ready to move there was less than usual to do and members of the team were getting fractious. Two of the Sisters had stopped speaking to each other.

They left Ismail for Odessa in the dark, shortly before Christmas and travelled perched on ammunition wagons. It was cold and the route was muddy but the wagons moved so slowly that they often preferred to walk.

Dr Chesney had found a hospital for them in Odessa but conditions were horrendous and food was terribly scarce. They were frighteningly short of money. There was not much call for their services in Odessa and after a few weeks, Ellie was annoyed to find they were to move again, to Jassy in Romania. Circumstances had changed for the worse. The Red Flag was flying and officials were increasingly insolent. Jassy proved to be full of typhus patients and they moved on to Tecuci where they looked around for somewhere to set up their operations. They finally found a place to camp and a disgustingly filthy building they could use as a hospital. While there, they heard a rumour that the Czar was to be sent to Siberia. She mentioned that Dr Berry, who had earlier worked in Serbia, had set up a hospital in a magnificent house a few miles away. She felt he did not have the knack of dealing with the Russians, tending to rub them up the wrong way.

They struggled on until September when Ellie wrote to her mother that the game was up and that she was coming home as fast as she could. The Germans were advancing, the Russians mutinying and to cap it all, a Russian bomb had landed in their midst. Luckily, it had not exploded. Ellie and Dr Chesney set off for home on 20 August 1917, disgusted with Russia, tired of the Scottish Women's Hospitals and fed up with living with strangers, only to be diverted to a hospital near Kragujevac. They stayed there until shortly after the Armistice, only to be sent to Bosnia for a frustrating few months to care for 2,000 sick Serbs, who had been prisoners of the Germans. Ellie finally reached England in April 1919.

Dorothy, Lady Kennard, was in Bucharest in October 1915, having had a 'wild wish' to leave England. She thoroughly enjoyed the social life in Bucharest, which continued even after Serbian refugees began to arrive in large numbers. The following May, she realised the situation was going to deteriorate, and that they would run short of supplies. She tried to get organised, spending hours writing lists of things she needed and sending them to England. Few of the items she asked for ever reached her. In July, although Romania was still neutral, all ladies were asked to volunteer with the Romanian Red Cross. British volunteers were able to choose where to work and she volunteered at a large military hospital, trying to learn as much as possible in a short time, as she had no nursing experience.

Waiting for the war to reach them was stressful. In preparation she packed away her silver and china, filled baths with water and piled blankets in the hall to be used to put out fires. She was jubilant when martial law was declared in August and excited to be at war, with wounded men and prisoners arriving in Bucharest. Excitement was soon tempered by reality. She felt sorely lacking in skill when she was put in charge of one section of the hospital, and worked long hours without feeling she really knew what she was doing. However, she did find operations fascinating. On one occasion, they had to treat a number of men from a barracks near the hospital who were wounded when their colleagues got over-excited and began shooting at random. There were repeated air raids, making her journey to and from work very dangerous. Later, concerned that the Germans were approaching the town, she decided to drink champagne at dinner, to stop the Germans getting it. She thought she was going to be able to leave the country and packed, wrapping three bottles of champagne carefully in eiderdowns. After the luggage had been sent off, she heard there were 30,000 people at the station waiting to get away, so she went to her apartment again, working for several more weeks before being able to leave.

* * *

Whereas some of the units working in Serbia were able to get to know members of the local community and to work in one place for months at a time, this was not a luxury enjoyed by workers in Russia. Margaret Barber had worked as a VAD in Serbia, but she joined a Red Cross unit in 1916, heading for Russia. They went to Lake Van for a short while, then moved to Petrograd before joining a Friends War Victims Committee hospital in Samara. Their time there started under the Czar, carried on during the Revolution and finished under the Bolsheviks. In 1918 she went to Astrakan on the Caspian Sea to work with refugees for the Armenian Red Cross.

Twenty-one-year-old Florence Farmborough went to Moscow in 1908, to teach English to the daughters of heart surgeon Dr Usov. She was very happy with the family and soon developed a love of Russia and Russian people. When the war started, Dr Usov was quick to join a Red Cross hospital under the patronage of Princess Golitsin. After a great deal of pressure from his family, and Florence, he persuaded the Princess to accept his daughters Asya and Nadya, and Florence, as members of the

Russian Red Cross VAD. Six months later, all three passed their Red Cross exams. For Florence, the greatest challenge had been that the written exams were in Russian. Each member of their group was presented with a Red Cross at a special service, although the priest who was officiating paused and checked that Florence adhered to an acceptable branch of Christianity before giving her Red Cross to her.

Not content with working in Moscow, Florence was determined to serve nearer the front. In 1915 she joined the Red Cross Unit of the 10th Field Surgical Otryad of the Zemstvo of all the Russias. She was appointed as a survival nurse in their 1st Flying Column. This was a mobile unit, equipped with a staff of forty-four and a series of twenty-four two-wheeled carts. They were sent on a four-week journey to Gorlitse on the Russo-Austrian front, where they set up a hospital.

Members of the flying column wore a uniform that contrasted with that of their colleagues on the Western Front. In addition to the usual dresses, aprons and headscarves they had sheepskin waistcoats, flannel-lined black leather jackets, high riding boots and black leather breeches. The only way for them to get around was on horseback.

The very nature of the flying column meant that they were constantly on the move, setting up and treating men for a short period, then moving on as the demands of the conflict dictated. One of the horrors of being linked to an army in retreat was having to abandon wounded men. When Florence's group had to evacuate Gorlitse, the walking wounded were sent on ahead and when the team left, they were followed by men crawling along, grabbing their skirts and pleading to be taken with them. The harrowing cries of the wounded they had left behind haunted them. This was not something experienced by any of the staff on the Western Front.

Florence was not the only British woman to join a Russian flying column. After Violetta Thurstan and her group were left at the Danish border by the Germans, Violetta read about the problems in Poland, where typhoid and cholera were adding to the soldiers' misery and where there was a lack of trained nurses. With three of her colleagues, she asked the St John Ambulance to let them go to Russia. After getting the necessary permission, passports, visas and cholera inoculations, they set off on the long journey through Sweden and Lapland to Finland. Violetta relished the journey; the starlit nights, snow and frost. From Finland, they travelled along a narrow track for a further fifty-two hours before reaching Petrograd.

The director of the Red Cross in Russia welcomed them warmly and sent them to stay in a Russian Community of Nursing Sisters to learn the Russian way of doing things. Although they realised that this made sense, Violetta and her companions were happier when they were sent to

Warsaw, as they were keen to get closer to the Front. Before they left, they had an audience with the Empress Marie Feodorovna at the Gatchina Palace, just outside Petrograd.

The women worked hard at learning at least the basics of Russian, as it was the only language spoken by the soldiers. French was the language of high society in Russia and although German was widely understood, there was a 3,000 rouble fine for speaking it. Partly to help them learn Russian as quickly as possible, the head of the Red Cross in Warsaw assigned the women to hospitals in pairs. Violetta and Sister G were sent to a large Red Cross hospital run by a Community of Russian Sisters. To their relief, the Sister Superior spoke English, and several of the other Sisters spoke French or German. The work was hard and trying to cope with the conditions and learn the Russian names of all the equipment made the early weeks especially exhausting. Sadly, the other pair of English nurses only lasted five days before going home.

Those who remained were soon very busy indeed, with twenty Sisters for 1,000 badly wounded patients. All the heavy work that would have been done by probationers in England, was done by orderlies or sanitars. About once a week the Sisters had to cover the night shift as well, so they worked for thirty-six hours with only a brief rest and a walk in the afternoon. Violetta commented that the local Sisters rarely took any exercise but that the two English nurses got out in the open air whenever they could. She caused consternation one night, when she opened the windows in a hot stuffy ward. The Russian Sisters feared for the safety of their patients, saying that they would never open a window before dawn.

Violetta believed that it was down to the Sister Superior that the hospital ran so smoothly in its terrible buildings with insufficient staff and inadequate resources. The staff worked as an effective team and both they and their patients were very fond of the Sister Superior. When they were told to prepare to take 400 patients, but could only make space for 200, the Sister Superior calmly said that they would all be made as comfortable as possible on stretchers overnight and space would be made for them the next day. Each man was undressed, examined quickly by a doctor, dressed in clean clothes and either taken to the operating theatre or given a bowl of hot soup. The Sister Superior worked through the night with her team, sitting with dying men to comfort them or lending a hand wherever it was most needed.

Some aspects of the Russian way of nursing came as a shock to Violetta and Sister G. They were amazed to find that even untrained or inexperienced nurses or inexperienced dressers regularly gave stimulating or powerfully narcotic drugs, such as morphine, codeine or ether, to their patients without referral to a doctor or even mentioning what they had done.

Like other British women working in the warzones, Violetta seemed intrigued by the behaviour of the local troops. The Russians, she noted, were impervious to how they looked as long as they were warm. She also remarked how friendly the officers and men were with each other. Discipline was strict when the men were on duty. At other times it was relaxed, with officers calling soldiers names such as their 'little pigeon' or 'comrade' while then men might address their officer as their 'little father' or 'little brother'. She contrasted their attitude to that of the Prussian troops whose officers treated their men badly and were therefore disliked by them.

One day Violetta and Sister G were sent to Lodz. When they arrived at the Hotel Bristol they found they were to join Prince Volkonsky's Flying Column, which reported to the Red Cross. Good transport was essential for a flying column and they had five vehicles to carry them and their equipment. Their job was to go out to collect the wounded and deliver them to a field hospital or ambulance train. The column's surgeon was an English colonel and the rest of the team consisted of Violetta and her friend, the prince, his wife and servant, some Russian dressers and students, orderlies and, sometimes, some Russian Sisters. Wherever they went, they had to take their bulky cases of cotton wool, bandages, dressings, anaesthetics, their field steriliser, operating theatre equipment, soap, candles, benzene and their personal luggage with them. As a flying column, they also had to take enough tinned food to enable them to be self-sufficient.

They took over a hospital in Lodz, whose regular staff had been told to evacuate. The stench was appalling, but it was too cold for even Violetta to open the windows for more than a few minutes at a time. The hospital and its outgoing staff had been stretched to breaking point. She longed for at least hot water bottles, and hot water to fill them, to give some comfort to the wounded and dying men who arrived steadily throughout the night, but all they could offer was shelter and hot tea.

As shells began to fall close to the hospital, horrifically wounded civilians were brought in, including a child with half its head blown off. An elderly Jewish woman was brought in having lost both legs in a blast and with a huge chest wound. No doubt numbed by the shock of her injuries, she was not in pain but spent the few hours before she died distraught at the loss of her wig. They soon had to start turning civilians away as it was all they could do to cope with the wounded soldiers.

Inevitably, the quantity and nature of the work took a physical and mental toll on all of them. Violetta commented that she was too exhausted, and numbed by her exhaustion, to be scared by the shelling. They were often so tired that their hands seemed to work automatically, without their brains being involved. She felt like a distant spectator and that watching the incessant arrivals of groaning men being brought in on blood-soaked stretchers, suffering unimagined tortures was intolerable. The filth, cold, stench, hunger, vermin, and the squalor of it all, added to their misery. Three days later reinforcements, in the form of a Russian doctor and some Russian Sisters, arrived to give them a few hours respite and they fell onto their wire bedsteads, fully dressed, and fell asleep. For a while, they were able to work alternate forty-eight-hour shifts with another flying column but by then, Violetta was too full of adrenaline to enjoy her break and after a short, deep, sleep was itching to go back to work.

As in a number of accounts of war service, Violetta's shows her enjoyment of, and enthusiasm for, her experiences. She naively wrote that war would be the most glorious game in the world if it were not for the killing and wounding. She described her time in Russia as one of high adventure and relished the comradeship and the ability to help and be helped. She was far from immune to the horrors war brought to Russia, but still enjoyed the campfires, frosty nights, the smell of horses, a keen hunger, and the sense of danger. It is hard to imagine that when she went back to England after the war she became a renowned craft weaving expert and settled in Cornwall.

When the time came to evacuate Lodz they struggled all night to get everyone's wounds dressed, and in the end, many patients had to leave untreated. Others had to be left behind with one orderly. At the suggestion of one of the drivers, Violetta pinned a note to each patient. Written in German, the notes stated that the man was a soldier and asked that he should be treated well. Just as the staff were finishing their packing, a Polish lady came and invited the princess, the doctor and the two English Sisters to her house, where hot baths and proper beds awaited them. They could not wait to wash for the first time since arriving in Lodz and to try to rid themselves of the three kinds of voracious biting insects that plagued them. Clean and refreshed they had just sat down to a delicious meal when Prince Volkonsky arrived and told them they had to leave at once. Assuming this meant that the Germans were close by, they left the rest of their meal, and their generous host, and went to the hotel to meet their Red Cross car, only to find it had been sent elsewhere. Dreaming of the meal they had abandoned, they sat in the once elegant restaurant, with a large hole in one wall, drinking 'coffee' made from the crusts of rye bread mixed with a little chicory, while waiting for a car to come and collect them.

In spite of all the evidence to the contrary, Violetta never lost the hope that each journey would end with a bath, a meal and a comfortable bed. She was nearly always disappointed. There were often no hotels and no restaurants and on occasion even the local Red Cross leader was at a loss to know where to billet them. Being led by a prince and princess did, occasionally, mean that they could pull rank and commandeer a floor where they could all doze, despite being bitterly cold.

Their new hospital quickly filled with wounded and the local Red Cross set up a kitchen to provide the men with soup and tea. However, in no time the Russians again had to fall back and the flying column had to start packing and pile onto the last train out. They left two dead soldiers behind as they did not have time to bury them.

In Radzivilow they were shocked to hear soldiers asking the hospital matron if there were any dead men's boots they could take. The matron explained that this was a common request and that she always tried to help. Boots were in very short supply.

They sometimes had no time to even unpack before the wounded poured in. When they were really close to the front, they had to nurse without even lighting a candle, as most rooms had no shutters or blinds and they did not want to attract German fire. On at least one occasion, they had to move on again after only one night. Violetta described how, having worked for sixteen hours without a break, there was enough of a lull for them to make and enjoy a quick meal at four in the morning, in a stinking room where the floor was awash with blood, mud and discarded dressings and crammed with men who had just been operated on. There were also two dead men on the floor, as it was too dangerous for anyone to take them out and bury them. They gulped down the black tea, cheese and black bread that had been spread on a sterilised towel on the operating table and in no time the next wave of wounded began to arrive.

Having toasted the New Year in Zyradow with glasses of tea, and with the almost unimaginable luxury of being billeted in a house with a bathroom, a bath and one bed for each member of the group, Violetta's year went downhill. Within a few days she suffered a shrapnel wound in her leg, was nearly killed by a German bomb and fell ill with pleurisy. The shrapnel wound was not serious and healed quickly. She felt that the German bomb, dropped from a Taube aeroplane, was her closest brush with death as she was walking across some open ground when she heard a whirr and looked up to see the plane release its bomb. When the smoke from the explosion cleared, she found she was standing on the edge of a large hole. Soldiers rushed over, amazed to find her alive, but it seemed that the deep mud into which the bomb had fallen had directed the blast upwards rather than sideways. She had to take two weeks' bed rest to recover from the pleurisy. She hated not being busy and, happily for us, she used her recovery time to write about her experiences so far, although, sadly, Violetta did not write about the rest of her war service. However, we do know that she went back to Russia at the end of 1915, to help organise hospitals for refugees from the German advance on the Eastern Front. She later worked in a hospital at La Panne, in Belgium, before joining a hospital unit at Ostrovo on the Kragujevac front in 1917.

In April 1916, Lady Muriel Paget arrived in Petrograd to help organise field hospitals to work behind the Russian lines. The team set up two tented units, a mobile field hospital and a casualty clearing station, supported by ambulance carts. In June the field hospital, administered and supplied by the Russian Red Cross, left Petrograd on a special train with thirty-seven carriages carrying 100 horses, 125 Russian orderlies, forty-four transport carts and ambulances, two mobile kitchens and English doctors and nurses from Anglo-Russian Base Hospital. For a mobile field hospital, this seems very unwieldy and reminiscent of a medieval caravan.

Conditions in Russia often shocked British workers. When she reached Lutsk, Lady Paget commented that casualties, filling all the public parks and open areas, were not receiving even basic first aid. Their wounds were black with flies and the stench, exacerbated by the hot weather, was appalling. She sent telegrams back to England asking for help in buying another 100, desperately needed, ambulances. About to leave Lutsk to go back to Petrograd, she observed that the British doctor in charge, Andrew Fleming, asked for a trepanning tool and was given a chisel.

Sarah McNaughtan, Mrs Wynne and Mr Bevan went to Russia to help without any official sanction, but were put to work at the Anglo-Russian Hospital in Petrograd while waiting for permission to take ambulances up to the front. Sarah, who had earlier worked near the Western Front, described the war as the crucifixion of the youth of the world and was appalled by the fact there were 25,000 amputation cases in Petrograd.

One day in November, they took a horse drawn ambulance to the Finnish Station. They were to meet the first group of prisoners who had been sent back from Germany because they were so badly injured that they would never be able to fight again. The first patients off the train were men who had had their eyes shot out. They felt their way, then waited for someone to lead them away. Next came the amputees. The men were thin, but dignified and looked old, even though the train had stopped to let them wash and shave before reaching Petrograd. They were taken into a hall where they were each given a present, food and wine.

Sarah and her colleagues eventually set off for Tiflis with their ambulances. Unfortunately, the ambulances froze fast onto the river in Archangel and had to be abandoned. They then bought a car, and when it broke down, continued by train. In January 1916, they reached Yerevan, where there were 17,000 Armenian refugees in a town with a peacetime population of only 30,000. The refugees were full of stories of 1,000,000 Armenians being massacred by the Turks in cold blood and women having been carried off to harems. The Russians tried to help, and gave the Red Cross unit just enough money to buy bread.

* * *

In their dealings with Russia, the Quakers made their usual efforts to identify the scope and nature of the problems, rather than doing what most teams did and plunging in without understanding the local situation. They realised that, apart from Poland, there were about nine frontier areas of Russia that had been invaded, creating millions of refugees who were driven eastwards. They described the refugees as people who had lost not only relations, friends and possessions, but also all the physical and moral landmarks of their lives, and had therefore been made helpless. In early 1916, they sent an advance party of four to investigate the situation and report back. They were overwhelmed by the welcome they received from the Russian Red Cross and local officials, who provided them with free travel and offers of buildings where they could set up bases for their work.

Their first centre was in the region of Buzuluk, which covered 700 square miles and had a population of 100,000, of which a quarter were refugees from all over the Russian Empire, as well as Austrian, Russian and Turkish prisoners. The thirty workers found that there were no doctors in the whole region. Sunday was the local market day, and the Quakers' hospital was particularly busy then as it was the only time that local people left their farms and could attend. The Quakers also visited seriously ill patients at home. With their usual desire to help people become self-sufficient and to ease the misery and apathy suffered by unemployed refugees, they set up local textile workrooms, helped people start growing vegetables, which were in very short supply, and in one area kept a cow so they could provide milk. They started several schools for previously illiterate children.

Some of the refugees needed more intensive help than others and more than 100 women and children were welcomed to a country house at Mogotovo, renamed The English House. The Quakers found that many of the refugees were grateful for a sympathetic ear, while they recounted the ordeals they had suffered on their journey to Mogotovo and their tales of their friends and family, who had died of cold in Tashkent during the winter. This listening was as important as providing practical help, such as felt boots and clothes.

The workers felt very cut off from England and one of them reported that the work he did in Russia was the most interesting and the saddest that he had ever been involved with. They were aware that their lack of Russian speakers was a frustration, as were the difficulties of getting around during the Russian winter. Russian officialdom presented a more complex challenge than anything they had faced elsewhere.

The team relished the challenge of working with people they described as displaying both a Mohammedan fatalism and a total ignorance of the laws of health. They asked for more experienced nurses to be sent out to join them.

The following year they prefaced their account of their work in Russia by saying that the Russian Revolution had begun, but not yet finished. Although the area where they were working was distant from the centre of the unrest, the revolution inevitably had an enormous effect on what they could achieve. They carried on with their much-needed medical work, treating outbreaks of pneumonia, influenza, anthrax (Siberian plague), malaria, typhoid, scabies, scarlatina, whooping cough, and a few cases of smallpox. They were always short of the drugs they needed, as they all had to be sent from Britain and communication was difficult.

During the following year the revolution reached Buzuluk. Famine was widespread. Local factional disputes made their work increasingly difficult and, when fighting reached the area, many of the refugees scattered. Even though the battle front reached the Volga and the Quakers had to hand over some of their medical and relief centres to the local authorities, they continued to run their hospitals, dispensaries, workrooms and an orphanage.

They concluded that the Bolshevik takeover initially stimulated local officials to work to improve conditions, but the situation soon deteriorated. The Bolsheviks closed the banks and stopped money, kept in Petrograd, from reaching the Quakers. From December 1917 to March 1918 no funds could be sent to them even though Quakers at home had raised £24,000 to help them fight the famine that gripped the former corn exporting area of Samara. Corn was available in Siberia, at a price, but could only be transported by train and officials in each area the consignments passed through tended to think that their need was the greatest, so that only a small amount of each consignment reached Buzuluk. Crops grown in Buzuluk were regularly ravaged by a type of marmot known as a suslik. The Friends realised that the suslik were easy to kill, so they offered the refugees a bounty for each skin.

They eventually felt that they had no option but to withdraw from the outlying areas and focus their work on Buzuluk itself. At the invitation of the local Soviet, they took over an old monastery outside the town and set up an orphanage and workshops.

As with many members of the volunteer groups who worked in the battle-torn areas of Europe, the Quakers felt it was well-nigh impossible for English people, who had suffered a few air raids and the loss of their favourite luxuries, to grasp the extent of the suffering many non-combatants had suffered in France and Russia. None the less, in 1918 they renewed their appeal for funds so that they could continue their work.

* * *

A prime example of the sort of upper-class British woman who must have made the British military establishment blench was twenty-five-year-old Margherita, Lady Howard de Walden. Trained as an opera singer, she left her three young children at home and travelled to Egypt with her husband when he was appointed second-in-command of the Westminster Dragoons. When he was sent to Gallipoli, Margherita and her friend, Mary Herbert, responded to an appeal for hospitals and nurses in Egypt.

They decided that the Maison Karam, outside Alexandria, was eminently suited for use as a hospital. They then travelled to England to get everything they needed, including staff, to run the Maison Karam. They ordered a mass of equipment, including hundreds of pairs of brightly coloured pyjamas, bedding, food, and chocolate. They also hired a matron and eleven qualified, private, nurses.

What they failed to arrange was official permission to set up a hospital. Just four days before they were due to return to Egypt, Margherita was summoned to see General Sir Alfred Keogh, head of the Army Medical Services. He refused to give her permission to start a hospital insisting, as usual when faced with a woman offering help, that the RAMC had everything under control and that he did not 'require or wish for any private enterprise in Egypt'. She burst into tears, embarrassing him so much that he gave her permission to go back to Egypt to visit her friends, but ordered her not to take any nurses or supplies. The next day Margherita, the matron and eleven nurses set out for Egypt with all their equipment.

When they reached Port Said, the captain said he had just received orders not to let them land. Realising what they had done, Keogh had cabled ahead. At the last minute, a ship came alongside and a woman in black stood up and called out in French that she was sent by Sir Ronald Graham, on behalf of the White Slave Traffic (this in English), and was looking for the group. They rushed down the gangway and climbed into her boat. Ronald Graham was adviser to the Ministry of the Interior and he had agreed to this manoeuvre.

Getting the Maison Karam ready was not easy. The rent was low but it was in poor condition. Every nook and cranny seemed to house yet another group of members of the extended Karam family, who had been allowed to live there according to Arab laws of hospitality and who were hard to displace. The house was elaborately decorated with ornate stucco and murals of sheikhs and camels but the drains were remarkable by their absence. As she supervised the work on getting the building fit for use,

Margherita was glad she had taken an active interest in the installation of new bathrooms at her childhood home on Brownsea Island and at her husband's family seat at Chirk.

Try as she might, Mary Herbert was not able to get permission for them to run a hospital but the authorities finally agreed they could open what was called Convalescent Hospital No. 6. Margherita came to feel relieved they were not going to run a full hospital.

After the landings at Suvla Bay in August 1915, patients poured into Egypt. The medical services struggled to cope and some of the men lay on the dock, in the blazing sun, for hours. Mary's mother-in-law, Lady Carnarvon, collected a group of her female acquaintances and, armed with sunshades, they went down to the quays with hot tea to cool the waiting men. Although the Maison Karam was only a convalescent hospital, the day came when they were unexpectedly sent a man with a bullet visible in his chest. The nurses said that something had to be done at once but refused to take action themselves as it was outside the remit of their training etiquette. To make things worse, they had no doctor that week. Eventually, two of the nurses agreed to tell Margherita what to do and she removed the bullet. The patient apparently endured this without complaint, and quite possibly without anaesthetic, and recovered.

Margherita did not generally deal directly with the patients but took charge of all the administration and acted as general supervisor. Not only were the men dressed in the striped pyjamas she had brought out from England, but their clothes were put in labelled sacks in the cellar so that the patients could not wander off. Some men did head for the town centre, attired in their distinctive pyjamas, and were brought back by the Military Police. There was a rumour that when her husband's regiment, the Westminster Dragoons, heard about the Maison Karam, they wore labels saying 'If wounded, please send me to No. 6.'

* * *

Medical units in the Balkans began to disband in 1919. Much of the equipment from the Scottish Women's Hospitals units was given to the Serbs to form the basis of the Dr Elsie Inglis Memorial Hospital in Belgrade. Funds were sent from Britain, Serbia and the USA to keep the hospital running. Various women who had served in the Balkans maintained their contacts with the area after the war and continued trying to help the Serbian people, for whom they had developed a strong affection. Several of them either established or worked in, orphanages or hospitals. Towards the end of the war Katherine and Isabel MacPhail, who had served with the Scottish Women's Hospitals in Serbia, Corsica and France went back to Serbia to work with children suffering from tuberculosis. They set up a hospital in Belgrade and later moved it to

Sremska Kamenica near Novi Sad. Katherine devoted many years to the hospital, only leaving when forced out by President Tito's government. Several of her former colleagues spent time helping her in the hospital. Isabel Emslie Hutton went to work in Crimea, with refugees from the Russian Civil War. Some women also found it was easier for them to get medical posts abroad than it was in Britain, where men were still reluctant to recognise them as equal colleagues.

5

Canteens and Comforts

By December 1914, almost 1,200,000 men had volunteered to join the British Army, augmenting the peacetime strength of roughly 750,000 soldiers. They were frequently on the move, around this country and to and from the various theatres of war. Men were sent to new postings, came on leave and went back again. Wounded and sick servicemen poured into the country. Those who recovered sufficiently went back to fight again. Shipwrecked mariners were brought home and then reassigned. The country seethed as busily as any ants' nest.

It was literally days after the start of the war that the first civilian groups realised that refreshment and recreation rooms for the vast numbers of mobilising troops were urgently needed. The military authorities knew this work was important but simply lacked the time and resources to get involved themselves. They were more than happy to let other organisations get to work and approved of the YMCA's efforts from the outset, possibly because it was such a male-dominated organisation. The authorities did what they could to help with the logistics involved, such as providing heavy transport and men to help erect tents and huts.

Official involvement was delayed until early 1915 when the Canteen and Mess Co-operative Society was allowed to set up a branch in France. The Society was the precursor of the Navy, Army and Air Force Institutes (NAAFI). It managed all of the 295 British Expeditionary Force (BEF) canteens. They were never remotely able to meet demand and there were regular complaints about their prices and the lack of a homely atmosphere. The feminine touch in the independent canteens meant a lot to servicemen.

The YMCA was the first off the block, but was by no means the only organisation to get involved. National leader, Arthur Yapp, realised that the YMCA could make a major contribution, drawing on their previous experience of looking after soldiers from the Boer War and setting up canteens in the field for the annual Territorial Army training camps. Within ten days of the start of the war, it had set up 250 recreation centres in the UK. Many of them were in tents sited where large numbers of troops would pass. Some of the centres were large. Flower Down in Hampshire, for example, catered for 7,000 men and 2,000 horses so it had both a hut and a marquee for recreation. By the end of the war, they had 10,000 centres in Britain, Italy, the Mediterranean, the Middle East, and France, all under their well-known symbol, the inverted red triangle. Later in the war, the Red Triangle was joined by the Blue Triangle an organisation set up by the Young Women's Christian Association (WYCA) to support the newly created Women's Army Auxiliary Corps (WAACS).

Hitherto a very male dominated organisation, the YMCA recognised that women would need to play a pivotal role in running the huts. Yapp and Princess Helena Victoria founded the YMCA Women's Auxiliary Force in December 1914. The Countess of Bessborough was the honorary secretary. Although most of the workers were women, there was a man in charge of each hut. These men were usually over military age or unfit to serve. As well as being in overall charge, they were responsible for ordering supplies and arranging entertainments. Both Princess Helena Victoria and the Countess of Bessborough made extensive tours of YMCA facilities in France and presented detailed reports, noting the specific achievements of individual huts or members of staff as well as their overall impressions. Reporting on her 1916 visit, the countess remarked that the lady volunteers went to France at their own expense to make a home for the men. She added that many of them had lost relatives in the war and left their children, families, homes and friends to create homely refuges for troops in foreign countries.

As well as refreshments, the huts dispensed comforts, little luxuries that had been donated and often made by people in Britain. Each gift was acknowledged, mostly by Lady Elizabeth Dawson and Lady Mackay Edgar. They also packed the comforts and despatched them to the huts for distribution to the troops. Each hut, here and abroad, was sent £3 to put on extra entertainment at Christmas. The volunteers, of course, had a uniform. In the case of the YMCA Women's Auxiliary Force the uniform adopted in 1916 consisted of a dark grey coat and skirt with 'butcher blue' facings and a black straw or velour hat. Volunteers could apply for a grant of £3 towards the cost of their uniform but, over a three year period, the committee only had to pay out £318 in grants. The drivers and secretaries were paid with a special grant from headquarters. A number of volunteers took their own motor cars to France and for the first two years they were given grants towards the upkeep of their vehicles.

Many of the early centres were under canvas but the autumn and winter of 1914–15 were extremely windy and wet, and hundreds of tents and marquees across the country were destroyed. The YMCA decided that buying more tents would not be practical and bought timber and corrugated iron huts instead. Each hut cost £500 and an additional quiet room cost £100. All the organisations that provided recreation rooms thereafter used a mixture of tents, huts and any other building that could be made available to them.

In the first two years of the war, the YMCA raised £830,000 from private subscriptions, including gifts from the king and queen and other members of the royal family. By the end of the war, donations had reached £2,500,000. Many gifts for huts were made in memory of someone who had died. Schools also took part in supporting the huts and raised more than £10,000 for the cause. The huts were designed to be used for entertainments as well as for providing refreshments and wherever there was enough space, there was a platform at one end. In one of their leaflets the YMCA claimed that wherever the army was, you would also find the YMCA. They set up 800 huts in England, 240 in France, fifty-eight in Egypt, thirteen in Mesopotamia, fifty in India, nine in Malta, five in Salonika and five in the Aegean Islands. Many of them were open twenty-four hours a day.

From 1916, soldiers arriving in Bournemouth in the early morning were able to take advantage of the YMCA's Kennedy Hut. Named after an Army chaplain from nearby Boscombe, the hut replaced a tent, which had twice been blown down in gales. It was the eighth YMCA hut to open in the Bournemouth area.

One of the strengths of the YMCA was that although it was religious, it was non-sectarian, did not allow proselytising in its huts, and did not push religion down the throats of men who simply wanted to use the other services provided. The workers believed they should cater for the whole man, starting with the body and working towards sharing their religious convictions. Yapp wanted to make religion a part of everyday life. Padres were there to run services at all the YMCA's huts. They offered support and handed out small testaments to any men who wanted them. They also made rooms available to various other denominations for holding services and for men who wanted a period of quiet contemplation or prayer.

The Church Army and Salvation Army made their Christian mission a more overt part of their work in their huts and tents. The Salvation Army recognised the need to provide cheap food, and free reading and writing materials, as well as spreading their message. The Church Army put evangelism at the forefront of their work; they resented the YMCA's high profile and financial success, as its leaders believed that these compromised the YMCA's original goals. In some camps, there were clashes between Church Army and YMCA staff over the format of evening services and the role music had to play.

Before very long the War Office saw how well some groups, such as the YMCA, were doing financially and wanted to set tough regulations. Workers quickly realised that running a hut successfully was a real challenge. They had to acquire and monitor their stock, take payment in pounds or postal orders and give the correct change in francs, they had to keep accounts, and serve for long hours. As a volunteer, the Reverend George Henderson said that it was much like running a busy shop. Many of them were, of course, doing this in a war zone.

In 1915 the Government and the Canteen and Mess Co-operative Society felt they were losing out to the greater popularity of most of the charity-run huts. The YMCA came in for particular criticism. The government wanted to stop the YMCA selling temperance drinks, to make the charity huts buy all their supplies through designated suppliers, to allow the Canteen and Mess Co-operative Society to run the business side of their huts and to pay an exorbitant tax to the Government. The YMCA protested strongly, asserting that it was a voluntary, philanthropic organisation that was simply focussing on the men and doing emergency work in abnormal circumstances for the duration of the war. They claimed that paying the tax would cost them £50,000 a year, which they would otherwise have invested in other huts. After almost two years of haggling, the Government gave way.

Various other groups and some more or less idiosyncratic individuals also ran large numbers of huts between them and, wherever they opened, they were almost always a hit. Diary entries are a vivid testimony to how much the men valued the refreshments and recreation facilities but were, if anything, even more grateful for the friendly, female contact that was on offer. It gave them a brief break from military surroundings and discipline, and many formed friendships with the staff, keen to meet them again when they returned to the area and sad if the staff had changed. Countless letters from soldiers and sailors also pay fulsome tribute to the efforts of the volunteer canteen workers. Funding came from individual donations and from a range of more unusual sources including the Variety Artistes Fund, the Bank of England and, in Rouen, the Cats and Dogs of Great Britain, with organisational help from Miss Maud Field of West Berkshire.

The British Women's Temperance Association reported in the winter 1914 edition of their journal, *The White Ribbon*, that since the start of the war they had set up rooms in a number of places where there were concentrations of troops, including Bedford, Birkenhead, Caerphilly, Newbury, Grimsby, and Tunbridge Wells. They were proud of the temperance work they had done in this way and wanted to expand their efforts as there was a huge need for refreshment and recreation rooms. The article reported that they only served freshly made tea and that teapots were greatly preferred to urns. They charged a halfpenny for a cup of tea or a scone, 1*d* for a glass of milk and 2*d* for a meat pie or a boiled egg. They boiled all their drinking water, which seems to be an unusual precaution and the fact that they believed this to be essential may be a comment on where their rooms were based. They were adamant that no religious propaganda should be displayed and found that a piano, a bathroom, and writing facilities were appreciated. They were committed to buying as much of their provisions locally as they could.

Huts were set up at military training camps all over the country. With commendable imagination, the YMCA set up a number of photographic studios so that men could have their picture taken, in uniform, and made into a postcard to be sent home to their anxious families. Local Boy Scouts were often recruited to help with the washing-up.

Before long, huts for soldiers and sailors had sprung up all over London and some people commented that there was hardly any open space that had not been taken into use in this way. The Shakespeare Hut was in Gower Street. The Bibesco Hut in Sloane Square served many men from the nearby Chelsea Barracks. The hut in Grosvenor Square for the Territorial Victoria Rifles apparently meant that the smell of stew wafted over the privileged square, to the displeasure of some of the residents. The hut in nearby Grosvenor Gardens, with separate facilities for officers and men, was donated by match manufacturers Bryant & May and was opened by Queen Alexandra. A hut on Wimbledon Common served the men camped there.

Foreign troops were not forgotten. After Minnie Rattigan came over from Australia with her husband in 1912, he joined the British Army. Minnie was one of the founders of the Anzac Buffet, set up under the London branch of the Australian Natives Association. The buffet provided free meals and entertainments to about 1,000 Australian servicemen a day in London. As with British buffets, this was a club run by volunteers and was in competition with the official Australian Soldiers' Club, which charged for meals and comforts. Equivalent clubs were run for South American, Canadian, New Zealand, and South African troops by their own ex-patriot organisations. A group of local women in Folkestone set up The Maple Leaf Club to provide a welcoming and homely place for the popular Canadian soldiers who were billeted around the town. A YMCA hut for the Canadians was later opened in Folkestone as well. On 5 November 1917 a ninth YMCA hut opened in the Bournemouth area. This hut, in Boscombe, was funded by the people of New Zealand, specifically for their soldiers who were billeted in the area. As it took some while after the Armistice for servicemen to be demobilised the huts continued to be important.

In London, members of the YMCA Night Motor Transport Column met late night trains and drove the arriving soldiers to the nearest hut that had space for them. Other members patrolled the streets looking for lost or strayed soldiers, generally from the Empire, who did not know where to go in the busy city. The volunteers took any who wanted it to the nearest hut. At times the huts were packed with sleeping men and at Waterloo, there were nights when there were men sleeping under and on the billiard table, on chairs, by the stove, on tables, and on the floor.

It was quickly recognised that servicemen's wives also needed support and clubs for sailors' and soldiers' wives were set up in towns all over the county. In London, Mrs Constance Peel, editor of the household department of *The Queen* magazine organised the Soldiers' and Sailors' Wives Club in Lambeth.

Many soldiers in Brighton were based at the Preston Barracks or billeted with civilians in the area. The Congregational Church Committee opened a canteen and rooms for writing and games in October 1914. It was immediately popular and soon outgrew the original space so that only a month later they expanded into the main schoolroom. They catered for about 150 men a night. They provided refreshments, at cost price, and free writing materials. Mr J. J. Beal donated all the writing paper and envelopes and Mr A. E. Gumbrill printed the huge quantity of notepaper free of charge for four years. They also provided monthly concerts at which local artistes performed for free. On Sundays they had a sing-song of religious music. Their Christmas parties were so popular that they had to have two, one on Christmas Day and one on Boxing Day.

Ever alert for new opportunities to help, a VAD in Southampton realised the large numbers of troops who camped near the town on their way to France, usually for just one night, desperately needed to be able to get something to eat and drink free of charge. A group of VADs managed to obtain a large tent where they set up a canteen. It was run by both male and female VADs and kept open day and night. When they realised that officers also needed somewhere to get refreshments, they opened a smaller tent for them.

Even with the best of intentions, some efforts were destined for frustration. Essex vicar, the Reverend Andrew Clark, reported that a group of ladies in Cheltenham had set up huts for soldiers in 1915, serving tea and coffee and taking turns to wait on the men at supper. After a few days, the lady in charge asked a group of men whether they had any complaints. Thinking, perhaps, that they would want to express their gratitude or perhaps ask for cake as well as tea she must have been chagrined by their response. They were reluctant to answer but when finally coaxed into expressing their opinion replied that they had two requests. They wanted spittoons to be provided and wanted to be served by girls from a similar background to their own and not toffs. Her response was not recorded.

The gentlemen of the village of Willingdon, just outside Eastbourne, in Sussex wanted to help the men from the numerous military camps in the area. They got permission to use the church school from 6 p.m. to 9.30 p.m. each day, with the added concession that the stoves would be lit in winter. They opened a clubroom for soldiers and appealed to local parishioners for games and books. In no time it had become very popular. It is easy to imagine that a period of relative peace and quiet must have appealed to some of the fresh recruits, away from home for the first time and living in crowded barracks.

Canteens with a slightly different role were set up by Girls' Patriotic Clubs. Their aim was to provide somewhere respectable where girls would meet their men friends, generally servicemen. By May 1915 they had set up twenty canteens and had had requests for more. Newhaven was an important port for troops travelling to and from France and the canteen that was set up there could take 250 people. It was also used by people on their way to visit wounded relatives in France. Programmes of activities – including cookery classes, first aid, sewing, drill and doing laundry for soldiers – were organised in many of these clubs.

With so many servicemen in search of relaxation and distraction it is surprising that more trouble was not reported, perhaps the fact that most huts did not serve alcohol helped to keep emotions under control. A rare and surprising riot, known as the Battle of Bow Street, was associated with the American Eagle Hut in the Aldwych in London. The large and well-equipped hut was set up by four American businessmen and was run by the wealthy American YMCA, catering mostly for American troops. In March 1919, police warned some troops who were playing dice outside the hut that gambling was illegal. When the men persisted, they were arrested and taken to the nearby Bow Street Police Station. A crowd followed, demanding that the men should be released. More than 1,000 people, some accounts say 2,000, took part in the riot that ensued during which the police charged the crowd with their batons. Many of the rioters were American and Canadian servicemen. About twenty people, including seven police officers, were injured. When the riot was over eleven Americans were handed to their military police to be court-martialed. American soldiers at the Eagle Hut were transferred to other huts and sailors were ordered to rejoin their ships. Four Canadians appeared at Bow Street Magistrate's Court charged with riot and a further six injured servicemen remained under guard in hospital until they were well enough to appear in court. The Eagle Hut closed in August that year.

Canadian troops were involved in a second riot early the same year. In 1919 Kinmel Camp at Bodelwyddan near Abergele housed 20,000 Canadian troops waiting impatiently to go home. Three-quarters of them had seen active service in France and Belgium. In February they were told that the ships that had been going to take them home had been reallocated to Americans. Anger was, understandably, widespread and on 3 March men, drunk on stolen alcohol, rampaged through the camp looting and smashing up buildings including the YMCA hut. Of the forty-one men who later faced a court martial, twenty-four were found guilty and sentenced to between ninety days and ten years in prison. Most were freed within six months.

Station buffets, set up and run by volunteers, provided a service that benefitted millions of men by the end of the war. Many of them were set up when local people saw how tired and hungry troops passing through their area were. The numbers they served are a graphic illustration of how much this service was needed, and appreciated, by all those who used it.

The *Daily Graphic* published an article in 1916 claiming that the Euston Station Buffet, which opened in London in February 1915, was the earliest. The writer may have failed to look beyond London for evidence as the station buffet in Perth and the one at Banbury in Oxfordshire certainly opened earlier. Miss Freda Day, quartermaster of a local Red Cross detachment was appalled by a letter in the *Banbury Guardian* of 10 September 1914 claiming that troops passing through the station were so desperately thirsty that they were drinking the water from the fire buckets. Freda, the stationmaster Mr Short, and Freda's uncle, Sydney Mawle, who happened to be the assistant director of the Red Cross in Oxfordshire, decided they had to do something for the men. Mr Short, acting on behalf of the Great Western Railway, agreed that they could set up a rest station and canteen in the general waiting room at Banbury Station. They set to with alacrity and recruited as many Red Cross nurses as they could. The next day they served lemonade to 500 men. The Red Cross nurses at the Banbury Rest Station & Canteen had their own motto: 'Hope Confidently – Wait Patiently – Do Valiantly'. They must have done all of these with aplomb as they served more than 3,000,000 men with drinks, food and cigarettes that were donated locally.

In 1915, the War Office designated Banbury as an official rest station for ambulance trains and Mr Mawle was put in charge. When an ambulance train left Dover or Southampton heading for Banbury, a telegram was sent to Mr Mawle to ensure that when the train arrived the team was ready. Every patient was given a drink and a small tray holding a sandwich, a newspaper, cigarettes, fruit, chocolate, bread, and butter and cake and postcards to write home. The postcards were later collected, stamped and posted by the volunteers. The train's medical staff and orderlies were also given trays. Between 100 and 350 patients would need to be served in just twenty minutes. Having run for almost the duration of the war, one of the team's final tasks was to welcome local soldiers home in August 1919.

When word got out that the first ambulance train was due to arrive in Birmingham, members of the local VAD raced to the station to offer food to the men. Thereafter they met every train, led by their commandant, Mrs Porter. Their whole way of working had a quasi-military organisation. Ambulance trains did not stop at Birmingham for long so efficiency was vital. When an ambulance train pulled in, two lines of nursing members were waiting with large trolleys laden with cakes, fruit, sandwiches and tea urns. When a whistle was blown, the orderlies went to each ward on the train carrying trays loaded with mugs of tea. Nurses followed them with food and fruit and they were followed by other members of the team with postcards, pencils, cigarettes, pipes and tobacco. Before the trains left the nursing members collected up the postcards and posted them. The work was funded by the people of Birmingham and the station authorities provided a room that could be used as a kitchen.

One of the most famous station buffets was at Preston. It opened in August 1915 and had a team of 300–400 workers, who kept it open day and night. As with railway companies elsewhere, the London & North-Western Railway Co. was keen to help and let the volunteers use a large room on main line platforms five and six. Whenever a train arrived, it was met by ladies with steaming buckets of tea or coffee and baskets heaped with food. Men who had a wait between trains could lie down with a rug and a pillow to have a rest and were carefully labelled so that staff knew who to wake for each departing train. Staff found that many of their mugs disappeared with each train and although the railway companies returned any that turned up, thousands were lost. Many were said to have reached the trenches. Replacing mugs made a serious dent in the buffet's finances. In the week before Christmas 1916, they served 12,500 men in thirty-six hours. As a way of thanking the station staff for their help and co-operation the workers in the buffet cooked them a hot-pot dinner, served in two sittings, so that every member of staff could share it. As well as the usual fundraising efforts, the Preston Station Buffet benefitted from some less common supporters – one 'Tommy's mother' sent a blanket and pillow, 'a prisoner' sent a donation, the Association of Lancastrians in London collected £70 at a special concert and a sailor, hearing they were holding a flag day for the buffet asked if he could take some flags back to his ship to sell; he raised £4.

In York, too, a report of how poorly visiting soldiers were being treated and that the normal buffet closed at 5.30 p.m. spurred Mrs Morrell and a group of local women into action. The Soldiers' & Sailors' Canteen opened on platform three at York Station in November 1915 and, given the number of troops based in or visiting York, it is surprising that nothing had been done sooner. The canteen consisted of two carriages donated by the North Eastern Railway Co. and provided cheap refreshments for servicemen. The team also had trolleys they could take to meet trains arriving at other platforms. Once the canteen had been set up, the team worked with intense commitment – opening twenty-four hours a day, and seven days a week, until it closed in May 1919. It has been estimated that they served 4,500,000 men, which is an average of 18,000 a week. In the first year alone, they spent more than £7,500 on refreshments. Like the Preston Station Buffet, they had a problem with wandering mugs and in 1917 had to spend about £12 a week replacing those that had vanished. Managing and fundraising for the canteen involved a growing team. Chaired by Mrs Morrell, it grew to include a president, four caterers, three secretaries, a treasurer, a surprisingly large team of forty-five managers and about 260 helpers.

Folkestone Harbour Station Canteen was one of the busiest, as literally millions of servicemen and thousands of nurses passed through the town on their way to and from the Continent. The town was proud of the fact that these men came from all over the British Empire. The Jeffery sisters were among the canteen's most dedicated volunteers. Margaret and Florence Jeffery were later awarded the OBE for their work. Visitors' books were placed on a table that was decorated with Allied flags and an estimated 42,000 men took the time to write in the eight volumes that were filled. Politicians and senior military officials on their way to or from the front were among those who recorded their visits. This canteen served a higher proportion of sailors and nurses than most because of its location.

Workers in the Dundee and Overgate canteens in Broughty Ferry raised more money than they needed to cover their costs, so they gave the surplus to other war charities. They also opened a hostel and an evening canteen in rooms owned by the YMCA. Every morning they loaded a barrow with buns and urns of tea and went off to serve refreshments to any men in uniform who passed through the Tay Bridge Station on the Khaki Train.

The station buffets in London positively bristled with aristocratic and well-connected volunteers, committee members, and patrons. Lady Brassey ran the Waterloo buffet while Lady Limerick was in charge at

London Bridge. At Waterloo, the vice president was Countess Brassey and volunteers included Lady Lloyd, Lady Willcocks and Lady Harcourt. Katharine, daughter-in-law of the Prime Minister Asquith, worked in the buffet at Euston. The Paddington Station Club, which opened in December 1914, was run under military supervision.

The involvement of aristocratic ladies, who were not used to the kind of work involved in the canteens, was parodied in a short play by Gertrude Jennings called *Poached Eggs and Pearls*. The play was first produced at the Apollo Theatre, London, in November 1916 and features a group of aristocratic volunteers, one of whom insists on wearing her diamonds and pearls, and a Miss Deacon, who is horribly accident prone and makes cocoa out of knife polish. Although described as a canteen comedy it is really not very funny. Perhaps the funniest moment is when Lady Clara advises the incompetent Miss Deacon to go and make pyjamas instead of working in the canteen and Miss Deacon replies that this would be improper work for an unmarried lady.

The Euston Station buffet in London, organised by Miss Margaret Boulton (as fundraiser) and Miss Marietta Feuerheerd (as manager), opened in February 1915 and had 30,000 customers a month by the end of the year. It was the first hut to have bunks in cubicles where the men could rest and was especially popular with members of the Artists Rifles who called in each day for meals.

Oddly enough, as one of the busiest of the London stations, Victoria was slow to provide a buffet for servicemen. An anonymous correspondent wrote to *The Times* in February 1915 saying how unpleasant it was to arrive in London on leave, late at night, to find all doors closed against you. The writer compared Victoria unfavourably with Boulogne where the Red Cross provided a popular buffet for soldiers. Before long The Victoria Soldiers' and Sailors' Buffet had been opened on land provided by the South Western & Chatham Railway Co. The Queen made a donation towards the cost of setting it up and, when she visited, brought a large cake with her. The buffet originally opened from 6 a.m. to midnight but this was soon extended to twenty-four hours a day to meet the demand from all the troop trains arriving at the station. Later in the war, when serving 5,000 men a day, the buffet got through a staggering 50 lbs of tea, 140 lbs of sugar, 45 lbs of potted meat, a 130 quarterns of bread, 400 lbs of cake, 26 gallons of milk, and 70 lbs of margarine. Provisions cost about £150 a week, which worked out at about 1½d per man served. Even when some foods were rationed and difficult for the general public to find, the buffets managed to get the provisions they needed.

Probably only a few of the travellers who use Waterloo Station in London notice a plaque on the wall of one of the pedestrian tunnels.

The plaque commemorates the fact that because there was no room for a buffet on the platform, it was run in a subway under platform 12. Waterloo was the last of the major London termini to have a buffet for servicemen. This was apparently because the throughput of 10,000 men a day was thought to be too many for a buffet to handle. There were rows of tables where volunteers in green overalls worked in three shifts a day making endless sandwiches. Only the washer-up was paid and she must have faced a Herculean task each day. There were eight workers on duty in the mornings, fourteen in the afternoons and eight in the evenings. They served about 8,000 people a day, and an amazing total of in excess of 8,000,000 British Imperial and Allied forces before the buffet closed in 1920.

As the buffet was in the subway, the volunteers were allowed to take trolleys onto the platforms to serve men who were going back from leave and for incoming Red Cross trains. Workers commented on the deafening noise when the men poured in and the silence when they left. In February 1918 the buffet was running short of funds and needed £10,000 to keep going. Entertainer George Robey gave a concert at the Coliseum to help them meet the shortfall.

The Salvation Army provided hostels near train stations and ports so that soldiers and sailors could have somewhere safe to stay while travelling and in a strange town.

The pressure on factory workers was immense. The demand for increasing quantities of munitions, textiles and other goods was unrelenting and dock workers loaded and unloaded ships as fast as they could. Shifts were long. The work was hard, often dangerous and thousands of women started working in heavy industries for the first time. Canteens offering a hot meal, cooked by someone else, were a real blessing. The writer of one leaflet created a vivid picture, describing the YMCA as a 'big motherly hen gathering servicemen and munitions workers under her wings for comfort'.

Essex vicar, the Reverend Andrew Clark, reported that a local lady called Marjorie Tritton, was to start volunteering in a canteen for workers at the Woolwich Arsenal. The canteen was run by Lady Lawrence, for the Munition Workers' Canteen Committee, and opened in May 1915 providing free tea, coffee, cocoa and bread and butter, three times a day. All the canteen workers were volunteers. Marjorie was on duty from 10 or 11 a.m. to 3 p.m. and her duties included brewing tea, cutting bread and butter, serving, and washing-up. The Munition Workers Canteen Committee went on to run canteens at many other munitions works and ended up with a team of more than 1,200 volunteers.

Mr James Caldwell gave Reverend Clark an alternative view of the canteen. He reported that the men in the Woolwich Arsenal hated the canteen but had to use it, as it was the only refreshment place allowed on the site. He said that the men did not want free tea and hated being served by young ladies as they felt shy of them; they wanted to be served by motherly working women who came from the same background that they did. Mind you, Mr Caldwell may not be the most reliable of reporters as he also said that women were no use in munitions works as they would crack up within a week.

Winston Churchill's wife, Clementine, was a YMCA volunteer responsible for organising canteens for munitions workers in north-east London. She not only organised the establishment of the canteens and ensured they ran smoothly but worked there herself on both day and night shifts, wearing the same ankle-length blue and white uniform as her colleagues.

During the early part of the war, twelve voluntary organisations ran about 500 canteens for munitions and dock workers, using thousands of helpers. As well as the big names, such as the YMCA, these organisations also included the National People's Palace Association, The Glasgow Union of Women Workers, the British Women's Temperance Society, and the Church of England Temperance Society. In 1916 this role was taken away from them when the Central Control Board was set up to organise canteens in munitions works throughout Britain, using paid workers. Large numbers of women must have felt rebuffed and frustrated to have their work taken over at short notice after they had put in so much effort – and there is no information about how many, if any, of them came to be employed by the Central Control Board.

The Catholic Club and the Catholic Women's League were the only Roman Catholic Societies that carried out widespread, organised work during the war. They had a total of 100 female and eighteen male volunteers. They began their work providing refreshment huts at bases in 1915 and eventually had twenty-six centres around Britain.

It would be a mistake to think the volunteers all fitted in well together and worked without problems. Not all volunteers were equally capable or adaptable. Gabrielle West reported in her diary that in 1916 the paid manager of the canteen at the Royal Aircraft Factory Farnborough was thoroughly fed up with her volunteers. Eighty per cent of them were married women and yet only one of the thirty-seven had even a rudimentary knowledge of cooking and housekeeping, as they were too posh to have learned these skills. The volunteers included the Duchess of Wellington's two nieces who were apparently enthusiastic but totally lacking in skill.

Middle class women in Dublin formed the Irish Munition Workers' Canteen Committee to provide subsidised meals at Dublin Dockyard and the National Shell Factories. Every worker was given free tea and a bun at the start of their shift. At other times tea, coffee, cocoa, sandwiches and sausage rolls each cost 1*d*. Fresh salmon and vegetables – on a plate – cost 5*d*. The Dublin leader was Mrs Highett who had been trained in London by Lady Lawrence and who based her efforts on the English system. As in many English canteens, most of the staff were VADs. The Dublin workers provided an extra service, not recorded as being provided elsewhere – they read newspapers out loud to staff during the meal breaks and this was apparently greatly appreciated by the workers. Here too, many of the volunteers were later replaced by paid workers.

If canteens and buffets were of enormous importance in Britain, their value to troops overseas can hardly be overestimated. In November 1914 the first YMCA group went to France to set up a hut at Le Havre. They soon extended their work to the main army bases at Rouen, Dieppe, Boulogne, Étaples and Calais, to the railway junction at Abancourt, and to Abbeville, Dunkirk, Paris and Marseilles and about 300 other sites along the lines of communication.

In June 1915 the YMCA was finally granted permission to operate within the Army areas and opened a centre in Aire. By the end of 1916, they had a chain of small canteens in France with a team of 1,500 and at times 1,750 workers. Most of the staff were women volunteers but there were also some men above military age or who were not fit enough for military service. The YMCA placed an advertisement in *The Times*, looking for women volunteers who could afford to pay their own expenses. They did not want women whose husbands were engaged in active service but married women and widows aged between thirty and forty-eight. Widows were considered most suitable. In the Étaples sidings alone, volunteers handed out over 200,000 cups of cocoa a month. YMCA staff in the area also kept pigs fed on kitchen waste, then slaughtered them to help to pay for the cost of running the huts.

The YMCA had some canteens that were surprisingly close to the fighting and, if they received a written request from an officer, they would take free cocoa and biscuits out to the men in the trenches. In 1916 goods for sale in the marquee near the front at Albert included biscuits, slabs of cake, dates, chocolates, sweets, oranges, tins of condensed milk, cocoa, Camp coffee, Hoe's sauce, tomato ketchup, tinned fruit, tins of sardines, herrings, salmon, sausages, and large piles of cigarettes.

Jessie Wilson was a suffragette and a trained gardener from Bradford who set off to London in 1915, aged thirty-four, armed with a letter of introduction for Mr Virgo at the YMCA. To her frustration, he was away and she was rebuffed by a member of staff who said they had enough women who wanted to go to France. She was sent off to the Ladies' Committee and again got a cold reception, being told that she could leave her name and address and that they already had 500 ladies on their books. After a long wait, she managed to buttonhole Countess Bessborough, who was on her way out to lunch, and got the offer of four to six months' service in France. Jessie offered to make herself useful while she was waiting for a departure date and was sent to see a Miss Batten at the YMCA hut at Euston. Jessie kept a diary throughout her service and later wrote that she learned a great deal during the two weeks she spent there. Her diary gives a vivid picture of the realities of working in one of the huts

After two weeks in the Euston Hut, she got a telegram summoning her to France, bought her ticket at a reduced price thanks to her YMCA permit, and set off. In Le Havre she met Miss Cust who was waiting with a car to meet the parents of a severely wounded man. Miss Cust informed her she was not expected and that nothing could be done with her until Mr Pilkington, the area superintendent, returned four days later. Frustrated, she went to a hotel but Miss Cust then reappeared and sent her to Hut 15 in Harfleur, right in the middle of a huge reinforcement camp.

Hut 15 was large, with a long, dirty counter, which had a boiler house at one end. The sawdust on the floor became a quagmire each day from the spilt tea and other drinks. The counter was piled high with chocolate, shoelaces, cigarettes, soap, chewing gum and other items the men might want. The soldiers surged, chaotically, around the counter and Jessie discovered that thousands of francs worth of goods went missing each month, while the staff were meant to give change at the current exchange rate in French, English or Italian currency, doing all the calculations in their heads.

The water supply was outside so that washing-up was a nightmare. After eleven weeks, Jessie could bear the filthy enamel jugs no longer and scoured them with soda until they were at least partly white again. She later created a small but attractive garden outside Hut 15, and Suttons, the seed firm, gave her all the seeds she asked for each year. Having initially been offered work for four to six months, it was actually ten months before Jessie got her first home leave and then she spent part of it raising £40 to buy mouth organs for the men.

Among the staff at Hut 15 were two men from the YMCA. Reggie Harrison was a delicate man, unpopular with the soldiers, who suffered from boils on his neck and who wanted to become a clergyman. The other man was Louis de Ridler, a complex man who could apparently have a reasonable discussion about social issues and then deliberately trip one of the orderlies. The Leading Lady was Miss Stainforth who had been there for six weeks before Jessie arrived. She had been one of the first women sent to a YMCA hut in France and Mr Pilkington later admitted that he and some of the other men had done all they could to keep women out. Jessie thought Miss Stainforth was a wonderful manager with real moral integrity. The military authorities insisted there must always be one male member of staff in a YMCA hut.

The other volunteers were a mixed group. Miss Hoare was keenly evangelical and played the organ and piano for services. Mrs Hope-Johnstone found sticking to the YMCA's rules very difficult and soon left and set up her own refreshment stall for soldiers in Montvilliers. Dorothy Hunter joined the team from the Central Hut in Le Havre in 1916. Jessie relished her company and they worked happily together for the rest of the war. Continuity of staff made a great difference to how a hut worked and to its general atmosphere. Everyone found frequent changes unsettling and men enjoyed going back to a hut to see their old friends on the staff.

Among the volunteers who did not stay long were a couple of very colourful characters. A small, stout lady turned up without warning. She was dressed in a green coat and skirt, a large hat with a white feather and was festooned with pearls including a pearl and diamond pendant. Although she was warm-hearted and willing, Mrs Christian's skills left something to be desired and they discovered she was incapable of even counting their stock of embroidered postcards. She was also very greedy, always the first at meals and determined to eat more than her share. Her friend, Mrs Birch, was charming and witty but so deaf that the men were unable to make her understand what they wanted. She was followed by Mrs Curtain, who had such poor eyesight that she could barely differentiate between the various makes of cigarette.

Everyone associated with Hut 15 found Christmas Day 1915 dismal. Although they had been short-handed for weeks, they were keen to do what they could to provide a Christmas celebration for their customers. However, they were repeatedly told that they did not need to worry about providing an entertainment as the Army had it all in hand. They believed what they were told and did not prepare anything. On the morning of Christmas Day they found the cook and orderly were dead drunk and had literally to be kicked out of bed. The boilers had not been heated. When the hut opened its doors, as usual, men flooded in, sad and homesick. The Army's idea of a Christmas celebration had been to provide dinner and tea and to reduce fatigues to a minimum. No entertainment had been arranged and the day dragged out as the men's misery grew. The YMCA learned a very valuable lesson and in subsequent years made sure that Christmas was celebrated properly in all their huts.

Lady Rodney was very worried that French towns were full of temptation for British soldiers and that there was nowhere wholesome for them to go when they were off-duty. To counter this she set up the Women's Auxiliary Committee to recruit female volunteers to run huts at base camps in France and provide games and comforts for the men. The Women's Auxiliary Committee was run by a group of titled and influential women and as all the volunteers had to be able to cover their own expenses, most of them were upper or middle-class. Some of them took their own motor cars out to France. Later in the war widows and mothers of dead soldiers were also recruited. Members could get a small grant to help pay for their grey uniform and hat.

The Church Army initially focussed on setting up tents and huts for servicemen in Britain but later extended their work to France. By 1918 they were running several hundred huts in France and Flanders with more than 800 workers. Their volunteers, like most others, had to pay their own expenses. After the Armistice they also opened huts in Germany for the Army of Occupation. Some of their huts were simply places where men could go and sit in silence for a while. Others provided refreshments. One, provided for the use of transport troops, was on a barge. At every site they offered religious support and services for those who wanted them, as well as a quiet area and a temperance bar. A Church Army hut cost £300 and a tent cost £150. They even had collapsible chapels. One of their fundraising ideas was to distribute collecting boxes that were shaped like one of their huts.

The first Salvation Army group to try to support the British Expeditionary Force overseas set off for Belgium in August 1914, presumably without sanction from the military authorities. The group was led by Lieutenant Colonel Mary Murray and reached Brussels just as the British Army began to retreat from Mons. Working alongside the Army was not, therefore, an option. Besides setting up recreation huts under their symbol of the Red Shield, a special aspect of the work done by Salvationists was the establishment of field kitchens with small ovens that could be set up anywhere, even close to the front line, to make sure that the men got a good meal.

Most recreation huts provided paper, pens and somewhere quiet to write letters. This was greatly appreciated by the troops and volunteers. One Salvation Army hut handed out 2,500 sheets of writing paper a week. Volunteers were quick to identify that the most popular meal among the British troops was egg and chips, while the Australians preferred a meat pie. Staff from all the organisations running huts, tents and canteens realised that it was important to make these bare and often temporary structures homely and welcoming. Their efforts, and the consideration behind them, were greatly appreciated. Many staff festooned the buildings with the flags of the allied nations. The Salvation Army, among others, tried to provide small tables, with tablecloths and vases of flowers rather than long benches and trestle tables that were reminiscent of Army mess huts.

The Scottish Churches Huts were a joint effort by the Church of Scotland and the United Free Church of Scotland. They ran huts on the same lines as other organisations in France, Malta, Egypt and then for the Army of Occupation in Germany.

In 1916, No. 7 Convalescent Camp, in the Boulogne Area, was the first to have a recreation hut run by the British Red Cross. Others followed, although only this first one had an attached kitchen. Almost all these recreation huts were staffed by VADs. The VADs at No. 7 Convalescent Camp were the first to come up with the idea of teaching soldiers to embroider. The aim was to occupy men who were shell-shocked or who were not terribly ill, but who were not well enough to concentrate on complicated work or reading. It proved to be a great success, as the embroidery occupied their minds, distracting them from their personal horrors for a while and VADs later introduced embroidery in other huts.

The Red Cross established canteens at various railway stations along the lines of communication in France. They were staffed by VADs with a commandant or quartermaster in charge and were open day and night so they could work with the staff on the ambulance trains that called at the station. When a train arrived, the VADs quickly provided cocoa, cigarettes, fruit, magazines, and clothing to the wounded, provided meals when necessary and changed dressings. The train's staff were not forgotten and the VADs provided them with food and shelter and undertook various commissions, including arranging for laundry and mending to be done and to be returned safely to its owner. This last service was especially welcome, as train workers never knew when they would be back at a particular station and it was easy for their laundry and mending to go missing. In some instances the canteens also served as medical inspection rooms for local troops and staff helped to treat local casualties.

As with other areas of voluntary work there a number of freelance efforts, mostly started by confident, determined women who wanted to get out to France to 'do their bit'. They attained varying degrees of official sanction. Miss Lily Butler opened a very popular leave club for men in Paris called A Corner of Blighty in Paris for Our Boys from the Front. This Club was particularly popular with Australian servicemen. In the Place de la Vendome, in central Paris, it ran for two years. There was no charge for its services and Lily Butler and her group of forty-five female volunteers also arranged outings for groups of the men. Lily Butler was sometimes known as the 'Mother of Blighty'.

When Lady Angela Forbes visited Boulogne in November 1914 she was so distressed to see soldiers left waiting on the quay for hours without food or drink that she went back to London, spent £8 buying provisions at Fortnum & Mason, returned to Boulogne and set up a buffet for soldiers. She later opened a canteen in Étaples for the workmen building the huge camp there. This was followed in 1917 by one for the thousands of troops in the camp and another at Étaples station. She liked to recount how one night, when she was on duty between 4 and 7 a.m. with only an elderly orderly to stoke the fires for her and a French girl making sandwiches, she fried 800 eggs. Her British Soldiers' Canteens came to be known as Angelinas, named after her.

Lady Angela and her putative lover, Lord Wemyss, worked hard to raise money for the canteens and managed to provide the refreshments free of charge, until the Red Cross began charging in their canteens. Lady Angela followed suit and managed to make a profit, which she later used to help fund training for disabled soldiers.

In 1917 Lady Angela was ordered to leave France and accused of unseemly conduct. The bizarre accusations against her were that she had said 'damn' and had washed her hair in the canteen. She appealed against the edict but the military authorities stood firm and the War Office took over her canteens and buffets. It seems that her ejection from France was more likely to have been due to her tendency to ignore red tape and her abrasive manner. She had made enemies, including Sir Douglas Haig, the Commander-in-Chief. She demanded an enquiry into her treatment but this was refused. In an attempt to clear her name, Lord Wemyss and Lord Ribblesdale, who may also have been Lady Angela's lover, raised the issue in the House of Lords in February 1918. Lord Ribblesdale recounted how the work had developed from a small-scale operation at the Gare Maritime in Boulogne and had grown until it had served 4,500,000 men. Lord Wemyss supported him and said that his own honour was caught up in the reputation of the canteens as he had been treasurer for three years. He said that he wanted to stop the slander of a good woman who had worked hard for the war effort. On behalf of the Government, the Earl of Derby acknowledged all Lady Angela had done, but said that the time came when it was right for the work to be centralised. He insisted the closing of her canteen was not meant to signify that her work had not been up to standard. He was adamant that the military authorities were not responsible for any of the wild rumours that were circulating and hoped the whole matter was closed.

One hut that was particularly near the front was run by a Scottish man, aged about fifty. He begged for help in getting fuel and chopping wood and raised both his living costs and the basic expenses of running the hut from donations. He sold cigarettes, chocolate, writing paper and other items but gave the mugs of steaming tea and cocoa away without charge.

After the death of his son, who had been in the Coldstream Guards, E. W. Hornung, left his grieving wife at home and set off for France. Famous as the writer of the *Raffles* books, Hornung was asthmatic, grossly overweight and an unlikely volunteer but going to France was his way of battling his grief. He set himself up in a hole in a chalk bank beside a road in the Arras area near where his son had been killed. Equipped only with a small stove, a few enamel mugs, tea, tins of sugar and condensed milk and a few books he began to serve hot tea to soldiers and to encourage them to talk about their homes. He later joined the YMCA and by 1917 had opened several coffee stalls in Arras.

Writer Sarah McNaughtan was described as small, delicate, elderly and highly-strung but willing to do anything that was asked of her. She was, in fact, fifty at the time and only just over 5 feet tall. After a stint with Mabel St Clair Stobart's hospital unit in Antwerp, she joined the Munro Ambulance corps.

One night she was asked to help unload ambulances at the busy Furnes Station. A chaotic scene greeted her. The station was crammed with stretchers and wounded waiting for the ambulance trains to arrive. Some of the wounds had been dressed with nothing more than field dressings, as the men had been brought straight from the battlefield. Many of the men had not eaten all day and asked her for food and water. She realised that nobody was actually looking after them while they were at the station. She immediately set to, determined to help.

During the day, she headed off to the market and, using her own money, bought food and coffee. She persuaded staff at the hospital to lend her portable stoves and cooking pots and commandeered part of a corridor at the station to use as a makeshift kitchen where she prepared soup and cocoa for that night's influx of wounded. When the first convoy of the day arrived at around 9.30 a.m. she carried out one of her boiling 'marmites' (large earthenware cooking pots) to the middle of the entrance and ladled out soup while a Belgian nurse distributed bread and coffee. Her efforts were hugely appreciated and before long she had taken over the whole corridor.

As word spread, off-duty colleagues from the hospital came to help, peeling and chopping vegetables for great vats of soup. Local shopkeepers delivered their left-over vegetables each evening. Impressed by their efforts, the stationmaster provided them with a proper room with shelves, cupboards and even electric light. She bought an electric hotplate and a trolley from Harrods, with her own money, to make it easier to distribute the soup to men all over the station. When she noticed that many of the men's socks were in shreds she ordered 1,000 pairs, knitted in thick wool, from Harrods and gave them out any man who needed them.

This intense work took its toll on Sarah, as it would have on anyone, but she also suffered from pernicious anaemia and Coeliac disease. The hospital chaplain noticed how tired she was and took to waiting up for her with some food or wine to greet her when she got back from the station. By the end of 1915 she was exhausted and went back to England. She later spent a brief period as a Red Cross volunteer in Russia but died in London in July 1916. She said that the period she spent in Belgium was the worst time she had ever spent and was incredulous to find that some people were enjoying it.

La Cantine Anglaise was set up by a group of English women in the former waiting room at Revigny Station. It was a free canteen, established to help the French soldiers, the badly paid poilus, whose own authorities did little to help them. Staffed by British volunteers, it had the sanction of the French Red Cross. It was at the end of the railway line to Verdun and was, therefore, exceedingly busy as reinforcements poured into the area. The canteen's services were given free and funded by private subscriptions. One of the most generous donors was steel magnate John Summers, who then used his influence to enable his daughter Maude and her school friend Lorna Neill, to join the volunteers even though they were only nineteen and therefore too young to serve overseas with any official group. Lorna recorded in her diary how thrilled they both were to be there, dressed in the white uniforms of the French Red Cross. She also recorded her horror at being shown photos of a soldier's wife and son before the war and a more recent picture in which they appeared haggard.

Each time a train arrived, the canteen filled within minutes. Free soup and coffee were provided but the poilus appreciated the fact that these English women had gone out to France to try to help them as much as they enjoyed the refreshments. The women served 10,000 men a day. Unlike the majority of canteens, they did not have a room where the men could go and sit. They were served through windows, which were draped with French and British flags. As well as serving drinks, the team handed out cigarettes and comforts. The Canteen of the Army of Verdun, was how one officer described the *Cantine Anglaise*. He said that, for men heading to the battle, it was where they breathed the last waves of warm sympathy that strengthened their hearts and for those coming back from the front it was the first place where they were greeted with a smile and glimpsed a life they had not thought to see again.

In the autumn of 1914 Lady Mabelle Egerton and her father took a load of Red Cross and St John Ambulance stores and parcels for the wounded to Rouen. While they were there, the deputy director of medical services asked Lady Mabelle if she would provide boiling water at the Rive Gauche Station for men passing through on their way to the front. The men carried dry rations but had no way of making a hot drink.

Within two weeks she was running a full-scale canteen and shop in an empty goods shed. The Rouen Station Coffee Shop, as it came to be known, catered for both officers and men and became well-known for Lady Mabelle's 'Officers' Parcels', which contained food for two days. Lady Mabelle only had a few helpers at first, and, if there was a rush, officers would help with service. It grew to be one of the largest canteens in France, famous for its efforts to provide everything the customers wanted, from cigarettes, candles and soap to mouth organs. In an anonymous letter, sent to the Coffee Shop, the writer succinctly described its importance. He wrote, 'Before we went forth to battle or to death, our last impression of women, home and love, which came to us in a strange land, was in the Coffee Shop at Rouen.' The organisation was impressive. They bought as many of their supplies as possible locally and the rest came from Britain. Provisioning the canteen was a major achievement as there were times when they had served 1,000 eggs before 8 a.m. and got through half a ton of bread in a day.

In 1916 the British military authorities recognised the importance of the canteen by providing it with a large hut. Unfortunately it took them further from the trains, so they also erected a small shanty at Line 11 to provide refreshments whenever troops were entraining there. In June 1917, the Church Army took over the canteen as a going concern and continued to feed large numbers.

Early in the war a Frenchman, Monsieur Duquesnoy, set up *L'Oeuvre de la Goutte de Café*, which provided very small canteens. The canteens were so popular that he and his wife appealed for funds to extend their work. M. Duquesnoy contacted the president of the British Committee of the French Red Cross (the British Committee) to ask for funds to enable him to open more canteens. The lady president saw this as an opening for some of the many Englishwomen contacting them wanting to go abroad to help but who had no specific training or experience. She agreed that the British Committee would set up and staff a number of canteens, remarking that the French lacked any organisations like the YMCA and the Church Army to set up huts and canteens and how badly the French poilu was catered for.

They British Committee ran canteens at railway stations and at various rest and transit camps. Apart from providing refreshments, they found that essential equipment included a gramophone and, wherever possible, a cinema, and space for concerts and other entertainments. In Monsieur Duquesnoy's original canteens, a small charge was made for refreshments but they were free in the canteens run under the British Committee. Volunteers often had to dress the men's sore feet and new socks were always welcome. Besides socks the British Committee sent out underwear, mufflers, gloves, handkerchiefs, and other items as requested.

The British Committee's first station canteen opened in a hut in the stationmaster's garden at Hazebrouck in February 1915. Staff were only allowed to feed French and Belgian soldiers. The lady in charge found that cocoa, made as strong as possible and with milk and sugar, was the most popular drink. The also provided milk for the babies of refugees.

They opened more and more canteens over a wide area. In 1916 alone they opened another twenty-nine. At Christmas 1915, staff at the St Dizier canteen begged and borrowed trees, decorations, tables, chairs, and table linen to make the hut festive. Then they put a small present at each place round the tables. Christmas dinner consisted of hot soup, cold ham, hot roast beef, haricot beans, bread and jam, red wine and coffee. The commandant donated cigarettes and cigars for everyone. The men were thrilled with the celebrations and the meal was followed by singing, recitations and records played on the gramophone. To the embarrassment of the staff some of the soldiers rounded off the evening by singing French love songs to them.

Lady May Bradford was a sixty-year-old VAD who went out to France in 1914 with her husband, Sir John Bradford, who was a surgeon at No. 26 General Hospital in Étaples. She developed an unusual and immeasurably important way of providing non-medical help to sick and wounded men. She made herself invaluable writing letters for men who were too ill to write themselves or who were illiterate. To make her service more personal she dressed in a formal suit and hat, rather than a VAD uniform and went around the hospital with her camp stool and writing materials. She worked from 1914 until after the Armistice with a break of only one week, when she was too ill to work. In this period she wrote more than 25,000 letters, an average of twelve a day.

Lady Bradford was renowned among the men and their relatives for her compassion and for the personal touch she added to many of the letters. She would spend long periods at the bedside of seriously ill men, not only writing the letters but comforting the dying. She described this as standing in for their mothers. As a Welsh speaker, she was able to send information about sick and wounded men from Wales to their relatives, who understood no English.

Although most volunteer-run canteens were in France and Belgium a few were set up further afield. Local volunteers in Sliema, Malta, sent up a canteen for sick and wounded soldiers. They also arranged weekly concerts and served more than 50,000 men.

Mrs Watkins led a group to Italy in 1915 to set up station canteens for hospital trains at Cervignano and San Giovanni Manzano on the Isogno Front. For two years, she raised most of the funding herself but did get some help from the British Red Cross Society. In 1917 she took over feeding the wounded men in the Dolegna Clearing Station. Her efforts so impressed the Italian authorities that they emulated her work and opened their first recreation hut. The supreme command was planning a further100 huts just before the retreat of October 1917.

Over time, it became clear that nurses also got ill, exhausted, and stressed and needed somewhere to recuperate. The first convalescent home for nurses was opened at Hardelot in 1915, in a house belonging to HRH Princess Louise. The Battle of the Somme, in 1916, took its toll on medical staff. They worked around the clock for extended periods, trying to cope with the wounded. This increased the demand for places where nurses could go to rest and the VADs were given the job of expanding this area of work. Before long, they had opened homes in Étretat and Le Touquet.

Staff at the Princess Louise's Rest Club for Nurses at Étaples had to walk 2 miles each way to buy supplies of eggs, milk and other supplies, as they had no means of transport. The staff slept in tents in the sand dunes, where they also planted nasturtiums, mignonette, and heliotropes. The club had to close for three weeks in 1917, as all the staff were quarantined when one of the VADs, Miss Evans, was diagnosed with cerebro-spinal meningitis. Miss Evans sadly died but none of the other staff got ill. In 1917 they were asked to manage a sick bay for WAACS at Wimereux. The sick bay was set up by the British Red Cross and run under a VAD superintendent. A series of similar sick bays were set up in other camps.

In May 1917 the YMCA arranged for Ethel Knight of the YWCA to go to France to set up Blue Triangle huts for the WAACS, on the same lines as the Red Triangle Huts for men. Within a year, twenty-three of these huts were up and running, serving all the main WAAC camps. There was a small quiet room or chapel attached to each hut. The huts were generally made as cosy and homely as possible to give the women a real break from their usual military surroundings. There were also clubs in seven towns, a rest house in Le Tréport, a tea garden at Le Havre and a marquee in the WAAC rest camp, known as the Lady Carisbrooke Marquee.

In 1915 Mrs Brice Miller offered to set up and fund a convalescent home for nurses. She set out for France with her daughter, assistant, chauffeur, and servant. Arriving in Le Touquet, she rented a house called Le Petit Château and opened her convalescent home. It only had eight beds. Like a number of independent volunteers, Mrs Brice Miller was not willing to continue her work once all organisations operating overseas had to affiliate to the British Red Cross Society. She felt affiliation would obliterate the individual quality of her convalescent home, so she closed it and went home.

Lady Ponsonby and the Hon. Mrs Cyril Ward set up a rest club for nursing sisters who worked in the hospitals at Wimereux. They soon realised how much facilities of this kind were needed and set up an organisation to provide additional clubs. As HRH Princess Victoria

agreed to be the organisation's president, the centres came to be called
HRH Princess Victoria's Rest Clubs for Nursing Sisters. The Wimereux
club continued, in the same premises, until 1918 then moved to a larger
building. The organisation opened additional clubs at Camiers, Étaples,
Rouen, Calais, Abbeville, St Omer, Le Tréport, Paris, Boulogne, Trouville,
and Le Havre.

Until a club opened in Calais, there were no facilities for the numerous
sisters in the town and the only place they could get a bath was in the
house of a local woman. The Abbeville Club was in a very pleasant villa
with a lovely garden. One of its special features was a large, tiled tea
room. In August 1917 they were so busy that a third VAD was taken on.
Sisters from ambulance trains and barges were honorary members of all
the clubs, rather than having to join each one individually. During air
raids on the town in 1918, the VADs were granted special permission to
shelter in a bomb-proof dugout at the Nurses' Home.

The club at Étaples ran into difficulties with its first lady superintendent,
a VAD called Mrs Latham. She seems to have been unable to either
understand or accept military discipline and wanted to introduce her
own regulations regarding such issues as smoking, and entertaining
officers. The problem was referred up to the princess herself, and she
agreed with the committee that neither smoking nor entertaining officers
could be countenanced. In June 1915 Mrs Latham was replaced by two
VADs from the British Red Cross Society. As a concession, they were
attached to the Sisters' Mess at a nearby hospital. The Étaples club was in
the middle of number of hospitals and so was ideally suited for the many
nurses, who had nowhere else to go to rest, read newspapers and get
something to eat. The club was damaged in the air raid on the hospitals
in May 1918 and, in one room, the only thing left standing was a portrait
of Princess Victoria. None of the staff was injured and the club was soon
repaired and open for business as usual. This was the last club to close, in
June 1919, but the organisation's work was not over as they then opened
a club in Cologne, for Sisters who were with the Army of Occupation.

Providing somewhere for VADs who needed a period of care was always
more contentious and the provision of facilities was never formalised.
Several hostels were provided in London for VADs who wanted to live
near their work or who needed to stay in town on their way to and from
duty. Each of these hostels was managed by a VAD commandant with a
staff of VAD general service members to do the kitchen, domestic and
clerical work.

Hard-working VADs, exposed to every kind of infection, sometimes
got ill and needed to be nursed back to health. Others were wounded in
the course of their duties and about 243 died from wounds. Inevitably,
a large number of VADs contracted Spanish Flu in 1918 and some died

A crowd of refugees in Victoria, London, in September 1914. The people in the foreground seem to be watching the refugees from outside the railings. (© Imperial War Museum, ref. Q53305)

The sheer scale of the effort needed to care for the refugees is illustrated by this photograph of 600 refugee children being given tea at Earl's Court in London. (© Imperial War Museum, ref. HU88813)

Above: Fund-raising was unending and this group of Boy Scouts and Belgian refugees were trying their luck at Newmarket racecourse. (© Imperial War Museum, ref. Q53361)

Left: A member of the City of London Red Cross, London Ambulance Column in 1917. Members met trains of wounded men arriving in London and transported them to hospital. (© Imperial War Museum, ref. Q30395)

Members of the Ledbury War Hospital Supply Depot making medical supplies. They were affiliated to the Belgravia Workrooms in London. (© Imperial War Museum, ref. Q108265)

Above left: VADs running to an ambulance train at Étaples, 1917. (Courtesy LOC)

Above right: Belgian refugees arriving in the Netherlands, 1914. (Courtesy LOC)

Lady Dorothie Feilding looking excited and enthusiastic in October 1914, soon after her arrival at Furnes in Belgium as a member of the Munro Ambulance Corps. (© Warwickshire County Record Office)

Just a couple of years later, this picture of Lady Dorothie Feilding illustrates all too clearly how the strain of working in such dangerous conditions had taken its toll. She was the first woman to be awarded the Military Medal for bravery in the field. (© Warwickshire County Record Office)

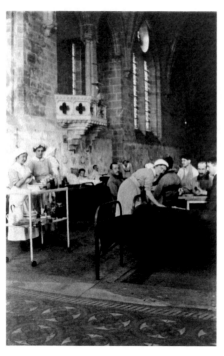

Above: A group of cheerful Red Cross VAD ambulance drivers, with an ambulance donated by people in Canada. The photograph was taken at the large base in Étaples, in June 1917. (© Imperial War Museum, ref. Q2438)

Left: One of the wards in the hospital run by the Scottish Women's Hospitals for Foreign Service in the Abbey of Royaumont, north of Paris, France. (© Imperial War Museum, ref. Q115371)

Nurses exploring the ruins of the flimsy wards in the hospital at Étaples that were reduced to matchwood after being bombed on 31 May 1918. (© Imperial War Museum, ref. Q11539)

YOU MUST HELP
SERBIA

Our Serbian Allies — homeless, robbed of every possession, thousands of them orphaned, all of them destitute—are dependent upon the generosity of the British Public for the very necessaries of life.

You will not shirk your share of British responsibility for unfortunate Serbia !

Give what you can to the

SERBIAN RELIEF FUND

Address Donations to the Earl of Plymouth, and Parcels to
Mrs. Carrington Wilde, at the Serbian Relief Fund,
5, Cromwell Road, London, S.W. 7.

Poster appealing for support for the Serbian Relief Fund, which was founded by Mabel Grouitch, the American-born wife of Serbian diplomat Slavko Grouitch. (© Imperial War Museum, ref. ART IWM PST 10928)

Right: The Duchess of Westminster in her nurse's uniform, although she and her friends wore evening dress to greet each group of patients arriving at her hospital in Le Touquet. (© Imperial War Museum, ref. Q108175)

Below: Nurses and patients playing cards in the tented hospital run by the Scottish Women's Hospitals in Salonika in 1916. (© Imperial War Museum, ref. Q31919)

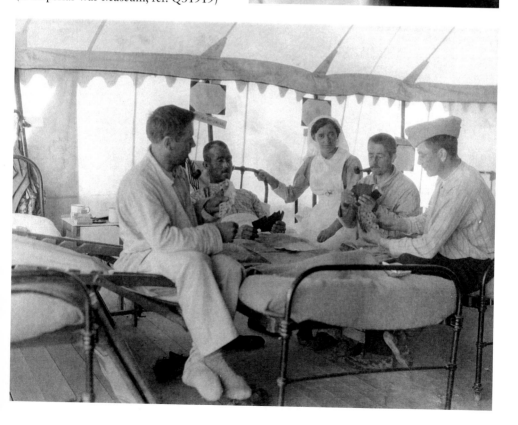

Cooks from the 6th American Unit of the Scottish Women's Hospitals preparing a meal on a stone hearth in the open air at their hospital in Ostrovo in 1916. (© Imperial War Museum, ref. Q32347)

Members of Mabel St Clair Stobart's unit taking a much-needed rest during the Great Retreat from Serbia in 1915. (© Imperial War Museum, ref. Q69143)

Right: Dr Hilda Clark was at the forefront of the Quakers' efforts to help civilians struggling to continue their lives in parts of France near the front. She continued her aid work in Austria after the Armistice. (© Religious Society of Friends (Quakers) in Britain)

Below: Miss Ross, who worked for the Friends War Victims' Relief Committee, outside one of the buildings in the model village they built at Sermaize, France. (© Imperial War Museum, ref. 8068)

Volunteers working for the Friends' War Victims' Relief Committee distributing mattresses and furniture from their Couvanges warehouse in 1916. (© Religious Society of Friends (Quakers) in Britain)

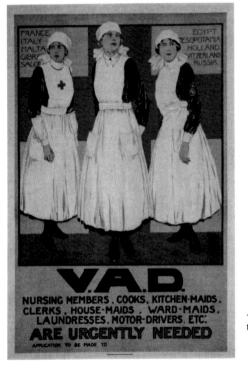

A poster advertising the need for recruits to join the Voluntary Aid Detachment. (Courtesy LOC)

This picture of Péronne was taken in March 1917 and shows the scale of the task of rebuilding large swathes of France that was faced by returning refugees and the authorities. (© Imperial War Museum, ref. Q4968)

The Mayor of Blackburn and other dignitaries before the opening ceremony of the Pont de Blackburn in 1924. (© Blackburn with Darwen Library and Information Service)

Quaker food train distributing food and clothing in Russia. (© Religious Society of Friends (Quakers) in Britain)

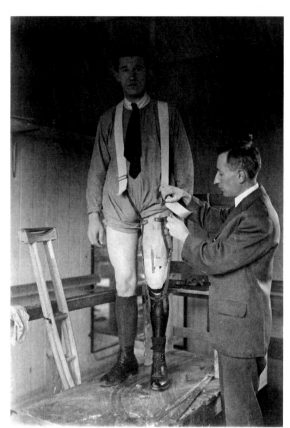

Left: A veteran at Queen Mary's Convalescent Auxiliary Hospital, Roehampton having the last fitting for his artificial leg before it was completed. (© Imperial War Museum, ref. Q33679)

Below: A group of blinded veterans making and repairing boots in the workroom at St Dunstan's Hostel in Regents Park, London. (© Imperial War Museum, ref. Q54583)

Above: Volunteers entertaining young servicemen in the Euston Station Buffet at Christmas 1917. As the sign shows, the Free Buffet was only available to men who were actually travelling. (© Imperial War Museum, ref. Q54274)

Right: A smartly dressed volunteer collecting used mugs from sailors at the Red Cross Buffet at Banbury Station. Many buffets lost large numbers of mugs when servicemen kept them as souvenirs. (© Imperial War Museum, ref. Q114908)

Above: Miss Kirk and Miss Loy must have had their work cut out serving this crowd of men at the Church Army Hut at St Omer. (© Imperial War Museum, ref. Q7967)

Left: Boy Scouts were very active collecting salvage and, as in this picture, donations of eggs that were sent to hospitals for sick and wounded men. (© Imperial War Museum, ref. Q30606)

The Army's need for sandbags was unending so volunteers made as many as they could. Mrs Mower is standing beside piles of bags made by members of the Hull Social Club for Soldiers' and Sailors' Wives. (© Imperial War Museum, ref. Q108250)

Above: Internees at Ruhleben racecourse near Berlin, milling around outside the YMCA hut and the theatre just after their release on 22 November 1918. (© Imperial War Museum, ref. Q109547)

Right: The Blue Cross Fund, formerly the Dumb Friends' League, carried out vital work caring for horses wounded in the conflict. (© The Blue Cross)

BLUE CROSS FUND
HELP THE WOUNDED
HORSES AT THE WAR

"OUR DUMB FRIENDS' LEAGUE"
A SOCIETY FOR THE ENCOURAGEMENT OF KINDNESS TO ANIMALS
DONATIONS IMMEDIATELY TO
ARTHUR J. COKE, Secretary.
58, VICTORIA STREET. LONDON, S.W.

Men who had been transferred from Prisoner of War camps to Chateau d'Oex in Switzerland greeting a group of their wives who had travelled out to see them. (© Imperial War Museum, ref. Q54695)

Weaving was one of the crafts that the Quakers established at Knockaloe Camp on the Isle of Man to help occupy the internees and enable them to earn a small income. (© Religious Society of Friends (Quakers) in Britain)

as a result. Several were treated for shell-shock, including two who were sent to Charing Hospital in Kent. Katherine Furse and Rachel Crowdy fought tirelessly to get some beds set aside in hospitals for VADs who needed nursing. In consistently refusing to agree to this the Hon. Arthur Stanley, who was placed in charge of the Joint Committee in 1917, said he was sure that a hospital would always find a bed if sick or wounded VADs arrived on their doorstep. Rachel Crowdy then submitted a list of fees for private patients at major London hospitals, adding that beds for VADs could not be guaranteed in these hospitals. She believed that they were running a grave risk of endangering the health of members if better arrangements were not put in place. Sir Thomas Hudson then committed the Joint Committee to paying for hospital beds for VADs who were invalided home.

In the early days of the war relatives given permission to visit their dangerously ill relatives in France had to travel unaccompanied, which was a huge additional strain. It was even worse for the bereaved who had to travel home alone. Typically, it was considered much harder for the female relatives of officers to travel unaccompanied, as they were gentlewomen, than it was for women visiting men of other ranks.

Almost all relatives arrived at night, and without warning, after they had got the telegram from the War Office inviting them to visit their dangerously ill relative. They set off a quickly as they could, often carrying no more than a toothbrush. Their initial permission was for a forty-eight hour visit, but this could be extended if the man remained on the dangerously ill list and if the relative's presence was thought to be helpful. Visits sometimes lasted for several months.

When the British Red Cross Society decided to provide a hostel for relatives visiting dangerously ill men in the Le Touquet and La Plage area, they were dismayed to find most of the hotels had been already been requisitioned for use as hospitals. However, they did manage to rent the Hôtel des Anglais, which had a shady garden and which was on the edge of the forest of Le Touquet. Staffed mostly by VADs, it had two wings connected by a long dining room. A large part of the building was used to house staff from the Duchess of Westminster's Hospital, the VADs who ran the hostel, the Étaples branch of the Missing and Wounded Enquiry Department, the department's staff, chaplains attached to the hospitals, voluntary drivers and other male workers. Almost all of one wing was occupied by an eminent physician, working in the Étaples hospitals, and his wife. This first hostel was seen as an experiment and was a great success.

Relatives were not charged for their stay. Some of the more wealthy visitors made large donations to the Red Cross, while others did what they could. Many could give nothing. Staff often felt their role was mostly with the less well-off who needed extra support. They welcomed guests of both sexes, of all ages, and from all classes. The hostel was open for three years and often had between 120 and 160 guests. The VADs were kept so busy that they had to provide five sittings at each meal. The VAD commandant was responsible for running the hostel economically and efficiently, and did fortnightly cash returns. The quartermaster ran the stores but mostly worked with the guests. The VADs did all other work. In October 1918, the hostel was handed over to the Army.

VADs also staffed a hostel for relatives of dangerously ill men in Le Havre. The house was well-placed, on the tramlines leading to the port and the station. It had a pleasant garden, which was used as an overflow dining room when they had to fit forty guests into a space designed for twenty-eight. The hostel was used by workers passing through Le Havre, as well as by relatives of dangerously ill men, and regularly welcomed VAD drivers from Étretat and Trouville and volunteers travelling to and from Salonika, Italy, Egypt, Malta, North Africa and Corsica, interned prisoners travelling home from Holland or Switzerland, parties of relatives going to visit prisoners still interned in Switzerland, and parties of Serbian children being sent to be educated in Britain. Apart from Red Cross workers, every guest was expected to put some money in the donations box. One evening, the boat to England was delayed. At short notice staff had to find space for six VADs from Salonika, a relative of a wounded man, three members of the FANY, five French Red Cross workers, two Church Army workers, a Serbian Relief Fund worker and one Scottish Women's Hospital worker, in addition to their regular guests. At its peak staff served almost 600 meals in a week.

Apparently, the Rouen Hostel was always open and never turned anyone away. One of its special features was a lovely, peaceful courtyard. The hostel was opened in July 1916 with a staff of five. This was the month of the start of the Battle of the Somme and within a week they had thirty guests. The work was heart-breaking, as relatives came to see men with horrific wounds, some of whom appeared to rally and then died. At the end of July they got two more members of staff. Mary Campion was the hostel's custodian. She recorded in her diary how well most of the relatives supported each other and how social differences vanished in the face of shared problems. She said they had commercial travellers, a shopkeeper, people from the suburbs, an army officer, parsons, lawyers, doctors, schoolmasters and actresses, all together. We can only assume that she also meant the female relatives of the professionals she listed. An elderly Scottish lady and her daughter were reduced to tears at the experience of being waited on for the first time in their lives. Until then they had always eaten in their kitchen, so the staff arranged that they should take the rest of their meals in the hostel kitchen where they felt more relaxed than in the dining room.

In June 1915 the YMCA opened its first hostel in France for the relatives of dangerously ill men. A YMCA car met the relatives at the harbour and transported them to the hostel. One of the volunteers was Betty Stephenson from Harrogate, who volunteered at the age of nineteen to work in a YMCA canteen in France. She later became a driver and drove relatives visiting men in the hospitals at Étaples. She was killed during the major air raid on the hospitals on 30 May 1918.

Over time, the YMCA opened a hostel at every base hospital in Northern France, helping about 200 relatives a week. The organisation gave financial help to people who could not afford to pay for the journey themselves.

The Women's Auxiliary Committee of the YMCA ran the Les Iris hostel for relatives, conveniently placed within easy reach of the many hospitals at Paris Plage and Étaples. It was managed by three sisters, the Misses Chapman, who drove their own cars around. Apart from relatives of the sick and wounded, they also gave hospitality to members of Lena Ashwell's Concert Party, who gave concerts for troops in the area. Some of the female volunteers from the hospitals in Étaples also lodged there and the Misses Chapman drove them to and from the camps each day.

Alice K. Austin and her sisters also worked in a YMCA hostel and described something of their work in a letter to the editor of the *St Leonards' Gazette*. He had originally asked for an account of work in a YMCA hut but as she felt that was already well-known, she wrote about the hostel instead. She recounted that although some hostels were purpose-built, the two they ran were in rented houses in Le Tréport close to various hospitals and hospital camps. One of the hostels was large, with forty beds, but on one occasion it had seventy-five guests. Luckily, this happened in summer so the guests were able to sleep in chairs, on the floors and even in cars until beds could be found for them in the town. The seventy-five continued to eat together in the hostel. Alice's sister did the cooking, using Army rations, with a great deal of ingenuity and helped by three French or Belgian maids.

On their way to France, relatives were housed in hostels run by the Salvation Army or by the YMCA in London. Staff saw them off on their way to Folkestone, where Salvation Army staff looked after them. In France, the YMCA looked after the relatives of non-commissioned officers and other ranks. Each organisation regularly helped the other with transport. On their arrival in France, the relatives were fed, warmed and comforted – then taken to the nearby hospital camp's YMCA hut whose hut leader took them to the wounded men. The Red Cross looked after officers' relatives.

Alice said that the lady superintendent was available to greet arrivals at all hours of the day and night and to sit with them over a cup of tea. Visitors were allowed onto the hospital wards for an hour in the morning, two hours in the afternoon and an hour-and-a-half in the evening. The evening would end with prayers for those who wanted them. Between visiting hours, time dragged for the relatives as, apart from doing bits of shopping for themselves and their wounded relative, they had little to do. Therefore they took turns doing the washing-up in the hostel and all made their own beds and helped with a range of other tasks. Both men and women often asked for some job to do to distract themselves a little from their situation. Things could not always go smoothly and one man kept coming in drunk and upsetting everyone else. When he was told that he would have to leave if he continued this, he said he would go home and tell everyone that the YMCA was no place for fun!

Staff also accompanied relatives to funerals, in cars driven by VAD drivers, and helped the relatives with their homeward journey. In common with other hostel workers, Alice expressed her great admiration for the relatives, many of whom had never been abroad before.

The Bristol Inquiry Bureau became the model for the country and eventually had hundreds of volunteers linked to the 2nd Southern General Hospital. The volunteers answered enquiries about patients in the city's hospitals and organised clean, respectable lodgings for the families of wounded soldiers close to the hospitals where they were being treated. For 'deserving' families who could not afford to pay their own expenses, the bureau paid the fares, board and lodging. Their work developed to include organising entertainments for convalescent troops and eventually served the whole of south-west England and Wales.

In February 1915 Lord Cecil asked the London Branch of the Red Cross to appoint VADs to make enquiries at London hospitals to try to find missing soldiers. There were initially twenty volunteers, plus typists, but this number grew and they had to move into larger premises several times, as modern warfare created an unprecedented number of men who could not be accounted for.

The VADs visited hundreds of hospitals on a regular basis, armed with lists of officers and men who could not be accounted for and made enquiries to try to get any information they could about what had happened to them. Led by Sir Louis Mallett and later by the Earl of Lucan, this Red Cross unit acted as the clearing house for all enquiries from the public and all reports from searchers here and abroad. In time, they opened offices in London, Paris, Boulogne, Rouen, Malta, Alexandria, and Salonika. Their work was largely regulated by the War Office but was not officially recognised until July 1915. They were then approved as the only organisation permitted to search for the missing in this way. An enquiry list was put together each month, then sent to all searchers – who passed any information they could glean back to the office. In July 1916, they began searching for all the missing and not just for those whose friends or relatives had contacted the authorities. The War Office provided the unit with daily casualty lists, which gave information such as battalion and company, and date of casualty, which was not available on the published lists. When the War Office heard of a casualty, they automatically referred the family to the Red Cross. The unit always sent relatives waiting for news an individually written letter, rather than an impersonal form, so each family would feel that their enquiry really mattered.

In Britain alone they eventually had about 1,200 searchers. After the Armistice, they continued their work in the reception camps in Britain and France, where POWs being repatriated were initially sent. Another section checked the lists of prisoners received from Germany through the Frankfurt Red Cross.

The office in Malta handled 4,500 enquiries and provided photographs of the graves of the men who had died in hospital and who were buried in Malta. The Egypt and Palestine office was extremely busy, while staff in Salonika had a particularly challenging job as the hospitals were scattered over a wide area and communications in the area were poor.

6

In Every Village and Town

In just two months after fighting started about 500,000 men rushed to volunteer to fight. Many women had an equally strong urge to do something for their country. Given the limitations that society imposed on them, many felt they had just three options; they could nurse, knit or organise. Mrs C. S. Peel, writing in 1926 with the value of hindsight, described how 'masses of rather inarticulate people quickly got together and committees seemed to exude from the mass and to coagulate more or less at random.'

Some women had already begun to play a significant role in local government and they and their colleagues turned their colossal energies and skills to running any number of charitable committees. In the early years of the war the titular heads of most aid committees, the chairman and treasurer, were still men. The bulk of the committee members and those doing the most were generally women. As the war progressed and conscription bit, some women even rose to chair charitable committees. A few chairmen of committees dealing with comforts or Belgian refugees had the grace to admit that, while the committee as a whole made decisions, the work was done by the women. By 1918 what they had done for Britain and her Allies was incalculable.

Before the war, pipes were more common than cigarettes, which were a luxury. Women smokers were considered distinctly fast, and many only smoked in private. By the end of the war, smoking was widespread among all classes and had been taken up by tens of thousands of women, who had more freedom and money than they had ever had before. It had become almost universally acceptable. Women's reasons for smoking were much the same as men's. Troops on leave or recovering from wounds in Britain generally smoked and this encouraged civilians to copy them. People at home were also eager to take advantage of smoking's reputation for easing stress and by the end of the war, tobacco had gone from being a luxury to being a necessity.

Doctors and scientists were already aware that smoking could be harmful and yet during the war it was encouraged to the point that cigarettes and tobacco were included in every serviceman's rations. By September 1914, each soldier in France and Belgium was issued with two ounces of tobacco a week. Tons of Britain's favourite Virginia tobacco were shipped to France so that French factories could make cigarettes for British troops.

Sir Thomas Fraser was among those who were uneasy about such widespread distribution of tobacco and tobacco products. He wrote a letter to *The Times* in October 1916 in which he said that medical people were well aware that excessive smoking was dangerous, damaging the nervous and digestive systems, heart and blood vessels. He was also worried about young men who had joined up as non-smokers but who had become habituated due to the free distribution paid for by tobacco funds. He felt that tobacco should be limited or rationed.

The impact the war had on smoking is graphically illustrated by the fact that within a year the cigarette trade had doubled, thanks to exports to the front. Although pipes remained widespread, cigarettes increased in popularity due to the fact that no paraphernalia was needed beyond cigarettes and a light. There was nothing else to get lost during a battle or during the endless marches from one place to another. Matches were a problem, as most people used ordinary ones rather than the more expensive safety matches, and they were ignited by friction against any hard object. The Postmaster General had to issue strict instructions on packaging and posting after several fires were caused by matches in parcels accidentally igniting. Soldiers often kept their cigarettes or tobacco in a watertight tin and Players received a number of letters from men claiming that their lives had been saved when damage from a bullet or a piece of shrapnel had been mitigated when it struck the tobacco tin.

When the German blockade had a serious impact on imports, some people questioned whether tobacco should be rationed to allow priority to be given to importing food. Wills and Imperial Tobacco persuaded the Government that rationing tobacco would be a bad idea and Wills argued that it would be bad for the economy because, if people could not smoke, they ate more. Pragmatically, Bonar Law also pointed out to Parliament that the income from tobacco taxes was important to the Exchequer.

The importance of cigarettes was illustrated by the work of the famous Army chaplain, Geoffrey Studdert Kennedy, better known as Woodbine Willie. He was a heavy smoker, although he was asthmatic, and when he was based at Rouen he used to walk along the troop trains handing out

Bibles and packets of Woodbines to the soldiers. He believed it was his job to stay close to the soldiers at the front, even setting up his 'vicarage' in a trench. He was never without a supply of cigarettes and used them as a way of breaking the ice and getting groups of men chatting both to each other and to him. He described his job as having a box of fags in his haversack and a great deal of love in his heart. When he died in 1929, ex-servicemen sent a wreath to his funeral with a packet of Woodbines at the centre.

Many makers cashed in on the opportunity for some good publicity by donating large numbers of cigarettes to troops. By August 1915, Bernard Barron, owner of the Carreras Tobacco Company, had donated 3,000,000 Black Cat cigarettes to soldiers at the front. Godfrey Phillips Ltd donated 2,500,000 cigarettes to the British Expeditionary Force and 50,000 to men on ambulance trains in Southampton. In 1918 tobacco consumption in Britain reached 56,800,000 lbs a year.

Tobacco rations notwithstanding, it was no time at all before servicemen were writing home asking to be sent additional 'smokes'. The Reverend Leighton Green, from Norfolk, was an Army chaplain who began or ended almost every letter home with a plea for cigarettes to give to the men he worked among. Families were keen to help and before long cigarette and tobacco funds had been started in thousands of towns, villages and pubs. On the smallest scale, individual men and women bought whatever cigarettes they could afford and went to their local station to hand them out to the sick and wounded arriving on ambulance trains. Liverpool-born Sydney Bond remembered his father taking him to local hospitals for the wounded and walking along tossing packets of five Woodbines to the patients. Servicemen's letters are a testimony to how much their extra 'smokes' meant to them.

Many national and local newspapers ran their own appeals for raising money to provide cigarettes and tobacco to troops and to sick and wounded servicemen. In October 1914, *The Times* reported it had set up a Smokes for Soldiers and Sailors Fund. Lord Kitchener had asked them to set up the fund to provide wounded servicemen with cigarettes and tobacco and it sent supplies to more than 200 hospitals and convalescent homes. On a smaller scale, the *Fishing Gazette* also set up a tobacco fund for wounded soldiers and sailors. The *Weekly Despatch* and the *Bexley Heath Observer* were among the newspapers that used cartoon cards to raise money. In December 1918, Glasgow held a Tobacco Day that raised £1,700 and attracted the donation of masses of cigarettes and tobacco.

Thomas Clark was a tobacconist in Wadhurst in Sussex who, like many other shopkeepers up and down the country, appealed for people to provide cigarettes for the troops by putting money in the donation box in his shop. He started his appeal in October 1914 and by December he was able to send 700 cigarettes a week to members of the Royal Sussex Regiment. By the end of the war he believed he had sent nearly 39,000 cigarettes. He may have also had an eye on the effect this fund raising would have on his own profits.

The theatrical world also tried to help and the *Performer* announced that its tobacco fund, registered under the War Charities Act was supported by nearly all the leading artistes. Many of the performers raised money by selling signed photographs of themselves.

Alongside, and sometimes linked to, the tobacco funds were endless comforts funds. These were set up to provide what we would consider necessities, as well as little luxuries, for the troops. There were funds to support the men from one village or town and funds linked to an ever-widening range of organisations such as the Wounded Pawnbrokers and Assistants' Fund, the Patriotic Fund for the Employees of Higgs & Hill Ltd, the Comfort Fund of the Society of Authors, Playwrights and Composers, the Great Western Railway Salaried Staff Special Assistance Fund, and the Herbert Road Traders' Association Fund in Plumstead, London. Many firms, such as the Nova Scotia and Oozebooth Mills in Blackburn and the British Quilting Company's Female Pierrot Troupe (military hospitals) charity in Rawtenstall set up funds that were supported by their employees.

The Cadbury family were Quakers but in spite of their own pacifism, believed that each of their employees had to act according to their own conscience. About 2,000 of their employees joined up and about ten per cent of those were killed. The firm did well from the war as the Government ordered huge quantities of Bourneville Cocoa and bars of Cadbury's Dairy Milk Chocolate for the troops. Cadbury's used some of these profits to send 20,000 gallons of milk a week to poorer families in Birmingham and supplemented the government allowance for the families of employees in the services to two-thirds of the married men's peacetime salaries and a third of that for unmarried men. Cadbury's paid the pension contributions for the men who had joined up, kept their jobs open for them for as long as the war lasted, made grants to the widows of men who were killed and the wives of men who were disabled, and worked to find suitable jobs for men who returned injured or helped them with retraining. The firm arranged for thousands of comfort parcels to be sent to their staff serving overseas and sent each of them a 1 lb bar of chocolate twice a year. The firm's education department sent out thousands of books, including many to help the men learn to converse in French. Female employees were encouraged to keep in touch with their workmates in the forces and to send additional parcels. Knitted goods were always wrapped around a small bar of chocolate. The women were also encouraged to do first aid courses and some then left to work in local military hospitals. The Cadbury family also allowed several of their properties to be used as auxiliary hospitals and convalescent homes.

Many funds included the word Tommy or Tommies in their title, using this affectionate nickname for the ordinary soldier, to encourage a wish to provide care and comforts for them. The *High Peak News* published a report about the local Tuck for Tommies Fund, announcing that donations of 4s would provide 'sufficient delicacies for ten fighting men'. The delicacies included sardines, Oxford sausages, potted meat, Nestlé's nut milk chocolate, and a pot of 'Campaigning Bovril'.

Some individuals set about providing as many comforts parcels as they could, often taking great care over the selection of the contents. In 1915 the Reverend Clark recorded in his diary that Mrs Vickers of Waltham House, Great Waltham in Essex, had sent a lot of parcels to troops at the front. She clearly thought long and hard about what she sent as each parcel contained socks, a tablet of soap, a tin of Vaseline, a small tin of Keating's insecticide powder, two bars of chocolate crushed into a tin, boot laces, a handkerchief, an indelible pencil, and writing paper. Cards from men who received the parcels showed that the insecticide was particularly popular. Some parcels also contained a small testament.

Mrs A. Volk of Brighton set up a depot in her drawing room for producing comforts for soldiers just four days after the war started. Much of what she and her helpers made and collected was for sick and wounded men in hospitals and convalescent homes. However, they could also boast that no appeal was ever refused. This attitude resulted in the despatch of some seemingly unlikely items such as two lounge chairs as well as musical instruments, cigarette lighters and footballs.

In April 1915, the rector of Newdigate in Surrey got a letter from his son Wilfrid, who was serving as a lieutenant in France. He mentioned how the contents of comforts parcels were often shared among a group of comrades and described sharing the sumptuous parcels that a Captain Drummond got from home every week. Wilfrid asked his family to send him a list of items including khaki handkerchiefs, a military notebook with attached pencil, and some Log Cabin tobacco. He added that chocolate was essential.

The busy Post Office allowed comforts to be sent by letter post rather than the more expensive parcel post.

It is probable that after the image of VADs comforting troops, the next most common picture of volunteers during the war would be of the much maligned knitters and their creations. Most authors who write about civilians during the war do little more than quote Captain John Liddell of the Argyll and Sutherland Highlanders. He wrote to his family in November 1914 that although the people who sent parcels of knitwear meant well, they clogged up the mail service with their huge bales and stopped anything else getting through. He said that the government parcels were preferred by the men as they contained 'top hole' garments and that some of the privately sent items were shoddy and very thin. His greatest condemnation was reserved for what he described as 'the atrocity known as the heelless sock.' This ignores what it meant to people who used knitting as a way of expressing their support. Writing after the war, Mrs C. S. Peel expressed her belief that it was soothing to knit and comforting to feel useful. It also ignores the fact that many of the servicemen got through a pair of socks a week and that the captain could no doubt afford to buy better socks than many of the men serving under him. The books that quote him ignore the fact that the Government later thought it worth channelling all this energy and issued approved patterns, which were followed by vast numbers of people. These writers also ignore the volume of surviving letters that express appreciation of the knitted goods they were sent. The men liked to feel that someone at home was thinking of them and some developed a correspondence with the knitters who had tucked a slip of paper with a short message and their name and address into the knitted goods they sent out. Gunner A. Hemsley wrote to Reverend and Mrs Leslie Stevenson in Wadhurst in the autumn of 1915 to say that the socks he had been sent were a great blessing as the main trouble was cold, wet feet.

The urge to knit, and the need for the finished products, swept aside conventions and knitting came out into the open. Men, women, and children knitted on trains, in concerts and wherever they got together. Lady Semphill urged women in Aberdeenshire to knit in church during the sermon. Emily Galbraith's father was a church minister and, soon after the war started, they toured Scotland together. She remarked how many people had started to knit for the war effort. When they were staying near Loch Fyne, a group of women, busily knitting, asked her father if it was acceptable to knit socks for soldiers on Sundays. They were delighted and relieved to get his approval for their efforts.

Many funds were linked to particular regiments. Lord Roberts set up a fund for Indian Troops and it was supported by the family of Sir David Stewart of Banchory. They often wrote to the papers appealing for funds. However, Lady Stewart appears to have all found the sorting, packing, and posting a bit much. She tried to close the fund but felt she had to keep it open when the Commander of the Indian Expeditionary Force in France wrote to her pleading for more socks. She did close the fund in July 1915, by which time she had despatched more than 1,000 pairs of cuffs, mitts, and gloves, nearly 1,700 pairs of socks, more than 600 mufflers and many other knitted items.

Official recognition for the importance of knitting came in November 1917 when the DGVO, Sir Edward Ward appealed to the women of

Britain to knit 1,000,000 items of all kinds to be sent to British troops that Christmas. Ward's staff issued standard patterns, identified specific needs and directed the workers accordingly. A letter was placed in the *Daily Telegraph* to say that Ward would be setting up a central organisation to deal with knitted comforts and that before it was up and running, knitters should concentrate on mufflers, in drab shades, in fleeced wool, 58 by 10 inches; and fingerless mittens with short thumbs, in drab shades, 8 inches from wrist to knuckle. Ward asked for them to be sent to Army depots in York, Stirling, Chester, Weedon, London, Southampton, and Dublin. The letter writer praised all that the many patriotic women had achieved through their knitting but said that central organisation was needed to maximise the utility of offerings through standardisation and commented that there had been a great waste of time and energy.

Volunteer organisations involved in making all kinds of items for the war effort seem to have counted their output compulsively from the outset. We therefore know the girls at the National School and Aske's School in Deptford made 4,000 pairs of mittens and that two ladies in Kilbarron in Ireland each knitted a pair of socks every week for the duration of the war, buying their wool from the War Office to save money. After the end of the war it was estimated that more than 1,000,000 women had knitted in excess of 15,500,000 garments. We should not forget that knitting was not exclusive to women and that the shepherd in his seventies who lived in the Lammermuir Hills steadily knitting socks while looking after his sheep was certainly not the only man to make his contribution through knitting. Girl Guides could earn merit badges for their knitting.

Various war hospital supply depots set up groups of women who repaired clothing for sick and wounded servicemen. The members of the Aberdeen Ladies Needlework Guild were active in many ways and recorded that they repaired 44,623 articles of clothing during the war. Sir Edward Ward also asked some depots to concentrate on making clothes, in particular underclothes, for women and children in the devastated areas of France. The Red Cross distributed these clothes.

Mr John Penoyre was not a knitter but realised that the vast number of men who joined up in late 1914 were short of uniforms. He worked in a barrister's chambers in the Inner Temple in London and set up Mr John Penoyre's Sweater Association. His aim was to collect boating and cricket sweaters and dye them khaki as substitute uniform for early recruits. This scheme was unexpectedly popular and about 18,000 sweaters were collected and distributed to commanding officers who had written directly to him. He also appealed for ladies' golf coats, long or short but not in small sizes. He placed appeal letters in various newspapers and sent a politely worded postcard of thanks to each donor.

To Mr Penoyre's surprise, his project was still in demand in 1916 and his Sweater Association was duly registered under the War Charities Act. In March 1918, the DGVO asked him to add indoor and outdoor games to the list of objects he collected and despatched.

For five years the Vegetable Products Committee for Naval Supply worked to gather fruit and vegetables, jams and preserves for distribution, without charge. Before the involvement of the committee, the only vegetables the men got were potatoes. The committee wanted to help keep the men as healthy as possible. The scheme had the support of the Admiralty and the War Office and although its original aim was to help the Navy, they also helped supply hospitals, camps, and depots. There were 845 branches throughout Britain, including a number in Ireland. Between them, they collected more than 45,000,000 tons of fruit and vegetables, excluding potatoes. It has been estimated that a further 5,000,000 tons were sent directly to naval depots rather than through the Central Committee. A value of £1,250,000 has been put on the committee's work and this was, therefore, money that the government did not need to find.

Local committees were to encourage local producers to grow more and to persuade people to send produce on a regular basis. The centres in Glasgow and Chelmsford were especially successful. The railways provided free carriage for each consignment. Members of the Women's Institute in Chelmsford, Haywards Heath and elsewhere collected the vegetables that were unsold at the end of their regular markets and sent them off to the Navy.

The first Wolverton Troop of Boy Scouts toured the local allotments in January 1918 and filled two handcarts with the vegetables they were given. These were taken to the local hospital. However, some local people were clearly worried that patients were being over-indulged and the medical officer, Dr H. Wickham, felt he had to write an open letter to the local papers emphasising the care the local quartermaster took to ensure he never spent more than the official allowance on food and that the diet sheets were scrutinised on a monthly basis by the administrator in Oxford. He added that he could not believe that any local people would begrudge the sick and wounded the right food to help them recover.

Appeals for help sometimes fell on remarkably barren ground. When Lord Harris, Vice Lieutenant of Kent, was asked to encourage people to get involved with the committee's work he replied, from the comfort of the Carlton Club in London, that he sympathised with the objects of the scheme but did not feel justified in officially inviting the people of Kent to respond and it was obviously the duty of the naval and military authorities to provide the forces with all they needed. Neatly passing the buck, he added that he was certain that a direct appeal to farmers' associations from the committee would have more effect than one from him. He concluded by saying, in effect, that he was helping Belgian refugees and could not do any more.

Civilians were also mobilised to collect eggs and the National Egg Society provided 44,000,000 eggs to hospitals over four years. The National Egg Collection Fund for the Wounded was formed in 1915 and boasted Queen Alexandra as its patron. Its workers collected in excess of 20,000,000 eggs through a network of more than 200 collection points. Between these organisations, 10,000 eggs a day were sent out to base hospitals in France. Schools, Boy Scouts and Girl Guides were among the many groups who got involved. Perhaps the schemes were so successful because it was possible for individuals and small groups to make a tangible contribution. In Hampton, just to the west of London, local children were recruited by Mrs Isabel Anthony. In January 1916 she thanked the pupils of Hampton Grammar School and the St James' Church Lads' Brigade for their help in collecting 4,974 eggs and £26 in cash. The following year she used a letter to the *Surrey Comet* to suggest that donors should write a short, personal message on each egg they donated. Chrissie Squire, in Bridport in Dorset, donated hundreds of eggs and decorated them with tiny pictures or poems and her name and address. Members of the Kidderminster War Hospital Supply Depot collected more than 10,000 eggs. In Swindon, ranked eleventh in the country, they collected 161,000. Some villages in Sussex only collected about half a dozen eggs a week but that number was a real effort for them. Farmers were able to send the eggs, carriage free, to local depots or to the central depot in London. People who kept chickens were asked to donate one in ten of the eggs laid.

The eggs were sent to hospitals and convalescent homes treating sick and wounded servicemen. Most of the eggs will have gone straight to the institutions' kitchens. However, letters show that some men did get eggs with messages written on them and that this personal contact mattered. In the middle of the war it was estimated that 200,000 eggs a week were needed to feed sick and wounded men in this country.

As with the Vegetable Products Committee, some appeals made by the National Egg Collection for Our Wounded were firmly rejected. The Essex vicar, Andrew Clark, recorded in his diary the arrival of further circulars from someone who, he concluded, might not know at which end a hen deposits an egg. He believed that it was pointless to try to rear poultry or pigs in the area, partly due to the price of animal feed and the shortage of labour. This was, luckily, a minority opinion.

An appeal for people to collect eggs or vegetables for the war effort was easy to understand. Other appeals were shrouded in secrecy, but were also well-supported. In the autumn of 1917 a government notice was sent to schools and Scout groups asking them to collect conkers, without their green husks. They were told that this was invaluable war work but not what the conkers were needed for. A bounty of 7s 6d (35.5p) per hundredweight was paid. This acted as such an effective incentive that there were not enough trains to transport all the conkers and many rotted in large piles outside railway stations. Volunteers, including schoolchildren, in Louth in Lincolnshire collected six tons. The headmaster of Willingdon School in East Sussex recorded in his log book that they had sent off three bushels of conkers that the children and local Scouts had collected. Back at the school the children had removed all the green husks before bagging the conkers and wheeling them off to the station on a handcart. Three thousand tons of conkers were delivered to the Synthetic Products Co. at Kings Lynn in Norfolk. Acetone was an essential component of cordite, used in making munitions. Before the war, acetone was largely imported from the USA, as it was made from large quantities of timber. In 1915, a technique was discovered for making acetone from grain and the Government set up works in Kings Lynn and Dorset but by 1917 the blockade was hitting food supplies and an alternative method of making acetone was needed. Conkers appeared to be the solution. Production only started in April 1917 and ended after three months, due to problems caused by the conkers foaming during fermentation. Many piles of conkers were simply left to rot.

Waste paper, tins, fruit stones and hard nut shells were also collected. In 1918 schools were asked to let children have time off to collect fruit stones and hard nut shells to be made into charcoal to go in gas masks for men facing mustard gas. It was important that as much jam as possible was made, to preserve fruit, and the volunteers of the West Kent Agricultural Committee in Westerham were keen to do their part. They borrowed a building from the Territorial Force Association and installed gas, bought or borrowed large pans and other equipment and made 5,200 lbs of jam. They worked day after day in the baking kitchen. Unfortunately, there was a shortage of jam pots and the volunteers had to resort to using carton containers, which were then in common use. Sadly, when the weather turned damp, these containers were shown to be inadequate and much of the jam was wasted. The members of Wivelsfield Women's Institute collected 1,120 lbs of medicinal herbs and sent them to manufacturing chemists. It is a shame there are no pictures to show what this weight of herbs actually looked like. They also collected conkers, wool, blackberries, and paper.

Many individuals identified what they thought was a need for a particular kind of help and set about providing it without waiting for any official guidance or support. Lady Roberts, daughter of the late Field-Marshal, Lord Roberts, realised that the Army had grown so fast that it did not have enough field glasses for its officers and non-commissioned officers. She issued an appeal for the loan of field and stalking glasses that was so successful that she was soon despatching about 300 pairs a month. People who did not have field glasses to lend were invited to send cheques so that Lady Roberts could buy what was needed. The optimistic idea was that the glasses would be returned to their owners at the end of the war and was yet another illustration of how people thought that the war would be over in months rather than years. In a separate initiative, the Cambridge and Isle of Ely War Hospital Supply Depot collected fifty-two periscopes, sixteen telescopes, sixteen telescopic sights, and ten pairs of field glasses and sent them officers on active service.

Another example of ingenuity was the creation of the Glove Waistcoat Society. Based in London, the society had branches in Australia, New Zealand and the United States. Members collected old gloves, and even old leather furniture and sent the leather to London. In the London workshop, women who needed employment because of the war, salvaged the leather and made it into 55,000 windproof waistcoats, which were sold at a low price to make the workshop self-supporting. The society also collected fur coats, which were in great demand on minesweepers, and salvaged small pieces of fur, which they made into gloves.

Miss Gladys Storey, an actress in her twenties, wanted to do something more than knitting and sewing and, as the first winter of the war started, she determined to send the men something nourishing, practical and comforting. She managed to get official approval for her plans and set about raising money to send consignments of Bovril to troops on active service. She funded her work through selling signed photographs of the Boer War hero, Field Marshal Lord Roberts, at sixpence each. Her efforts were reported in various newspapers. In spite of rumours claiming that she was involved in a promotion scheme for the makers, she was not sponsored by them or by anyone. The makers did, however, donate some supplies of Bovril. She sent her first consignment to troops in France in December 1914 and later extended her work to soldiers in Salonika, Mesopotamia and Gallipoli and military hospitals in Mombassa. Letters of thanks soon poured in showing that she had been right in identifying something she could do that would bring comfort to troops. She managed to keep her administrative costs at a negligible level. In the Second World War she started another Bovril Fund.

Mabel Williams heard about the mud in France and decided that the troops at No. 1 Base in France must need oilskins and rubber boots. She launched an appeal and managed to send 700 pairs, which were warmly received. The commandant wrote urging her to sustain her efforts as they needed another 3,000 pairs. She renewed her appeal in January 1915.

Miss Hope-Clarke of Wimbledon was busy doing sewing for soldiers when she found a hole in her thimble. Looking through her sewing box, she found two more thimbles that had holes in them and it struck her that thousands of women, all over the country, must also have thimbles that were no longer fit for purpose. She decided to collect as many unwanted gold and silver thimbles and trinkets as possible so that she could sell them for their metal value and use the money to help the Forces. Her aim was to raise £400 to fund an ambulance. She launched the Silver Thimble Fund through a letter to *The Times* in July 1915. She had an immediate response and the first, hand-delivered parcel of trinkets was delivered to her home. Within a month she had raised enough to buy an ambulance. Interest in the fund soared and parcels poured in. Miss Hope-Clarke and her sister were joined by a group of volunteers including Lady Maud Wilbraham, who dealt with the money and accounts. Queen Alexandra agreed to become the fund's patron. Although Miss Hope-Clarke's house remained the headquarters from which the fund operated, around 160 collecting centres were set up in distant countries such as Australia, China, Canada, and South Africa as well as in nearby France. They made over thirty appeals, which brought in more than 60,000 thimbles. In one week in March 1916 they collected a ton of old bracelets and other items at Central Hall in Westminster. People were quick to send in objects such as wedding and engagement rings, which were far from unwanted. The most spectacular gift was a chest of silver that had been in a bank vault, untouched, for sixty years. The contents included a number of vessels as well as cigarette cases and some items that dated back to the Crimean War in the 1850s. The Silver Thimble Fund raised more than £60,000, which enabled it to pay for fifteen motor ambulances, five motor hospital launches, two motor dental surgery cars, and gave money to the Red Cross and servicemen's charities. The launches, one of which was called Wimbledon, were used in Mesopotamia where local men were serving in the East Surrey Regiment. Two of the ambulances were called Wimbledon and Merton. The Fund also gave money to the Star and Garter Home in Richmond, St Dunstan's, the Soldiers and Sailors Help Society, the Navy Employment Agency, the Seamen's Hospital in Greenwich, sponsored beds in the Sops Hill and Nelson hospitals in Wimbledon and helped other war hospitals. At the time of the Armistice they were trying to raise funds to provide a complete radiological outfit. At the request of the War Office, they then stopped work.

The Tibbett sisters from Southampton were both VADs. One worked for the Red Cross and the other for St John. Early in the war, they created a role for themselves and kept to it for the duration. They started handing out cigarettes and chocolates to wounded Belgian soldiers who were arriving at the port. Soon afterwards, they heard that a ship loaded with British wounded would soon be docking and asked the military authorities for permission to hand out comforts to the men as they disembarked. Permission was granted and from then on, they met virtually every hospital ship that arrived and were the only women allowed on the berth. The sisters devised a special pouch, which they wore filled with postcards, pencils, notepaper, matches, boxes of cigarettes and chocolate, which they distributed as they went to every soldier who arrived. For a while, they and their friends covered the entire cost of this work themselves but a fund was later set up in Southampton to provide the plain chocolate and cigarettes. A few critics questioned both the Tibbetts' motivation and their effectiveness. They were accused of thrill-seeking, by wanting contact with the soldiers, at the expense of doing worthwhile work thoroughly. The authorities must surely have felt that their efforts were valuable or their permission to enter the dock area would have been withdrawn. One critic was Lieutenant Colonel T. H. Clayton-Nunn, who complained in his diary about the women who boarded his hospital train in Southampton. His acerbic account described, scathingly how 'the two elderly ladies in short tweed dresses and thinking themselves young and comely were giving out chocolate and cigarettes to the officers and men...' When one woman asked him if he was glad to be back in England he retorted that he was not. It is tempting to suggest that his attitude was, at least in part, the result of pain and exhaustion.

It is clear that soldiers, in particular, quickly developed a belief that if they appealed for a particular item, civilians at home would move mountains to provide it. This extended into areas that might traditionally have been thought the responsibility of the authorities. It is interesting that the military authorities apparently realised they should simply accept, with tacit gratitude, what was being provided. It was natural for friends and relatives to provide comforts and tobacco but the assumption might easily have been made that adequate numbers of sandbags would be provided by the authorities. The scope and nature of the war made this impossible and civilian help was welcomed, although never officially solicited.

After Margaret Tyler got a letter from her brother, in France, telling her that sandbags were desperately needed, she wrote to her local paper, the *Hampstead and Highgate Express*. Her letter asked the editor to 'tell the women of England that they can themselves make defences for their loved ones at the Front. What they are asking for is a million sandbags, empty of course'. As it was then mild at the Front, her brother had said that they did not need any more mufflers or caps and wanted all the people who had so kindly knitted comforts to turn their energies to sewing sandbags. He gave some figures that illustrated just how many sandbags were needed. A 'nice commodious house for a few officers in their gun position' needed 2,000 sandbags. Tens of thousands were needed to protect a single battery and he estimated that a mile of trenches could need 100,000. He added that when the troops moved on they did not have time to empty the sandbags and take them with them so always needed a supply of fresh ones. He said that they should be about 3 foot by 2 foot and made of coarse linen or canvas. He added that the normal colour was white.

A lot of people began to send sandbags to Margaret Tyler's Hampstead home. She sent out instructions for how to make a good sandbag in the official size of 33 by 14 inches. She instructed that the seams should be oversewn and not made with chain stitch. She also said that they should have wide turnings and strong seams as sandbags get thrown about a lot. She was soon sending off about 4,000 sandbags a day.

Gunner A. Hemsley, from Wadhurst in East Sussex, wrote to the Reverend and Mrs Leslie Stevenson, recounting the delight their recent parcel had given him (he had been able to put a clean shirt on for the first time in seven weeks). He asked them to keep on making sandbags, saying they could never have too many. He wrote that a few layers of sandbags over their heads gave them an unbelievable feeling of safety. One Infantry lieutenant wrote that his division alone used about 1,000,000 a month. He said that sandbags saved many lives and that his battalions needed about 2,000 a day for their present trenches.

The need was so great that wounded soldiers in some hospitals switched from embroidery to sewing sandbags. Postal orders and cash came in from people who were not in a position to sew sandbags themselves but wanted to help in the way they could. A group of women in Newdigate contributed 1,700 sandbags and issued a prize to the woman who made the most. The winner was seventy-six year old Mrs Elsey, who made 161 sandbags.

Men on active service, recovering from wounds or illness or languishing in Prisoner of War or internment camps, needed anything that would help counter boredom and distract them from their present situation. Many books were sent by friends and relatives and within a year of the start of the war, the Red Cross and St John Ambulance War Library had started collecting books and periodicals, the YMCA operated lending libraries in many of its huts and the Fleet Library was sending books to sailors. Mary Chomley set up an informal book scheme for Australian prisoners, working from the London offices of the Red Cross and she got much of her stock from a cousin who ran a book shop.

There were a few even larger scale initiatives, which included the Camps Library, the Fighting Forces Book Council, and the Prisoners of War Book Scheme (Educational). The Fighting Forces Book Council had official approval and worked closely with the Society of Authors, the Publishers' Association, and the Home Reading Union. Sir Edward Ward, later the DGVO, and writer Dame Edith Anstruther, set up the Camps Library in October 1914, after Lord Kitchener asked Ward to see what could be done to improve the welfare of Imperial troops in London. They rented a building in central London and recruited a team of volunteers. As with many other charities, it was launched through an appeal in the press. Within twenty-four hours, large quantities of books had started to arrive. The road outside the headquarters was repeatedly blocked by horse-drawn cabs and carriages dropping off parcels. Every nook and cranny in the building was soon stacked with piles of boxes of books waiting to be unpacked and sorted. Soon they were receiving 75,000 books a week. Prominent supporters included Kipling, George Meredith, Conan Doyle, Marie Corelli, and John Galsworthy.

When members of the British Army heard what was being done for Canadian, Australian and New Zealand troops, they asked for the same support. This expansion of their work meant that the Camps Library had to move into larger premises, lent by the Belgian Army in London.

The Camps Library got strong support from senior Army commanders. After Douglas Haig became Commander-in-Chief, he wrote about his belief that people who had not visited the Armies overseas could not understand how much books meant to men in the trenches, in billets and in hospitals. He encouraged people in Britain to buy books, enjoy reading them, and then donate them to the Camps Library, adding that any movement that encouraged reading had his full support.

For the first two years of the war, they were able to pack the books into wooden boxes that were donated in large numbers by wine merchants, typewriter merchants, and shops of all kinds. However, supplies of wood later dried up and boxes were in short supply. Donations eventually dwindled, in spite of fresh appeals in the press and in the windows of large shops. Each package of books that was sent out included a card asking the recipient to send it to their friends or relatives to persuade them to send donations. One issue faced by the Camps Library was that people were finding it difficult to pay for the postage on the bulky parcels of books they were donating. After seeing the problem for himself, the Postmaster General came up with the idea of using post offices as local depots where people could drop off books, which would then be transported to the Camps Library offices free of charge. Freight costs were also a problem for the Prisoners of War Help Committee, which found itself owing American Express more than £2,500 in early 1916. Carter Patterson carried books from the organisation's headquarters to the stations without charge for months but when the volume of packages increased significantly, Her Majesty's Stationery Office (HMSO) took over.

The Queen supported the Camps Library by sending a donation each year. Books were donated in many languages, such as Japanese and Gaelic, as well as English. Most were in good condition but some were in such a state or so inappropriate that they were only suitable for salvage. Among the more bizarre donations were a book on how to cut a stylish woman's blouse, one on how to organise a mothers' meeting and an antiquated list of members of a club. Books of old sermons were regularly donated but hard to place. Personal papers, such as a draft will or a passionate plea from Edwin to Angelina, were inadvertently left between the pages of books, without any way the sender could be identified and the papers returned. Some donors enclosed touching messages to the recipients.

Most donations were fiction and among the most popular items were vast numbers of cheap mass-produced editions that fitted easily into a uniform pocket. Travel and adventure books were also popular as were books on old wars, poetry, history, geography, agriculture, science, and gardening. Four boxes of books were sent to each unit every few weeks and smaller parcels were sent to Army chaplains. With the Armistice, donations plummeted and the War Office had to step in with a financial donation to enable organisations to continue providing books to men waiting for demobilisation and to members of the Army of Occupation. By the time it closed in March 1919, the Camps Library had collected and distributed 16,500,000 books and periodicals to soldiers and POWs.

The British Prisoners of War Book Scheme (Educational) was set up with a slightly different target than the Camps Library. Its founder, Alfred T. Davies's initial aim was to create a library for civilians interned in Ruhleben near Berlin. It was later expanded to include all British POWs. Prisoners' requests for books were varied and although most were for fiction, a former miner asked for books on coal mining, a man who had been a cooper for the herring fisheries wanted books about barrel-making and others wanted books to let them continue their pre-war degree studies. Davies and his team wanted to encourage POWs to use the opportunity to improve their knowledge and education while also trying to distract themselves from their immediate situation. They kept a card index showing what sort of reading material each man had requested and what he had been sent. This prevented duplication and also helped them build up a picture of each man's reading tastes and educational ambitions.

Lady Alice Taylour donated most of the money that got this fund started. The vast majority of books were donated but members of the public also donated money, to help the fund buy stock. The fund was registered under the War Charities Act in 1916 and was provided with rent-free accommodation in London by Davies's employer, the Board of Education.

In 1918 the Danish Red Cross offered to help the British Prisoners of War Book Scheme by setting up a book depot in Berlin to provide books for British POWs. They had already received many requests for books from camp Help Committees, including one from a camp holding 1,200 men where they did not have a single book. Ordering books from Britain took a long time but the Danes had been able to buy 500 light literature books from Bernard Tauchnitz in Leipzig and get them to the camp within a week. They wanted to formalise this arrangement using British funding. Officials in London were concerned that Tauchnitz might use such a scheme to make a profit, palming off unsold German books to the detriment of British authors. Staff at the Prisoners of War Book Scheme resented the idea that the Danes might encroach into their territory, claiming that they knew better than the Danes which books the POWs might want, spectacularly ignoring the problems in the existing system.

It would be a mistake to think that books reached POWs smoothly. They were always censored and the Germen authorities sometimes took months to distribute them. Books or authors were banned on the whim of a particular commandant. Some were also damaged maliciously, covers being ripped off or specific pages being removed.

Under the terms of the Prisoners of War Book Scheme, books were due to be returned at the end of the war. However, many prisoners wrote to the schemes' headquarters asking if they could keep the volumes they had been sent. It was impossible to refuse such requests, which were a testimony to the success of the scheme. Some of these treasured books have been passed down to successive generations as heirlooms.

The Fighting Forces Book Fund was set up in 1916 to help young men whose studies had been curtailed by the war and who wanted to use the long periods when nothing much was happening in their sector to further their reading.

Christmas is an emotional time of year. With the realisation that the war might not be over by December 1914, many people wanted to send parcels to servicemen to make their Christmas a little less bleak and to show them that their absence had left a gap in the celebrations at home. Naturally, countless families sent parcels to their loved ones overseas, but there were also numerous Christmas Parcel Funds to enable communities to express their, joint, concern. With each year that passed these funds multiplied and grew in size.

Different communities in Derbyshire set up funds to send Christmas parcels to their own men overseas. In Matlock Bath, one of the fundraising events was a whist drive and dance at the Pavilion. It was remarked that women outnumbered men at least three to one at the event and that the men were almost all ineligible for military service for one reason or another. The nearby village of Cromford raised money through children's concerts that included patriotic recitations and a tableau of Britannia and her Allies. They sent twenty-six tuck boxes to France, twelve to the Dardanelles, four to Serbia and forty-three to soldiers still in England. The boxes going overseas contained a pork pie, a cake, a pocket stove, a tin of café au lait, Oxo, chocolate, tobacco, and cigarettes. The men in this country received smaller parcels.

In preparation for Christmas in 1915, the Duke of Devonshire, as Lord Lieutenant, and the mayors of Derby, Chesterfield and Ilkeston set up a fund to enable them to send a parcel to each Derbyshire man on active service. Each parcel cost 5s 6d and contained food and other items such as Vaseline, candles and shaving soap. They were despatched in good time so they could reach all the men before Christmas.

The people of Newport Pagnell in Bedfordshire were enthusiastic and energetic fundraisers for a number of wartime causes. When they determined to send Christmas parcels to local men on active service in 1915, members of the local Pleasant Sunday Afternoon Brotherhood held a concert in the Electric Theatre. Musical performers included Miss Beatrice Walley of Crewe, winner of the Crewe and Chester Eisteddfod; Miss Bertha Richens, of Emberton; and the Reverend Father Walker. Charles Conyers combined jokes and singing with ventriloquism. Sadly, in spite of all this talent, the show only raised £3. Nothing deterred, the following year a Christmas Presents Committee was set up to raise £150 so that parcels could be sent to every man from the town then serving in the forces. The committee staged a wide range of events to support their aims. They did the same in 1917.

In the period leading up to Christmas in 1914, the Soldiers' and Sailors' Families Association (SSAFA) was told to expect a consignment of presents for children from the United States. Similar consignments had been sent to all belligerent countries. SSAFA was in a quandary, not sure whether to distribute the presents to the families with most children or to those that were in the greatest need. In some villages, the presents were given to families of serving men and in others, to widows and orphans. In Aylesford, a volunteer took time collecting the names of seventeen people who were suitable to receive a gift but in the end, only eight presents arrived.

The gifts were meant for children but it is clear that some of the parcels contained items better suited for adults, and some items that were not fit for donation at all. One lady wrote to SSAFA on 29 December 1914 to acknowledge receipt of a piece of netting, a towel, a tin of sanitary fluid, a bag of rice, a woman's undergarment, a pair of woman's shoes, 1 pair of stockings, an old, torn blouse, an old sash, three pieces of ribbon and a pinafore, which were apparently part of the gifts for children (her underlining) from the United States. A lady from Hopebourne received a parcel but did not know who it was for and wrote to SSAFA for guidance. Mrs Beauchamp from Hawkhurst wrote to say she had received gifts from the USA for distribution but was returning the gloves as they were both for the right hand and she could not possibly give them to anyone. She felt it would have been better to send nothing than to send two right-hand gloves. She returned them in the hope that someone might have been sent two left-hand gloves. One of the gloves is still in the Kent County Archives. Mrs Beauchamp felt that it had been a mistake to make such a fuss about the Santa Claus ship from America, as all the publicity had raised people's expectations far too high. A letter from Southfleet Rectory bemoaned the fact that the gifts they had been sent for distribution contained only second-hand clothing for women and nothing for children. The writer asked if they could be passed to Belgian refugees instead.

Some families were very happy with what they received. A number of recipients wrote to SSAFA bemoaning the fact that the parcels gave no indication of who the donors were, as they would have liked to write a letter of thanks. SSASFA admitted to being disappointed in both the quantity and quality of the gifts.

Local funds for alleviating distress were set up in most towns and villages, usually under the auspices of the local council. They concentrated on helping families whose main breadwinner had gone to fight, those who had been put out of work by the war, and widows and orphans. Women volunteers took a leading role in identifying who was in need of help and in distributing the aid from these funds.

Football clubs received numerous requests for help. They were asked to let their grounds be used for charity matches, sometimes with their players taking part, and to allow volunteers to sell flags or make collections for an ever-increasing range of charities. Everton Football Club selected the causes it supported carefully. In the first months of the war it made donations, from its own funds, to the local branch of the Prince of Wales' Relief Fund and sent ten guineas to Princess Mary's Sailors' and Soldiers' Christmas Fund. It also set up the Everton Football Club Army and Navy Footballs and Football Outfits Fund, which was later registered under the War Charities Act. It provided footballs and outfits to groups of men and to individuals but did turn down some requests. They seem to have been especially keen to support the Liverpool Prisoners of War Fund, the British Red Cross, the Liverpool Fund for

Blinded Soldiers, Sailors and Civilians and setting up club rooms for discharged soldiers and sailors.

The Dick Kerr factory in Preston originally made light railway equipment but, like many other factories, switched to munitions work and employed a large number of women. The managers felt the women needed a means of letting off steam and encouraged them to play football in their lunch breaks. The office manager, Alfred Frankland, watched the women play and asked the works manager if he could arrange a charity match between the women and another women's team. He optimistically hired Preston North End's Stadium for the match. On Christmas Day 1917, in front of a football-hungry crowd of 10,000, they beat the team from the Arundel Couthard Foundry 4-0. The match raised more than £600 for the local hospital. After this, women's teams proliferated and the Dick Kerr's Ladies' Team became famous. At every game they raised considerable sums for charity. After the end of the war, Alfred Frankland claimed that they had raised in excess of £50,000. The team continued to play after the war.

Family contacts were behind The Hampshire Football Association's decision to set up its own Wounded Soldiers Fund in October 1914 to send comforts to wounded soldiers in hospital in France. The fund was the brainchild of Mr W. Pickford, whose sister-in-law, Sister K. E. Flower had gone to France in August 1914 to nurse with Queen Alexandra's Imperial Military Nursing Service Reserve. The fund initially sent parcels to her hospital but she later moved to a number of other hospitals, each of which they also supported. They sent off an average of six cases a week, each weighing 56 lbs. As well as food and cigarettes, they sent razor blades, games, magazines and books, gramophones with records, soap, hot water bottles and air cushions. It was registered as an official war charity in 1916.

The *Daily Chronicle* was one of several newspapers that appealed for footballs and other sporting equipment for men at the front. One of their appeals was seen by two young lads in Warrington who promptly donated their football. In periods when they were away from the front, soldiers could easily get bored and sport was a popular means of whiling away the time and keeping fit. The MCC sent cricket equipment to seventy-six military and naval units and to POWs.

The Officers' Families Fund made regular appeals for funds and their fundraising efforts were helped by having the Queen as patron. Their remit was to help officers' relatives who were 'in financial embarrassment' or other trouble. They also helped military widows. They prided themselves on sending help without complicated formalities or long delays. Having been lent a number of houses for various periods, they loaned them to military wives or widows and some allowed children too. The fund's organisers put hosts in touch with potential guests. They set up a clothing depot in Berkeley Square, collecting and distributing clothes for women and children. Queen Mary decided that some of the best clothes donated to her Needlework Guild should be passed on to this fund. There was a separate depot for men's clothing.

All the older regiments, and many of the newer ones, had organisations for supporting their troops and their families. Although the Machine Gun Corps Comforts Fund was only started quite late in the war, members raised more than £13,000. They passed £2,000 of this to the Machine Gun Corps POW Fund. Mesopotamia was reputed to have one of the worst climates in the world, with rapid changes from suffocating heat to torrential rain and freezing winds. Tropical diseases were common. The Mesopotamia Comforts Fund for British Troops was set up to provide comforts for the masses of Imperial troops who were sent there with very little preparation. The fund worked closely with Lady Chelmsford's Fund in India. Distribution depots were opened in Basra and later in Baghdad. They received a large number of requests for mosquito nets and khaki drill sunshades, which were made in some of the war hospital supply depots in Britain.

Members of the Rotherham and District Soldiers' Comforts Association concentrated on making knitted articles. Most of their working groups were attached to places of worship and, apart from the Roman Catholic Church, all denominations took part, as did the Women's Liberal Association, the Women's Suffrage Party, the Primrose League and the Brabazon Society. There were also various groups of home workers. Local soldiers on leave were always offered fresh clothes, good socks, a shirt, a muffler, and a knitted helmet to take back to the front.

The men of the Queen's Own Cameron Highlanders were supported by The Camerons' Comforts Fund, founded by photographer Andrew Paterson, who personally packed the comfort parcels, often working into the early hours. He also organised the Camerons' Fair, which raised more than £4,000 for the fund. In 1917 the *Highland News* published various letters of appreciation including one from Lieut. Colonel R. L. McCall, writing on behalf of his battalion. He wrote that the knitted gifts were particularly welcome as the cold weather had set in. Soon after this, another consignment was despatched, which included more than 3,000 pairs of socks and more than 1,300 mufflers as wells as shirts and other items.

Nowadays, it is widely recognised that royal involvement makes a significant difference to a charity's success. Royal involvement in charity was unusual before the First World War and it was King George V and Queen Mary's determination to support their people during the war that led various members of the Royal Family to get actively involved in charity work.

The Prince of Wales lost no time in setting up The Prince of Wales' Fund, later known as the National Relief Fund or the Prince of Wales' National Relief Fund, to help alleviate anxiety and distress caused by the war. There was some lack of clarity over who was to receive help but its main aim was to help the dependants of men on active service and people suffering from 'industrial distress.' The prince was the fund's treasurer. He launched an appeal through *The Times* and within a week, donations in excess of £1,000,000 had reached him at Buckingham Palace. The fund was supported by fundraising efforts all over the country and local papers published lists of donors and the size of their donations to encourage or shame other people to follow suit.

Members of the Society of Friends at Fritchely, near Crich wanted to support the fund. However, the Friends who wanted to work for the fund wrote a letter seeking reassurance that it was not run under military supervision and that relief work undertaken by the fund could in no way be seen as a substitute for military service. They simply wanted to help alleviate distress caused by the war. They noted that some of their members had already been criticised by local people for their refusal to help the Red Cross because they saw that it worked under military direction.

Acting in her role as President of SSAFA, the king's mother, Queen Alexandra, wasted no time in appealing to women to help support the families of soldiers and sailors who had been left without adequate means of support. SSAFA had branches all over the country and workers often collaborated with the Prince of Wales Relief Fund to avoid duplication of effort. SSAFA is still supporting servicemen's families.

Queen Mary's Needlework Guild (the guild) was established almost as soon as the war started. It had the ambitious and all-encompassing aim of alleviating 'all distress caused by the war'. In fact, the guild concentrated most of its efforts on making and distributing goods for hospitals and clothes and comforts for servicemen. By the Armistice there were 630 branches, with more than 1,000,000 members in Britain, The Hague, North America and countries all over the British Empire. Between them they produced 15,500,000 items with an estimated value of well in excess of £1,000,000.

The guild was based at St James's Palace, which was soon stacked with materials and finished items. One of the strengths of the organisation was its ability to respond quickly in an emergency. After the first gas attack at Ypres, in April 1915, members of the guild worked flat out in St James's Palace to make 3,000,000 eye pieces for gas masks out of cinema film.

Not all the volunteers were equally skilled at needlework but they were committed and enthusiastic.

The guild soon came into conflict with the National Union of Women Workers, who claimed that it was putting professional sewers and knitters out of work and exacerbating female unemployment in the textile trades. The palace was quick to respond to this criticism and stressed that they were making items that the Government was not getting from factories. It announced that its intention was to work in partnership with other organisations and not in opposition. Thereafter, they consulted representatives of working women to make sure that they did not impinge on their ability to earn a living.

When the war ended, the guild had considerable uncommitted funds. The Queen wanted there to be a lasting legacy to its work and decided that it should endow a maternity home for servicemen's wives. The maternity home opened in 1919, in a house in Hampstead, London, lent by Lord Leverhulme as a temporary base. The foundation stone for a permanent home, on land provided by Lord Leverhulme, was laid in October 1921.

Queen Alexandra's Field Force Fund was approved by the War Office. This meant that when commanding officers sent the fund a request for particular items, they could be sent out free of charge. The system avoided waste and also ensured that men got the things they needed most. It also ensured parcels were not set to battalions whose members were already well-supplied by their friends and relatives.

The fund quickly took over a bonded warehouse in London so that they could get dutiable articles, such as tobacco, tax-free. This must have been an enormous saving as they sent 5,000,000 cigarettes to troops, as well as 1,600 tons of other comforts. The contents of their parcels varied over time. To begin with, when many of the men were short of basic items, they sent vests, pants, socks, shorts, pipes, and tobacco. Once they were assured that men had the basic clothing and needed different items, a parcel would contain a handkerchief, a toothbrush, a towel, soap, toilet paper in a wallet, a packet of sweets, boot laces, stationery in a wallet, a pencil, a candle, socks, and matches. Volunteers wrapped the parcels carefully, first in brown paper, then in waterproof paper and then in bales, before they were sent to men in all areas of fighting. After the Armistice, they continued to send parcels to the Army of Occupation and to troops in Russia and the East. The fund's administrators were aware that they had not done much to help Indian troops during the war. In 1919 they decided to present each of the 500,000 serving Indians with a gift. Indian troops in Mesopotamia were excluded from this as they apparently got support from India.

Each gift was accompanied by a personal message from Queen Alexandra in Urdu and Hindi.

Princess Mary's Gift Fund was started in October 1914. The princess wanted to send a Christmas present to every man serving in the forces, tailored to meet their particular religious needs and designed to provide something of lasting use. Nurses were included as beneficiaries of this scheme. Princess Mary also wanted to help workers in trades that were suffering because of the war and originally planned to fund everything out of her own allowance, but this was not practical, so she lent her name to a public appeal. The fund's committee was stuffed full of the great and good, including the Prime Minister Winston Churchill, Lord Kitchener, Earl Roberts, High Commissioners from various colonies and a member of the Rothschild banking family. Committee meetings were held at the Ritz in London.

Each recipient got a brass box, embossed with a picture of Princess Mary and holding an ounce of tobacco, twenty cigarettes, a pipe, tinder, a lighter, a Christmas card, and a photo of the Princess. Non-smokers received the brass box, a pack of acid tablets, a khaki writing case holding a pencil, paper and envelopes, a Christmas card and a photograph of the Princess. The Ghurkhas got the same as British soldiers, the Sikhs got a box filled with sweets and a card and all the other Indian troops got the box with sweets and a packet of cigarettes with a tin box of spices and a card. The original gift was considered unsuitable for nurses in France so they were given the box, a bar of chocolate, and a card.

Fundraising went well. The gifts were meant to be ready for Christmas 1914 but the sheer quantity and a shortage a suitable brass for the boxes meant that production and distribution took much longer. Brass was also needed for shell cases. A large quantity was being imported from the USA on the Lusitania when it was sunk in May 1915. Supplies of some of the contents ran into difficulties and the committee quickly bought a range of substitute gifts; bullet pencil cases, tobacco pouches, shaving brushes, combs, packets of postcards, knives, scissors, cigarette cases, and purses. The sailors, who should have had the lighter in theirs, instead got a bullet pencil in a silver cartridge case decorated with Princess Mary's monogram. The delays meant that in many boxes the Christmas card had to be replaced by a New Year's card. Distribution was later widened to those who felt left out, including POWs and the next of kin of men who were killed in 1914. There were eventually 2,500,000 people entitled to receive this present from the princess. Some soldiers sent the boxes, unopened, to their families, others treasured the box and a surprising number still have their contents intact.

Most wives of British Army commanders were involved in voluntary work. Lady Smith-Dorrien, wife of the then commander of the 2nd Army made a unique and particularly valuable contribution. In April 1915, a nurse told her it was proving impossible to safeguard valuables belonging to sick and wounded men in casualty clearing stations and hospitals. Lady Smith-Dorrien contacted her husband to ask if a supply of closable bags might ease this problem. She got a response from the 2nd Army's Assistant Director of Medical Services, General Porter, asking for an immediate supply of 50,000 bags. Lady Smith-Dorrien must surely have been both gratified and a little daunted by this response. She appealed for help and set up a depot in her London house. They later needed larger premises for the work. Depots were also set up in Scotland, Bedford and eventually the USA as well, with a total of more than 12,000 people sewing the bags. At first they were made of unbleached calico but bright fabrics such as cretonne were later favoured as they made it easier to distinguish between the bags. The men nicknamed them Blighty Bags. Lady Smith-Dorrien accepted donations to help with expenses and to provide materials to workers who could not afford to pay for them themselves. To save money, she bought large quantities of fabric, and the tape on which the men's names could be written, wholesale, and then resold them cheaply to the workers. From the middle of 1916, the bags were distributed through the office of the DGVO with 40,000 a month being sent to medical stores depots and smaller numbers going straight to hospitals and casualty clearing stations. By the end of the war, almost 5,000,000 bags had been made and despatched to the forces.

Musical instruments were always in demand and requests poured into many of the organisations working to help soldiers. Mouth organs were the most popular as they could easily be slipped into a pocket. Larger instruments were more likely to get lost or damaged. However, men in several POW and internment camps asked for, and were given, enough instruments to start an orchestra. The Musical Instrument Collection was started by Madame Novello Davies and was based in London, with branches in various towns. Instruments were collected and forwarded to London where arrangements were made to send them to France, Italy, Salonika, Mesopotamia, Egypt, India, and to the Navy. Most of the instruments were sent in crates, with the DGVO arranging transport. At the request of Sir Douglas Haig, the fund provided instruments including banjos, violins, piccolos, zithers, castanets, tin whistles, and thousands of mouth organs, to various camps in France.

Many people were acutely aware of the dangers faced by various animals taken from their homes to serve overseas and a number of animal charities set out to supplement what the Army Veterinary Corps

(AVC) could achieve. At the start of the war, the Royal Society for the Prevention of Cruelty to Animals (RSPCA) offered its services to the military authorities. They also set up the new Fund for Sick and Wounded Horses with the aim of reducing animal suffering and providing swift and humane treatment to animals forced to serve in the war. The RSPCA was the only animal charity that was authorised by the Army Council and able to collect funds on behalf of British war horses. It was also the largest animal charity operating during the war. It was made an auxiliary of the AVC and in time, more than half of the RSPCA's Inspectors joined up, many of them serving with the AVC.

During the war, the RSPCA raised more than £250,000 and was able to provide four complete veterinary hospitals, each of which could take up to 2,000 horses and mules. The society also paid for stabling at other veterinary hospitals and forward treatment stations, twenty-eight motor ambulances and 180 horse-drawn ambulances. In addition, they provided logistical support to the AVC including three motorised lorries, fifty corn-crushing machines and tens of thousands of waterproof loincloths and rugs as well as 50,000 books on lameness and first aid. They worked in France, Italy, Mesopotamia, Salonika, and Egypt. Once gas attacks had started, they began paying for specialist veterinary equipment and isolation units for treating horses that had been burned or gassed.

Many stray dogs were befriended by soldiers and the RSPCA made a point of caring for them when the men moved on or died. They also set up kennels in Boulogne where dogs could be cared for when their masters were going home on leave. At the end of the war, they helped men get dogs they had adopted back to Britain. They set up the Soldiers' Dogs Fund to meet the costs of quarantine and care for the dogs until the men were demobbed and could take them home. *The Evening News* supported this fund. The RSPCA even built special kennels to house 500 of these dogs at Hackbridge in Surrey.

The Animal Defence and Anti-Vivisection Society set up the Purple Cross Service for Wounded and Sick Army Horses. Its managing committee positively bristled with earls, countesses, lords, and ladies. Their offer of help was rejected by the British authorities but accepted by the French. They worked to reduce the number of horses suffering by setting up base and field hospitals for them, and maintaining a team of qualified vets in the field. This society also provided horse ambulances, materials, and equipment. They were relieved when they got permission for a group of qualified men from the Purple Cross to go out and kill badly wounded horses left on the battlefield. They also looked for abandoned and disabled horses and helped people care for them. They wanted the Geneva Conventions to be adapted to give

Purple Cross staff the same level of protection that was enjoyed by Red Cross workers.

Our Dumb Friends League had been active during the Balkan War of 1912 and was re-launched as the Blue Cross Fund soon after the outbreak of the First World War. The president was Lady Smith-Dorrien. The fund worked in France, Belgium, Italy, and Britain and aimed to do for wounded animals at the front what the Red Cross did for men. They ran a number of hospitals for dogs 'irrespective of their nationality'. When they offered their support to the British Army, they received the usual response, that the military authorities did not need civilian help. The authorities had confidence in their own Veterinary Corps. The Blue Cross therefore turned to the French, who were keen to take them up on their offer of help. By the end of the war they had raised about £170,000.

While many people put energy into trying to help animals caught up in the conflict, various animals apparently felt the need to play their part in helping humans. Maud Field and her brother's fox terrier, Tom, founded the Cats and Dogs of the Empire Fund in July 1915, after she read an article in which the Kaiser was quoted as saying that Germany would fight to the last cat and dog. Maud wanted to encourage the cats and dogs of the Empire to play their part. Tom issued an appeal asking every cat and dog to donate sixpence. In just four months they collected £1,000, which was used to provide a YMCA Soldiers' Hut at the Front. The hut was large and well-equipped. Each animal that donated £5 could have his picture hung on the hut wall and the dogs also provided two gramophones. Maud Field assembled an album of photos of the animal subscribers, which was sent out to the hut to amuse the soldiers using it. After Tom's master died, while he was a POW in Wittenburg, Tom began raising money to help POWs in Germany. Subscribers included guinea pigs, a chicken called Solomon, a 30-year-old cockatoo, a cat, a spider, sixteen horses, a 'school of teddy bears' and a naturalised dachshund. A writer in the *Daily Chronicle* said it was in some ways the most remarkable of the funds that had been set up since the war started.

By the middle of 1915 the British Forces Post Office was handling up to 70,000 parcels a day through Le Havre and there were six trains and four boats dedicated to transporting them. There was also a temporary sorting office in Regents Park. In the week before Christmas 1915 they handled between 300,000 and 400,000 parcels a day. By 1917 it was normal for them to be handling 300,000 parcels a day. The Postmaster General was urged to reduce the cost of postage but refused, as he realised that if he had given in the volume of post would have increased until they were no longer able to cope. Some individuals got large numbers of parcels. The Royal Fusiliers were nicknamed 'The Chocolate Soldiers' because they got so many parcels from home containing luxury items such as foie gras, plover's eggs, game and champagne. Siegfried Sassoon's aunt sent him a box of kippers, and some Devon creams twice a month. Fortnum & Mason's and the Army & Navy Stores in London sent hundreds of parcels a day. It is a tribute to the postal service how much fresh food reached its destination in good condition. Post could reach the base camps in France in just two days, if there were no unusual delays. It was sometimes more difficult to get them from the base camps to the men in the trenches, not least because of how often the location of a particular unit changed. By 1917, troops were aware that their families were under huge strain at home and that food was increasingly costly and hard to find. Some wrote home urging their families not to send so much to them as they received adequate, if basic, food from the Army and did not want their families to suffer extra hardship by sending food parcels.

Reaching Beyond the Wire: Supporting Prisoners of War and Internees

When the war started none of the governments involved can have had any idea just how many prisoners they would take and therefore have to look after. As far as Britain was concerned, about 185,000 of its men, around one sixth of its battlefield losses, consisted of men taken prisoner. Approximately half of them were captured in 1918. Britain and France held about 720,000 Prisoners of War (POWs), Germany 2,900,000 and Russia 2,500,000. The average life-expectancy for POWs was far longer than for men at the front and this was something that many POWs were acutely aware of, especially those who were taken prisoner early in the war.

Most British prisoners were released quickly after the Armistice and by 15 November, many had reached Calais. A holding camp to take 40,000 men was quickly set up at Dover. By 9 December, 264,000 had been repatriated. Many had been released en masse to find their own way home, some dying of exhaustion along the way. They were all given a message of welcome and thanks from the king. All returning officers had to write a report explaining how they came to be taken prisoner and to show they had done all they could to avoid it. By January 1919, most POWs had been repatriated but when the British authorities asked for the return of the final 35,000 men registered as having been taken prisoner, the Germans could only produce 22,000. The missing 13,000 men had died in captivity.

Under the Second Hague Convention, countries holding POWs are meant to treat prisoners in the same way as their own soldiers with regard to board, lodging and clothing. In reality, conditions often fell short of this standard. The British public rallied to send parcels of food and other goods to their men who had been taken prisoner. French, Italian, and Russian prisoners fared less well, not least because their countries were actively being fought over. Some POWs in Britain did receive parcels from home. The naval blockade caused food shortages in all the belligerent countries and the food parcels received by British POWs meant that they were often better fed than the local civilian population. This caused great resentment and there were increasingly frequent stories of petty revenge by guards with all the tins in parcels being punctured, sausages split open, chocolate broken into small bits and everything being mixed together. Food became so scarce in Germany that a significant number of prisoners and civilians starved to death.

Again, under the Second Hague Convention, the Red Cross and other humanitarian societies had a right of access to distribute aid. The International Committee of the Red Cross Prisoner-of-War Agency in Geneva was the largest non-governmental organisation helping prisoners. Faced with rumour and counter-rumour about the mistreatment of prisoners, the neutral countries, in particular Switzerland, and until 1917, the United States of America, played an important role in inspecting camps.

James Gerard, the American Ambassador in Berlin, said that the Germans were totally unprepared for dealing with POWs. He was so worried by their conditions that he went out and bought all the blankets and underclothes he could get hold of in Berlin and gave them out to Allied prisoners. He also bought walking sticks, crutches, and eggs for the neediest prisoners at Doeberitz. Gerard worked hard to improve conditions for POWs and internees until he had to leave Germany when America entered the war. He reported that by the time he left there were 2,000,000 POWs, of various nationalities, in German hands who were materially helping agriculture and industry.

Local fundraising for POWs started early in the conflict and struck a chord with the public. Door-to-door collections and appeals, asking each household to donate at least a penny, were very successful. Many children went without sweets so that they, too, could make a donation. Plenty of tales of cruelty, neglect and hardship reached home, giving the appeals an extra impetus.

After he was exchanged in 1915, Private George Wells, from the 1st Cheshire Regiment, recounted how he was not allowed to write home, or request parcels, for six months. While he was waiting for his first parcel, he did not have a change of clothes and was bitterly cold, as the Germans had taken his greatcoat. His feet swelled due to marching barefoot in snow and rain but he received no help or treatment until three British doctors arrived in the camp as prisoners. They had to amputate both his feet at the instep. Private Wells died from his wounds in 1918.

One of the major issues POWs had to contend with was the quantity and quality of their food. Many later said they would not have survived without food parcels from home. Several American and even one German nutritionist claimed that the rations POWs in German received were inadequate, short on fat and protein, dull and monotonous. By 1916, the situation had improved a little but as the impact of the naval blockade grew, rations were in very short supply. Large numbers of civilians starved. It did not help matters when one newspaper reported that enemy prisoners in Ruhleben were not only eating fairly well, but were suffering few privations other than the loss of liberty. Even the prison guards resented the well-stocked larders of the British internees, while they went without necessities. One of the prisoners later recalled how German soldiers went through the rubbish picking out odd pieces of bacon and fat. They were particularly fond of the fat in the corned beef tins, which they scraped out and ate with relish.

Every regiment had its Prisoner of War Fund, set up as soon as word got back that men were being taken prisoner. The bulk of the work was done by groups of women many, but not all of whom were related to men in the regiment. Although initially on a small scale, the volume of work undertaken by these groups expanded beyond anyone's expectations and was essential to the survival of many POWs. These charities later registered under the War Charities Act. Many civilians took on the responsibility for paying for parcels for one or more prisoners. Huge numbers of volunteers were needed to keep POWs supplied with parcels.

The Royal Scots Association was the first Regimental Care Committee in Scotland and raised £62,000. The Aberdeen and District Prisoners of War Bureau was set up to provide support to the families of Gordon Highlanders who had been taken prisoner. It was later expanded to include men from other regiments and services and it spread to include Aberdeenshire, Banffshire, and Kincardineshire. Using many personal links, it built up a list of POWs and, if possible, their state of health. The bureau was invaluable, acting a point of contact for servicemen's next of kin and giving them information about what they could send and how to send it. It also co-ordinated sending parcels that had been donated by benefactors unrelated to a specific prisoner.

Christina Fell was the hard-working and efficient honorary secretary of the Regimental Care Committee for Prisoners of War of the 4th Battalion the Kings Own Royal Lancashire Regiment, based in Ulverston. When she was notified that a man had been taken prisoner, she wrote to his family to let them know that the man's name had been added to her list and that he would be sent six parcels of food every four weeks, each worth 8s, in addition to 26 lbs of bread worth 7s 6d. She asked the family to make any contribution they could towards the cost and assured them that any donor's name would be added to the parcel. She asked the family to let her know the prisoner's height and boot size so he could be sent a full set of clothing. She explained that although relatives were not allowed to send parcels of food, they could send a 'personal parcel' once every three months. She reassured the family that she would let them know if she was told that a man had been moved to a different camp, and that the family could send the man as many letters as they wanted, free of charge, providing the flap was tucked in and not stuck down. They did not forget that some local men served in different regiments and provided parcels for them as well, if their relatives wanted their parcels to be sent from the local centre.

The contents of clothing parcels were carefully thought out. They contained a jacket, a pair of trousers, a pair of boots, a pair of canvas shoes, two shirts, two pairs of pants, two under-vests, a cardigan, a pair of gloves, two towels, three handkerchiefs, a pair of braces, a greatcoat, a cap, and a kitbag. Repeat parcels were sent every six months, apart from the greatcoat, which had to last a year and the kitbag, which was only sent once. They also sent 4s worth of tobacco or cigarettes a month to each man.

One of Christina Fell's fundraising initiatives involved sending letters to all churches in the area asking if they would allocate the collections made on the first Sunday of February to the Regimental Care Committee Fund. They also had an Adopt a Prisoner scheme and encouraged people to get together to sponsor a prisoner for £36 a year if they could not afford the full cost themselves. During 1917, the fund managed to collect almost £3,000, roughly £250 a month, to help them care for the 600 men from the regiment who were POWs in Germany and Bulgaria. According to the annual report, the cost of food for parcels had risen from £26 to £36 a year for each man. The writer added that the amount of food they were sending was just enough to keep the men from 'starvation and the misery of acute hunger'. Other regiments had comparable schemes.

Christina Fell received many letters of thanks from prisoners. One from Corporal G. A. Wilson in Scheveningen in March 1918 is clearly part of an on-going correspondence. As well as referring to the joy of being relatively free in Holland after his time in a German prison camp, he made a number of suggestions about parcel contents. He asked her to try not to send tinned food as tins were taken to a central store and issued as needed. When a prisoner was moved to another camp, often at very short notice, the tins got left behind and it could take several months for them to catch up with their owner. He also said tins had to be opened at the store and the empty tins were taken away each day for use in munitions factories. He commented that oatmeal, Quaker Oats and rice were always welcome, adding that when his parcels arrived regularly he ate much better than he had done as a civilian before the war as he had a large appetite. However, there were times when he had to go as much as five months between parcels and he accused the Germans of stealing them. He was very bitter about the way parcels were handled in his last camp and claimed that at the time he left there was a cellar full of cigarettes and tobacco.

Sergeant H. Robinson wrote from The Hague in October 1918. He was not sure if anyone would tell her when prisoners were exchanged to Holland and wanted to be certain she knew she no longer needed to send parcels to him. He referred to the fact that some earlier parcels had gone missing but thanked her for everything she had sent him.

In November 1917 four parcels were returned from Germany as the men had died in hospital. In each case, the contents were intact. When W. McNeill wrote to Christina Fell from Hamelin in August 1918, he thanked her and her committee for everything they had done for him. He was pragmatic in his attitude to the fact that some parcels had gone astray and commented that the surprising thing was not that some got lost but that so many arrived safely under war conditions. He also thanked Miss Fell and the ladies of her committee for the visits they had made to his family.

The committee worked from centres in Ulverston, Lancaster, and Blackpool, sending off consignments of parcels six times in every four weeks. Bread for the POWs, paid for by the committee's appeal for funds, was supplied from Berne and Copenhagen. During 1917, HM Post Office Censors for the War Office inspected the Ulverston Packing Centre five times and gave it glowing reports. People got involved in whatever way they could. Mrs Brocklebank donated all the boxes and string for the parcels and many people gave sacks of paper shavings to be used for packing. Over a three-and-a-half-year period, the committee supported 330 men. The committee's final report paid tribute to the people who had packed all the parcels, especially Mrs Gaisford and her team who had dealt with up to a ton of food a week. They also thanked staff at the Ulverston Goods Station and the local press for their help over the years.

Funding these schemes was by no means plain sailing. When the Lord Lieutenant of Warwickshires's appeal for funds gained only a lukewarm response, the Royal Warwickshire Regiment's Old Comrades' Association was worried about how long their work could continue. The appeal was renewed, with the comment that the first one must have been overlooked by the generous people of Warwickshire. Hopefully the renewed appeal was more successful.

In stark contrast to the regimental care committees, some appeals were very local or even focussed on just one man. Such appeals were often very short-lived and could claim exemption from registration under the War Charities Act. After Private George Booth of the 2nd Sherwood Foresters was sent to a POW camp in Hamelin, Germany he wrote to his mother complaining that their food ration consisted of only a small loaf of prison bread and a cup of black coffee every third day. He asked his mother to send him food parcels. She mentioned this to Mr Rowbottom, who was the manager of the Matlock Bath Pavilion. One night he reported the story to his cinema audience and collected £1 4s 6d, which was passed to a local confectioner who then sent five weekly parcels to Private Booth. Whether his mother found a way of sending further parcels is unclear. Some of his regimental colleagues wrote home asking for books, to distract them from their misery, as well as for food parcels.

William Tasker from Ellesmere Port was a jockey, riding professionally in Belgium before the war. After the war started, he hid for several months before being captured. He spent two months in a small room with fifty other men before being sent to Ruhleben. He said that without his food parcels from the Ellesmere Port Prisoners of War Society, he believed he would not have survived.

The people of Wadhurst, in East Sussex, set up a fund to support local men and in 1916–17 they spent more than £17 on blankets, £34 on bread and about £140 on groceries. The church of St Peter and St Paul in Wadhurst provided the fittings to equip chapels in four POW camps.

Shops were quick to realise that support for POWs was an opportunity for them to increase their profits while appearing patriotic. Newspapers and magazines contained numerous advertisements for their Food for Prisoners of War services with parcels available at various prices. These were alongside their promotions for parcels for serving officers and men.

The stories of food shortages in the camps caused considerable distress among relatives of the men who were held. In 1918 the Reverend Andrew Clark reported that Kenneth Sadgrove, the son of one of Reverend Clark's colleagues, was a POW in Germany. Kenneth had written to his parents saying the only food the Germans gave them was acorn coffee, a small piece of black bread and potatoes. The Sadgroves therefore paid £4 2s a month to the Central Prisoner of War Committee, which then sent Kenneth six parcels a month and 26 lbs of bread or biscuits. Kenneth was adamant that his parents should not pay for the parcels and had arranged to send them £5 a month through the Army bankers Cox & Co. The family also got six permits to let them send additional parcels through the post.

Not every prisoner was happy with his parcels or with the system for sending and distributing them. It has been suggested that some of the more extremely negative reports about conditions, including parcels, came from men who were suffering badly from the mental strain of being a prisoner. C.F. Priestly of Soothill wrote to his wife in February 1917 complaining about his parcels. He moaned that he was sent cigarettes when he did not smoke. He did admit he was getting good bread from Denmark and had a good stock of various items. He felt it was a mistake for the contents of parcels to be standardised, showing a spectacular lack of understanding of what was involved in assembling and sending parcels to tens of thousands of POWs. He also claimed he had seen a parcel for a man who had gone home a year earlier and more than 100 for men who were not there. These parcels were given to the relief committee to be used by men who were not on the list for parcels. He also complained that although the clothes he had asked for had arrived, some of them were second-hand and there were even holes in some of the socks.

By June 1915 there were ninety-three regimental care committees and twenty-six local associations working to help POWs. There was no co-ordination between the groups, resulting in a measure of confusion and overlap. There was a suggestion that the Home Office should take responsibility for co-ordinating support for POWs, but they declined. According to a report by the British Red Cross, some prisoners had a glut of parcels while many got too little and some parcels were found to contain forbidden articles including information useful to the enemy. The report concluded that the excess food going to some prisoners was roughly enough to feed a whole German division. Meanwhile, members of the public were getting worried about those who were still short of food. With the approval of the War Office, the Prisoners of War Help Committee was set up. It was a voluntary organisation, without any official powers, based at The Savoy in London, with the aim of helping transmit money, comforts and relief to POWs.

The committee's position was ambiguous. In answer to a parliamentary question, the Under Secretary of State for War, Mr Tennant, said that the committee acted under instructions from the War Office even though it was not a War Office Committee. This lack of clarity made the committee's position untenable in the long-term.

In September 1916, the War Office finally accepted that its involvement was inevitable and set up the official Central Prisoner of War Committee. One of the committee's first tasks was to carry out a full census of parcels sent to POWs in one month. They concluded the overall amount of food being sent to POWs was excessive and that distribution was uneven. While some men had been sent up to sixteen parcels in two weeks, others had received little or nothing. The military authorities had raised the fear that goods were being sent that might be of use to the enemy. The committee was based in Thurloe Place in London and was actually run by the British Red Cross Society and the Order of St John. As the numbers of prisoners grew, so did staff at Thurloe Place until there were 750 workers, half of whom were volunteers, and the War Office had had to take over extra buildings to accommodate them. The committee was authorised to take on the role of a care committee for civilian internees and POWs who did not have a care committee. They were also able to pack parcels if care committees and local associations asked for their help.

They created a standard emergency parcel that was designed to keep two men alive for a week, and they were allowed to keep 12,000 of these parcels at POW camps across Germany. The parcels contained tins of beef, tea, cocoa, biscuits, cheese, tins of dripping, tins of milk and cigarettes. The committee also prepared parcels with specially selected contents for prisoners in Turkey and Bulgaria, for Indians, invalids and vegetarians. Parcels without tins also had to be assembled to meet the rules in some camps in Germany. The committee had to adapt its parcels to meet the changing rules of different countries. Turkey banned the sending of blankets and candles. By the end of the war, more than 2,500,000 parcels had been sent to POW camps abroad at a cost of £6,500,000. A third of the money came from the General Fund of the British Red Cross Society and the rest came from the public.

Captain McMurtie of the Somerset Light Infantry said that after the parcel system got going and they stopped being hungry they began to get heartily sick of tinned food and supplies of dry biscuits. These came in large quantities to be eaten when bread supplies failed but some camps accrued such large stocks that in at least one case a large amount was given to a French officers' camp where the men were very hungry.

The committee sent parcels of games and entertainments, which again had to be tailored to meet local conditions. A prisoner from Doeberitz Camp wrote they were not allowed to play tennis or cricket but would like rope or rubber quoits, books for the library and music for the string orchestra. The committee also tried to help to make sure letters to and from POWS were delivered safely. The Red Cross appointed a Swiss haulage firm to transport parcels and it handled two million parcels for POWs over four years.

There was a lot of resistance to the creation of the Central Prisoner of War Committee from regimental and local associations who were upset at losing the freedom to help in their own way. Some committees dropped all relief work. A parliamentary joint committee was set up to check that the committee was doing a good job. Its report concluded that the committee had rushed too much to impose the new arrangements, had caused problems and should have drawn on existing experience. Some people felt regulation by the committee, and by the requirements of registration under the War Charities Act of 1916, intruded into their right to operate however they saw fit. The treasurer of Lady Garvagh's Prisoners Fund took exception to the Central Prisoner of War Committee's insistence on knowing the full details of all the fund's committee members, many of whom were titled. Mr Bird, of the Central Prisoner of War Committee stood firm.

The importance of the parcels and the success of the scheme was shown when men in Holzminden camp made a collection for the Red Cross. The POWs contacted their friends and relatives in Britain and asked them to make donations. This raised over £2,000.

Berne, in neutral Switzerland, was the base for several early organisations set up to help POWs by sending them food and clothes. These included the British Legation Red Cross Organisation (British Legation Depot), which was set up by Mrs Grant Duff, wife of His Majesty's Minister in Switzerland. The British Legation Depot was, in effect, a war hospital supply depot with twelve affiliated working parties in areas where there were concentrations of Britons. The groups worked with a considerable degree of independence and sent their finished garments to Berne. Volunteers at the headquarters in Berne controlled the patterns and quality of the articles, and tailored what each group was asked to make to their particular skills. The finished articles were sent to British and French hospitals as far away as Boulogne and Calais as well as bundles of underclothes to Lyons and to the Cardinal of Rheims for distribution to the destitute. At the request of Lady Wemyss, they sent one consignment to a hospital ship in the Mediterranean.

Lady Grant Duff also set up a depot in Berne for sending food parcels to individual POWs. The depot was funded by British residents in Berne. They initially concentrated on meeting requests from regimental committees and private subscribers but the administration involved, and dealing with thousands of postal orders a month, was so onerous that Mrs Duff Grant contacted the Prisoner of War Help Committee to suggest that the administration should be centralised in Britain. When the Central Prisoner of War Committee was set up in 1916, the Berne Depot was quick to affiliate with it. Many of the smaller organisations based in Switzerland closed.

Mrs Duff Grant was careful to liaise with the authorities in London to let them know what she proposed doing and avoid any clash of interest. This close co-operation became even more important when the conditions in camps in Germany became known and letters from POWs showed how hungry they were. Although the Prisoner of War Help Committee and regimental associations did what they could, the geographical position of Switzerland made it an ideal base for sending bread to POWs. Mrs Grant Duff decided to make this the focus of the Berne Depot's work and later provided 100,000 men with bread. All the wheat for the POW's bread was imported, as grain was in very short supply in Switzerland. Swiss bakers worked in about forty kitchens to make the bread, which was baked twenty minutes longer than was usual in Switzerland. This made it stay fresh for four to six weeks but led to some complaints that it was too crusty. In 1918 a biscuit was developed to replace the bread. The biscuits were softened in water before being eaten and proved popular with the POWs. The work grew quickly and the Swiss made railway wagons available, free of charge, for transporting the bread to Frankfurt for distribution. The Berne Depot later had to take on a row of eight shops and a large music hall to get enough space for its work. A supplementary supply bureau was opened in Copenhagen.

A problem arose when Mrs Duff Grant got a letter from a camp commandant in Germany saying that a parcel had arrived containing abusive literature and that if it happened again no more bread would be allowed into the camp. Neither the addressee nor the camp was on the Berne lists so the identity of the sender remained a mystery. Luckily, nothing so potentially serious happened again.

St Dunstan's, the charity set up to help blinded servicemen, also helped POWs in Germany who had lost their sight. The charity worked through the British Red Cross Society, advising on what the blinded prisoners needed most. Aid provided in this way included correspondence courses in Braille, books printed in Braille, special dominoes and playing cards, and eye-shades and eye drops for those recovering from blindness.

One of the remarkable achievements of the International Committee of the Red Cross and the Swiss Government was persuading the belligerent nations, Germany, France, Britain, Russia and Belgium, to sign an internment agreement in 1914. Under this agreement captured military and naval personnel, who were too seriously wounded or sick to be able to continue military service, could be repatriated through Switzerland, helped by the Swiss Red Cross. The American Ambassador in Berlin, James Gerard, was very active in the development of this scheme and its progress. The first men were repatriated in March 1915. By November 1916, 8,700 French and 2,300 Germans had been repatriated.

Prisoners hoping for internment under this scheme were examined by travelling commissions of Swiss doctors, who visited the various POW camps. Once a prisoner had been selected they had to appear in front of a panel consisting of two Swiss doctors, two doctors from the holding country, and a representative from the prisoner's own country.

By the end of 1916, almost 27,000 men had been interned in Switzerland. The criteria used for selecting men for internment changed over time, no doubt influenced by the sheer number of enemy prisoners the various countries had to deal with as the war dragged on. The scheme was first extended to include men who were very badly wounded or seriously ill but who were expected to recover enough to go on serving, albeit not at the front. In mid-1917, men who had served more than eighteen months in captivity and had barbed-wire disease were also eligible for transfer to Switzerland. By the end of the war, nearly 68,000 men of various nationalities were interned in Switzerland.

The internees were under the guardianship of the Swiss Government and each nation had an officer or diplomat attached to the embassy specifically for liaison over interned men. From 1916 Lieutenant Colonel H. P. Picot filled this role for the British internees. He considered that the Swiss authorities did a remarkably good job looking after the internees.

When Picot heard that the internment of certain groups of British POWs in Switzerland had been agreed, he contacted the energetic Mrs Grant Duff. She had anticipated his call and the Berne Depot had already held a special meeting and had put together sets of shorts, vests, pants, socks, pyjamas, handkerchiefs and linen wash bags for 500 men and dressing gowns, bed jackets, ward slippers and handkerchiefs for 200 hospital patients. Bundles of regulation kit, ordered by Picot, arrived from Britain just before the first internees reached Switzerland. The Berne Depot set up a sub-committee to look after the internees, with some help from the British Red Cross Society, and to supply them with various requisites.

The first group of British POWS arrived in Constance on 28 May 1916, dazed, exhausted and ill. At Constance Station, and in every village along the route, crowds turned out to welcome them. The dazed men cheered back. It was after midnight when they reached Berne but there were still thousands of people waiting to greet them. At 3 a.m., after they had eaten the supper prepared by the Berne Depot and had a short rest, the exhausted men were given presents and loaded onto yet another train. At 7 a.m., they finally reached Montreux, where Red Cross volunteers and trained Boy Scouts carried or helped them walk to the Hôtel Suisse. Many of the men found it hard to believe their change in circumstances could last and kept asking if they would be sent back to Germany once they had recovered from their wounds. The volunteers were quick to reassure them.

The British internees were held in three locations in south-western Switzerland. The largest group went to Châteaux d'Oex while Leysin was for men with tuberculosis. A camp at Mürren, high up in the mountains held around thirty-five officers and 600 men of other ranks. Mürren was almost cut off by deep snow for around seven months a year and many of the men had to be confined to barracks for their own safety when it snowed. One internee said that it only took five minutes to walk from one end of the village to the other so the men must have been very aware that they were still prisoners, albeit in a friendly prison. Eighty-eight Britons are buried in the war cemetery at Vevey beside Lake Geneva.

In Ulverston, Christina Fell got a letter from Joseph Askew who had passed his commission for Switzerland on 18 December 1917 and finally left his prison camp eight days later. He wrote that when he and his comrades reached Berne, at 6.30 p.m. on 27 December, they were greeted by dignitaries, including the British Ambassador and his wife, before being given tea in the station restaurant. Every man was given a gift from Queen Mary and Joseph wrote how wonderful it felt to know that they had not been forgotten during their captivity. When a lady asked him about his first impression of Switzerland, he replied that it was like leaving hell for heaven and went on to say how wonderful it was to have the grip of a hand and pleasant smile instead of a kick and a curse. Like other POWs reaching Switzerland, he was amazed at the crowds of Swiss people who turned out to welcome them.

He was sent on to Mürren and got a really warm welcome from the men already interned there. At the Jungfrau Hotel, he and his comrades could hardly believe their eyes at the sight of all the food laid out for them at a splendid dinner. He was impressed to find that a range of practical classes was available, including watch repairing, light leatherwork, motor driving, painting, joinery and beadwork (making fancy necklaces) and that the Army School had a branch to help men get certificates of education. He said that the YMCA hut was splendid and there was even a cinema show there twice a week and occasional concerts, kindly arranged by officers and the ladies of the entertainment committee.

It was some time before Joseph was well enough to join any of the classes, as he had to spend several months in bed suffering from general weakness and dizziness. This did not stop him reporting enthusiastically about all the sports that were available to the internees. Sport was as important to the men in Switzerland as it had been when they were in the camps in Germany. It helped keep them fit, gave them a focus and was a distraction, and gave them a safe outlet for some of their frustration and aggression. In Switzerland, they could ski, toboggan, skate, play ice hockey, and participate in torch-lit fancy-dress ice carnivals in winter, while in summer there were football, hockey, and cricket matches between the various hotels.

Askew also reported that a 'splendid dentist', Mr Woods of Liverpool, was there with his wife. James Gerard gave a fuller picture of Woods' work for the POWs. Woods, described as being most amiable and kind, had longed to make a contribution to the war effort and when he heard that men were being transferred from POW camps in Germany to internment camps in Switzerland he recognised his opportunity. With his wife's full support, he offered to visit the various British camps in

Switzerland, carrying out operations and making dentures and splints for jaw injuries. There was a real need for his help, as all dentures had been confiscated from prisoners leaving Germany. He said he would comply with any restrictions that might be imposed, closed his private dental practice in Liverpool and set off for Berne with a load of dental equipment. He originally offered his services for a month but this was extended to three and then his appointment as Head Dental Surgeon to the British Interned was made indefinite. He stayed until the autumn of 1918 when the camps closed, having given his services as a volunteer for two years four months. Woods was based at Miirren but later set up an extra surgery at Interlaken. In August 1917 he was joined by Mr W. I. Law, who took over Leysin and Château d'Oex. His expenses were paid by the North Midland Branch of the British Dental Association and the British Red Cross Society. Mr Woods was entirely self-funding and carried out 9,725 operations and 6,673 restorations. He insisted his aim was to provide treatment that was just as good as he would have given in own consulting room at home. He managed to see ninety-nine per cent of the interned officers and eighty per cent of the other ranks. He also gave lectures on the importance of dental hygiene.

The Swiss had very little time to prepare to receive and help 30,000 seriously sick and wounded men, many of whom also had mental problems. A Swiss medical officer was in charge of discipline and worked closely with the senior British officer in each centre. They soon agreed that in many areas the senior British officer would be in charge of day-to-day matters. The Swiss were responsible for the camp administration. Although many internees could simply be billeted in hotels, various buildings had to be adapted at short notice for use as hospitals. The Berne Depot fitted up an operating theatre, known as the Kitchener Theatre and donated by any anonymous Swiss gentleman, in the Soldanelle hospital at Château d'Oex.

The Swiss Sanitary Service, in charge of the medical care of the internees, came in for a lot of criticism for refusing outside assistance and, in particular, for refusing to allow British nurses to help. Swiss doctors would not allow female nurses to work in military hospitals. When the Allied Red Cross offered to provide large numbers of medical staff, the Swiss Trade Unions blocked the plan. The Allied Red Cross eventually offered to pay for Swiss nurses, and this offer was accepted. In reality, the Swiss coped remarkably well with the influx of sick and wounded men. One problem area was the fitting and supply of artificial limbs. There was a Europe-wide shortage of both limbs and experienced fitters and Switzerland was no exception. Lady Dorothy Dalrymple worked hard supplying peg legs to men at Château d'Oex.

The second batch of internees to arrive in Mürren were in better health than their predecessors and Lieutenant-Colonel F. H. Neish, the senior

British officer in the area, found himself in charge of a group of young men keen to be active after their time in prison camps in Germany. In association with the Berne Depot, he worked hard to set up workshops and arrange classes for the men. The classes were so popular that additional instructors soon had to be sent out from England.

It took some time for schemes to be put in place to engage both the minds and bodies of the internees and some of the men found their first months in Switzerland very frustrating. Classes in motor engineering, and the relevant workshops, were largely sponsored by the management of *The Autocar* in London, who also gave materials and machinery. Various Swiss firms also lent equipment. Picot was disappointed that more men did not take advantage of the training on offer but conceded this was often due to their mental state. He also felt the regular soldiers were not concerned about what would happen to them after the war, as they expected to remain in the Army and were therefore uninterested in learning new skills. The YMCA hut at Leysin was used as a workshop for motor engineering and woodworking.

Picot said everyone who had been behind barbed wire for more than six months showed some symptoms of neurasthenia and that about ten per cent of them were in a very poor condition. This syndrome came to be known as 'barbed-wire disease'. Symptoms progressed from irritability and a refusal to trust those around them, to loss of the ability to concentrate and then a tendency to sit for long periods doing nothing at all and being unwilling to speak. Disturbed sleep was common. Many lost the ability to remember people or events from before the war. Doctors hoped that the symptoms would fade after the men arrived in Switzerland but recovery was often slow or non-existent. Visits by relatives could make a big difference to the men with mental problems but some visitors were horrified to find that their relative's personality had changed beyond recognition.

The Reverend A. Sutherland and 'a lady' worked with the World's Alliance of the YMCA at Geneva, the Berne Depot, the Patriotic League in Lausanne and private friends and managed to raise enough money to rent premises and equip a recreation club, which was called The Foyer. It gave the men somewhere non-sectarian where they could read the papers or books, write letters, listen to music and smoke. It was so popular that it quickly outgrew the premises so the British Red Cross Society offered to set up a large hut, which would be staffed by VADs. Word later leaked out that it had been funded by Sir William Cresswell Gray of West Hartlepool. The Gray Hut was built in the winter of 1916–17 and after it opened in January 1917, The Foyer closed. When internment came to an end, the Gray Hut was handed over to the Swiss for use as a holiday centre for children.

The YMCA's work in Switzerland was organised by Mr Hobday and Mr Whitwell and their efforts were a huge success. Their hut in Miirren was said to have been the largest in Switzerland and the highest in world. It had a canteen, cinema, billiard and bagatelle tables, stage, library, quiet room, and a magic lantern for lectures. Social life for the men in Mürren revolved around the hut. An entertainment committee was quickly set up and arranged weekly concerts and a theatrical group. Lectures and mock trials and numerous classes in subjects such as embroidery, languages, and basket making were put on. There was also a large plot of land, where the men grew vegetables to supplement their diet. When a camp opened at Interlaken, the YMCA installed a canteen under Mr and Mrs R. Hughes in one of best hotels in the town.

A number of British residents in Switzerland were also determined to help the POWs. Miss Annan and Miss Metcalfe ran Homes for Men at Rougemont and Rossinieres. They provided the initial outlay, rent and running expenses and did all executive work and looked after the men themselves. Miss Annan also organised basket making and fancy work classes to occupy the internees and let them earn a little money. Mrs Anderton of Vevey got involved in various schemes for the welfare of troops and was decorated for her work by the Pope. Miss Simpkin had a chalet near Interlaken, by the Lake of Thun. She offered it to the authorities as a convalescent home for men with shell shock and heart problems. She took twenty men at a time and looked after them with great kindness.

In the spring of 1917, Picot was approached by Mrs Cook Daniels and Miss Martin who had opened a hand-made carpet factory at Lake of Thoune employing French and Belgian internees. They offered similar work for up to fifty disabled Britons and took them to their workshop at Gunten in the Bernese Oberland. The workshop continued until the end of the war and the carpets soon earned a good reputation. The men were paid wages out of any profits that were made. The ladies also opened a club and a canteen for the men, at their own expense.

As soon as word leaked out about which officers were to be sent to Switzerland, some of their wives set off to meet them. Picot could see how contact with their families helped the officers, and he thought it would be good for the non-commissioned officers and other ranks to see their wives or family members too. He approached the War Office for help. Lord Northcliffe, who had visited Miirren, backed the idea. He collected money through *The Times* and set up the machinery for the care of the women, both in transit and while they were in Switzerland. He also donated 750 lbs of tea a month for the internees, sending it through the British Red Cross Society. This was very welcome as tea, greatly appreciated by British troops, was unavailable in Switzerland. It was issued free to hospitals and for a charge in all the Red Cross and YMCA huts.

Groups of sixteen to twenty relatives were taken out each fortnight for a two-week stay, accompanied by volunteer chaperones. The YMCA helped run the scheme and the Central Prisoner of War Committee leased a house in Bedford Square, where the groups gathered before setting off. When they arrived in Switzerland, one of the interned officers was appointed to look after them and the Berne Depot took responsibility for their entertainment and their lunches, dinners and teas. Always ready to take on extra responsibilities, the ladies from the depot also provided meals in Berne for all prisoners en route from Germany to Switzerland or, if repatriated, to Britain.

The first official group of visiting relatives reached Château d'Oex in September 1916. It was a memorable occasion and a crowd turned out to greet them and lead them in a torch-lit procession to their hotels. The town was en fête for the whole two weeks of their visit. Over the years, 600 wives and mothers made the trip.

Holland also housed a number of British internees. In October 1914, 1,500 men of the First Royal Naval Brigade, who had been helping the Belgians at Antwerp, were cut off and could not get back to Britain. To avoid being taken prisoner by the Germans, they crossed into Holland and were interned at Groningen. Since they were already caring for tens of thousands of Belgian refugees, the Dutch authorities must have been less than pleased when they had to find space for British internees as well. A camp, soon nicknamed HMS Timbertown, was built on the parade ground of the local barracks in Groningen.

In 1918 some wounded prisoners from camps in northern and eastern Germany were exchanged and interned in Holland. The War Office gave the YMCA permission to run huts in Holland for both interned officers and men. About 2,000 men were billeted in houses and hotels on the outskirts of Scheveningen and The Hague. In an imaginative move, all the staff in these huts were the female relatives of the internees. As not all of them could afford to travel to Holland and support themselves while working in the huts, the YMCA set up a specific fund to pay the expenses for those in need. Workshops were also set up to help keep these internees occupied.

A British Red Cross Hospital was set up in The Hague to minister to British internees. Staff included two VADs, Miss Bradney and Miss Charlesworth, who earned high praise for their ability take on the work of trained Sisters when necessary. Staff were particularly busy in October and November 1917, when there was an influx of men with pneumonia. Another hospital opened in Rotterdam in 1918, specifically to care for repatriated POWs. It had 1,000 beds and when Miss Bradney and Miss Charlesworth transferred there, they were again praised for acting as trained Sisters, working night and day and remaining cheerful throughout. A further twelve VADs went out to the Rotterdam hospital. By the end of the war, there were 40,000 British and Commonwealth troops interned in Holland.

In December 1914 there were 9,103 Britons living in Germany but 70,000 Germans and Austrians in Britain. Having large numbers of resident enemy aliens posed a problem for the authorities in each country, who were understandably worried about spies. Britain started internment first and continued in stops and starts until all enemy aliens of fighting age had been rounded up. Germany soon followed suit and their process of rounding up and interning enemy aliens was carried out quite smoothly over a three-week period. The men were each allowed to take a few personal belongings including one sheet, one pillow case and two light blankets. The rest of their property was to be held separately until they were released or repatriated. Some of the internees had been born in Germany, thought themselves German and hardly spoke English.

Internee Sir John Balfour remembered being spat at and having insults shouted at him throughout his journey from Baden-Baden to Berlin. He said even members of the German Red Cross refused to hand out food and drinks to the internees. There are also a number of reports of German Red Cross workers refusing to hand food and drink to wounded POWs although most of the police were polite and a few guards shared food with them or tried to protect them from onlookers. Many of the internees in Britain received worse treatment from the authorities and from members of the public. Most internees in both countries had a double burden. The felt humiliated at being imprisoned and shame at not fighting for their homeland. This made their rehabilitation harder after the war, as they suffered a severe loss of status within their respective societies, while suffering from many of the same problems as former military prisoners.

When the Germans first considered interning British civilians, the military authorities said they should not be held near Berlin, to minimise visits and inspections by the representatives of foreign powers. In spite of this, Ruhleben Racecourse became the largest civilian internment camp in Germany. It was just 2 miles west of Berlin, near Spandau. Over the remainder of the war, approximately 5,500 men were interned there, with a peak of 4,273 in February 1915. Because it was so close to Berlin, Ruhleben was, indeed, the most visited, widely publicised, and most frequently written about camp in Germany.

Ruhleben was unusual in that most inmates arrived on one day, 6 November 1914, rather than in dribs and drabs over a period of months. The turnover of internees was comparatively low, enabling the men to form a relatively stable community and mitigating some of the worst effects of internment. People of all classes and from all over the British Empire were sent there. Internees included fishermen, West Indian sailors, Jewish tailors from London, music hall artists, football players and golfers, jockeys from the racecourse at Hoppegarten, businessmen, well-known musicians and actors, artists, journalists, as well as various criminals and conmen who happened to be in Berlin or Hamburg when the war started. About one in twenty of the internees was openly pro-German. Many others had German wives and children.

Conditions at Ruhleben were very bad at first. The men were packed into the stables, six to a grubby loose box, with up to 200 men crammed into the open lofts above them. The only heating was from the hot water pipes that ran through the boxes. There was little ventilation and inadequate lighting. Snow drifted in. The tiers of bunks were packed close to each other. During that first winter, the men complained they were never able to get properly dry. The yard outside was unpaved and quickly became a quagmire. By March 1915 a pool more than 130 feet long had formed. The following summer this area baked hard and clouds of dust enveloped everything. Bad as they were, conditions at Ruhleben were better than in some of the military camps, including Münster where the men lived in the open while building their own camp.

When the American Ambassador, James Gerard, first visited Ruhleben in March 1915, he recoiled in horror from what he saw. He made his views felt there and then, and also wasted no time in writing to the authorities, urging them to improve conditions. He had an impact and before long several new barracks had been built, allowing the men who were in the open lofts to be moved into better surroundings. Many of the internees bought wood so that they could build bits of furniture and further improve their own living conditions. Gerard also complained about the poor sanitation which, he claimed, was a danger not only to the camp but also to Berlin. There was one cold tap between 300 men, who also had the opportunity to take just one tepid shower a month in a nearby station. Thanks to Gerard, two new toilet blocks were built, one at either end of the camp. They were still inadequate, stank and often broke or froze in winter but they were a real improvement on the previous facilities and did provide enough hot water for shaving. A few months later warm showers were made available weekly or cold showers at any time.

The pro-German internees were all billeted together, as were the black sailors who had been taken off ships in Hamburg. In a way that most people today would find deeply shocking, many of the British internees felt deeply insulted to be in the same camp, interned under the same conditions, as black people. They felt that the Germans had done this to slight them and in retaliation for the fact that the British had put

Germans in camps with black guards in Africa. The Jewish prisoners were also billeted in separate barracks and there was some anti-Semitism among the guards.

From September 1915, the inmates were basically self-governing as the soldiers withdrew to the circumference of the camp. Each barrack had a captain and the captains formed a committee, which ran the camp. Barrack captains had to speak English and German fluently and to have the confidence of the others men in the barrack. From January 1915 the head of the captain's committee was Joseph Powell, a cinema owner from Leeds. Powell was not popular with some of the upper class internees who objected to him having any authority over them and the fact that he was allowed into Berlin to run errands once a week and visited the US Embassy.

The barrack captains were not only part of the committee but were also in charge of basic discipline and overseeing the work of officials, such as the barrack vice-captains, postmen, firemen, cashiers, and laundrymen. All the inmates were responsible for keeping the camp clean. Gerard was shocked to discover that most of the internees refused to do any cleaning and a fund was raised to pay some of the poorer inmates to clean for their colleagues. Work parties were formed to do the heavier and dirtier work such as cleaning latrines and emptying rubbish bins. The men who did this were paid about five marks a week.

The early Commandant was Count Schwerin, a retired army officer, who was assisted by the equally elderly Baron Taube. They were relatively humane and in 1916 Count Schwerin remarked to a visitor, 'You mustn't suppose that the camp was always like this. When the men were first brought here, the place wasn't fit to keep pigs in. All that you have admired in the camp they have themselves created.'

Filling time and finding ways of distracting themselves from the reality of their situation was vital to internees' well-being. Within a month of arriving at Ruhleben, they had founded an Arts and Science Union led by a group of university-educated men who organised a programme of lectures and helped internees wanting to do private study. Before long, they had also started the Ruhleben Camp School, which ran classes, reading circles, debates, and discussions on a wide range of subjects. Over time, 297 different courses were offered. Classes ranged from the elementary to postgraduate in subject and level and before long about 200 teachers were teaching about 1,400 students. The school was backed up by a large camp library with more than 5,000 books, which had been sent out from Britain by various charities, or bought by the men themselves. Internees gathered living material for their biology courses from the pond then in the middle of the racetrack. A Canadian internee arranged for his former professor to send them microscopes and other equipment. Adolf Engler, director of the Berlin Botanic Garden, also sent them specimens.

The Ruhleben inmates also developed two lively dramatic societies, performing plays in English and French, and an operatic society. They were supported by an orchestra of good quality musicians, some of whom had taken their own instruments to Ruhleben. Others either arranged for their instruments to be sent from home or were given new ones by various charities. A number of artists held exhibitions, even selling works to fellow internees as souvenirs. Two camp magazines were produced and circulated.

Sport was enormously important, as it was in military camps. James Gerard helped negotiate for the men to be able to use an increased area of the racecourse grounds and they used the additional space for sports facilities including a five-hole golf course. Some of the internees could afford to buy sporting equipment but the group also received numerous generous donations from home and they soon had a full sports programme. Football teams were organised in fourteen of the barracks and a competition was set up. The first match of the season was held in March, with Baron Traube on hand for the kick-off. Tennis was popular and seven tennis courts were laid out on the straight sections of the track. Rugby, hockey, boxing and cricket, including an annual Yorkshire versus Lancashire contest, were also played with enthusiasm. An added advantage of all these sports was the time it took all the committees and sub-committees to organise them.

The first issue of the *Ruhleben Camp Magazine*, published early in 1916, included an article urging the camp gardeners to think of spring. There were hints on preparing soil for sweet peas and mention of nasturtiums, violas, petunias, asters, begonias, geraniums, marguerites, and bush roses. Apparently, cuttings or small plants could easily be bought from a market gardener in nearby Spandau. The author suggested trailing convolvulus up the front of the barracks, since disguising the austere nature of the camp was one of their aims. Seeds could be ordered from England and the men were urged to make window boxes out of the packaging their parcels came in. Another article suggested planting schemes for the communal areas. The gardeners were encouraged by a gift of seeds from the Crown Princess of Sweden.

The Ruhleben Horticultural Society was formally set up on 25 September 1916. Just a few days later, T. Howat wrote to the Royal Horticultural Society (RHS) asking to be allowed to affiliate their society to the RHS. He explained that due to circumstances, they were unable to pay the usual affiliation fee but hoped this would not stop them enjoying the advantages of affiliation. The RHS quickly agreed to the affiliation and arranged to send parcels to Ruhleben through the Red Cross. After an appeal to nurseries across Britain, donations of seeds and bulbs poured in. The RHS was soon able to send off five cases and one parcel of seeds and bulbs with six pamphlets on gardening matters. Eleven more cases soon followed and were gratefully acknowledged by Howat. That they only sent six pamphlets may indicate that the RHS had underestimated the number of enthusiastic gardeners at Ruhleben. The RHS continued to support its latest affiliate for the rest of the war.

When frost killed the German potato crop in 1916–17 and the naval blockade reduced imports, shortages were severe and there were a number of food riots in Germany. The men in Ruhleben began to work hard at growing vegetables, investing communal money to cover the initial expenses and the rent of additional land. They also bought thirty loads of very poor quality pig manure from the Wacht Kommando and all they could get from the Fort, which they mixed with some basic slag, bone meal and potash salts and dug in to improve the soil. Due a very dry patch, and the late arrival of their watering cans, they lost many of their early seedlings. Vegetable seeds were sent out by the RHS and Suttons of Reading. As soon as possible, the internees set up frames and a greenhouse and even bought a second-hand boiler. At their peak, they produced 33,000 lettuces and 18,000 bunches of radishes in a year. After 1917 they actually sold produce to Berlin and sent the money they earned back to their families.

One of the German officers tried to claim fifteen red cabbages for the officers' mess and issued an order that all outer cabbage leaves should be handed over for cattle fodder. Red cabbages were hardly available in Berlin at the time. The captains committee unanimously refused, as the cabbages had been grown from seed sent from Britain on the specific understanding that only interned men would benefit. However, they did agree to hand over the outer cabbage leaves in return for manure but some men believed that the leaves were eaten by the hungry guards rather than the cattle. The Ruhleben Horticultural Society had great plans for 1919 but just a week after the Armistice many of the men were on their way home.

It was not easy for British charities to give direct help to the internees and the Quakers felt frustrated that they were not allowed to visit the camp as the authorities felt that the American YMCA was doing all that was needed. On the other hand, leaders of the various camp departments were allowed periodic visits to Berlin to buy supplies and transact business. The American YMCA was able to help and donated and built a YMCA hut at Ruhleben in December 1915, providing the men with a well-lit, comfortable place to go – complete with a large hall, classrooms, and a reference library.

In October 1914 a group of German professors in Berlin bravely appealed for funds to help support enemy aliens in distress and cited the work the Quakers were doing for Germans in Britain. They made a another appeal in 1916. Albert Einstein was among the Germans who donated money. Their efforts were mostly directed at supporting those who had lost income through internment but they also helped to find work for internees who were released.

The Swiss Dr Elizabeth Rotten and her Committee for the Advice and Assistance of Germans Abroad and Foreigners in Germany, based in Berlin, did all they could to help the wives and families of internees in Germany. At Christmas 1917, they helped internees at Ruhleben organise a party for some of their children. The Rotten Committee also sent presents to children who lived too far away to attend. The Rotten Committee provided a considerable amount of equipment and a large number of books to the internees and provided holidays for some of their wives and children. Some camp leaders were suspicious of offers of help, but for groups willing to accept it, Dr Rotten's Committee tapped every possible source for materials.

Just three days after the start of the war, the Society of Friends set up their Emergency Committee for the Assistance of Germans, Austrians and Hungarians in Distress (Friends' Emergency Committee) to help enemy aliens who lived in Britain and who had been made destitute by the war. They also helped the families of missionaries from German East Africa who had been ordered out of their homes, with only the clothes they stood up in, and sent to Britain so that the men could be interned. Their supporters include the Archbishop of Canterbury and several bishops. The National Peace Council helped them get rooms in St Stephen's House, Westminster, which became their base. After steady expansion, they expanded into ten rooms, equipped with borrowed furniture, where forty staff, mostly volunteers, worked. The offices featured homely touches, such as flowers on the tables, designed to create a welcoming atmosphere.

The Quakers were fully aware that the Friends' Emergency Committee's work would be unpopular with many people but firmly believed they had a duty, as Christians, to help the innocent. Enemy aliens who had no embassy or consulate to support them fell into this category. Quakers also believed that mitigating some of the wounds the war would cause would give peace a better chance in the future. The Home Office supported them from the outset and the American Embassy also backed them. Home Office support was vital, as their work drew a lot of criticism and they were never sure how much of what they did was strictly legal. After all, the Treason Act of 1351 was still on the Statute Books and stated that it was treason to help the king's enemies, here or abroad. Several members of the Friends' Emergency Committee were later imprisoned as conscientious objectors, however, some tribunals agreed that the work the Friends' Emergency Committee did was of national importance and sent men to work for them as an accepted form of alternative service.

By the end of November 1914, they had raised almost £6,000 and had already received more than 2,800 applications for help. Before giving more than an emergency grant, the Friends' Emergency Committee insisted that applicants get at least two reputable references and used local Quakers to investigate individual cases.

The Quakers were not alone at trying to help stranded aliens. The Central Council of Refugee Societies, the International Women's Relief Committee and the Prisoners of War Relief Agency all did what they could. They wanted to mitigate the worst effects of the Government's policy of internment, especially as most of the internees were the main breadwinner in the family. They all had to work within a society where they were regarded with suspicion at the least and, at the worst, outright hostility.

The first desperate cases the Friends' Emergency Committee dealt with were actually referred to them by the Home Office. The report gave several examples of the types of people they had helped. These included a group of students from Bohemia, who had been at a summer school and got stranded. There were literally hundreds of waiters, many with excellent references, who had been sacked for being German. As they had mostly lived in the hotels where they worked, they had also become homeless and a number were sleeping rough, in areas where they were increasingly unpopular. Their desperation and fear must have been palpable. The Quakers arranged soup kitchens and tried to help in any way they could. One British journalist and his wife took in a German journalist and his wife, who had been stranded here while visiting her parents. Their children were left in Germany. A number of Quakers took distressed aliens into their homes for a while and hostels were set up in two furnished houses. One Quaker furnished her large garage, so that people who were delayed while waiting for their travel permits could stay there. After the sinking of the *Lusitania*, the families of many of the men who had been interned were driven out of their homes and one Friends' Meeting House temporarily housed seventy people.

Baron 'X' and his wife were visiting England when the war started. He was quite ill and their expensive tastes meant that they soon ran out of money. Baron 'X' was among the enemy aliens rounded up soon after the war started and interned in Olympia. The Baron found himself sleeping on a rug on the unwashed floor of the very cage where, just two weeks earlier, he had played with some monkeys while visiting Olympia as a tourist. He was released, distraught, after two days and he and his wife turned to the Quakers for help. The Quakers put them up in a boarding house. The poor Baroness apparently changed from a self-centred aristocrat into a far more considerate person. She was very grateful for the Quakers' support as her husband's health deteriorated, her four brothers were killed in the war and her sick mother kept writing letters beseeching them to go home, which they would dearly have loved to have done. The last straw came when the Baron was arrested during a raid on the German Hotel and spent a night in the police cells. His mental health gave way and he had to be taken to the County Asylum. After a few days there, he died. A permit to return to Germany, with a letter explaining that the suspicions that had led to his arrest were a case of mistaken identity, reached the Baroness just after her husband's death. The authorities apologised but all that remained for the Baroness was to take her husband's body back to Germany for burial.

One worker took on the task of visiting pawnshops to redeem belongings that had been pawned, in desperation, by people who were then sent to Germany or interned. They were given the pawn tickets and at least some contribution from the people concerned towards the cost of getting the goods back. The Quakers would always try to redeem wedding rings for people being repatriated to Germany, or articles such as razors or tools that might help the men to earn a little money while they were interned. They also got requests, frequently endorsed by a letter from the camp commandant, to go to a particular address to collect belongings that had been left behind and forward them to an internee.

While the Friends' Emergency Committee reached a point of saying it could not take on any further tasks, it recognised that some individual workers wanted to do more for the families they were supporting. It agreed to finance outings organised by the workers. These included tea at a Visitor's house, small parties or a trip to the countryside. In the early years of the war they also arranged Christmas presents and parties in various towns and sent presents to families in remote areas. This involved a lot of work, but meant a huge amount to the recipients. One year they were given £60 to be spent on Christmas dinners. They decided to use the donation to buy postal orders of 2s to 3s 6d, which they sent to internees' families. They received a mass of effusive letters of thanks, as even such small gifts were invaluable to the recipients.

The Friends' Emergency Committee's workers, led by a Mr and Mrs Bridgewater, helped many women who were taking their children to Germany and leaving their husbands interned in Britain. Most of the families had very little money. The Friends' Emergency Committee set up a hostel in two large houses in London, run by Rachel and Catherine Braithwaite – who were helped by other Quakers. Travellers got a warm welcome at whatever hour they arrived. Groups of up to forty women and children were put together for the journey. The Quakers made sure the children were suitably dressed for the journey, spending nearly

£5,000 on clothes in 1918 alone. After the war, the Friends' Emergency Committee was keen to praise the officials at Tilbury, who treated these groups with great kindness and courtesy, as valuable customers. The manageress let women who were ill rest in her private room before they embarked on their ferry.

Many enemy aliens wanted to go to America. One man, who haunted the offices at St Stephen's House, had earned his living with a troupe of ten performing dogs and wanted the Friends' Emergency Committee to pay their fare to America. The committee felt this was not proper use of their money but realised that if they sent him without the dogs he would have no way of earning a living. They approached the Society for the Protection of Animals for help but they were only willing to chloroform the dogs to kill them, and not to pay for tickets. Enough money was eventually collected to pay for five of the dogs to travel to America. The man later wrote to the Quakers to thank them and to say that he and his reduced troupe had received their first booking.

Lack of good food made children very susceptible to infections and many of the internees' dependants were very short of food. The Quakers decided they needed to get some children away for recuperation. They experimented with using a small YWCA hostel in Willesden. Then Mr and Mrs Pethick Lawrence lent their cottage at Holmwood, in Surrey, and a lady in Letchworth offered to welcome some children into her home. Others were sent to spend time at the seaside at Clacton and Ramsgate and for two years, a house at Margate was filled with children who were threatened with tuberculosis. The doctors selecting children for these holidays found that up to a third were too sick to go. Common complaints included rickets, incipient tuberculosis, skin diseases, weak hearts and nervous troubles. As the years passed, the need for these places increased. The children usually went for a break of about a month. One member of the Friends' Emergency Committee also set aside a whole floor of his country house to give groups of twelve children a break of around three months at a time. His wife and daughter helped to care for them. By 1917, 700 children had been sent away to benefit from a break of this sort.

The Quakers found that the average length of time people asking for help had lived in Britain was eighteen years and most of the children had been born here. Many families who had been used to a good standard of living suddenly found they were paupers, struggling to pay the rent. Local Quaker Committees were set up to help all over the country. In Liverpool, they sheltered German women and children at the time of the riots that followed the sinking of the *Lusitania*. Quakers worked particularly hard in towns such as Bradford and Leeds, which had large populations of foreigners. Some families in rural areas were in extreme hardship, as they stood out more in thinly populated areas where there were fewer chances for them to get any work.

There were, of course, some difficult and bizarre cases. Fellow internees were delighted when a visiting general asked a man in one camp what he had done before the war. He replied that he has been a colonel in the British Camel Corps in Egypt. How far the visitor appreciated the irony of a former colonel in the British Army being interned as an enemy alien is not known. The Quakers' Industrial Adviser, James Baily, once met a young British-born sentry guarding the camp where his German-born father was interned. One of the Quakers' volunteers had her brother interned in Ruhleben and her step-father and step-brother interned in Knockaloe, on the Isle of Man; her mother was technically an enemy alien through her second marriage.

The sudden internment of thousands of men who had been the head of their households resulted in numerous problems for those left behind. A group of Quakers quickly developed expertise in helping to unravel a myriad issues relating to businesses, insurance, debts owed to the internee, mortgages and even marital relationships. The interned men felt enormous relief and gratitude for this help, as their awareness that their families struggled, while they were powerless to help, made the pain of internment much worse.

Although the Government started paying a basic subsistence allowance to the wives of interned men, they made no allowance for clothing. The mothers of growing children struggled to replace, mend and adapt clothes and to provide footwear for their offspring. The Quakers had a contact who owned a boot factory in the West Country and who provided them with many boxes of boots. Neither clothes nor boots were given out without the recommendation of a Visitor, who knew the family and a decision by the Case Committee. The Quakers often had to spend £80 a week on boots alone. Local committees all over the country sent in clothes they had made and the girls in various Quaker boarding schools knitted boys' jerseys. A special section carefully made baby clothes. For women treated as pariahs by their neighbours and former friends because they were married to someone of alien birth, contact with the Quaker's Visitor was itself a vital patch of warmth and humanity in their difficult lives. In turn, the Visitors were often horrified by the conditions in which these families existed.

Among those who were not interned at first, were a number of skilled tailors whose long-standing employers had been loath to lose them but who felt unable to employ an enemy alien. With their usual determination to find practical solutions to problems, the Friends' Emergency Committee again turned to their network of contacts for help. Arthur Crosfield of Liverpool bought rolls of good quality cloth from another

Quaker. He then employed some of the tailors to make boys' clothes for the Quakers' War Victims' Committee to send to France. The system was soon running well, with the men being paid the normal piece rate for their work. The Quakers liked the irony of one of Germany's enemies employing Germans to make clothes for another of Germany's enemies.

In time, almost all the men were interned and their places were taken by women. Money was always needed to buy materials and keep the workshops going. One large donation came from a French pacifist who, it turned out, had given an equal sum to the Berlin Committee for Foreigners in Germany. The Friends' Emergency Committee also received a large donation from a businessman in Germany, who hoped it would promote a greater understanding between the two nations and moderate the sufferings caused by the war.

The perceived need to intern large numbers of so-called alien civilians caused huge logistical problems for the authorities. In October 1914, Chief Constables were told to stop arrests while more accommodation was found. As and when places became available, the War Office notified the police. The next serious round of internments was in May 1915, when about 1,000 men of military age were rounded up each week. By November, 32,440 men had been interned. Numbers rose until the summer of 1916 after which they levelled off.

The internees were sent to a number of, more or less, unsatisfactory makeshift camps. At Deepcut in Surrey the men had to live in tents. The 700 men sent to a filthy old wagon factory in Lancaster had no heating or artificial light, little bedding and only basic sanitation. In an ironic parallel with Ruhleben, Newbury Racecourse was turned into an internment camp, with six to nine men packed into each stable. The men were locked into the unheated stalls from sunset to sunrise. As at Ruhleben, the area around the stables soon became a quagmire. Other camps, used for varying periods, included Frimley in Surrey, a factory at Handforth near Manchester, a former jute sacking factory in Stratford, East London, Reading Prison and a former workhouse in Islington, London. The main camp in Scotland was at Stobs and after all the internees were transferred to the Isle of Man, it became a military POW camp.

Large numbers of internees were sent to Olympia and Alexandra Palace in London. Olympia was used as a clearing house until December 1914 and then closed. Two exhibition halls were divided into twelve camps, each housing over 100 men and separated by heavy ropes. Those who could afford it paid £1 a week to stay in better accommodation in the restaurant. Private Hughes, who was one of the guards, said that this special area was nicknamed The House of Lords and that about twenty aristocratic and rich men lived in relative comfort, able to buy in extra food and furniture. He added that five men had such blue blood, or such large purses, that they were allowed to go out into the yard with a guard for half an hour a day. The War Office decided to keep several thousand internees from London at Alexandra Palace so that it would be easier for their families to visit them. Local people resented enemy aliens being interned at Alexandra Palace and thought it should have been used as a convalescent camp for soldiers instead.

When they ran out of space in the available camps, the War Office requisitioned nine transatlantic liners, moored at Ryde, Gosport and Southampton. Class differences were even perpetuated on board ship. There were three classes of cabin and three classes of internee. Those who could afford it could pay extra to get better food and waiter services. The waiters were third class internees earning a little much-needed money. Many men from Newbury paid 1s a week to be interned on *The Canada* at Ryde.

There were regular rumours about poor conditions in camps in both Britain and Germany. After one bout of rumours, officials from the American State Department visited a number of British camps including Newbury. They found no signs that men had been ill-treated and reported that the commandant at Newbury was on good terms with his prisoners and that living conditions were being improved.

Artist and writer Paul Cohen-Portheim was among the men taken to the old jute factory at Stratford after the sinking of the *Lusitania*. He was shocked to find how tightly the men were packed into a large room with broken panes in the glass roof. He was soon transferred to Knockaloe on the Isle of Man, where he enjoyed the views from the camp and the mixture of internees, but hated the crowded conditions. Encouraged by some of his comrades and by rumours of cushy conditions, he petitioned to be transferred to the 'gentleman's camp' at Lofthouse Park, Wakefield. His transfer was agreed, but he was shocked by the hostile crowd that greeted his group at Wakefield Station. He found that Lofthouse Park was, indeed more comfortable than Knockaloe and soon settled in. Internees paid 10s a week to be there and could draw £3 of their own money from the camp bank each week. The money was deposited by relatives and friends. The internees were able to buy items from local traders to personalise their accommodation and create their own, unofficial, cubicles in the dormitories. The canteen even sold beer and sherry by the glass. After the American YMCA provided a large hut, to be used as a reading room and library, Cohen-Portheim commented that only the YMCA and the Quakers stuck to any notion of Christian charity in wartime. The hut was also used for lectures and other events.

Notwithstanding the YMCA hut, he found life in his new camp very dull, likening it to a lower middle-class suburb, and he missed the open landscape of the Isle of Man. He believed it was the incessant community rather than imprisonment per se that led to barbed wire disease. He said it was a false community as there were no women or children, no old people and no young people. It was very class-ridden, with the German nobility keeping together in one part of the camp. He said that anti-Semitism was common among the internees. The men were never alone and it was never quiet. He noted that men lost all reserve and sense of decency, hatred was common and it was sparked by people's little foibles. Keeping active was the only way to keep the problems at bay. Over time, some of the richer internees ran out of money, putting those they had employed as servants out of work and competing for a smaller pool of jobs themselves. Tensions rose.

Every camp had a Markel Committee named after Dr K. E. Markel, who did a huge amount of work for the internees. Dr Markel was responsible for supplying most of the personal needs to men as well as equipment for them to use. The Markel Committees certified requests from prisoners and passed them to Dr Markel. When goods arrived in camp, the Markel Committee would distribute them. Markel donations included books, surgical equipment, food, clothes, musical instruments, music and sports equipment. The committees also provided emergency help for military prisoners who arrived hungry and exhausted. Prisoners and camp officials all knew that if Dr Markel could help in a particular situation, he would. He raised most of the money for his work from Englishmen who had strong ties with Germany and Austria. Markel was also the official representative of the German Red Cross Societies in Britain and helped make sure their aid was properly distributed.

Working with enemy prisoners and internees was considered too sensitive for the British YMCA to get involved. However, the American YMCA stepped in to provide huts and give other help wherever they were allowed to.

Numerous early, unsatisfactory camps only closed after two camps opened on the Isle of Man. The first was in Cunningham's Young Man's Holiday Camp in Douglas, and was initially tented. The other, which became the largest internment camp in Britain, was at Knockaloe on the west coast. At its peak Knockaloe housed 23,000 men, thus increasing the population of the island by half. Shockingly, joining a crowded charabanc from Douglas to view the internees became a popular excursion for islanders. How the internees must have hated being viewed as if they were animals in a zoo.

One visitor described the camp as being like a glorified chicken run. The huts looked like large henhouses and the men wandering aimlessly around the compounds, in mud or dust, looked like chickens. Knockaloe was divided into four camps and each of them was subdivided into a number of compounds, each housing about 1,000 men. The occupants of each compound were divided into companies, each with their own leader. The men had to submit to frequent head counts to help prevent escapes.

The first connection the Quakers had with Knockaloe was through visits made by their General Camp Traveller. His reports made shocking reading. Men were arriving before the camp was complete. Sanitation was bad, huts were leaky and unheated. The area around the huts was wet, muddy and miserable. There were no proper washrooms and the men had to use a bucket to collect cold washing water from a pump. The food was poor and inadequate. Resentment was heightened by the men's inactivity, which gave them endless time to brood on their incarceration. About ten per cent of the men had friends or relatives who could send them money and they were allowed to draw £1 a week from the camp bank to buy extra comforts. The remaining ninety per cent had no additional resources and vied for the chance to work for the richer internees and earn a little money.

The team at St. Stephen's House always felt a particular need to help the men at Knockaloe. Not only was it the largest civilian internment camp but it housed most of the poorer men and was so remote that their families were unable to visit them. Problems for the men were made worse by the repeated refusal of the Isle of Man authorities to permit the YMCA access to the camp or to allow them to provide recreation huts. Anyone wanting to help the men had to deal with many level of officialdom, which might include a officials from the Home Office, the War Office, and the Isle of Man Government, the general camp commandant, the sub-commandant, the assistant commandant, a sergeant, a sentry, a camp leader, a hut captain, the adjutant, the quartermaster or the doctor.

The worker who had the greatest impact on the lives of the internees at Knockaloe was James T. Baily. He was an expert handicraft teacher, who volunteered to accompany the General Camp Visitor in the summer holiday in 1915 intending to get some of the men involved in handicrafts. He found that the demand for his help was so great that he offered to work full-time for the Friends' Emergency Committee until the end of the war. His employers, Kent Council, granted him leave of absence.

The War Office soon decided that workers could not actually teach the internees. Instead, they had to restrict their work to helping the men set up their own classes and workshops and to providing materials. James Baily was appointed the Industrial Adviser and soon had an increasing stream of requests for help. The camp authorities had provided a large hut in each section of the camp, to be used as a dining room, and let the men use this space for various social purposes, including craftwork. Things went fairly well but there were problems with a build-up of material and supplies being delivered to the wrong compounds. In late

1915, this led to a letter ordering the Friends' Emergency Committee to stop sending materials to the camps. Baily had to smooth things over and realised that the Friends needed their own store. A large hut was built, just outside the camp, and served as their base. Each morning, a guard took representatives from the camp's Industrial Committees to the hut with their hand trucks to collect any materials that had arrived for them. The hut was later expanded so that it could also house the stock of items made for Dr Markel's Committee, for whom the Quakers acted as intermediaries. The Quakers working at Knockaloe increased to five, four of whom brought their families to stay on the island.

Sailors had a long tradition of making items to while away the hours on board ship. Some of them quickly started making all sorts of models and ornaments after they were interned. Others followed suit, after a little encouragement. In 1916 the Friends' Emergency Committee reported that about 5,000 men were being provided with occupation in this way, and that a special fund of £4,000 had been raised for this side of their work. Before the camps closed more than £20,000's worth of the men's handicrafts had been sold by the committee. This is particularly remarkable when you think that many of the items were small and sold for as little as a penny. The internees and prisoners also made items for their families, as souvenirs of their incarceration, or sold them to their fellow internees or to the guards. Some camps developed specialisms. Military prisoners at Leigh Camp made delicate inlaid work using coloured woods and these were sold to German officers in other camps. The men at Alexandra Palace concentrated on making wooden toys. The men were relieved to be able to earn small amounts of money to send to their families.

Quality control was a thorny issue and the Quakers' Visitors helped the camp's Industrial Committees monitor the goods that were sent out for sale. It was hard for them to refuse an item that a man had laboured over in the hope of earning some money for his wife and children but some articles were completely unsalable. Popular items included delicate animals made from cuttlefish moulds filled with melted 'silver paper', jointed wooden animals and inlaid match cases. The Quaker Visitors reached a point where they never wanted to see another box of any size, shape or colour, as they were inundated with them. They became equally unenthusiastic about the vast numbers of vases or napkin rings made from the shin bones of cattle, which had been bleached and carved. However, men also crafted beautiful pieces of furniture, some made to order, elaborate carvings, jewellery and complex mechanical models, which sold for high prices. One workshop was equipped with knitting machines, mainly so that men could make socks for their fellow internees out of unravelled knitwear that could no longer be repaired. After the war, some of the men who had been interned in Knockaloe set up a business in Germany in making new stockings out of old, each marked with their trademark showing the three legs of the Isle of Man, wearing their stockings.

Selling the finished items was an additional challenge. They were only allowed to send items out of the camps as long as they were not sold through normal markets and were not advertised. Sales had to be arranged through personal contacts and through a showroom in St Stephen's House. A Prisoners of War Relief Committee in New York was sent large consignments of goods to sell, until they became overstocked. The Crown Princess of Sweden worked to help POWs of all nationalities and organised an exhibition in Stockholm selling items made in POW and internment camps in various countries. Thirty-three cases of goods from Britain, worth more than £1,000, sold within two hours. Smaller consignments were sent to Norway and Denmark for sale.

Among the internees with previous experience of woodworking was Charles Matt. Before the war, Matt had been foreman over eighty men in a furniture-making factory in London. With a group of other professional cabinetmakers he was given permission to use two huts at Knockaloe as workshops. This group was commissioned to make a set of furniture designed by Charles Rennie Mackintosh. It was for a house called New Ways, which Rennie Mackintosh had designed for Mr W. J. Basset-Lowke, an industrialist from Northampton and one of the founders of the Design in Industries Association. The furniture was beautiful, very modern and made to an exceptionally high standard.

The Quaker workers were periodically called on to help settle disputes between individuals, or groups of men. They earned widespread trust from most of the internees and so were well placed to act as intermediaries when disputes arose, as they were bound to when thousands of men were forced to live in close proximity to each other for a long period. Sometimes, the workers also liaised between the authorities and the internees.

Until his sudden death at Knockaloe in early 1917, the commandant was Colonel Panzera. He was liked and well-respected by the Friends' Emergency Committee's workers and by most of the inmates. His attitude is illustrated by the warmth of the Christmas message he sent the internees in 1916. As well as acknowledging that it would be inappropriate to wish the internees more than the best Christmas they could have under the circumstances, Colonel Panzera wrote that he hoped that the New Year would bring peace so that they could be re-united with their families. He hoped that peace, prosperity and happiness would eventually eradicate memories of their current unhappiness. He also expressed his appreciation of how the 23,000 internees had generally behaved, making his staff's work easier than it might have been. He wished that he could have gone round to speak to each of the internees.

The main organisations working for the internees got together each Christmas to mark the festival. Sadly, the restrictions on what they could offer were tightened each year until no food or presents could be taken in. The Friends' Emergency Committee had a policy of never trying to take food into any of the camps, as the internees' families were in greater need of this kind of help. They helped with the administration of the Christmas event and gave each man a calendar with a message of goodwill. From 1915 onwards, one wealthy sympathiser gave between 6*d* and 1*s* per head to all prisoners and their guards each Christmas to help them celebrate. Each year Christmas was celebrated as the 'last Christmas in Camp.'

As at Ruhleben, some internees in Britain turned to gardening. This helped to keep them occupied and fit. It also enabled them to improve the appearance of their surroundings and supplement their diet with home-grown produce. The Old York Scholars' Association raised a special fund each year so they could award grants to internees to help them buy seeds, plants and tools. The Quakers also gave them grants and where outdoor gardening was impossible, they provided bulbs that could be grown indoors. In the later part of the war, workers at the Markel Fund encouraged internees to grow potatoes and other vegetables. The fund financed this scheme.

One of the Knockaloe internees had been a professional boxer and self-defence trainer whose former pupils included men from Scotland Yard. He was Joseph Pilates. When he was initially interned, in Lancaster Castle, he taught boxing and self-defence to his fellow inmates. He was then transferred to Knockaloe where he worked in the sick bay. He was told that he could help the patients exercise, as long as they stayed in bed, so he developed special frames using bed springs, which helped the men exercise. This and the system of floor exercises he developed at Knockaloe formed the basis of the Pilates exercise method after the war.

When conscription meant there was a shortage of workers, the Government relaxed the rules on employing aliens. The Friends' Emergency Committee saw this as an opportunity to set some of the men to making useful items, rather than fancy goods. Men who had been unwilling to take employment on government-run schemes were more enthusiastic about working for the Quakers, whose workers they had grown to respect. Getting the schemes up and running was complicated. Every single proposal to make goods for sale had to be submitted, in detail, to the Home Office for approval. Permission was granted for the internees to make a range of articles including dolls' wigs, Montessori educational materials, small model ships and planes.

Basket making was done on a larger scale. There were three skilled basket makers among the internees and they had soon trained another 100 men. Baily worked with the Island authorities and groups of internees were allowed out, under supervision, to cut willow for baskets and to clear the ground for future planting. Baily hoped basket making would continue as a new and thriving industry on the island after the war. Unfortunately, it did not survive for long after the Armistice.

Creatively, Baily also got internees making things for people who had also suffered during the war. The men at Knockaloe made large numbers of shoes and hosiery, which were sent to St Stephen's House for distribution. They also made bed-tables, leg-rests, and other items for camp hospitals. When a member of the Friends' Emergency Committee donated the materials, a group of internees made a revolving shelter for the use of tubercular patients. At the Markel Committee's request, suits of clothes and boots were made and stored ready to be given to the men when they left the camp.

Internees also made things that would help people in the devastated areas of France. This was not easy to arrange but they were eventually able to set up a workshop where men made furniture for French peasants who had lost everything due to the war. Yet again, the Committee was able to call on fellow Quakers for help. One Quaker from Birmingham lent some woodworking machinery, another provided the capital needed to get the project up and running and Baily drew up designs for furniture that could be folded up and packed flat for ease of transport. The dressers, buffet cupboards and kitchen tables were given to people living in temporary homes that had been supplied by the Friends' War Victims' Relief Committee. The Quakers made it clear to the internees who they were making things for and told the recipients who had made the furniture. They chartered a small cargo steamer to take the cargo of furniture to France.

Although the Quakers were not allowed to teach handicrafts to the internees, the rules were bent on a few occasions. At Knockaloe, a Swedish lady was allowed to use the Friends' Emergency Committee's hut to teach two internees how to weave. These men then instructed their fellow internees. Handlooms were built in the camp and the men made large numbers of decorative tablecloths and other items. One of these looms found its way to a technical museum in Germany after the war.

A number of so-called 'friendly aliens', both civilian and military and including Poles, Alsatians and Danes, were interned at Feltham in Middlesex. The Friends' Emergency Committee found someone with technical knowledge who was allowed to teach some of the men how to make and use carpet looms. They then made and sold brightly coloured pile rugs.

In wartime, people who help enemy aliens are widely derided and regarded with suspicion. In 1916, the *Evening News* published a vicious attack on the Friends' Emergency Committee calling its members 'Hun Coddlers' and suggesting their main activity was taking food and luxuries to internees. In reality, that is exactly what they were not allowed to do, but the name stuck. The *Daily Mail* and *John Bull* were also vitriolic and persistent in their attacks on those helping internees and their families. Anonymous letters and threats were written on parcels of clothes arriving at St Stephen's House. One letter threatened to shoot the secretary on sight. Individuals sometimes turned up to rant in person. The abuse abated after the first year but did not stop completely. From time to time, the Friends' Emergency Committee tried to place letters in the press about the favourable conditions in some POW and internment camps in Germany. Unfortunately, only the *Westminster Gazette* and the *Manchester Guardian* would ever print them. The Quakers realised it was not in the interests of those promoting the war to hear anything good about the enemy. Most newspapers preferred to give the idea that Germans in British camps lazed around in luxury while Britons in Germany were tortured and starved. This sort of campaign in the papers may also explain why several long-serving Camp Visitors suddenly had their passes withdrawn, without any explanation being given. One retired schoolmaster, who worked as a Visitor, was described as being obviously mentally deranged because of a remark he made at a tribunal. Another was considered dangerous, as he was a declared pacifist. In spite of their good relations with their contact at the War Office, there was no appeal against such decisions. A new Visitor could, however, be appointed.

Horatio Bottomley, editor of *John Bull,* was rabid in his hatred of Germans, Austrians, and anyone who showed them any compassion whatsoever. In an article headlined 'Teaching Treacherous Teutons' he launched a vitriolic on Baily, his work, and the Government for allowing it to be done. The story was taken up by other papers and Baily's wife and family, back in Ashford, had to deal with all kinds of unpleasantness. When Mrs Baily took a parcel destined for the Isle of Man into her local Post Office it would be passed along the counter to everyone with many facetious remarks. Some people in Ashford called on the Kent Education Committee to dismiss Baily. Luckily, the director refused to put the recommendation forward, as only a few months earlier they had granted him leave of absence to the end of the war. The director believed if they dismissed him he would have right to sue them for wrongful dismissal.

Some of the guards at Knockaloe objected to the presence of a pacifist civilian in the camp and some assumed Baily was pro-German. One guard even said that he would like to put him up against a wall and shoot him. Soon after this, Baily was called to appear before a tribunal as a conscientious objector, as his age group was due for call up. After much thought, he decided that he would not fight but would do alternative service in ambulance or relief work. To his amazement, his name was called out as 'exempted from military service because engaged in work of national importance'. When he asked why, the clerk would not tell him. It turned out that Lieutenant Colonel Panzera had written a personal letter to the tribunal, asking to be able keep Baily for his work at the camp, in the interests of discipline. Baily later said that while he was grateful for this, he would rather have had the chance to argue his case.

Many prisoners and internees were scared of going mad. It was very difficult for the Camp Visitors to have a rational conversation with a man about his problems once he had developed barbed-wire disease. In camps where the men were kept busy the incidence of barbed wire disease was very low but in camps where there was little to occupy the men it could be as high as ten per cent. Without the work by Baily and his fellow Quakers, the incidence of barbed-wire disease in Britain would have been far higher and, as Gerard noted with Britons transferred to internment in Switzerland, without early help some men were unable to recover.

After the Armistice, most internees wanted to get back to Germany or Austria as quickly as possible. Unfortunately, it was another year before they had all been released. This was a very difficult period. The men were completely focussed on their release and it was hard for the Quakers to persuade them to do any work. Some of those who had coped well until then, developed mental health problems. They were also upset by repeated articles in the popular press, insisting that none of them should be allowed to stay in Britain. In the end only about 3,000 of the interned civilians were allowed to stay in Britain. They were held in various camps for months more and were finally released in batches. The relief of rejoining their families must have been tempered by the realisation of the hardships their relatives had suffered and the problems they faced rebuilding their lives.

The Friends' Emergency Committee continued to help in any way it could. Realising that it would be hard for former internees who wanted to stay in Britain to find work, they set up a register of the men's skills and tried to find sympathetic employers. They eventually found work for almost all the men on their books.

8

Helping Civilians Overseas during the War

At the Friends' Meeting for Suffering, in September 1914, Quakers Dr Hilda Clark and T. Edmund Harvey stated their belief that civilians in the war zone, initially Belgium and France, needed help. The Quakers reinstated their War Victims Relief Committee (The Friends' Committee) that had previously done relief work for civilians during both the Boer War and the Franco-Prussian War of 1870, working under their badge of a double red and black star. Over the next nine years, they did relief work in nine European countries. They had about 270 workers in their London office and warehouse, and about 600 working overseas. Many, but not all, their male workers were conscientious objectors. From 1914–1923 the honorary secretary of the Friends' Committee was Ruth Fry, who later wrote an account of their work.

One of the things that makes the Quakers' work stand out is their determination to research what help was actually needed rather than simply launching in to do what they wanted to, or assumed was needed. Ruth Fry said providing aid was complicated and that giving money, food, and clothing was not enough. The Quakers never forgot their belief that man cannot live by bread alone and always considered the psychological as well as the physical well-being of the people they tried to help. They also wanted to help people move away from a dependence on aid and back to independence. Although the French quickly accepted the Quakers' offer of help, liaising with the French authorities was a real challenge until the two sides found a satisfactory way of working together. The French authorities became very supportive of the Quakers' efforts and provided building materials, petrol for cars and equipment, and maintenance for the hospital in Châlons sur Marne. The *Comité du Secours National* promised to give them a £120 a month to support their workers.

The Friends' Committee opened a number of departments. The purchasing department worked hard to get the best value on everything they bought, which was an increasing challenge as the war dragged on and prices for everything rose. The publicity department provided speakers to give illustrated talks about their work to stimulate interest and donations. The London office raised almost £393,000 in Britain and was sent additional funds by Quakers in America. The clothing department worked from a large warehouse, lent by Messrs Spottiswoode & Co. This department collected, sorted and distributed hundreds of thousands of garments to Belgian refugees in Holland, and to French, Armenian, Russian and Serbian refugees. The American Red Cross was among their largest donors. One of the busiest departments dealt with passports and permits. Each worker going to France needed a passport and a certificate from the Red Cross, which had pastoral care of Quakers working for the French Red Cross. If they were working in the war zone, they also needed a *Carnet d'Étranger* from the military authorities.

Most of the workers were volunteers, many of whom paid for their own travel, equipment and living expenses. However, some medical staff were paid an honorarium. The workers were given free rail travel by the French authorities. As a concession, workers who were waiting to make their case for exemption from military service on the grounds of conscientious objection were allowed to attend a tribunal in France rather than travelling back to Britain to be heard.

Ruth Fry said there were three types of refugees: *sinistrés, émigrés* and *repatriés*. They initially planned to help the *sinistrés*, who had lost everything, but soon realised they also needed to help the *émigrés,* whose homes were occupied and who had to live as unwanted guests elsewhere in France. The third group, who also needed help, were the *repatriés* who had stayed in their homes for a while under the occupation but who were later sent back to unoccupied France via Switzerland and became émigrés.

The Quakers identified four areas where they felt their help would make a difference: general medical work and district nursing, building shelters, agricultural aid, and general social work. They also recognised that to stop many people losing heart, their immediate priority had to be helping people prepare for the impending winter. In France, the Quakers were often referred to as the English Mission.

The first groups of volunteers went to the area north-east of Meaux and to La Ferté Milon to hand out clothes, boots and blankets. Although the French Government gave refugees an allowance similar to that given to soldiers' wives, it was barely enough to pay for food and lodging. Most refugees had left their homes with only their summer clothes and, as winter approached, there were thousands of people around

Châlons-sur-Marne who had no blankets or warm clothes to help them through the winter. Some women had stayed in the remains of their villages, tied by caring for sick relatives, or because they themselves were invalids or pregnant, or because they were even more scared to desert their homes than to stay and try to preserve what they could.

During January and February 1915 the Quakers visited fifteen villages and, having checked what was needed, handed out 3,250 articles of clothing, 178 blankets and 370 pairs of boots, helping 1,242 people. Among the bales of clothes that were sent out from the London warehouse were some garments where the donor had slipped a message or a small gift into a pocket.

The volunteers worked in small groups, each of which was allowed considerable autonomy by the committee in London. This freedom was important if they were to be effective, as communication with London was very difficult and telephones and telegrams were reserved for official use only. The permits issued to each volunteer were only valid for a few weeks at a time and restricted their movement. These limitations must have regularly tried the Quakers' patience. Before long there were more than seventy workers in Châlons, Fère Champenoise, Vitry le François, Sermaize, Fontenelle, La Ferté Milon and Paris, where they took over a warehouse to house stores waiting to be distributed. In Bar-le-Duc, the authorities managed to get exemption from military service for a doctor so he could work with the refugees.

After just a few months, the Quakers published a report on their efforts so far and concluded that they needed to raise at least £250,000 for their work in France. By that point, they had raised £30,000. Administrative costs were kept very low, as they were lent all premises free of charge and most of the workers were volunteers. Gifts, ranging from a packet of needles to a lorry, according to the giver's resources, poured in from Quakers in England.

As early as November 1914 a group of thirty-two volunteers, including doctors and nurses, set off for the Marne region to start relief work. As well as medical projects, their work included installing new wells to restore access to clean water.

Châlons-sur-Marne was not badly damaged itself but was a centre for refugees from the Ardennes, Meuse and Marne areas, where old men, women and children huddled in barns, stables and anywhere else where they could take shelter, often sleeping on straw without any blankets. The sound of firing was constantly in the background. The team soon identified that the greatest need was for maternity care and support for mothers with young children, as all the local doctors had been called into the Army to replace military doctors who had been killed. The Préfet was desperate to ensure that dearly wanted babies did not die in the hovels where their mothers were sheltering so he asked the Quakers, under Dr Hilda Clark from Street in Somerset, to start a maternity hospital.

The Quakers were offered a wing in the vast Asile Départmental des Veillards, which housed the elderly and people with epilepsy. The regional authorities paid for the conversion and maintenance of the building. Some of the former residents were used as rather dubious servants. There were twenty-eight beds for women and a crèche for the older children. A second ward was ready to open by January 1915. Many of the babies slept in hammocks made by Belgian refugees involved with the Quakers' schemes in Holland. Staff often had to drive out to the nearby villages in their own cars to fetch expectant mothers, as all other transport was reserved for the military. One mother, collected from a tiny overcrowded house, only owned three garments in the world. By the summer of 1915, the number of volunteers in the area had grown to 150. Thanks to gifts from Quakers in Britain and the USA, team members were able to give each new mother a layette and, when it was absolutely necessary, a cradle and blanket.

Staff tried to keep in touch with all the mothers who had given birth in the hospital and monitored the progress of their babies. Presumably because most young men were away fighting, the number of births in the Châlons area had dropped so far that by the end of 1915 there were only about ten a month. This meant only one ward was needed and the other could be devoted to women from the area around Rheims, where the hospitals were often shelled. Every time there was an alert in Rheims, the patients had to be carried to the hospital basements and it was felt that this constant disruption slowed their recovery even, as the Friends' Committee's Second Report put it, if their recovery was 'not abruptly cut short by a shell'.

The hospital had to be evacuated to Méry-sur-Seine in July 1918 after a bombardment and damage from aerial torpedoes. Fortunately, the authorities had been able to warn them that an attack was imminent and they had managed to remove the patients. Staff opened an emergency post in a champagne cellar in Châlons, where several babies were born. In the summer of 1918, the Châlons Maternity Hospital, where the Friends had overseen more than 500 births, was proudly handed over to the French.

When local villages were bombarded, the Quakers took in hundreds of children whose parents had had to flee and take cover in the woods. One day forty children arrived with little notice. Each had been carefully identified with a label, which they had proceeded to chew during their journey. Many of the children were filthy and by the time they and their clothes had been washed the labels were illegible and the children anonymous.

The Quakers provided spectacles to 530 French people who had either lost their glasses during the war, or who had never had any. One writer reported that at least a quarter of the women had told the volunteers that the weakness of their eyes was due to the volume of tears they had cried since the start of the war.

The bombardment of Rheims, which lasted more than a year, traumatised many of the children so badly that they begged to be taken to the relative safety of Châlons. The Quakers tried to find places, away from the battle zones, where the children could stay and were delighted when the Comtesse Morillot offered to lend them her home, the Château de Bettancourt-la-Longue, near Châlons. An anonymous donor, who turned out to be the author of *Peter Pan*, J. M. Barrie, paid for a convalescent home for fifty children to be set up in the château and covered its running costs for the first year. The home was managed by Barrie's friends, the writer E. V. Lucas and his wife. Children, rescued by workers from a number of villages, were given sanctuary there. One of 'Maman' Lucas's weekly tasks was overseeing the children while they wrote letters to their mothers or to their fathers in the trenches.

Apart from one hospital nurse, the home was run by volunteers, some of who were friends of the Lucases. Mrs Lucas was in charge. There were also an orderly and a chauffeur. The latter was invaluable, as the château was 20 miles from Vitry and the closest shops. The Comtesse de Morillot insisted that a French lady should live on site to keep the girls on the straight and narrow, and to ensure their religious instruction was not neglected. At the end of the year, Mrs Lucas had to go home and Barrie did not extend his funding but as the home was providing an essential service, the Quakers had to take it on themselves.

They also worked hard to help with the appalling lack of viable housing. They initially set out to repair damaged buildings but soon switched most of their efforts to building prefabricated wooden houses for villages around Vitry-le-François and Fère Champenois, destroyed during the Battle of the Marne. Staff accommodation and a workshop were set up in a disused school in Vitry. The local authorities provided the timber for the houses, as part of the compensation that was payable to the displaced people. The Quakers employed a number of male refugees, who were not of military age, to help with the work.

The first house was ready by Christmas 1914 and local mayors were quick to put in requests for buildings to be put up amidst the ruins of their communities. The old houses had been so badly damaged that they could not be re-used. Often the only part of a building left standing was the brick-built chimney.

Sermaize-les-Bains had lost 900 of its 1,000 houses. Numerous wooden houses were erected there, and the working population moved in. The houses had from one to four rooms, double walls and robust plank floors, casement windows and strong, locking doors. However, as they didn't have ceilings and due to a shortage of materials they were only roofed with tarred paper, they were very cold. Once the Quakers realised how unsatisfactory these roofs were, they switched to using tiles whenever possible. The houses survived the next attack on Sermaize in 1917.

The Quakers expanded their building work to a number of other towns and villages, including Fère Champenois and Esternay. Esternay itself was not badly damaged but was surrounded by ruins, so the Quakers set about repairing damaged houses as well as building new ones. When they went to build houses in a new area the mayor would help draw up a list of the people whose need was greatest. Workshops were set up in a barn or other building and the carpenters got to work. Although the French authorities paid for timber it was hard to come by, as supplies were often commandeered by the military. Each house soon became a home.

At Pargny and Sermaize the Quakers built small garden cities for people who did not have their own plot of land. Twenty-four houses were built along curved roads. Due to a shortage of timber the walls had timber frames and brick infill. Each house had a front and back garden. The plan was that the houses would be for long-term use by the old and infirm after the war.

David Garnett was not a Quaker, but chose to work with them. He later wrote that the suffering he saw at Sommeilles, near Sermaize, turned him into a conscientious objector, believing that none of the issues mattered as much as putting an end to the atrocious suffering. Sommeilles was a hilltop village overlooking the Argonne Forest and was the closest point to the front that the English Mission was allowed to work. A week before the Battle of the Marne, Sommeilles had been taken by the Germans – who had then systematically destroyed it, burning houses, throwing incendiary bombs into every building and killing all the livestock. Some inhabitants were killed and others taken hostage and sent to Germany. Later, when the Germans were driven out, there were still a few families eking out an existence in the village. All that was left of the town hall was a pair of smiling stone lions, a flight of steps and a handsome portico. Yet, between the ruins, Garnett was amazed to see neat gardens with rows of vegetables and foraging chickens. The remaining people were growing food wherever they could. The Quakers set about erecting some of their frame houses as quickly as possible and a French society provided stoves and furniture.

In the summer of 1916 they opened another workshop, at Dole in the Jura, which was out of the war zone and closer to good supplies of timber. Being away from the front made it easier for the Quakers to get workers' permits and they soon employed 100 men. When the American Quakers joined in, in the autumn of 1917, this workshop was too small and another was opened at Ornans in Doubs, using machinery that had been sent from the United States.

When eight-year old Antoinette's grandmother returned, after ten months as a prisoner in Sedan, the family was in a bad way. Antoinette's father was away in Verdun, sick and dispirited, and he refused to allow the family to spend any money. Her mother was almost too depressed to do anything at all. Young Antoinette was the only one with any energy and was determined to get a new home for the family. She coaxed her mother into letting her go to talk to the Quakers about getting a house. She told them she had half a franc and would pay for the wood herself, and that she wanted a two-room house with a kitchen and bathroom. Moved by the girl's appeal, they agreed to help the family.

In the summer of 1917, the Friends' Committee's report remarked that the level of destruction in the Somme and Aisne regions had to be seen to be believed. In the Marne, most of the damage had been caused by fire but in the Somme and Aisne, it was by shelling that was largely deliberate and systematic so that in some cases, the church and every house in a village had been deliberately blown up with dynamite. The French authorities would not allow any of the people who had fled from the onslaught to return until some kind of dwelling had been built for them. The Quakers were the only organisation involved in building houses on any significant scale. By the time of the German advance in March 1918, the Quakers had built about seventy houses and helped plough 300 acres. Like the local people, they had to flee the area when the Germans advanced – but stayed to help wounded soldiers after everyone else had left. The damage caused by the German advance cost the Friends alone in excess of £7,000. After the Armistice, they went back to the area to help with reconstruction.

There were people who questioned whether it was worth repairing or replacing houses in areas that were quite close to the front but the Quakers were convinced that giving people some semblance of normality and a way of providing for themselves was well worth the risk.

The prefabricated house frames were sent to a village by lorry and unloaded into a heap. Assembling them was not difficult and French carpenters then added the windows. People gradually came to love the Quakers' houses and rivalry developed over who received the one, two- or three-room houses. Most people who were given one of the huts were thrilled but one woman complained that the light in her new hut was intolerable after the pleasant darkness of the cellar where she had been living. Another old lady moaned that the roof of her new house leaked so David Garnett and Francis Birrell went to investigate. Sure enough, there was a pool of water in the corner of the room. They realised that the pool had been produced by the lady's free-ranging Belgian hare, and she had to apologise.

Local people were generous in providing the workers with as many vegetables as they could and the Quakers sent out cocoa, chocolate, sardines, tinned salmon, tinned herrings, tinned milk, and more chocolate, from England. The French authorities provided bread, which was often a month old.

The Quakers were acutely aware that they needed to get farming up and running again to prevent the recurrence of destitution. Their first efforts to help French farmers were in Esternay. The team was led by a New Zealander, Theodore Rigg. As usual, they planned carefully. The farms in the area had been small, growing barley, oats, wheat, and potatoes. The Quakers commented that there was a marked lack of co-operation between farmers; each with their own tools and with no thought of sharing equipment with each other. The Quakers had to address the shortage of farm machinery and tried to get communes to share a pool of equipment, but they all wanted it at once. The Quakers concluded it was better to have a central pool of equipment that could be lent out as needed, each piece with its own driver. They also set up workshops to salvage and repair existing machinery and gave out chickens and rabbits for local people to breed so they would have food for the coming winter.

By April 1915, the Quakers had distributed 20,000 packs of seeds containing peas, beans, cabbage, lettuce, beetroot and onions, and repeated this each year. They also brought in more than 8,000 kilos of artificial manure and 80,000 cabbage plants that had been raised in a Quaker nursery at Sermaize. Not content with helping local farmers and gardeners, the Quakers cultivated some plots of land themselves.

Because the area had been denuded of horses and cattle, there had been an increase in wild boar – themselves thought to be refugees from the Ardennes. They created an additional problem to which there was no easy solution.

Ruth Fry noted that more and more farmland was falling out of cultivation each year with weeds spreading and spoiling such crops as were planted. Because of this, the Friends' Committee decided to expand their work to helping farmers throughout the year. When Rigg moved on to work in Montenegro and Albania, his successor, Edward Guest, went one step further and began ploughing in the Verdun area even before the *sinistrés* began to return. The Quakers were concerned that by ploughing they might blur property boundaries but the local mayor and council said that they should not worry. When the *sinistrés* returned they were delighted with the work that had been done as it had given them a head start in bringing their land back into productive use.

The French Government distributed a considerable amount of seed corn, so the Friends decided to concentrate on the needs of smaller farmers and growers. In the spring they distributed, free of charge, five tons of seed potatoes and 1,700 packets of seeds, each containing fourteen varieties of seeds. As it was clear that the land could not be restored to productive use until it had been cleared, they brought in more than 800 tools including rakes, scythes, spades and hoes, which they gave away. Enabling people to grow their own vegetables again had a huge impact. Helped by the Agricultural Relief of Allies Association, the York Old Scholars' War Time Service Fund, the Essex and Suffolk Quarterly Meeting and the American Relief Clearing House, they also provided large amounts of heavy machinery. Where no labour was available, members of the unit stepped in to run the machines themselves. A volunteer on one machine threshed over 1,500 sacks of corn.

They helped young refugees in Sermaize to grow their own vegetables as well as seedlings, which were then distributed to other centres. Families living in the disused Hôtel de La Source in Sermaize had their own allotments. When they realised the local people had been very dependent on their chickens and rabbits before the war, they put one skilled refugee woman in charge of rearing rabbits and poultry for distribution. She was so successful that they were able to send out 250 chickens every three to four weeks and hoped to provide 200 young rabbits every three to four months.

There was no doubt how much their help was appreciated and when one team was leaving a village, they found that their car had been decorated with flowers and more were pushed into their hands.

The Quakers were worried the people they were helping would come to depend on charity and so they asked everyone to pay what they could. In some areas, they held weekly stock sales, with goats brought from other regions of France and Southdown sheep from England. They made beehives in their Dole workshop then stocked them with bees, aware how important bees had been in the Ardennes and northern Meuse areas before the war. The York Old Scholars Association sent 25,000 fruit trees to the Quakers, who shared them between 130 communes.

In 1870, the Royal Agricultural Society had helped French farmers. In 1915, a week after the Battle of the Marne, they set up the Agricultural Relief of Allies Fund to provide similar help during the latest conflict. Representatives from the organisation visited the Marne and Meuse regions and reported that the scale of damage could not be exaggerated. They said it was amazing that any cultivation was taking place and expressed their admiration for the women of France and what they were achieving, cultivating land to within a few miles of the trenches.

The society made an appeal for livestock including Southdown rams and Large White boars, which were sent out to the Marne and Meuse areas.

The king headed the list of donors, sending five shearling rams from his famous flock at Sandringham. Each time the French regained an area, the committee sent aid. They sent consignments of agricultural machines and implements, seed wheat, oats, barley and potatoes. Live poultry and rabbits were sent to start a breeding programme to supply meat for the table. Approximately 10,000 fruit trees, carefully selected for the soil and climate, were sent to replace those that had been destroyed. Before the Germans had left the area around Péronne and Bapaume, they had sawn through the roots of the trees in all the orchards to make sure that they could not regrow.

By December 1915, aid provided by the organisation included sixty-one rams, eleven boars, two goats, 1,800 head of poultry, as well as twenty binders, forty harrows and fifty ploughs. By the end of the war, they had sent aid worth about £265,000. Farmers in Britain providing enormous help to their French counterparts.

The Royal Horticultural Society set up a large fund to provide help to French farmers and the Lincolnshire firm of P. Johnson sent out enough seeds to plant 7,000 vegetable gardens.

Organisations in the British Dominions were also quick to help. The Canadians were particularly generous but representatives from Australia, New Zealand and South Africa also visited France and set up their own committees to provide agricultural aid.

On an informal basis, various groups of British soldiers helped farmers at different points during the war. Some helped repair equipment, while cavalry troopers helped ensure the ploughing was done on time. Australian troops helped with the harvest around Villers-Brettoneux, reaping and carting, as well as sowing new crops. Another group began rebuilding the local school, but peace came before they had finished construction.

Furniture was in very short supply. One very old great-grandmother lay slowly dying in her granddaughter's one-roomed hut that the family had built. The granddaughter approached the Quakers to ask if they could provide a bed for the old lady. The only help they had received up to that point had been seeds for their garden, which was doing well. Within an hour of the request being made, they had been given a pillow, a bed jacket, blanket and nightdress for the old lady and some clothes for each member of the family. By evening, the old lady was lying on a new mattress. When the summer got hot, she was tormented by flies so the Quakers hung fly papers around the room, then cut two windows in the walls to allow a through draught, hung a muslin veil around the bed and checked the surrounding area for any unhealthy deposits. A nurse called regularly, even though there was nothing she could do to keep the old lady alive. All this care certainly eased the last three months of her life and helped her family feel that they were not alone.

The French Government managed to give some grants towards the cost of furnishing the houses built by the Quakers. A few individual Quakers also sent money for furniture. In some areas, the Quakers bought furniture, which they sold to the *émigrés* at cost price, paid in monthly instalments.

It was a matter of status among the refugees to have a decent bed and bedding, and there was fierce competition between families, each wanting to have the best. The bed linen was particularly important to them and one family had buried 150 pairs of sheets in a false bottomed cellar for safety, before the Germans arrived.

In Bar-le-Duc, the Quakers set up a Linen Chest Club for refugees. Each family paid 1.50 francs and provided a packing case. They were then given three or four sheets, four pillow cases, six towels and a blanket, and were encouraged to embroider their initials on each item. A carpenter then added hinges and clasps to the packing case, turning it into a useful piece of furniture for the family. Nearly 700 of these chests were created.

During 1916, the Quakers continued their work in France but also turned some of their attention to Belgium. Their efforts included carrying out investigations in every town and village in the parts of the country that had not been occupied, recording how many refugees there were, where they were living, what conditions they were living in, how many were ill, how many were orphans and whether there was a school. Their research showed that large numbers of babies were dying so they set up fourteen milk distribution centres and infant mortality started to fall. They also opened two orphanages and several schools, including separate ones for Flemish-speaking children, as Flemish was not allowed in the French schools. Hard-pressed members of the Friends' Ambulance Unit found time to do relief and sanitary work in a number of Flemish villages and helped restore clean water supplies.

When a Chartreuse monastery at Le Glandier, Pompadour in Corrèze, was emptied of monks so that it could house 600 Belgian children, the Quakers were asked to help look after and entertain them. The home was in the charge of a captain and paid for by the Belgian Government and the American Red Cross. When the Quakers arrived, the children were pale, anaemic, homesick and described as a disorderly rabble. However, with good food, care and activities to keep them occupied, they improved steadily. In 1919, they were sent back to Belgium, accompanied by Quakers as far as Liège.

The Quakers providing general aid often had to be ready to cope with a sudden influx of refugees. They felt the saddest people were the refugees from the Ardennes or from around Verdun. The refugees felt lonely after arriving in a safer part of France and had often been separated from other members of their family. Many of the older people were visibly depressed.

Bar-le-Duc was not badly damaged but quickly filled with shocked refugees who had fled their burning homes. All the refugees longed to be able to return home and many of the old people asked, repeatedly, if they would be home by Christmas. The area was used as a clearing station for refugees from Verdun, who were then sent on to other parts of France. The Quakers did all they could to keep people from the same village together and tried, at the very least, to stop their condition and spirits sinking any lower.

The Quakers set up a workroom in a large room provided by the mayor with the dual role of keeping women and girls busy, working together, and producing much-needed clothes. All the materials were bought from mills in the town. Some of the clothes were then sold, giving the women a much-needed, if small, income. More than 100 women, who were used to working hard on their farms, found the chance for purposeful work with a group of other women very welcome.

Several other workrooms were set up in the surrounding area. Margery Fry got a group of women doing embroidery on sacks, in brightly coloured wool. Canadian flour sacks were the best for this because of their finer weave. Before the war, lace-making had provided an important income for women. When they learned how many lace-making pillows had been lost by the refugees, the Quakers provided 269 new ones and also found outlets for selling the finished lace. In Bar le Duc, Rachel Alexander set up a workroom for white embroidery, which was so successful that the women continued the work when they went back to their own villages after the war.

Although French regulations governing who could run schools were stringent, the Quakers did manage to start a few open-air crèches for children under six, taking children who had run wild for a year. It was agreed the authorities would not ask too many questions about what the Quakers did, as long as the Quakers did not encroach too far on the normal curriculum. Caring for these traumatised children, who were not used to any organised activity, was very challenging. It was also rewarding for the volunteers, who did not include a single trained teacher. Before long, most of the children looked forward to their time with the Quakers. Their parents were relieved and grateful to have some respite and to know their children were getting a basic education. One mother said she had twice taught her son to read since the war had started, and twice he had forgotten what he had learned because he had no chance to practise. In one village the classes had to be stopped over the winter as there was no room where they could be held and it was too cold for them to continue outside. Volunteers commented that when they arrived, the children had forgotten how to play.

It was inevitable that when people fled their homes some of the oldest and frailest would get separated from their families in the ensuing turmoil. Fourteen old ladies, who had been driven from their homes by air raids on Bar le Duc, were taken in by the Quakers who set up a refuge for them in an old farm at Charmont in 1917. The eldest of these ladies was apparently a 'delightful old lady' who had been well-off until all her houses were destroyed.

The Quakers realised that both goods and money were in very short supply, so they opened a number of shops in western Meuse, which stocked essentials including food, household goods, tools and seeds. They even ran mobile shops that visited remoter villages. The goods were sold at cost price. By 1920, when they were handed over to the Meuse Co-operative organisation, the shops were flourishing. One share, worth twenty-five francs, was given to each family who had been customers, to encourage them to keep the co-operative working. There were initially about 3,000 members.

Where the Quakers led, other organisations followed and began to help, although not in any great number until 1917. The Quakers remained, by far, the largest British group trying to bring help to the damaged areas of France. Their achievement was huge and up to the German offensive in March 1918, they had helped about 35,000 people from 12,000 families in 282 villages. They had erected 540 of their wooden houses and 36 barns. They had also provided clothes, bedding, seeds, tools, fertilizers and furniture.

Volunteers from other groups also remained dedicated to their roles even when the front line moved and they had to regroup. Members of the French Wounded Emergency Fund worked with the British Red Cross in fifteen villages between Péronne and Ham. When the Germans advanced in March 1918, the workers helped local people flee and then stayed to help wounded soldiers. They were still there when the Germans were pushed into retreat at the end of the summer. One Scottish lady, supported by a committee in Glasgow, went out to Flanders where she devoted herself to rescuing children from villages that had been bombarded. She sent many of the children she rescued to safety in Switzerland and was later awarded the *Croix du Guerre* in recognition of her achievements.

* * *

The Quaker volunteers did not confine their efforts to France and Belgium. In October 1915, aware that it was impossible to assess the situation from a distance, Theodore Rigg and three others left Esternay and set off to Montenegro and Albania, hoping to do aid work there. Before they could reach their destination, they met the remains of the

Serbian Army in full retreat in terrible conditions. Nothing daunted, they appropriated a building, straw to sleep on and some fuel and started to do anything they could to help the seemingly endless stream of civilian refugees and retreating soldiers. After a while, they moved on and did the same in several other places. In one place, they acquired four large tents and arranged for 2,000 kg of bread to be baked and distributed. In another, they distributed bread and beans to 900 refugees and, when the refugees were about to sail for Corfu, delivered bread, blankets and clothes to the ships.

The winter of 1916–17 found Rigg and four colleagues in Russia, firstly in Moscow and then in Samara. They often had to travel by sleigh as they tried to reach wherever the next wave of refugees was pouring in from the Western Front. After a while, they were joined by a group of American relief workers from Philadelphia, one of whom, Esther White, joined Rigg in his efforts to set up orphanages for children displaced by war. They worked together until 1919.

When the Bolsheviks took over, local officials were initially keen to show how well they could run things and conditions improved. This was, however, temporary – and was followed by severe food shortages. Funds dried up after the Bolsheviks closed the banks and for three winter months, no money could be sent from Petrograd to the team. In spite of all the difficulties caused by the Revolution, the Quakers continued running hospitals, an orphanage, dispensaries and workrooms in a number of villages throughout 1917–18. However, they finally concluded that they had to withdraw from the villages and concentrate their work in Buzuluk. The local Soviet then asked them to take over the orphanage in an old monastery outside the town, which they did. They also set up workshops in an attempt to help local people to earn a living.

Quakers in England raised £24,000 to help fight the famine in Russia but getting money out to Russia was extremely difficult. Grain could, however, be bought in Siberia and then transported by train to wherever it was needed. Unfortunately, it was often removed from the trains when officials in the areas they passed through decided that their need was greater than that of the planned recipients.

As well as manmade problems, the Quakers, and the refugees they were helping, faced an assault from the suslik and other pests. The suslik was a grain eating ground squirrel, which ravaged crops. On hearing that they were easy to catch and kill, the Quakers organised suslik hunts – paying the refugees for each skin.

The Quakers made a strong impression on the Russian authorities, and were allowed to continue their work after other organisations, whose staff were thought to include spies, had been made to leave the country. One official said he thought the Quakers were 'psychologically incapable of espionage'. It was clear to everyone that their desire to help was founded on their fundamental belief that they needed to assist suffering people, no matter how their governments behaved.

* * *

Ruth Fry said that Belgium was invaded by an army and Holland by a people. While 250,000 Belgian refugees made their way to Britain, 500,000 crossed into the southern Netherlands. The Dutch were sympathetic and hospitable but the sheer volume of refugees meant the welcome soon wore thin. Bergen Op Zoom had a normal population of 15,000 but over just three days, a tidal wave of 300,000 refugees passed through the town. Dutch Common Law dictated that in a city where there were aliens in distress, the Burgomaster had to give them one night's lodging and a ticket to the frontier. The lawmakers had never envisaged an influx of refugees on the scale that happened in 1914 and Burgomasters were soon writing to their Government begging for help. It was simply not possible to deliver all the refugees to the border and many were dispersed to towns all over the country.

The Quakers were acutely aware of the situation in the Netherlands and wanted to help. They sent T. Edmund Harvey and Dr Dyson, to the Netherlands in September 1914. They found the situation was tense and that the Dutch were in a very difficult position, worried that the Germans were about to invade the Netherlands. It was widely believed the presence of large numbers of refugees from an occupied belligerent country would not help the Dutch position. Luckily, tension soon abated and the Quaker volunteers were able to go to Flushing to keep a maternity hospital open. They continued to support the hospital for about nine months, during which time more than seventy babies were born there. As a busy port, Flushing was not considered a safe place for unaccompanied young women, so the Quakers also set up the Home Belge, which was designed as a refuge for homeless girls who were making their way to Britain.

The Dutch established a number of *Vluchtoorden*, literally translated as 'flight places'. These were emergency camps, each of which was designed to house 20,000 people for an undefined period and which were like small towns. The largest of these camps were at Gouda, Ede, Uden and Nunspeet. Other camps, for interned soldiers, were set up at Amersfoort, Harderwyek and Groningen.

Refugees in Gouda were housed in greenhouses rented from a local nursery. As Ruth Fry soon realised, greenhouses were poor substitutes for homes. Like the low wooden huts provided in other camps, the greenhouses were freezing in winter and baking hot in summer. The living conditions were very basic. Each family had a cubicle just 15 foot square, partitioned off by a curtain. The Quakers stepped in to offer what help they could and were always dependant on the goodwill of the camp commandant, as his word was law. On the whole, the Quakers' efforts were welcomed with enthusiasm and support by both the Dutch authorities and the refugees.

Frederick (Fred) Rowntree and Philip Burtt joined the volunteers who were working in the four main camps in early 1915, convinced there was a great deal they could do to make life less tedious and depressing for the refugees. They also wanted to help young boys use their time to train for their future, so their time in the camps was not wasted, and were particularly keen to help the large numbers of boys who had come from the slums of Antwerp and other cities. The Dutch authorities were very supportive of their plans.

Looking to the future, Fred designed some very simple one-storey semi-detached wooden houses, with a sitting room and two bedrooms. They were designed so they could later be joined together to make a larger house. The intention was for the refugees to be able to take the houses back to Belgium when the war ended. They were called '*Maisons Demontables*' and Fred demonstrated how ten men could erect a house in just three hours. The Quakers financed the construction of more than 100 of these houses at a cost of £50 each. Painted green and white, they broke up the stark monotony of the camps. The volunteers lived in one of these houses in each camp, and the carpenters who built the houses were allowed to live in them rent free. Every house was provided with a bed, table, chairs, cupboards, bedding, curtains, doormat, pail, utensils, and brushes, all of which were made in the camp.

The Dutch government had been given £27,000 by the Danes for the support of the refugees and used the money to enable the Quakers to build a whole village of houses at Ede. It came to be known as the *Deensche Dor,* the Danish Village. Some roads, such as Fred Rowntree Straat, were named after the volunteers. House building was extended to Uden, financed by the Dutch Government.

The Dutch employed as many refugees as they could on jobs around the camps. The Quakers also provided work, but were asked not to pay wages that were high enough to temp refugees away from the official camp jobs. The Quakers' workrooms were therefore filled with people who were not fully fit and those who wanted to learn a handicraft and were therefore willing to work for a lower wage. The Quakers carefully selected the people they thought would benefit most from training and employed about 150 workers in each camp.

Women and girls were taught to make woollen rugs, dresses, appliqué work, embroidery, raffia shoes and baskets. Men were taught fretwork, inlaid woodwork and how to make wooden toys, fibre mats (largely for use in the camps), baskets and brushes. Alfred Powell and Martin Walker taught chair-making. Brush-making was taught by Thomas Cox, an English brush-maker who volunteered to go to the camp at Uden as a teacher. Before he was allowed to start work, he had to undertake not to undercut the prices charged by Dutch brush-makers. He initially had the usual language problems and had to manage with sign language until he discovered that one of the refugees had been a brush-maker before the war. He then arranged to pay this man a little extra as his assistant and translator. They painted the backs of the brushes in the colours of the Belgian flag, which went down well. Brush-making was very popular and Cox soon had a waiting list of recruits. He was impressed by how keen even the middle-aged and elderly men were to learn a new trade. They exported some of their brushes to Britain until such imports were banned.

Buying materials for the workshops was often a problem and they sometimes had to be imported from Britain. The raffia work suffered a blow when the authorities decided that raffia was needed for making secret camouflage fences, and the Quakers and their workers had to make do with inferior materials instead.

It was not long before they could see a clear improvement in the mental state of the people who were occupied in this way. Working regular hours, and finding friendship with their fellow workers and teachers, contributed enormously to their sense of well-being. The Quakers regularly came up with new jobs and activities to keep people fully occupied and to alleviate the boredom that was a problem for both refugees and volunteers. Many volunteers remained in the camps for several years, with very few chances to take any leave in Britain. Most of them soon learnt to get by in French and sometimes Flemish as well.

Volunteers at the camp in Gouda were asked to take on making 1,500 seaweed mattresses for the refugees. They had employed thirty additional workers and were ready to start work when they arrived in their workroom to find it piled with stinking seaweed. They were told a further twenty wagon loads were on their way, so the incentive to work quickly must have been enormous. The camp at Gouda was the least formal but the refugees were eventually dispersed to other camps to get them out of the greenhouses.

The Quakers were also acutely aware the refugees needed recreation as well as work. They set aside quiet areas for pursuits such as reading or writing letters, and ran popular English classes. The also gave grants for the provision of libraries at Ede and Uden. Several Scout groups were set up and were a real asset, as they gave younger refugees the chance to learn the usual Scout Law, signs and knots as well as going on Sunday outings to nearby woodland. Scouting gave the boys an escape from their everyday lives and a taste of adventure. Burleigh Fincken, leader of the team at Nunspeet, described how the children would turn up dressed in the closest approximation to the proper uniform that their mothers could manage. He was impressed by their enthusiasm and the delight they took in saluting smartly. He noted, with disappointment, that they were not set on 'playing the game' in the same way as their English counterparts and that a group of six or seven boys would often pounce on a weaker opponent and leave him black and blue and badly scratched.

'Friendly Girls' groups were also set up but their activities seem to have been less exciting. Ruth Fry reported the girls would exhibit their younger siblings, clean and tidy for once, so that they could get their nursemaid's badge. The boys' outings beyond the perimeter of the camp sound far more fun.

In 1917 the Dutch authorities moved out of the camps at Ede and Nunspeet and asked the Quakers to take over full supervision of the Danish Village. Edith Attenborough and Agnes Rutter took on this task, and Agnes gave cookery lessons to the residents. Unfortunately her budget was limited to 6*d* a day and this tried her ingenuity in coming up with appealing menus.

Just five days after the Armistice, aid workers were called to the village of La Besace, near Sedan. As they approached the village they had to cross a battlefield covered with dead bodies. About 3,000 people, who had been driven out of their homes in local villages by the Germans, had been herded into a concentration camp outside La Besace. Many had died of exposure. As a final blow, the Americans had bombed the village, unaware of the civilian camp. The bombing only stopped when the Curé raised a white flag. In areas like this, it only became clear how desperately help was needed after the fighting had stopped.

The Armistice did not end the need for help in the areas devastated by the war. Representatives of many of the thirty to forty British, French and American aid organisations that were working in France in November 1918 stayed on to help with the reconstruction that was all too obviously needed. Volunteers in Eastern Europe also continued their efforts to help thousands of people in extreme need well after fighting on the Western Front had stopped.

9

Rebuilding Communities after the Armistice

By the end of the war, food was in short supply in Britain. People had grown as much as they could, with women drafted onto the land to fill the gaps left by men who had gone to fight. However, imports had dropped dramatically due to the ever-present threat posed by German U-boats. A worrying number of cargo vessels had been sunk. The British blockade of Germany had hit hard and during the war 763,000 German civilians died due to lack of food, thirty-seven per cent of them in 1918.

While discussions at Versailles dragged on, Germany continued to starve under the Allied blockade. General Plumer, the officer commanding the British Forces of Occupation, telegraphed the War Office to say that the situation was grave, with women and children dying from disease and starvation. He was concerned the people were in such deep despair that they would prefer death from bullets to starvation. Serving with the Army of Occupation, Antony Newell wrote to his wife about General Plumer's telegram adding that everyone out there agreed with the general and felt that the situation was rough on the women and children. In defiance of orders, but with the tacit agreement of their officers, British troops gave starving civilians food from Army stores.

There was a plan to moderate the blockade and let the Germans use their gold reserves to buy food. This proposal was blocked by the French President, Clémenceau. He insisted Germany's gold reserves should only be used for paying reparations to France and Belgium. After a further two months of delay and of people dying, Lloyd George insisted the gold should be released and food began to reach Germany.

After the Armistice, the Quakers recognised that war victims were everywhere and in some areas, distress had only increased as soldiers were demobilised and as people returned to the wreckage of their homes and industries. The Quakers set up an office in Berlin and started a

Foreign Fund to help the former so-called enemy countries. It ran until the end of 1919 when it was closed, as they then felt it was wrong to differentiate between the allies and enemies.

In the sixth report of their War Victims Relief Committee, covering the period from October 1918 to March 1920, the Quakers said until Europe turned to the path of sanity and reason and arranged for credits instead of soldiers, acute distress would remain. They also realised that relief work was only a palliative. A cure could only come from economic reconstruction and goodwill between nations. While Europe waited for this to happen, children starved. The Quakers' pragmatic, compassionate approach undoubtedly saved lives and relieved distress in many areas.

In the first eighteen months after the Armistice, the Quakers' London Committee sent 874 tons of aid worth almost £128,000 to 128 German towns. They also sent large amounts of cod liver oil and condensed milk, each bottle of which came with a card explaining where it had come from. Another 113 tons was sent by individual Quakers. This work was initially in direct opposition to government policy. The cod liver oil was sent in response to a report by Robert Lunnon that rickets was widespread and that in Cologne he had found one six-year-old child whose leg bones were so soft that he could bend them. Their bones were so weak that they produced no images on X-rays. Deaths from tuberculosis were increasing, as the debilitated people had little resistance to disease, and lack of milk was a serious problem. Their food programme for German schoolchildren came to be called *Quakerspeisung*.

In Cologne, the Quakers concentrated on feeding children, aged from two to fourteen, and expectant mothers who were malnourished. The Germans paid half the costs and 20,000 children were fed through this programme. The Quakers believed feeding university students was also vital and reported that 'the gratitude expressed for the little help we have been able to give has been most humbling.' They started in May 1920, providing a midday meal for 100 students. Arthur and Plesaunce Parsons were behind a scheme at all universities, except Berlin. Food to the value of one Mark, later one-and-a-half Marks, per student attending for a midday meal, was sent to universities and technical high schools, which already had dining rooms for poor students. The neediest students, put forward by staff, were given free meals. By the end of February, they were providing this food subsidy for 16,550 students each day. Arthur Parsons died on 18 December 1920; apparently due to the strain of his service to the War Victims Relief Committee. The work was taken over by the World Student Christian Federation.

In March 1920, the Quakers sent Helen W. Dixon and Marion C. Fox to assess the condition of refugees expelled from their homes by the incoming French. They found the refugees living in grim conditions.

Many had been crowded into a military barracks for a year and needed help moving out to settle on land provided by the government. They helped nearly forty families resettle and form the nucleus of a new community, also providing them with tools, stock and food. Helen Dixon set up a depot from where food and clothes, sent from England, could be sold at half price to the families of schoolteachers and other white-collar workers, who were in real distress but who tended to fall outside the remit of other aid organisations.

***

Hilda Clark and Marie McColl were sent to Vienna in May 1919. They were shocked by the conditions they found, which were due to the years of suffering during the war, to the continuation of the blockade after the Armistice and to the effects of partition after the war ended. Before the war, there had been 5,000 more births than deaths each year. During the war there were 16,000 more deaths than births. Only a fraction of the amount of coal, milk, and clothes that were needed was getting through. Three members of the Quakers started relief work in July 1919 but the number of workers soon rose, reaching a peak of around sixty. They set up a network of depots, linked to existing welfare centres in each district of Vienna. Doctors identified women in need and gave them a card, which entitled them to a greatly subsidised ration of food each week. They got two tins of condensed milk, 4 oz of sugar, 4 oz of fat or butter, 8 oz of oatmeal or semolina, about 3 oz of cocoa and 4 oz of soap. Due to limited supplies, this ration had to be restricted to one child under the age of six per family. Even so, they started by feeding 25,000 children, and hoped that within a couple of months this would have risen to 50,000. Doctors began to carry out systematic examinations of children and, by the end of October 1919, well in excess of 83,000 had been examined – only 8,665 were found to be in 'normal' condition, 32,267 were undernourished, 33,589 were badly undernourished and 8962 were very badly undernourished. Most of them were issued with food cards.

The Quakers distributed as much clothing as they could get, from a room in the former Emperor's palace, but also set up workrooms to make garments at trade union prices. Families who qualified for food rations were also entitled to clothes. Each member of the family could buy two items of clothing at a nominal price. In one month, 30,000 people were sold clothes and several hundred elderly people had their food and fuel supplemented by the Quakers.

During the summer months, very poorly nourished children from Vienna were sent to special homes in the country, where they spent from three to six months. Quakers in England undertook to finance individual children, enabling nearly 3,000 to spend time in the country.

The Quakers again worked hard to help farmers get back on their feet. To help tackle the lack of milk in Vienna, they helped get nearly 300 cows for municipal stalls and subsidised the sale of milk through Infant Welfare Centres. The cows had to be imported, as they were so scarce in Austria. Perhaps the fact that 250,000 cow's stomachs were needed to make each of the Zeppelins, produced by Germany and Austria, had contributed to the scarcity of cows. Swiss cows were far too expensive, so 256 cows and six bulls were bought in Holland. Three of the bulls were gifts from Dutch sympathisers. Another Quaker gave two pedigree Swiss bulls for a town farm in Innsbruck and planned to add thirty cows to the gift. Most of the cows were sold on to various co-operative societies. Ten cows were given to a hospital at Salzburg, though it is not clear which member of staff added being a dairy worker to their job. Large amounts of fodder had to be imported to feed these important cattle.

The Quakers also set up a special fund for supplying goats and provided them to nine children's hospitals. More than 1,000 head of poultry, of the 'best egg-laying breeds', were imported from England to give a boost to the Austrian stock of birds that had deteriorated during the war. Quakers also helped set up government-run breeding stations. They felt agriculture was one of the best ways of helping the Austrians get back on their feet and only the availability of money limited the help they offered.

* * *

The Polish border with Russia was fluid after the war, meaning that the Quakers were constantly readjusting their work. One of their larger projects was in the district of Werbkowice. By July 1920 they had twenty one workers there, helping cultivate more than 1,000 acres of land and running soup kitchens and a dispensary. However, their plans for distributing clothes in the autumn were disrupted for several weeks when the Russians advanced. After a few weeks on the road, the Quakers were able to establish a base in nearby Malice. As well as handing out clothes, they came to an arrangement with the Polish Government under which Polish Army horses were released for work under the Quakers' mission.

In Warsaw their work included setting up and running two schools to help deal with the growing problems caused by children and demobbed boy soldiers with nowhere to go and nothing to do. While trying to help as many communities as they could, the Quakers were always careful to ensure that the best possible results were achieved; in many cases giving a grant was contingent on other organisations helping as well. They also tried to work with existing institutions wherever possible, rather than setting up new ones.

Both during and after the war typhus was a widespread problem and from 1919 the Quakers worked tirelessly to help. Rather than simply nursing the victims, they set about meticulous cleansing in various villages in Galicia at the request of the Polish authorities. The number of people catching the disease dropped significantly. During the winter of 1918–19 fifty people a week caught typhus in Zawiercie but this was reduced to one or two through the Quakers' work. While one group disinfected houses, another group examined heads, cutting hair and treating any infestation they found. They also provided baths and disinfected clothing. Their reports show that they were deeply shocked by the squalor in which many of the Poles lived. Two of the Quakers died of typhus and one of pneumonia. Two others caught typhus while nursing Bolshevik prisoners at Bialystock, but survived.

Suffering was widespread in Poland and, in many areas, got worse after the war. The Quakers felt that the intelligentsia, including university students, were suffering particularly badly and that the future of the nation lay in making sure that they could function. The Quakers provided clothing, kitchen utensils, books, and food to students in Warsaw, Krakow, Lwow, and Posen. The position improved dramatically when the American Quakers undertook to feed 30,000 students each day. The British Quakers then focussed their help on students in Lwów.

* * *

The Quakers' work in Serbia was drawing to a close by 1921. They had not had a separate unit there, but had worked with the American Quakers. As well as setting up a thirty-bed hospital in Pec, they had done their usual range of welfare work including house-building, farming, and general relief work.

Due to the political situation in Russia, the Quakers' direct work there ended in 1919 but they made repeated attempts to be allowed back. In March 1920 two Quakers were allowed to reach Petrograd with a consignment of food and drugs. A few more permits followed. The Quakers identified the main needs as milk, fats, cod liver oil and soap, which they then sent in large quantities. They were also allowed to distribute goods that were sent by the American Red Cross and the American Relief Organisation.

Working under the new government in Russia was a delicate matter and the Quakers had to take great care that there should be no misunderstanding as to nature of the Society of Friends. They wanted it to be made clear that help for Russian children was just an outward expression of love and sympathy for a stricken people. It had no political significance and did not mean that they accepted the political aims for which the Russian Government stood, nor the means by which it had come to power. Their annual report noted that 'the result is mutual understanding and a very friendly co-operation.'

As in many countries, the suffering of children made a particularly strong impact on the Quakers and they were aware this had to be addressed for the future well-being of each society. Arthur Watts reported that of 38,000 Moscow babies needing milk each day, only 7,000 were getting it. Infant mortality had risen to 400 per 1,000 births. It is clear from their reports that the Quakers would have liked to be able to provide far more help than they could in Russia.

* * *

The Save the Children Fund (The Fund) was set up in 1919 and was the result of work by sisters Eglantyne Jebb and Dorothy Buxton. Eglantyne had been arrested and fined for distributing a leaflet with the headline 'A Starving Baby and Our Blockade Caused This' in Trafalgar Square. The sisters then decided campaigning was not enough and action was needed. After a public meeting at the Albert Hall, the Save the Children Fund was established, with Eglantyne as honorary secretary. Although it was not designed to be a permanent creation, it is still needed and working hard today.

Their ambitious campaign, Fight the Famine, was very successful, attracting donations ranging from a few shillings to £10,000. Money raised by The Fund was passed to existing relief organisations. The Quakers were represented on The Fund's executive committee. Money was targeted at organisations working to alleviate starvation among children in Germany, Austria, Serbia, Hungary, France, Belgium and the Armenian refugees in Turkey. Help was certainly needed and one of The Fund's schemes involved the 'adoption' of 1,200 children who were then given fortnightly rations of food.

* * *

After the Armistice, French people poured back to their land as fast, or sometimes faster, than their government wanted them to, focussed on reclaiming what was left to reclaim and rebuilding the rest. They joined those who had remained on the land where armies had battled to and fro for four years. There were, inevitably some tensions between the two groups. A considerable number of refugees who did not own their own land stayed away, having found work and a life in other parts of France.

Many of the French people, especially the farmers, were very conservative and wanted to get back as close to what they had lost as possible. You only have to compare photographs of many of the villages before the war and today to see how the new buildings replicated those that had been destroyed. It was therefore vital that the aid organisations emulated the Quakers and investigated what help would make the most difference before starting to provide it. They also needed to pay attention to regional styles, materials, and history. Caveats aside, help was needed on a vast scale. The Picardy Plateau suffered acute water shortages for years. The damage to railways, canals, bridges, and roads made delivering aid very difficult. By mid-1920s some areas of extreme devastation, including the battlefields north of Épernay, had still not been fully cleared of corpses. The French Government gave priority to reconstructing railways, roads, canals and industry, and took great pride in how quickly many factories were working again. House building had a lower priority. All the French State aid agencies closed in the early 1920s, after demobilisation finished, in spite of the fact that people still needed help and felt desperate.

The returning refugees, known as *sinistrés*, fought so hard to get their land back that a large part of the area, known as the Red Zone, which had originally been judged to be beyond salvage, had been brought back into active cultivation by the 1970s through determination and hard work. A few villages could not be rebuilt and were designated as having been 'killed for France'. Others had to be moved to a new site. Recent reports that water supplies in more than 500 French villages are still being contaminated with perchlorates, from First World War bombs, illustrate the depth of the problem the *sinistrés* faced.

After the Armistice, the Quakers continued to work in the areas where they were already involved, working with both the people who had remained throughout the war and the *sinistrés*. Within the British Army Zone, north of the Somme, there was little movement to return until the war was over. This was partly because of how badly the area had been damaged, but also because the British were using 10,000 hectares of land to grow crops for the Army. The British also used some of the land for military preparations and storage. Everyone was keen to get their land cleared of the colossal detritus of the war so that they could start to grow food again, although at times the job they faced seemed overwhelming. Once the war was over the *sinistrés* flooded back, the people of Picardy being known within France for the exceptionally powerful emotional link they have with their land.

In 1919 the *Manchester Guardian* made an appeal for funds to help with the reconstruction in France. The money raised through the appeal was handed over to the Friends Emergency and War Victim's Relief Committee to administer. The newspaper sent over a special correspondent to see the work in progress and write about it for the paper. In his first report, published on 29 November 1919, he remarked that the Quakers had been working continuously from 1914 to alleviate the suffering of refugees. He was clearly moved by what a group of pacifists had achieved in war-ravaged France, writing that: 'It would be hard to find any form of service more beautiful and adventurous than this, which went on in the war and yet was not of it.' He commented that on many occasions they had worked under shellfire and had repeatedly helped to evacuate the sick and elderly. Quakers had become refugees on several occasions but had soon returned to their work.

The reporter noted that the areas of the Meuse, Marne and Somme, where the Quakers had been working, were eighteen months closer to regaining prosperity and happiness than the other parts of the war zone. He said that you could look across a desolate landscape 'scarred with shell wounds and bound with tangles of rusty barbed wire' and in the distance you could see a cluster of huts with curls of smoke coming out of the chimneys. These huts had been built by the Quakers and were hugely appreciated by their occupants. They also opened small co-operative shops in ruined buildings and cellars to help meet the needs of the people.

In a second report, the correspondent reminded readers that previously insignificant little farms, houses, gardens or vineyards or natural features had become important strategic points during the war, fought over at huge cost, and then more or less abandoned. French people were returning in increasing numbers and starting to salvage their country. Here and there, small patches had been cleared and life resumed. He remarked that they were starting on a long journey, changing a set of values that had seemed fixed. 'Battlefield tourism' started very quickly after the war and tourists showed their sympathy and pity for the local people. However, chalked graffiti showed what the French thought about this and called for less pity and more help. Rather than a quick donation, they needed considered support. Two million French people were said to have been driven out of their homes. At least half had made their way back by 1920. They had scavenged whatever they could from the battlefields to make shelters that would keep out some of the harsh winter weather. They had made beds out of wire taken from camouflage, adapted discarded military huts to make shops and workshops and, in most villages, one of the best huts would have been made into a café, highly valued by the local people as a refuge from their rudimentary homes.

After the war the Quakers employed German POWs on several of their projects and were most satisfied with their work. The French Government paid them a small amount, but it could only be spent in the camp canteens and the French authorities would not let the Quakers supplement this sum. The Quakers were not happy with this and therefore sent two of their members off to Germany to pay money to the prisoners' families instead.

In 1919 the Quakers turned some of their energy to the area west of Verdun and the site where the village of Neuvilly-en-Argonne once stood. The Germans had taken the village in 1914 and from then until the end of the war, it had either been in no-man's land or part of the French front line. There was not a single building left standing and matters were made even worse by the fact that the Americans had opened a depot nearby where they carried out controlled explosions of captured ammunition and explosives. The Quakers brought sixty-four prefabricated houses by train from their Dole and Ornans workshops. In Neuvilly, teams of four laid the foundations and erected the houses.

Soon after the Armistice, the French Government allocated overseeing reconstruction in ninety parishes to the British Committee of the French Red Cross. Further districts were assigned to other organisations. Co-ordinating it all was very difficult as numerous foreign organisations arrived in the country wanting to help in their own way. Sixteen British women Red Cross workers were based at Vitry, on the desolate Artois Plain, between Arras and Douai. They lived in wooden huts, surrounded by a world of mud, and no better than those of the people they were trying to help. From here they collected in the stores sent by their headquarters and distributed them throughout the area. Each family receiving help was personally visited so that its needs could be assessed. Vans were then piled high with clothing, bedding, furniture, and food, cooking and farming utensils and set out. The staff had the discretion to vary what was given if they identified that a family had a different or particular need. Communities supported in this way included 187 families in Vimy, 207 people in Givenchy and the nineteen people who made up the combined population of Fresnoy and Gavrelle.

Individual members of staff from a range of organisations, including the Scottish Women's Hospital at Royaumont, decided either to stay on in France or to travel to Germany to help, affiliating themselves loosely to one of the other organisations, such as the Red Cross. They had developed a strong affection for the French people and wanted to help with the challenges of reconstruction, knowing that medical staff would continue to be in short supply.

Industrialist Henry Bronnert and his wife set up the French War Charities Committee of Manchester in 1920. They planned to bring children from the devastated areas to northern English resorts for a holiday, much as children from Chernobyl have more recently been brought to Britain for a respite. However, in 1921 and 1922 the organisation found it could not raise the necessary funds, as there was so much unemployment in northern England. Therefore they turned to towns in the south of England for help. The mayor of Bromley in Kent was quick to step forward and, with the help of the Kent County Education Authority, was able to host a group of thirty girls in a hostel, in College Road in Spring Hill. Philanthropic organisations in Portsmouth got together with the Training College Hostel at Milton to take another group. Aldershot invited fifteen boys and fifteen girls, some of whom came from the district of Mesnil-Martinsart, which had been closely linked with the Hampshire Regiment during the war. Rather than a civic response, it was the British Red Cross Society for Devon who hosted a party of children in a convent in Exmouth.

The Garden League for Devastated France was founded in 1920 with the aim of helping French peasants who had made their way back to their pre-war homes. The league sent 1,200 garden tools and implements, large quantities of vegetable seeds and other plants and more than 1,000 fruit trees. They encouraged schools and other institutions in Britain to adopt school gardens in designated French areas. The work went well and its very success made the organisers realise how much more help was needed. One of their publicity ideas was the message that every plant from a British garden that grew and flourished in its new French home would be a lasting remembrance of a good link between the two nations.

Lilias Countess Bathurst inherited the newspaper the *Morning Post* in 1908 and took a keen interest in the paper. Her editor was H. A. Gwynne, an opinionated and difficult man who quarrelled with lots of people including politicians and military leaders and was very self-important and almost paranoid at times. Part way through the war he apparently believed that Britain would have benefited from a military dictatorship. He was so much more interested in shaping national politics than in editing the paper that in July 1918, Lady Bathurst had to ask him to spend less time on political intrigue and more on editing the paper. However, they worked well together. Lady Bathurst was considered one of the most powerful women in the country, with strongly right-wing political beliefs and an entrenched opposition to women's suffrage, even after the war. Luckily for history, she and Gwynne exchanged a lot of letters as she would not allow a telephone in her Cirencester home. Gwynne had no faith in anyone but himself.

Gordon Knox, who was the *Morning Post's* correspondent in France, visited Ville and Passel, on behalf of Lady Bathurst in March 1920, to see what help the people needed. Lady Bathurst apparently had an interest in the area, having been there on a sketching holiday before the war. The Union des Femmes de France was organising support in the area and had identified a real need for a school canteen for the children who went to school in Ville from a wide area. Sadly, they were unable to fund one themselves. For two francs a day, the Union des Femmes de France had said they could run a canteen providing soup, meat, vegetables and dessert, with medicine if necessary, five days a week. Mr Knox also said clothing of all types was needed in Ville, especially heavy corduroy trousers and long-sleeved flannel shirts, rough coats and bedding. Although local people badly needed agricultural tools, he passed on the advice that it would be better to send money so the tools could be bought locally, and probably more cheaply than buying them in England and sending them out. Mr Knox had, at Lady Bathurst's request, made enquiries about what livestock was required and reported that horses, cows, pigs, goats, rabbits and chickens were all needed. He said that goats were particularly popular and that their milk was desperately needed for the children.

The Passel schoolmaster, M. Fouchon, was acting mayor and provided lots of useful information about what help was needed in his letters to Lady Bathurst. He also worked closely with Mr Knox. He described how one old lady of eighty, whose back was completely bent, had managed to dig over her whole garden. The mayor and the Union des Femmes de France felt that two kinds of help were needed. Firstly, they asked if a few carts, ploughs, wagons and harrows could be given to Passel, under the mayor's control, to be lent or hired out to people as they needed them; if cared for properly, these could act as a sort of endowment as the fees could be used to replace stock or machinery in the future. They also asked for a range of items that could be given or sold at trifling prices to the individual inhabitants. Apparently flannel shirts were definitely not wanted in Passel as they somehow had a good stock of them. They did need sheets, woollen socks and stockings, workmen's dungarees, goats, poultry and rabbits. Again, he said, livestock and some items of clothing such as *sabots* would better be bought in France. The Union des Femmes de France had an arrangement in place for buying goats from the South of France and delivering them to the villages in the north so there was no need to import them. In spite of M. Fouchon's insistence that it was better for the livestock and many other items to be bought in France rather than being shipped from England, it appears Lady Bathurst was not convinced. A number of receipts show that she bought fabrics and other goods at Harrods, hardly the most economical of suppliers, and had them shipped to France.

Knox commented it had been found that if people were given lavish supplies of clothing they stopped valuing them, would not repair them and got in the habit of saying, 'No matter, we will go to the *Croix Rouge* and get another.' He wondered whether the Red Cross should therefore consider introducing a small charge in some cases. He said the organisation for identifying needs could not have been bettered. He raised the possibility that individuals in England might like to take a specific interest in one family. However, the Union des Femmes de France had said all the aid should be channelled through them. This was because there had been a considerable amount of abuse of private aid, so the authorities had nominated one aid organisation in each area and all aid had to go through them.

He made a particular appeal for sewing machines, which would not only enable women to make clothes for their own families, but also to produce goods for sale, helping them to become self-sufficient. He suggested they should be sent over for sale in the villages and that the proceeds could then be used to buy materials. He estimated that the damage to Passel was in the area of 2,000,000 francs, which equated to about £40,000.

Lady Bathurst got behind fundraising in Cirencester for both Passel and Ville and there is a positively sycophantic letter from Mr Gilmer, secretary of the British League of Help for the Devastated Areas of France, written in April 1922, praising her for the sum of £545.17s.0d that had been raised. He went on to say that while the bell given to Passel and the clock given to Ville would be lasting memorials to the generosity of Cirencester, he hoped there would be some suitable and permanent record to her 'wonderful personal effort'. She entered into a correspondence with the acting mayor M. Fouchon and sent him money to be used to buy goats. Mr Gilmer repeated Mr Knox's point that it was better to buy goats and chickens in France, partly to reduce the trauma of travel for the livestock. He was checking carefully what each family's needs were and stressed that some people preferred poultry to goats. However, while Passel had kept large numbers of geese before the war the demand was actually for hens. Geese and ducks were not wanted. He reported enthusiastically on the canteen for schoolchildren at Ville. Again, they had carefully checked the needs of each child to be sure who were in need of supplements, iron tonics and cod liver oil. He begged Lady Bathurst to try to send some white bedspreads, as they were a small luxury that women had valued highly before the war and they now grieved to have to make do with tatty grey covers. Piles of sheets would make them even happier. Lady Bathurst kept careful records of all donations, even of the fact that her husband donated two vests.

Marcel Braibant represented the cantons of Asfeld and Château-Porcien to the Conseil-Général for the Ardennes region. After *The Times* had published a couple of articles about the devastated areas, he wrote to the newspaper in March 1920. He reported that the thirty-five villages in his cantons were occupied by the Germans from 1914 to 1918 and most of them were centres of fierce German resistance in the last weeks of the war. He quoted the French President Poincaré, who had said, 'our devastated regions are in a state of distress that no human words can describe.' Apart from the wartime damage, they were short of money, transport and manpower to start the work of reconstruction. They were still struggling to make much of an impact on clearing away all the rubble so that reconstruction could begin.

They were getting some help from the people of Nîmes, whose delegation of ladies had found that the women were wearing chemises and petticoats made of bits of old sacking that had been cut off discarded sandbags. They had also had help from towns in Alsace and Provence. The British Royal Agricultural and Royal Horticultural Societies had already sent some seeds. Braibant pleaded for clothing, food, goods and bedding and was the first to suggest that British towns might emulate some in southern France and adopt French communities and thus build a lasting bond between the two countries. The editor of *The Times* added his support to this plea, saying almost every town and village in a strip of land as long as the distance from London to Inverness and as wide as from London to Tonbridge had been destroyed. He added that the French Chamber of Commerce in London was ready to facilitate any adoptions.

A few days later, Admiral Sir Charles Dundas had his own appeal published in the *Morning Post*. Repeating parts of M. Braibant's plea, he added that Mezières was even shelled by the Germans after the hostilities had been suspended, as the German troops had not been told about the Armistice. After the German evacuation of the Ardennes had started in October 1918, the Germans had retreated 'filled with the rage of wild beasts.' They took the entire civilian population with them, some of the old and sick being pushed in wheelbarrows. The Germans then pillaged the houses before burning them and mining some for good measure. Sir Charles added his voice to the call for an adoption scheme.

It is hard to know what response there would have been to this appeal if it had not been hijacked by Lady Bathurst's paper, the *Morning Post*. It could simply have been seen as yet another charity wanting money to do something in France, where lives and money had been poured in an endless stream for four years. Britain was facing its own economic difficulties after a war that it is estimated cost well in excess of £33,000,000, with rising unemployment and large numbers of veteran, widows, and their children to be supported.

In April 1920 Mr Gwynne told Lady Bathurst that he wished he could only get someone in every district to do what she had done for Ville and Passel. Lady Bathurst backed the idea in the belief that such links might help prevent future wars. While many people in Britain felt the French should be deeply grateful to the British for liberating them from the Germans, there were others who held an opposing point of view. They believed it was the British who owed a huge debt of gratitude to France. Fighting the war was not an altruistic crusade to liberate France. Britain and its colonies were fighting to prevent Britain being invaded and ultimately the Empire from coming under German domination. They argued that we were, in fact, using French towns, villages and farmland as a battlefield for goals that were primarily, but not exclusively, in Britain's interest. They were also aware that a large amount of the damage in France was done by British weapons.

Mr Gwynne suggested discussing the idea with the French Embassy and, assuming he got their approval, to ask the Lord Mayor of London and the mayors of all large towns in England to hold public meetings as a way of getting the adoptions started. Gwynne stated that: 'The underlying idea of the scheme is the repayment of our debt of honour to France by assisting her in the task of restoring to something like a semblance of their former state those war-scarred areas in the North.'

From these discussions and ideas, The League of Help for the Devastated Areas of France (The League of Help) was formed and quickly gained the support of The Anglo-French Society, the Association of Great Britain and France, and the *Entente Cordiale*. John Gilmer, from the Anglo-French Society, was appointed as secretary of the League of Help. It is interesting that in Britain the links that were forged were called adoptions whereas in France the term 'godparent' was, and is, preferred. From the outset, the leaders of the scheme were keen to emphasise that it was 'not a matter of relieving beggars but of helping workers get on their feet again.' They also differentiated between the kind of help participants would offer, and payment for rebuilding that would eventually be extracted from Germany.

While sorting out who to invite to be on the central committee, Lady Bathurst apparently suggested they should try to get the backing of the Prime Minister, Lloyd George, and get government policy behind them. Responding in typically robust fashion to this suggestion, Mr Gwynne said he did not believe the Prime Minister would be appropriate, as he believed him to be an opportunist who was corrupt and unstable. Lloyd George was eventually asked to be one of the League of Help's patrons rather than a member of the central committee. Winston Churchill, MP, and the French Ambassador M. Paul Cambon were also patrons.

The Lord Mayor of London, Colonel the Rt Hon. James Roll, invited all other lord mayors and mayors to a meeting at the Mansion House on 30 June 1920. The meeting was addressed by Marcel Braibant and by Lady Bathurst. A manifesto was then published, restating their believe that the task of restoring the devastated areas was one in which the British people were honour-bound to take part, since the struggle in France was waged just as much in defence of British lives and British homes. They determined to enlist the full power of the press by making articles available to all papers that wanted to promote the scheme. At this point, twelve large towns had signed up to the scheme. Local committees were to be set up in all the towns and villages that wanted to participate.

The central committee's role was essentially liaison and promotion. They made speakers and lantern slides available to towns considering an adoption, linked potential adopters with suitable adoptees and helped sort out problems with shipping and French bureaucracy. They suggested the selection of a particular French town might be based on it being where local men had fought and died; where there was close affinity with pre-war industry, such as that between Albert and Sheffield; a similar name,

such as Eton and Eton (Meuse); or personal links. Doncaster adopted
St Leger because of the famous race of the same name held at Doncaster
racecourse. Mayors and other civic leaders were encouraged to visit
France to see the damage, and the French Government was persuaded
to provide cars to drive them around as they inspected the former
battlefields and decided whether or not to adopt a community. The
League of Help for the Devastated Areas of France was registered under
the War Charities Act on 10 May 1921. Its stated purpose was 'to secure
assistance for French towns and villages in the devastated areas in the
form of adoptions.' It was based at Scala House in Tottenham Street in
London, which was also the home of the Anglo-French Society.

Within a year, the League of Help could report that fifty-nine
communities in Britain had adopted seventy-nine towns and villages in
France. However, the committee was keen to note that industrial unrest
in post-war Britain had hindered fundraising efforts. The first annual
report commented that the ruined territories would, in England, have
stretched from Dungeness across the whole of the Thames estuary
between London and the neighbourhood of Sheerness and Southend,
and then spread north-westwards in a belt covering many of the most
important industrial districts of the Midlands and Lancashire.

In 1921 a delegation of British mayors from towns that were not yet
signed up went over to France to see the devastated areas for themselves.
Leaders of the League believed effective fundraising could best be
led by people who had actually seen what was needed and met some
of the people struggling to rebuild their lives. John Gilmer and other
members of the committee went along to act as interpreters and guides.
Ellen Chapman, Mayor of Worthing, was also able to help with the
interpreting, as she was a fluent French speaker.

Although ninety-nine British towns finally signed up to the scheme,
there were whole counties where not one community took part and
others where very few did. When the council in Lewes, in East Sussex,
was asked to consider an adoption, their reply was, apparently, that they
were too busy with other things. What they were so busy with is not
obvious. On 7 August 1920, the *Manchester Guardian* reported that the
Macclesfield Town Council had considered a request from the League of
Help to adopt a French village and had 'decided not to take such a course,
the Council being of the opinion that with rates at virtually 20s in the
pound the town required the whole of its money for local developments.'

The initial decision was to invite mayors to act as figureheads but it
was never the intention that the fundraising would be a civic activity.
The committees that were formed were not formally part of the local
authorities. Unfortunately, this has meant that councils did not have a
duty to preserve the records of the adoptions and most of the paperwork

has been lost. In some cases, local authorities made considerable donations themselves as well as, or instead of, collecting from the general public. These civic contributions were most common in the north of England.

The League of Help did not meet with universal approval, usually because people felt that any available money should be spent helping British veterans rather than French civilians. A few angry letters appeared in the press. A writer to the *County Express* in Stourbridge felt that although gratitude was due to France, it should not stretch to sending money or goods while many veterans were having to sell their homes to provide food for their families. Stourbridge did go ahead with the adoption of Grandcourt but decided to buy goods locally to send to France so that they helped the local economy as well as the French.

When the Mayor of Stourbridge visited Grandcourt he was shown around by the Comte de Nalèche. The comte announced he would work out a scheme for Stourbridge to fund and argued that there was no point sending out farm tools until the land had been cleared of war debris. So far so good. However, he then announced that he knew a gentleman, not a contractor, in Miraumont, who would clear the land. The amount of land he would clear would depend on how much the people of Stourbridge could raise. This made the Stourbridge Committee uneasy but they still sent out £250 after which they sent farm implements seeds and household goods.

In September 1920, the Hove General Purpose Committee gave hearty approval to the mayor's proposal that Hove should 'adopt' a French town in the devastated area and send some of the ordinary necessities of life to the distressed inhabitants. The local newspaper later stated

> there must be many an ex-serviceman in Brighton and Hove who will thrill at the news that the war-ruined village of France that Brighton and Hove have decided to adopt is Bourlon … Bourlon village was a mere heap of rubbish, blown up again and again so that the ruins were flung away from where they first fell.

This did not go down well in some quarters and when the full council met to ratify the adoption, Mr H. Burgoyne said that while he had sympathy for the people in France he had more sympathy for those at home and there were dozens of ex-servicemen in the town who had sold their furniture and homes to get money. He stated he was against sending anything to France while people at home were starving. This was seconded by Alderman Stringer. The mayor said he hoped they would stick to the original resolution because he believed that to throw it out would be against the wishes of the people of Brighton. Alderman Carden denounced the objections in no uncertain terms saying he could not 'understand such mean and contemptible behaviour.' The amendment was lost at a vote and the adoption was approved.

In the same month a cold shower was poured on the belief that ex-servicemen would be behind the scheme. The chairman of the Council's Care and Disablement Sub-Committee wrote to the *Brighton Herald* to say that veterans would not thrill until they knew their disabled comrades were first fully provided for. Another writer said that ex-servicemen did not want to talk. They wanted to work.

Once the adoption had been approved, the Mayor of Hove visited Bourlon and found the children were being educated in huts and the people living in cellars. He reported that the drawn faces and vacant expression in the children's eyes confirmed how they had suffered when taken prisoner, and in some cases wounded, by the Germans. The mayor claimed no place had been as damaged as Bourlon. He was not the only mayor to make this claim for their 'godchild'. There was an element of status associated with the level of damage in the village selected for help.

Hove went on to send a range of goods to Bourlon including five milch goats, as milk was almost unobtainable there. The goats had to have veterinary checks before being sent out and to be certified free from Foot and Mouth. The Ministry of Agriculture then certified them as fit to travel. Complications getting them through customs followed, all illustrating why other places sent money so animals could be bought in France.

The Mayor of Hove was contacted by a lady who wanted to be put in touch with a child in Bourlon, preferably one who was crippled. She wanted to send clothes, etc., directly to that child. The mayor passed the offer on to his counterpart in Bourlon, with the suggestion that had been made to him that girls from Bourlon might like to come to Hove as servants. The mayor said he himself would take one if the Mayor of Bourlon thought it was a good idea. There is no record of the response to these suggestions.

One reason why neighbouring Brighton decided not to adopt a French town and why Hove had trouble raising a large amount for Bourlon may have been linked to the number of Belgian refugees who had been housed in Brighton and Hove during the war. It is possible that local people felt that it was time to look after their own.

When recommending to local people that Westminster should adopt Gavrelle, near Arras, the council was keen to emphasise that the adoption was designed to help the people of Gavrelle to help themselves and that it would not involve a charge on the rates. This assurance was repeated at many meetings up and down the country.

John Gilmer could be abrasive at times and when Southport was considering an adoption he ruffled feathers by declaring that Southport had been 'untouched by the war'. Lord Derby stepped in and smoothed things over. Gilmer had wanted the town of Festubert to be adopted by Windsor, the home of the Guards, as there was a Guards cemetery at Windy Corner near Festubert. However, both Southport and Turton in Lancashire voted, on consecutive nights, to adopt Festubert. Turton gave way to Southport as it was richer and could do more good.

A newspaper in Hastings printed a negative article commenting that there had been a plethora of organisations starting up after the war, including some that were controversial, such as one wanting to bring Austrian children to Britain. J. Adams, who had twice visited devastated areas of France and Belgium, was frustrated by this attitude and felt Hastings Council dragged its feet in committing to an adoption. Once they had made a commitment, they struggled to raise money.

The success or failure of an adoption and the amount of money raised depended strongly on the personality and commitment of the person heading the appeal. In the case of Worthing, it was the mayor, Mrs Ellen Chapman, a remarkable lady, who was a dedicated Conservative and suffragist and who was known, among other things, for hunting her Pekinese dogs across the South Downs like beagles. She also spoke fluent French. One of the towns the League suggested Worthing might consider adopting was Richebourg L'Avoué in the Pas de Calais. Richebourg is not well known but it has a special place in the hearts of Sussex people. On 30 June 1916, the day before the start of the Battle of the Somme, there was an action there involving the Royal Sussex Regiment. One of the officers was the poet Edmund Blunden. The action was a disaster with appalling casualty levels, and 30 June 1916 came to be known as the Day that Sussex Died. Worthing lost no time in selecting Richebourg and in deputing Mrs Chapman to contact the mayor to ask what help they needed.

As happened in many towns, a public meeting was held before the adoption was ratified. The disappointingly small audience was addressed by Mrs Chapman; the local MP, Lord Winterton; and Admiral Sir Charles Dundas, who represented the League of Help. Sir Charles spoke of the need for France and England to remain friends in the future. He said the French press had raised objections to the scheme and that the British knew the Germans were trying to build a rift between France and England. He added that the French had grounds for annoyance with England – we charged them £15 a ton for coal while paying less than £3 for it ourselves. We also put a hefty tax on wine! During her speech, Mrs Chapman played on rivalry between communities, suggesting that it would look bad for Worthing to lag behind other towns in the help it gave. She stressed that the French Government was rebuilding the destroyed villages and charging the costs to Germany and that the

League was anxious to provide more immediate practical assistance. Earl Winterton said all 423 houses in Richebourg had been destroyed and the population was less than half its pre-war level. He added that the union would no doubt be difficult as the French and English often disagree politically but that by helping, Worthing would lessen the chance of future friction.

The adoption was ratified and a provisional committee appointed. Mrs Chapman opened the fund with a donation of £50. This was followed by a promise of £20 from Lord Winterton and £10 from a Colonel Randolph. The rest of the audience managed a total of £20. Without press backing, it is unlikely that any of the adoptions would have been a success and the *Worthing Gazette* and the *Worthing Herald* immediately endorsed the fundraising campaign, noting that although charity begins at home it should not end there. They published detailed accounts of all events associated with the adoption as well as lists of donations.

The Mayor of Richebourg was quick to write to Mrs Chapman expressing the delight and gratitude with which the news of the adoption had been greeted in Richebourg. He invited her to visit the town, but asked for two to three days' notice, adding: 'If your generosity would offer us some clothes, I can assure you that it would be appreciated, for the misery is great in our devastated cities.' The people of Worthing lost no time in collecting clothes to send out to Richebourg. Sadly, Mrs Chapman had to cancel her visit in April 1921, due to ill health, but two councillors did go and reported on the conditions they saw. Captain Mercier again stressed the fact that the scheme was to help people who deserved to be helped. He reported he had been impressed by how dignified the people he had seen in France were and wondered if the people of Worthing would cope as well in similar circumstances. Supporting him, Major Fox, from the League of Help, said it was a good old principle of British charity that it was the duty of the poor to help the poorer; and he would like to urge even poor people to help those who were poorer in France. The French had clearly gone out of their way to lay on suitable entertainment for their visitors but none of the group commented on the fact that the French had expended much of their scant food supplies on providing the first lunch to have been eaten in the local café since the war.

Clearly, some people in Worthing were making their objections to the adoption heard. When Mrs Chapman next addressed a meeting promoting the scheme, she felt the need to say how upset she had been to hear the objection raised by some people that this movement should not have been taken in hand when they had so much distress at home. She added, 'nobody could deny that we had troubles of our own but had

England been in the position of France today we should have been very grateful if she had extended the hand of friendship to us.' By April 1921 they had raised more than £500, which they proudly announced was more than any other town in Sussex.

Not only did Mrs Chapman visit Richebourg that summer, where the mayor, M Boulianguez, entertained her in the flat-roofed shack that he called home, but in July, the mayor and his son visited Worthing as her guests. While in Worthing, M Boulainguez made a speech thanking the town for its generosity and stressing just how much the help meant to his townspeople. He also spoke of their relationship with British soldiers from Sussex and the care for the graves of those who were buried around Richebourg. The contrast between the two towns must have been overwhelming and it is perhaps not surprising that on his return home he wrote to Mrs Chapman:

> How I love to carry my thoughts back to Worthing. How I long once more to see that beautiful town of yours, with its wide and well-kept asphalted roads, its fine seafront and its splendid hotels. All these delighted me and I often think that I have left Paradise to return to hell.

Mrs Chapman continued to play very active role in the adoption, even when her term as mayor had ended and the *Worthing Herald* reported 'that no portion of her public duty has afforded the Mayor more complete gratification than the practical help she has been enabled to extend, with the support of the inhabitants, to Worthing's adopted town of Richebourg.' In 1922 Mrs Chapman attended an international congress of civic representatives in Paris, held under the auspices of the League of Help, with the intention of creating an International Association of Mayors or other municipal representatives. Mrs Chapman's trip did not start well. The promised boat to Calais did not exist and she and her secretary had to embark for Boulogne instead. Then they suffered further delays due to problems with French customs officials, and confusion over train times. Other British mayors present included those from Oxford, Portsmouth, Doncaster, and Halifax. Because Mrs Chapman spoke French with some ease, she was asked to respond to the speech of welcome on behalf of the delegates. She was horrified to see areas were the destruction was even worse than in Richebourg and had a narrow escape when visiting Rheims cathedral with a group of French and British mayors; the vibration of their voices caused a huge block of stone to fall from the ruins, luckily missing the group.

Manchester is obviously a very different case to Worthing, with a post-war population of more than 1,000,000 and extensive industry. However, there too the success of their adoption of Mezières can largely be attributed to the commitment and energy of one person. In this case it was not the mayor but Henry Bronnert, an industrialist of French birth who had settled in Manchester. Bronnert had been a keen supporter of Red Cross efforts to help the French population during the war and the adoption scheme seemed to him to be a good way of extending this work.

The authorities in Mezières had set aside an area for reconstruction and Manchester undertook to help fund the construction of a development of seventy-six houses, pledging to raise £50,000. Each house cost about £400 and the town was to be like a garden city with wider, more airy streets than those that had been destroyed. The houses were to be designed by the English firm of Mee & Higginbottom. As part of the fundraising efforts, an exhibition about Mezières was held in Manchester Town Hall in November 1922. Donors to the fund included the Calico Printers Association.

In 1922 a group of English construction workers went out to help with the building. Their travel expenses were paid by the Joint Council of Ex-Servicemen. The fifty men had been carefully selected from thousands of applicants. Before they left, they were entertained to lunch at the Ivy Club and Mrs Bronnert gave each of them a small English-French dictionary. Mistakenly thinking that the offered books were Bibles some of the men were wary of accepting them until they realised their mistake.

Manchester actually raised £140,000 and seventy-six new villas were built. Each of them had a bathroom, four large rooms, an attic, a cellar and washhouse and electric light. They were built very quickly and the French government paid for another seventy-six houses. The rent from these houses went to support the local hospital. The new area of Mezières was called Manchester and, in 1923, one of the main roads was named the Boulevard Henry Bronnert. The hospital in the Manchester Quarter opened in 1930 with wards named after the Manchester men who had led the adoption including the mayor Tom Fox and Henry Bronnert.

Fundraisers turned to all the methods that had been tried and tested for a myriad charities during the war. Miles of pennies were constructed, concerts and entertainments held – and schools, churches, boarding houses and hotels did collections. In the city of London, fundraising was on a different scale and events included an Anglo-French polo match at Ranelagh, where the prizes were presented by Madame Poincaré, a boxing tournament at the Albert Hall and an Anglo-French tennis tournament at Wimbledon. The London Ladies' Committee of the League of Help held a luncheon at Claridges Hotel for guests including the French Prime Minister, Poincaré.

Southport's fundraising for Festubert was unusual, as the mayor showed a marked lack of interest in the scheme. He was focusing on his re-election campaign. A local paper, the *Southport Visitor*, largely ran the fundraising, supported by the *Southport Guardian*. Their aim was to raise enough money to build a memorial hall in Festubert. They quickly raised £938 5s 6d. Frustratingly, there were delays in building the hall, which dismayed the Southport committee members, who wanted public credit for their efforts. It finally opened in September 1922 and was initially used to house homeless people before being turned into a hospital.

Letters of thanks poured into the League of Help's offices in Scala House, and some of the more fulsome were published in its annual reports. One of these came from the Curé of Hermies, who wrote to the Mayor of Huddersfield:

> Your Mr Engineer Chesterman, like Moses in times of old, under the influence of his magic wand, has caused to burst forth in a good place from the midst of our ruins a source of water, limpid, pure and abundant, which our poor people have not been accustomed to drink since our wells were demolished and contaminated by the war. Waves of harmony, the delicious music of a spring of living water – these are more than enough to make us forget our past misfortunes and to give us back the taste for life.

There cannot be many local authority officers who have been likened to Moses.

It is, however, normal to want help to be received with gratitude and some towns were dissatisfied with the thanks they received. Evesham sent cows and a goat to Hébuterne in June 1921. This gift was acknowledged by the League of Help. However, when nothing had been heard from Hébuterne by October, Evesham made a complaint to the League of Help. Mr Gilmer then wrote to Hébuterne, but got no reply. Some months later, the chairman of the Evesham Committee wrote to Gilmer expressing his reservations about sending the additional £50 they had raised, as they had had no response from France. Gilmer acknowledged the problem but said that it was not, sadly, unique. It is possible that the Mayor of Hébuterne was among those who were illiterate and if he had nobody to help him write letters and translate those from England into French, it is easy to understand how correspondence may have been neglected.

Some towns insisted that a lasting monument to their generosity be created and it is clear that some local politicians were also keen for their personal contribution to be marked. This often took the form of the renaming of a street or square in the adopted town, such as the Rue Rice-Oxley in Souchez, the Rue de Birmingham in Albert, or the Pont de Blackburn in Péronne in France. In England, street names such as Bayencourt North and South can still be seen in Bexhill.

Hastings District decided to adopt Sailly-au-Bois, Coigneux, and Bayencourt. In practice, Rye adopted Coigneux, Hastings, Sailly-au-Bois, and Bexhill, Bayencourt. Fundraising in Bexhill was slow. Local people had had enough flag days and appeals to last a lifetime. However, after news of the adoption was published some donations came from soldiers who had served in the area. One of these was from a solicitor, Major Carter, in Birmingham. Although Birmingham had adopted Albert, he said that he wanted to help Bayencourt because it had been a haven of rest for the Infantry Brigade he served with in 1915–16. They had spent eight out of every thirty-two days in the village, getting respite from the trenches at Fonquevillers. He said he knew every house in the village. He sent the Bexhill committee contact details for other battalions of the Warwickshire Regiment who, he thought, might be interested in helping.

There was concern that the Mayor of Bayencourt was illiterate and Major Carter contacted his friend André Croisier, a former French soldier, who was the schoolmaster of a neighbouring village, and he and his wife helped the mayor with the paperwork. One of the Bexhill team met this couple and liaised with them. The Curé in Bayencourt refused a request to get involved or deal with the money from Bexhill on behalf of his flock, as he was annoyed that it was for the people and not the church. His refusal was curtly written on the back of his card.

The Bexhill Committee was told it was also important to get the clothes right to avoid children being 'chafed'. In fact the people of Bayencourt seem to have been exceptionally particular about the clothes they wanted, sending swatches of cloth, precise instructions as to cloth, cut and colour and sketches as well as lists of garments of particular sizes that they wanted. The Bexhill committee was advised to wrap parcels in canvas rather than brown paper to avoid pilfering. Major Carter suggested the best way of helping would be to send someone out to France with the money to meet the mayor in Doullens or a similar town to buy suitable clothes together. The Mayor of Bayencourt begged for sheets, even slightly worn ones, or cotton so they could make their own. They were also desperately short of shoes for the children walking to school. They were also in dire need of agricultural machinery.

The Mayor of Bayencourt seemed somewhat surprised to be asked for photographs of his town, as he did not think that any had ever been taken. A Miss Webb from Bexhill went and took half a dozen photos of Bayencourt, which she gave to the Bexhill committee in a small album. Bexhill councillors were clearly perturbed by the tone of the letters of thanks they received from the Mayor of Bayencourt, which they described as 'very effusive'.

The East Sussex Record Office file relating to the link between Bexhill and Bayencourt includes a rather bizarre letter dated 1921 from one of the committee, a Mr R. Gaby, to a Mr Rogers. In the letter, which displays a complete lack of empathy or imagination, he asked Rogers to try to get film of the village Curé with his maidservant, his ox and his ass with some more or less authentic ruins. He felt this would generate a lot of interest. Béthune was one of the towns where a prolonged British presence drew sustained shelling by the Germans. In 1918 the bombardment meant that the town had to be evacuated and by October 1918, when their ordeal ended, the people of Béthune faced the fact that fifty per cent of the town and ninety per cent of the historic centre had been destroyed. The population started to return in December 1918 but the carefully planned rebuilding did not start in earnest until 1920.

Béthune was adopted by Bristol and the Lord Mayor, Sir Ernest Cook, started an appeal for funds. Donations came in slowly and it took three years before they had enough money to do anything significant. They eventually built a group of houses, which were to be let to *sinistrés* who had lived in Béthune before August 1914 and who were then assessed on their contribution during the war. Each family house had four rooms. A tablet on the front of one of the buildings recorded that the gift was made, 'In memory of true comradeship during the war of 1914–18.' In 1944, an article in the *Bristol Evening Post* wondered whether the almshouses were still standing. Bethune had just been liberated again. The houses were still standing in 2010, although there was no sign of the plaque.

Several towns recognised that many communities still had a desperate need for fresh water supplies several years after the end of the war and agreed with their French towns that any funds raised should be used to provide a good water supply. A severe drought in 1921 made the situation worse and damaged the reconstruction of both agriculture and industry. Hastings contributed to a new water tower at Sailly-au-Bois, which opened in 1926. The French Government and the Department of Lot and Garonne each paid a third of the cost. Gloucester and Bexhill were among the other towns who helped pay for water towers and pumps.

The water tower and pump in Bayencourt stands close to the war memorial. They cost 55,000 francs of which Bexhill gave 22,000, the French government gave 19,000, and local people gave the rest. When the work was nearly completed, it transpired that they were about 10,000 francs short. The Mayor of Bexhill launched an appeal for a further 8,000 francs, which he wanted to take over as a surprise, unsolicited gift. In fact, about only a little over half of this sum was raised in Bexhill. Even so, the Mayor of Bayencourt was amazed to receive this additional gift. When the Mayor of Bexhill attended the inauguration of the water tower and pump in June 1924, he reported that, 'I can truthfully say they are all very grateful, and the installation of the water supply is a real, sound, pukka job.' There was no doubt how grateful the people of Bayencourt were. The War Memorial was inaugurated on the same day and the local children, dressed in historic costumes, formed a procession through the village. The mayor reported that clearance of the area was well advanced but little reconstruction had yet been done. Ironically, after a year of drought, the formal opening of the water tower and pump was delayed for forty-five minutes due to heavy rainfall.

Rye, in East Sussex, has a particular distinction. Mr J. A. Adams, who was also active on the Hastings Committee, set up a committee in Rye to raise money for Coigneux. The people of Rye raised £578 to help rebuild the school in Coigneux and then put up a plaque in the Town Hall in Rye celebrating their achievement. It is not clear where the money for this plaque came from, hopefully not from the French funds.

The scale of undertaking varied enormously and, on occasions, the aspirations were not matched by the fundraising. In some towns an appeal was launched, after a couple of months a cheque was sent off to France and the fund was closed with the local people clearly feeling that they had 'done their bit'. In others the fundraising efforts ran for several years.

Clothing, tools, livestock, fruit trees, and seeds were the goods most in demand. Cash, of course, was always welcome. Some of the donations were the expected threshing machines and other farm machinery. Worcester, Canterbury, and Maidstone, all in parts of England that were rich in orchards, sent apple trees to their 'god children'.

Some authorities were imaginative in choosing what aid to give. Portsmouth paid for a maternity hospital in Flers, and Blackburn paid for a replacement bridge over the Somme at Péronne, to be called Le Pont de Blackburn. Bradford Corporation donated the interest on an investment of £4,000 to Bailleul for a period of five years to help set up a trade school. Burnley pledged to give £200 annually for five years to the villages of Miraumont, Courcelles, and Colincamps. Newcastle sent 150 pigeons to Arras (to compensate for all the birds that had been killed to stop them being used to send messages during the war) and also provided £12,000 in cash. Paddington sent a harmonium to Neuville-Vitasse. Worcester sent £665 to Gouzeaucourt, part of which was spent on a windmill and the remainder on books, 'suitably inscribed', and annual prizes for schoolchildren to be called the Prix Worcester.

In some cases the types of gift sent reflect the level of damage in the selected area of France. The lack of even the bare necessities of life in some areas is illustrated by the way that Blackpool concentrated its efforts on sending clogs, boots, and clothes to Neuve Chapelle.

In 1921 councillors from Halifax Borough Council visited Metz-en-Couture in northern France. They decided to provide the village with a £5,000 interest-free loan to help reconstruction and provide clothing and livestock. The French Government guaranteed the interest on the loan. To help build up the local pool of livestock, Halifax sent a Durham bull and an Ardennes stallion to Metz. The stallion was in the care of the Mayor of Metz and sadly died quite quickly. The fate of the bull is not known. In return for this help and support the grateful Council of Metz-en-Couture agreed that the village square should be re-named Halifax Square. For some reason, the naming of the village square was put off and was only done in 2011 after Adrian Denham, grandson of one of the original delegation who visited Metz, contacted the mayor. The Mayor of Metz has tried to put new life into the link with Halifax but his efforts have been frustrated by the fact that Halifax has been swallowed up by Calderdale. In 2011 Keith Watson, then Mayor of Calderdale, was reported as having said, rather bluntly, that 'they promised they would do it and it's nice that they are finally doing it.'

The opening ceremony for the new bridge over the Somme in Péronne was out of all proportion to the small size of the bridge. The people of Blackburn raised 90,000 francs for the bridge, which was inaugurated in October1924. A triumphal arch had been erected, under which the visitors processed before standing in their heavy robes in the broiling sun listening to a long list of interminable speeches and translations. The inauguration was followed by an elaborate formal luncheon with a menu including iced melon, a mousse with a turbot sauce, leg of roe deer in a sauce with green beans, ducklings, sorbet, roast turkey, and ice cream, accompanied by wines and champagne. Although it is hard to believe the guests had much appetite for it, there was a formal dinner in the evening followed by a firework display. The road leading to the bridge was christened the Boulevard des Anglais. In Blackburn streets were re-named Péronne Crescent and Maricourt Avenue.

By March 1919, many of the people of Souchez had returned and were living in ex-army huts and other wartime shelters. They were surrounded by trenches and shell holes, graves with little wooden crosses and webs of barbed wire. Souchez was in the Red Zone, where the damage was most severe. The destruction of the town was so appalling that, on 13 August 1920, it was designated by the French Government as having been totally destroyed and as having shown, in spite of grief, a magnificent courage and patriotism. Souchez was awarded the *Croix de Guerre*. The local people rejected this designation and said it felt like a second assassination of their community. They got to work with determination and courage. They began to fill in the trenches, removed unexploded shells from their land, and exhumed and reburied a large number of corpses. By 1920,the farmers were able to reap their first post-war wheat harvest. The local mineworkers worked hard to get the mines working again. In 1921 the area around Souchez included in the Red Zone was dramatically reduced.

They were helped by a group of poor villages in the Dordogne but the gifts were small and included one of just ten francs. They needed more help and, in 1920, Souchez was adopted by Kensington in London, in memory of the Royal Kensington Regiment. An exploratory visit by a delegation from Kensington was led by the mayor, Mr Rice-Oxley, who retained a keen involvement in the adoption. The population of Kensington was generous with their support and, over a number of years, raised almost a 164,000 francs, in addition to donating voluminous cases of linen, clothes, toys and other necessities, help for the town band, and a new clock to go outside the mayor's office.

Part of the money raised was used to buy some communal land and to build two houses for families in hardship. They were to be called the Maisons de Kensington forever. The road leading to them was called Rue Rice-Oxley and the Place de la Mairie became the Place de Kensington.

In early July 1921 a group from Souchez spent five days in London. They were overwhelmed by the hospitality they received. Reporting on their experiences after the visit, they said that they had stayed in one of poshest hotels in London and that their whole visit was spent in receptions, official dinners, visits, and soirees. They were presented to Princess Louise, Duchess of Argyll, daughter of Queen Victoria, and one whole day was spent visiting Windsor, where they had a dinner hosted by the Mayor of Windsor in their honour. During a dinner in London, the orchestra played French music all evening in their honour. They spent one evening at the theatre watching a play in French from the royal box. In the interval a projection on the curtain let the audience know that a group from Souchez was in the royal box and the whole audience applauded and clapped even louder when the Mayor of Souchez waved his tri-coloured scarf. Cries of *Vive la France* rang out.

In 1924 a second delegation from Kensington visited Souchez, accompanied by twenty children who were also taken to the Red Zone to see the extent of the damage there. The last formal link between the two communities was in 1931, after a meeting of adopters in Paris. In 1963 a newspaper article reported that many of the residents of Souchez were unable to explain the street and square names to visitors. The newspaper put them straight. Today there are information boards in the square outside the mayor's office recounting the story of the adoption.

In January1925 the *Observer* reported that, 'The imagination was stirred the other day by the news that the Kentish town of Tonbridge, having adopted the gloriously famous battle village of Thiepval, had learnt that there was no Thiepval left to adopt.' The report said that there was no doubt that Tonbridge would easily find another town to foster and that the real tragedy was 'the bare official announcement that Thiepval is no more and never will be, except in memory.' Although the article said that the Préfecture of the Somme would be asked to suggest a neighbouring village that could be helped instead, Tonbridge seems to have abandoned the idea of an adoption.

Everything did not run smoothly with Eton's adoption of Eton (Meuse). The Mayor of Eton (Meuse) had written to his counterpart in the English Eton asking for help. The adoption was formalised but very little money was raised. In June 1921 A. A. Somerville (a former Etonian and Conservative MP for Windsor) wrote to Mr Gilmer at the League of Help saying that the Old Etonian world seemed very lukewarm about the appeal and that the Provost was feeling downhearted. He asked if Mr Gilmer, with his Old Etonian contacts in the League of Help, could do anything to assist. Nothing seems to have happened until Mr Gilmer wrote to Lady Bathurst about his concerns, in April 1922, complaining that 'the godparent seems to be very sleepy!' He said he had written to a Mr Somerville suggesting he should draft a letter to the press to be signed by a few notable people, including Lord Bathurst. The letter explained how badly Eton (Meuse) needed help and that the boys of Eton College and their parents had raised about £100 but went on to call for further assistance. It suggested that if £2,000 or £3,000 could be raised, a modest village hall might be built bearing both the arms of Eton and the *Croix de Guerre* that the French Government had awarded to the French village. The appeal appeared in nine newspapers, although *The Times* apparently acknowledged its receipt but did not print it. It was also sent to the parents of current pupils. Lady Bathurst made the first donation to the renewed appeal. They eventually managed to raise £1,500.

The Birmingham Committee sent a deputation to Albert to see what was needed and quickly sent gifts of building materials, seeds, tools, money, clothing, and bedding. However, they also identified that there was a need for almshouses and set about raising the necessary £4,000. The mayor, Alderman Bower, started a Shilling Fund also known as the Albert Memorial Fund. They drew up plans for almshouses for eighteen people. At various meetings, the mayor stressed that the people of Birmingham should be grateful that they had not suffered as the people of Albert had. The almshouses were to be a lasting memorial. In spite of donations, including £120 from Cadbury Brothers, they had not reached the hoped-for target by New Year's Day. By January 1926 they had only raised £1,300. The Lord Mayor made a new appeal and the *Birmingham Post* wrote an article saying how shameful it was for a town as prosperous as Birmingham to fail to raise the necessary sum when smaller towns had reached their targets. When they still failed to reach the target, the mayor made yet another appeal and Cadbury's again made a generous donation, as did the Birmingham City Police, Neville Chamberlain and Austen Chamberlain, MP. They eventually raised enough for building to start and Gerald Forty went over to Albert to finalise the details. It was his first visit for four years and he was amazed at the progress that had been made. The almshouses were called the Pavilion de Birmingham. It seems that links ended in 1932, after the Mayor of Birmingham again visited Albert. Veterans tried to revive the link in the early 1980s, without success. Sadly, when Albert selected a twin town, it was Ulverston not Birmingham.

After the Duchess of Sutherland visited the area around Bailleul, she announced she was going to devote the 40,000 francs left over from her ambulance funds to relief for the area. She estimated that about a 100,000 francs, about £1,200, was needed to convert a semi-ruined chateau just outside the town into an orphanage and launched an appeal for funds. She also wanted to set up a 'preventorium', a place where children, predisposed to tuberculosis, could be sent to be well fed and monitored in the hope it would not develop. She said that she had the approval of The League of Help and the British Legion for her appeal even though Bailleul had been adopted by Bradford.

The City and County of London Committee ratified the adoption of Verdun at a meeting at the Mansion House in December 1920. The Lord Mayor said they had been slow to decide which town to adopt as it had taken time to identify the wishes of such a large community. He said that London had to make a contribution that fitted her status and reputation and could not afford to stand back. They decided to adopt Verdun as it had suffered more than any other French city and was 'the soul of the French fight.' According to one speaker, London was the soul of England. With the funds they raised, they built a new waterworks and a boulevard in Verdun. In acknowledgement the Lord Mayor was made a Freeman of Verdun.

The pre-war population of Bray-sur-Somme was 2,000. This was reduced to 800 after the Armistice and of the 600 houses, only twenty-five had not been completely razed. After the adoption by Eastbourne was confirmed, Cllr Wood visited Bray and found that as well as the usual kinds of help the people also had an urgent need for window glass as there was not a single piece left in the town and none was available in the area. He urged people in Eastbourne to start collecting, even before the details of the appeal had been finalised. After 1,000 francs had been raised, Cllr Wood said that he did not think anything else was needed, at least for the time being. However, as well as the money they did send a load of rye seed, clothes and twenty-five cases, weighing a total of 1,200lbs, of tinned pork and beans. The main square in Bray was renamed the Place d'Eastbourne. It has since been renamed again.

Cllr Wood said the people were living in left over wooden army huts, which were never watertight or free from drafts. He commented on the commendable spirit of brotherhood he found in the town and said that although there were piles of shells and other detritus all around the town, the people were already growing vegetables on some plots. Unfortunately the winter of 1920–21 was very wet and the stooks were soaked and rotting in the fields.

There was some muttering in Eastbourne that the rates should not be used to help Bray so the mayor was at pains to assure people that not one penny of the rates was involved and that the deputation who visited Bray had paid for themselves. In November 1921, the Mayor of Bray estimated there was still another six or seven years' work to go before they could regain any kind of normality. Cllr Wood did a vast amount of work for the fund and Eastbourne raised more per head than other south coast town, but less than many inland.

Correspondence from 1926 suggests the Mayor of Bourlon tried, unsuccessfully, to revive the link with Hove. The links that were meant to last forever, tying Britain and France together, were quickly forgotten. In 1994 Monsieur Sénéchal, a nonagenarian clog-maker living between Richebourg and Neuve Chapelle, remembered Worthing's adoption of Richebourg well, and said how much the tools had been appreciated. He knew of an old man who still had the toy he had been given. Although he had been a child, Monsieur Sénéchal had been taken prisoner by the Germans and reminisced cheerfully about the ferocity of the Ghurkhas, the height of the Bengal Lancers and seeing the Prince of Wales and Rudyard Kipling at the unveiling of a local memorial to the fallen. He regretted the fact that local children were no longer taught about the link with Worthing.

Gilmer and the League of Help were keen to develop links between Britain and France. As part of this they took a party of schoolchildren to France in 1923. Gilmer wanted to take 1,000 children for a fortnight but in the end only 350 went. Before children from Hove were allowed to join the group, the council sought assurances that they would be housed in good-quality accommodation during their visit. This anxiety probably arose from the conditions the Mayor of Hove had seen on his earlier visit to Bourlon. Return visits were made by groups of children from several of the adopted towns.

Through the League of Help, a few Australian towns also adopted and supported French communities. Adelaide helped Dernancourt. A suburb of Adelaide was called Dernancourt and 11 June is still celebrated as Adelaide Day in Dernancourt. The children of Victoria raised £12,000 in memory of the 1,200 Australian soldiers who had died recapturing Villers-Brettoneux in 1918. The money was used to build a new school.

In 1920 the Mayor of Poilcourt wrote to the Mayor of Sydney that their efforts were frustrated by a lack of labour, materials and money but they had not lost heart. They wanted to rename their town Sydney-sur-Retoruen but the local authorities would only agree to Poilcourt-Sydney.

The inhabitants of Pozières prepared a list of 'wants' for any town considering becoming their godparent. The list included a loan of money for communal buildings and a gift for the building of a sports ground and a large assembly hall. They wanted a large college to adopt their school, a cathedral to adopt their small church and a cash loan for reconstructing buildings, the purchase of a threshing machine for communal use, and the gift of materials for trades people and artisans, clothes, furniture, and help in kind. It certainly seems that they were aiming high and looking for more than they had before the war. There is no record of what they actually received.

Many of the links between French and English communities did not last much longer that the fundraising phase and the formal openings of the new facilities that were built in France. No new adoptions took place after 1922. The course of the League of Help's efforts and the way in which the adoptions faded into history are paralleled by many a modern appeal. We give, as they did, while the images are fresh in our minds and then move on to the next project and the next. In the 1920s, as now, there were more committed pockets of help where fundraising and support continued after the initial impetus had faded away. Some links lasted until they were broken by the Second World War. The modern twinning of British towns with the communities they adopted after the First World War show just how important these links can remain.

Keighley's twinning with Poix du Nord is said to be the oldest in Europe. The links go back to interchanges in 1905 and grew from mutual interests between Gaston Ducornet, who had a mill in Poix, and Ferdinand Binns, director of a mill in Keighley. The link was broken in 1914 when Poix was occupied by the Germans. Binns was Mayor of Keighley in 1920, when Keighley Council formally adopted Poix. The people of Keighley raised £5,000 and, on 21 May 1921, Binns laid the foundation stone of a new community building, called Keighley Hall. A parchment laid under the foundation stone says that the mayor and people of Keighley, in Yorkshire, had adopted Poix du Nord in compassion for the sufferings endured by the Commune during the German occupation and in the hope of uniting the two towns in lasting friendship. A newspaper report added a rider that 'it may be hoped that the inhabitants of Poix will be instructed in the correct pronunciation of Keighley.' History does not record whether the guidance was duly given but the hall, prominently labelled the *Salle de Keighley*, still stands today. The link was interrupted by the Second World War. In the 1970s there was an attempt to re-establish the connection but by then Keighley had been swallowed by Bradford. Links between certain families continued for a while longer but have now declined.

The League of Help for the Devastated Areas of France achieved a great deal in a very short period, raising a total in excess of 7,250,000 francs. The first suggestion that the headquarters of the League of Help should be wound up had come from Lord Derby as early as 1922. He was concerned by the economic downturn and the fact that their work needed to be seen in that context. Some of those involved were also concerned at the proportion of the funds coming in that were being used for rent and administration. That year, the League of Help had to leave its base at Scala House in Tottenham Street at short notice and relocated to 3 Cromwell Gardens in Kensington. Mr Gilmer, telling Lady Bathurst about the move, said that it would be fine once he dared to light a fire but that the smell of gas was too dangerous for him to risk it.

The League of Help made a fresh attempt to raise funds the following year, without much success. Mr Gilmer became increasingly worried and called an emergency meeting to consider the future of the League of Help, which had to be adjourned due to poor attendance. Lord Derby suggested that the League of Help should be wound up. Their funds were so low that they could not continue for more than a few more weeks, but the sense of the meeting had been that they should try to continue until relations between France and Britain were on a firmer basis. Nothing happened immediately, although Mr Gilmer noted that there were no fresh adoptions in 1924.

As the registration authority for London (under the War Charities Act), the London County Council was responsible for monitoring the charity's returns. In 1924 and 1925, the League of Help only submitted unaudited accounts. This was in contravention of the terms of its registration under the War Charities Act. It did not present any accounts at all in 1926. In March 1927 the London County Council decided that the League should be closed down by its officers or submit to forcible closure. In addition to concerns about the lack of audited accounts, the London County Council was worried that Mr Gilmer's salary was not shown in the accounts and that his return to being the 'honorary' secretary had not been approved. The chairman and treasurer had appointed paid staff without having the power to do so and the names and addresses of new officers had not been submitted to the London County Council as they should have been.

Lord Derby apparently shared some of these anxieties and had written to Colonel Powney in December 1926 to the effect that he no longer had much to do with the central organisation, confining his involvement to the City and County of London Branch. Up to then he had been very active in encouraging adoptions. Like some of the other members, he made it known that he was unavailable to attend the meeting on 27 May 1927 that formally wound up the League of Help.

However, the fact that the central office had been wound up did not have a noticeable effect on the adoptions that had taken place and some fundraising did continue, so that projects could be completed. It is clear that fundraising grew increasingly difficult as the length of time from the war grew and as unemployment and economic hardship spread in this country.

10

Veterans and the Legacy of War

At the eleventh hour on the eleventh day of the eleventh month, the fighting in Western Europe ended. Peace came to a region that had been changed forever, through years of fighting and all the concomitant damage. The Liberal Party's manifesto for the 1918 General Election promised that their first duty was to ex-servicemen and to the dependants of the fallen. They said that every effort would be made to protect them from want and unemployment. The election produced a Liberal/Conservative coalition led by Lloyd George. Its promise to make a 'Land fit for heroes' was soon shown to be more of an optimistic aspiration than an achievable commitment.

Britain was a badly damaged nation. The war had cost the country approximately £8,500,000,000, making the National Debt soar. Bomb damage was estimated at about £570,000,000. Many industries had been badly affected and factories had been converted to do war work. Restoring them to their previous function took time, effort and money. Markets had to be re-established. Unemployment soared from three per cent in 1919 to twelve per cent in 1923. In January 1922, about 55,000 of the 2,000,000 men who were unemployed were veterans. The last instalment of the war debt was not paid off until 9 March 2015

More than 6,000,000 people had served in the forces and 750,000 of them died. Of those who returned, nearly 1,750,000 had suffered a disability of some kind and half of these men were permanently disabled. The British people recognised they had a debt to these veterans and to the widows, orphans, and parents of the men who died. For the country to pay this debt was another matter.

It was apparent, from the early weeks of the war, that the Government had no mechanism for dealing with men who were disabled as a result of their military service. Even so, it was not until 1917 that the first Minister of Pensions established the cumbersomely named Joint Committee of the Ministry of Pensions on Institutional Treatment to arrange appropriate treatment for disabled men who had been discharged from the services. Among the committee's tasks was helping and advising local authorities on how to set up rehabilitation homes and treatment for the men. In reality, the Government did not have the money to fund ongoing care, so the Red Cross allocated some of its funds to this work. Other charities did what they could to fill the gap.

There was a distinct division between the totally disabled, who would need institutional care for life, and the partially disabled, who could live independently. Their pension was assessed accordingly. In the days before sulphonamide drugs were introduced, men who had survived spinal injuries were especially vulnerable to infection and needed institutional care for the rest of their lives. Personal wealth had a major impact on the sort of future disabled men could expect, as wealthier men could pay for good artificial limbs, motorised wheelchairs, personal attendants, adapted cars, and other aids. Some veterans were stuck in institutions, because their families were unable to cope with them at home or afford the necessary adjustments. The writer John Galsworthy campaigned for retraining to be provided for disabled men.

At the end of the war, there were 6,000 British charities, registered under the War Charities Act, whose aim was to help disabled soldiers and sailors. This was almost one organisation for every 1,000 disabled men. There were still 500 of these charities in 1936, spending £6,000,000 a year between them. Their spending was about one tenth of the State's expenditure on these veterans. There is no record of how much charities spent on supporting and educating war orphans.

Before the war there were philanthropic charities, such as the Soldiers' and Sailors' Families Association (SSFA) and numerous regimental associations that were set up to look after veterans and their families. Before the war had even ended, a new type of charity had appeared with the creation of organisations run by and for veterans themselves. The Government was very anxious about the proliferation of these charities and other organisations, some of which had strong political affiliations. Worried by the example of Russia, they feared the establishment of these groups might lead to an attempt to the overthrow of the British State.

SSFA was set up in 1885 at the instigation of Major James Gildea, who appealed for funds to support the families of men in a force that had been sent to Egypt. In 1895, the charity extended its work to providing Alexandra Nurses to help the families of serving men. This was followed by the creation, in Wimbledon, of the Royal Homes for Officers' Widows and Daughters. Shortly after the First World War started, the Government asked SSFA to look after the families of men on overseas service. With the help of 50,000 volunteers, they administered £2,000,000 from the National Relief Fund. With the establishment of the Royal Air Force, the organisation updated its name to reflect its new responsibilities, becoming the Soldiers' Sailors' and Airmen's Families Association in 1919.

The lack of housing for veterans who could no longer support themselves or their families quickly became a serious issue. The speed with which demand outstripped even the organisations that were set up to help, is illustrated by the work of the Scottish Veterans' Garden City Housing Association, which is the oldest and largest charity offering housing for veterans in the UK. It was founded in Edinburgh in 1915 with the aim of building reasonably priced homes for veterans with permanent mental or physical disabilities. The charity was started by a group of professional men and businessmen in Edinburgh, who wanted to help disabled veterans who had little or no hope of finding either accommodation or work. It was chaired by Edward T. (Lord) Salveson, who himself lost two sons in the war. The founders wanted men who had gone from the tenements of Scottish cities to serve in their country's forces to be compensated for their suffering by moving to new homes in garden city areas. They thought there would be a manageable number of disabled veterans needing their support and that they would be able to help them all.

Most of the organisation's fundraising and building was done by small voluntary committees across Scotland, each of whom acted with considerable autonomy. Their plans included a jam-making factory and a piggery as well as homes, a village hall and a shop in each development. Each cottage was to have a large garden and a beehive and some were to have a small shed fitted out for basket-making.

The foundation stone of the first home, at The Piggery, Longniddry, East of Edinburgh, was laid by Lord Kitchener's sister, Mrs Parker, in 1916. The land had been donated by the organisation's first president, the Earl of Wemyss and March. The founders already realised that there were so many casualties that helping them all would be impossible. They had to tailor their plans so that they could provide 'the best of artisan housing', with large gardens, for as many of the homes as they could afford. Longniddry was the only development that was realised according to the original plans and the first veterans moved into their homes in late 1917.

Donors included various Caledonian Societies and First Nation Tribes in the USA. Some of the homes were funded as memorials to individual men, including James Harvey Bryson, who was killed near Cambrai in 1918. King George and Queen Mary planted a cherry tree at Earl Haig Gardens in Edinburgh in 1923. By 1928, the charity had built 159 homes. The organisation is still growing, with 624 homes throughout Scotland, which they aim to rent to veterans at below the local authorities' social housing charge.

The Douglas Haig Memorial Homes charity was founded in 1928 with the aim of providing housing to ex-servicemen from the UK and Channel Islands. Its work was intended to be a memorial to Earl Haig, who had had many critics during the war, but whose work for veterans attracted widespread praise and gratitude. From the outset, the charity benefitted from the Prince of Wales's support and public donations underpinned its work. It has grown steadily and in 1995 amalgamated with the Housing Association for Officers' Families, which had been set up by Mrs Willie James in 1916. Now known as Haig Homes, the charity has approximately 1,400 properties, mostly in groups of six or more. They are generally for disabled veterans who have families and are adapted to meet the disabled ex-serviceman's needs. Their commitment is to provide the men with a home for life.

Some charities that aimed to provide homes for veterans were on a local, rather than national, scale. The Disabled Soldiers' and Sailors' (Hackney) Foundation was set up in 1918 to provide homes for local married men who had been disabled during their military service. The foundation acquired a group of ten cottages, bordering a green, which were taken over by Haig Housing in 2014 and are still rented to disabled ex-servicemen at an affordable rent.

Queen Mary was among the first people to voice concern about how severely disabled servicemen would cope with the rest of their lives and she asked the British Red Cross Society to find a 'permanent haven' for them. To that end the Auctioneers' and Estate Agents' Institute generously bought the old Star and Garter Hotel on Richmond Hill and presented the deeds to Queen Mary. She in turn handed the building to the British Red Cross Society. The basic philosophy underpinning the work of the Star and Garter Home has always been that 'there is no such thing as a hopeless case'. It is shocking to think that when the first sixty-five residents were admitted, in 1916, their average age was twenty-two so they had most of their lives ahead of them. After intensive therapy and support, some of them were able to go home while others remained in the home where they were given ongoing support. The Star and Garter Home soon had such a long waiting list for artificial limbs that the Red Cross began to supply them and by December 1919, they had issued nearly 12,000. In 1922 the Star and Garter Home separated from the British Red Cross Society and became an independent charity. The British Women's Hospital Committee paid for a new home to be built and the king and queen opened it in 1924. It is now known as the Royal Star and Garter Home. The old building is still in use as the charity's headquarters.

Gladys, Marchioness of Ripon, was heavily involved in charity work linked to St George's Hospital in London. She was committed to establishing a hospital-cum-home for disabled veterans. Sadly, she died in 1917, before her goal could be achieved. When Mr and Mrs J. D. Charrington, from the Charrington brewing family, offered to extend the loan of Gifford House, in the fashionable 'millionaire's row' in Roehampton, to 1920, Lady Ripon's dream could become a reality. Gifford House had been used as an auxiliary hospital during the war, staffed by VADs, and so relatively little adaptation was needed. It re-opened as the Queen Alexandra Hospital Home in Roehampton in 1919. Nursing care was provided by VADs and male orderlies helped with manual work and catering. Although the war was over, the patients still wore 'hospital blue' suits and lived under military rules. The Charringtons continued to take an interest in the Hospital Home and each time Mr Charrington visited, he would hand one cigarette to each patient. The governing body struggled to find a permanent base for the Alexandra Hospital Home and when the Charringtons offered to sell Gifford House to the committee for £30,000, the fundraisers could not find enough money. The Red Cross Society wanted the patients to be transferred to the Star and Garter Home, being built nearby. In 1933, the Hospital Home moved to Worthing where its permanent base was renamed Gifford House. Like many such institutions, the hospital-home has always struggled to raise enough money to support its work and has depended heavily on the efforts of its volunteers. Mrs Verena Hay, who was one of Lady Ripon's close friends, dedicated twenty years to working for it. Members of the Royal family, including Queen Alexandra, also lent their support. The home came to be known for the imaginative use of physiotherapy and occupational therapy. It still cares for about sixty ex-service personnel.

In 1915, a specialist hospital for limbless sailors, soldiers and airmen was opened in Mr Kenneth Wilson's home, Roehampton House, in London. After he heard about Wilson's work the American banker, John Pierrpoint Morgan Jnr, offered his late father's home, Dover House, for use as a hospital for limbless officers. Set in 140 acres of ground and almost next to Roehampton House, Dover House was ideal. Both hospitals were affiliated to the King George Hospital in London and Queen Mary agreed that they should be known as Queen Mary's Convalescent Auxiliary Hospitals. By November, both hospitals were full with another 1,259 men ready, or almost ready, to be admitted and temporary wards had to be built in the grounds of Roehampton House to help them cope with the increasing demand.

As well as being fitted with artificial limbs, and being trained to use them, the men had physiotherapy to help them get fit and strong again, and training to help them find employment when they were able to leave. In February 1916, an appeal was launched for funds to allow a specialist limb-fitting service to be set up. Until then, prosthetic limbs were sent to most patients through the post, after they had been discharged and sent home. The prosthetic limbs could rarely be used without adjustment by a specialist limb-maker. Since most of the men lived a long way from a specialist centre, many limbs lay unused, their owners having to depend on a peg-leg or crutch instead. As a result of the appeal, the hospital was able to set up a limb-fitting service for officers living in almost all English counties. Those living in Wales or in counties along the Welsh border went to the Wales and Monmouthshire Hospital for Limbless Sailors and Soldiers (renamed the Prince of Wales' Hospital in 1918), in Cardiff. After the war, the Ministry of Pensions took over the management of the specialist artificial limb-fitting service.

Another person who realised that some of the injuries inflicted during the war called for new, specialist, treatment centres was Charles Kenardine. He had been one of the founders of Queen Mary's Convalescent Auxiliary Hospitals in Roehampton and, by 1917, had realised there was an acute need for a centre to care for men with horrific facial and jaw injuries. Kenardine suggested a new hospital should be built in the grounds of Frognal in Sidcup, Kent. The land was bought by the Government. The Red Cross and a range of charities, both in this country and abroad, raised money for the hospital to be built and run. An appeal in the *London Evening Standard* raised enough money to build a canteen, a cinema and a recreation hall. As Queen Mary took a keen interest in the hospital, it was named The Queen's Hospital, Sidcup. It opened in July 1917 and was soon designated the central military hospital for maxillofacial injuries for British and Imperial Expeditionary forces. The Queen's Hospital had 560 beds and before long, six other hospitals, with 450 more beds, were affiliated to it. The Queen's Hospital was directed by Sir Harold Gillies, an imaginative plastic surgeon who became famous for devising many innovative plastic surgery procedures and helping the devastated men begin to face the rest of their lives and the outside world. Before long medical and dental teams from Canada, Australia and New Zealand were going to Sidcup for specialist training. Between 1917 and 1920, 5,000 men underwent more than 11,000 operations at Sidcup. Most of the nursing staff were trained nurses but VADs also worked there, in less specialist roles. It was a severe challenge for the VADs to manage to look the severely disfigured men in the face without flinching but they knew they had to do it so that they did not embarrass or humiliate the men who were already suffering so much. In 1920, The Queen's Hospital stopped treating military casualties and became a civilian hospital.

In the early years of the war, surgeon Sir William Macewen was at the forefront of efforts to set up a large specialist hospital in Scotland for men who had lost one or more limbs on active service. While they were looking for a suitable site in or around Erskine, near Glasgow, the owner of Erskine House, Thomas Aikman, offered to lend his Clydeside mansion for the duration of the war – and for twelve years after it ended. Generous as this offer was, it was superseded when Sir John Reid, a member of the organising committee, bought the house and gardens and gave them to the charity. The people of Scotland were keen to help and had soon raised £100,000 to help set up the hospital. Princess Louise, Duchess of Argyll, agreed to be its patron and the hospital was named after her. Gifts continued to pour in. The Princess Louise Scottish Hospital for Limbless Soldiers and Sailors opened in October 1916. It has been estimated that one in five veterans who were disabled in battle was treated at Erskine. Demand was so high that huts had to be erected in the grounds to provide additional accommodation. Staff were keen to develop new ways of helping the limbless men and Sir William wanted artificial limbs to be manufactured in Britain rather than abroad. He enlisted the help of local shipmakers, Yarrow. Using workshops at the shipyard, hospital staff and skilled staff from Yarrow's worked together and developed the Erskine Artificial Limb. Thereafter, much of the work making the limbs was done by patients in the hospital workshops. By 1920, they had supplied and fitted 9,500 limbs. The site no longer includes a hospital, but the charity continues to provide care for any service person who has been injured during war – as well as convalescent care for those who have been sick. It has also built more than forty houses in the grounds to provide homes for veterans. It still depends on volunteers for much of its fundraising.

After the entertainer Harry Lauder's son was killed on active service, he was not content with touring the front to entertain the troops at his own cost. He also set up the Harry Lauder Million Pound Fund. Its goal was to help Scottish men who had been maimed on active service to get back to health and it also helped them with their transition to civilian life.

In 1921, the Limbless Ex-Servicemen's Association was set up in Glasgow to help veterans who had lost a limb. Branches were soon established in Edinburgh, Dundee, Hamilton, and Aberdeen. Word spread to Northern England and the Scottish organisers helped establish groups in Manchester, Leeds, Burnley, Oldham, Hull, Southport, Accrington, Bradford, Halifax and Wigan, in 1925. In the following years, some of the English groups were unhappy with the way the Scots were running the organisation and in 1932, a conference was held in Manchester at which the charity was renamed the British Limbless Ex-Servicemen's Association, generally known as BLESMA. The charity lobbied hard to get improved pensions, artificial limbs, and conditions for disabled veterans. Intriguingly, it did not spread to Southern England until the Second World War.

Lots of groups set up their own charities to help local veterans, which registered under the War Charities Act. The Blackburn and District Boy Scouts Association set up a Disabled Soldiers and Sailors Fund. In Manchester, the Partially Incapacitated Soldiers (New Careers) Fund was set up to help men retrain. These local funds tended to be short-lived and were either closed or amalgamated with larger charities.

In 1913 newspaper proprietor Arthur Pearson, who had founded the company that published both the *Daily Mirror* and the *Tit Bits* magazine, lost his sight through glaucoma. He then started to work for the National Institute for the Blind (now the RNIB) and, after becoming their treasurer, planned to set up a hostel where blind people could work to overcome their disability and live meaningful and rewarding lives. Before he could turn his plans into a reality the war started and servicemen who had lost all or part of their sight began to be sent back to this country. Pearson realised the numbers of men suffering in this way would only increase and he came up with the idea of a hostel where blinded servicemen could have space to recuperate and then could learn how to support themselves and lead fulfilling lives.

While they were looking for a suitable property, the American financier, Otto Kahn, offered to lend his home, St Dunstan's Lodge, in Regents Park, London, to the Blinded Soldiers and Sailors Care Committee. The committee, chaired by Pearson, took over the mansion and its fifteen acres of grounds. While it was being converted, the committee set up a temporary hostel in a house they were lent on Bayswater Hill. They moved into St Dunstan's Lodge in March 1915.

St Dunstan's Hostel for Blinded Soldiers and Sailors (St Dunstan's) was set up as a charity and much of its funding came from the British Red Cross Society, the Order of St John of Jerusalem, and the National Institute for the Blind. However, it also depended heavily on public donations and fundraising. The medical side of St Dunstan's was run by a matron, one trained nurse, orderlies and eight nursing VADs. The hostel also used VADs in a number of non-nursing roles. They did the housework, helped with administration, typed letters dictated by the men, read letters to them, ran the linen room and laundry, made beds, and waited on the men in the dining rooms. One of the VADs set up a music room where she and a dozen helpers encouraged the men to take up music as a hobby. Their ragtime band, known as St Dunstan's Own, gave a large number of public performances. Many of the men loved dancing and twice-weekly dances were held with VADs partnering the men.

Staff went out to the Second and Third London General Hospitals to reassure men who had been blinded that when their injuries healed they would be able to go to the hostel to be supported while they learned to adapt to their new circumstances. The first thirty men to move in included three Belgians and two Irish officers. By March 1916, there were 150 residents. Numbers grew so quickly that in October they had to expand into the nearby Regent's Park College, which they were lent on a temporary basis to house another 100 men. This annexe had its own matron and staff.

St Dunstan's offered training in a wide range of skills including typing, Braille, Braille shorthand, telephony, basket making, joinery, poultry farming, market gardening, boot repairing, and mat making. All but six of the seventy-two teachers working at St Dunstan's in 1918 were volunteers. At the end of their training, the men took a typing and shorthand test consisting of producing a business letter and writing a 500-word essay. They could only pass if they made less than one error and three corrections. If they did pass, and most men achieved high speeds and accuracy, they were given their own Remington typewriter. The typewriters were specially adapted so that the shift key was operated by a knee. A number of the instructors were also blind. Sixteen women, supervised by a VAD Commandant, taught the men netting. This was partly as a hobby, but also enabled them to make hammocks and pea and bean nets for sale. St Dunstan's also ran hostels where the men's female relatives could stay while visiting. In order to provide the men with entertainment and to improve their physical and mental confidence, a number of sports were organised. Professional goalkeepers from the Arsenal Football Club went along to help the residents practice shooting goals. Rowing on the Thames was also popular with VADs acting as cox for teams of rowers.

Recognising that the need for support did not end when men left St Dunstan's, the National Institute for the Blind decided to set up an after care branch to help men after their training period was over. All St Dunstan's residents were given a special watch by the National Institute for the Blind. Not only was it large, but, at a touch of a spring the cover flipped back allowing the user to feel the time, which was marked with raised dots. When they left St Dunstan's each man was also given a radio.

In 1920, Otto Kahn gave notice that he wanted St Dunstan's Lodge back and in 1921, the charity moved to St John's Lodge, another mansion in Regent's Park, which had been used as a hospital during the war. Demand for places grew steadily and the Federation of Grocers' Associations gave St Dunstan's West House in Brighton, to be used as an annexe. Outposts were also opened in Torquay and other large towns. Sadly, some of them did not last long, as St Dunstan's was hit by the economic slump of the 1920s. However, they were keen to find employment for their men and set up an employment bureau, placing the men who had trained as telephonists and in taking shorthand dictation. Although 130 men had trained as masseurs and worked in military hospitals during the war, they faced difficulties after the Armistice, when those hospitals started to close. St Dunstan's therefore set up a massage and electrotherapeutic clinic in Finsbury Square, London, where some of them were employed. In contrast, 200 of the men took up poultry farming at Dollis Hill and Kings Langley in Hertfordshire.

Sadly, Arthur Pearson died in 1921. He was replaced as chairman by Ian Fraser, who had been blinded by a bullet while serving as a captain during the Battle of the Somme. St Dunstan's was re-named Blind Veterans UK in 2012 and is still helping thousands of ex-service people with centres in Llandudno and Brighton.

In 1916, inspired by work in France and Italy, the Village Centres Council was set up to ensure that adequate care and training for disabled veterans was provided when they left the forces. They specialised in helping men who would be able to recover from their wounds. In December 1918, a letter in *The Spectator* stressed that the need for their work increased, rather than reduced. Their fundraising efforts were unremitting. The local committee bought Enham Place with its 1,000-acre estate, near Andover, in Hampshire for £30,000. It was then adapted to provide housing, rehabilitation, and long-term employment. The organisers were very aware of men with 'neurasthenia' or shell-shock who might benefit from spending time in a peaceful, rural setting. Fifty men, and their families, arrived in 1919. King George V made a personal donation to the funds and he and Queen Mary visited Enham in 1922. Some of the men only stayed a short time but others, called Settlers, stayed with their families for life. In 1921 Village Centres Cottages Ltd built more cottages and bungalows on the estate. The site was renamed Enham-Alamein in 1945 in recognition of the generous gift of £225,000 from the Egyptian Alamein Committee. The money was used to build a new village on the estate.

In November 1918 the people of Lancaster held a public meeting at which they decided that they wanted to have two types of war memorial. As well as the classic stone monument, they decided to create a memorial village where local men who had been severely disabled as a result of their war service could live with their families and where they would be employed. The priority was helping men who had served in the King's Own Royal Lancaster Regiment, although other Lancastrian disabled veterans were also welcomed. Thanks to energetic local fundraising efforts, it was less than a year later that work was able to start on the first building in the Westfield Memorial Village. Larger individual donations were essential in making the village a reality. It was officially opened by Earl Haig in 1924. The village was the brainchild of landscape designer, Thomas H. Mawson, and an industrialist, Herbert Lushington Storey, who hoped that similar villages would be set up elsewhere in Britain. Storey donated the land for the village. The first two cottages were paid for, anonymously, by industrialist Joseph Bibby. He had lost two sons in the war and the cottages, Morton and Leslie, were named after them. Alexandra Cottage was funded by the 'Lancaster Ladies'. Other cottages were also sponsored as memorials to specific men. Herbert Storey Cottage was the only one built to celebrate a soldier's safe return; that of Herbert Storey's son, Kenneth. Mawson believed that through segregation and sheltered workshops, crippled men could be protected from competition with the able-bodied. He believed that green spaces would be essential to the men's well-being and planned that the village would have workshops, recreational facilities, and allotments in addition to accommodation. Rents were kept very low. In reality, the workshops soon closed as the residents managed to find work in the surrounding area. Mawson's vision of public buildings that were fully accessible to men in wheelchairs, bath chairs and wheeled litters remained a dream.

About 55,000 men got tuberculosis while they were in the forces and a similar number not long after they had been discharged. The Barlow Committee recommended that the Government should spend £1,000,000 on special settlements for these men, inspired by the one that had been set up by Dr P. C. Varrier Jones at Papworth, Cambridge, in 1916. They were to offer a combination of medically supervised work in sheltered industries with healthy country living. The British Legion campaigned for the implementation of the report's recommendations but by 1925, the Government had only voted £20,000 for this work. Once again, charities tried to address the shortfall.

The British Legion set up its own Preston Hall Village near Maidstone in Kent, specifically designed for veterans with TB. Preston Hall had been a wartime TB settlement and the Legion added a hostel for single men and cottages for men who became 'settlers' and whose families joined them. The cottages had verandas to give the men sheltered access to fresh air. One bungalow was sponsored by the members of the Empress Club's Voluntary Aid Committee, whose members included Princess Sophia Duleep Singh, an active fundraiser for wounded and disabled veterans. It was directed by Dr Varrier Jones. The Housing Association for Officers' Families built Southwood Court, in Barnet. It was designed by C. S. Soutar, the official architect of Hampstead Garden Suburb, and opened in 1920.

Both the Officers Farming Association and the Ex-Servicemen's and Women's Land League were set up to help veterans train and take up life on the land. The movement was promoted by the Disabled Society. There were several centres where veterans could learn about poultry farming.

One relatively short-lived scheme was the Ashstead Pottery in Surrey, set up in 1923 by Sir Lawrence Weaver and his wife, Lady Kathleen Purcell. Sir Lawrence was the president of the Design and Industries Association. Their aim was to train veterans as art potters. They started by training just four men but expanded until they employed up to forty disabled ex-servicemen making a wide range of crockery and figurines. The men came from all over Southern England and initially lived in local lodgings. Purcell Close was later built to house workers who had families. The potters had a stand at the British Empire Exhibitions at Wembley in 1924 and 1925, exhibiting both their skills and their wares. The pottery suffered, like so many other businesses, during the depression. Sir Lawrence's death and increased competition also took their toll and the pottery closed in 1935.

Much of the purpose-built housing for veterans that was built after the war was funded by public subscription. Fundraising was often led by well-known actors or backed by regimental associations. Mrs Hilda Leyell, a well-known actress, set up the Golden Ballot lottery for war charities and the proceeds helped fund Westfield Memorial Village, Lancaster. Tobacco industrialists and boot manufacturers who had done well from the war were generous donors to charities for ex-servicemen.

War Seal Mansions in Fulham was founded in 1915 and registered under the War Charities Act the following year. Its committee included well known figures such as Sir Jessie Boot and Gordon Selfridge. The idea and impetus for the construction of this integrated housing providing housing for disabled ex-servicemen and their families, with on-site treatment for their injuries, came from theatrical impresario and founder of the Royal Variety Performance, Sir Oswald Stoll. Stoll also donated the plot of land on which the flats were built and covered all the costs of promoting the scheme. Fundraising for the project was even reported in the New Zealand press. A lot of money was raised through donations and by the sale of War Seals costing a halfpenny. People were asked to buy the seals and fix them to every letter, postcard, or receipt they gave out, thus publicising the scheme at the same time as raising money.

Shell shock, or neurasthenia, affected a large number of servicemen. In 1915, the British Army in France decreed that if a man's shell-shock could be linked to an explosion, his casualty report should have the W prefix. This indicated that he was classed as wounded and could wear a 'wound stripe' on his arm. However, if his breakdown could not be linked to an explosion it was not thought to have been caused by the enemy and he was labelled Shell-Shock or S for Sick. This meant that he was not entitled to a military pension or to wear a wound stripe, both of which were very important not only to the men's perception of themselves but also to how other people saw them. The need for specialist centres, where shell-shocked men could be treated quickly, near the front line, in a suitable environment and by psychotherapeutic measures, was identified in August 1916 by Charles Myers, the newly appointed Consulting Psychologist to the Army. The very fact of his appointment indicates that shell-shock was seen as a major problem, even if its causes were not properly understood. He also used hypnosis when treating some of his patients.

Sadly, Myers' compassionate views were held by a minority and later that year Gordon Holmes was put in charge of the northern section of the Western Front. Like many military men he had a far tougher, less empathetic approach than Myers. His attitude was in tune with prevailing military views and so it was adopted. By June 1917 all British cases of 'shell-shock' were evacuated to a neurological centre and were labelled as NYDN–Not Yet Diagnosed Nervous. However, because of the Adjutant-General's distrust of doctors, no patient could receive the specialist attention they needed until Form AF 3436 had been sent off to the man's unit and filled in by his commanding officer. This created significant delays in treatment, after which the authorities claimed that no more than ten per cent of the cases that had initially been described as 'wounded' could be attributed to a physical cause, insisting that the remainder were emotional. This greatly undermined the recognition of shell-shock as a war-related injury.

In the immediate aftermath of the First World War, there was possibly more public awareness of shell shock and mental damage than there was in successive decades. Awareness faded and many of the veterans who went home, supposedly fit and healthy were hiding their mental wounds. Problems in relating to their families and communities, inability to hold down a job, domestic violence, homelessness, and alcohol abuse are higher among veterans than those who have not fought. Some doctors recognised that it was important that men suffering from shell-shock were not placed in general hospital wards. If they were not segregated they would often find their symptoms and 'nervous tics' were belittled or made them the butt of jokes from the other patients. In some cases, they were badly treated by fellow-patients, who thought they were malingering.

One of the first places that was specifically set up to treat men with shell-shock was the Home of Recovery in Highfield, in North London. It opened in May 1917, with 100 beds and was meant to be used as a model for other institutions. The building was leased by the Red Cross, for £500 a year, and the Government paid the running costs. The staff included a number of experienced VADs, who had been carefully selected for this difficult work. The home was set in 12½ acres of grounds and most of the patients were involved in intensive gardening and supporting trades. The gardening was designed to be therapeutic but also to provide the possibility for future employment. Men not actively engaged in gardening were taught new trades. Carpenters learned to make cold frames for the gardens and packing crates for the produce. Basket-makers produced hampers and baskets for transporting fruit and vegetables and iron-workers made tools that were used in the gardens. In separate workshops, men were taught motor mechanics, shoemaking, and how to be electrical fitters. When the men were discharged, they were given help finding work. In 1918, the home was handed over to the Royal Air Force. Homes of Recovery were also opened at Allerton Hall, Leeds, Abbotswood House in Gloucester, and at the Remedial Exercise Room in London.

Stockport had two shell-shock hospitals in the Brinnington District and this led to the creation of the Stockport Special Shell-Shock Hospital Fund. Some men recovered with time and care but by the end of 1921 there were still over 6,000 shell-shocked men being cared for in asylums throughout Britain. They were granted special status but the British Legion's later request, that they should be housed in separate wards, was turned down by the Government.

The main charity dedicated to helping veterans suffering from the mental wounds of war, founded in 1919, and more active than ever, is the Ex-Services' Welfare Society; now known as Combat Stress. Its initial commitment was to treat (and train where necessary) all ranks who were suffering from neurasthenia and mental breakdown. The need for its services has increased dramatically in recent years with the understanding that many more personnel suffer from Post-Traumatic Stress Disorder (PTSD), and other mental disorders than had been previously thought and that the onset of obvious symptoms, and thus diagnosis, can be delayed for decades after the traumatic event. While some of its services now receive funding from the NHS, Combat Stress, like most charities, is heavily dependent on huge fundraising efforts. In spite of setting up outreach teams, it is unable to meet the increasing demand for its services.

Training for sick and disabled veterans was not only provided in association with hospitals. The YMCA started the Red Triangle Farm Colony at West Howe near Bournemouth in February 1917. This was the first colony of its kind in Britain, set up to provide training for ex-servicemen who had been invalided out of the services because they had tuberculosis. The site was bought from a local doctor, who had set up a sanatorium and farm there in 1910. The Red Triangle Farm Colony opened with twelve men, who were not fit to return to an indoor or sedentary job. It had thirty-five acres of land and the men were taught to run a smallholding; keeping pigs, and growing fruit and flowers. They worked regular hours and were monitored by a doctor. The farm buildings included sleeping huts, a dining room, recreation room, and kitchens. Unfortunately, there was a serious fire at the colony in November 1917 but the YMCA managed to rebuild and continue with the project until 1920.

The Old Metals Collection Scheme was set up to fund the establishment of a permanent Home and Trades Training School for soldiers who had been disabled through their military service. With branches all over the country, the scheme appealed for people to donate any scrap metal or trinkets. The Southgate branch asked people to support them in creating a Welfare Plan for Disabled Patriots, men who had been broken by the war.

Many veterans were in a desperate situation. Some found that their pre-war jobs were no longer available or that men who had not fought had been promoted ahead of them. Thousands of young men had been called up before they had had a chance to learn a trade and they found themselves disadvantaged compared to those who had stayed at home. Numerous small charities and volunteer-run schemes were set up to try to help these men. However, in an economic slump, competition for jobs was fierce and unemployment in the country as a whole soared in the 1920s.

The Lord Roberts Memorial Workshops, also known as the Incorporated Soldiers' Sailors' and Airmen's Help Society, was set up in 1915 to provide work for veterans who had lost a limb. The first workshop was in the Brompton Road in London. While the men were busy in the workshops, their wives and daughters worked in the painting room. Lord Roberts was known as a campaigner for help for ex-servicemen, and especially those who were disabled as a result of their war service. He had died in 1914 while visiting troops in France. The workshops were named after him. The charity's aim was to help the amputees. Machinery in the workshops was adapted to meet the needs of men who had lost a limb. Other workshops opened from 1916 and, by 1920, there were eleven. In each workshop, the products were geared to fit in with local industries. In Birmingham they made metal toys and in Bradford, woollen toys and printed items. The Colchester workshop made household items and porcelain toy bricks. Liverpool and Belfast made small furniture and toys. All of them made 'Lord Roberts' cigarettes. The Fulham Workshop, just over the road from the War Seal Flats, specialised in making dolls' houses.

In 1915, Annie Bindon Carter enrolled as a volunteer at Wharncliffe War Hospital on the edge of Sheffield. She had trained at Sheffield School of Art and enlisted the help of her fellow students to run occupational health art classes, three times a week, for men who were recovering from major injuries, such as the loss of a limb. While running her classes she was inspired by one patient, who she helped to learn to paint, even though his right hand and his left hand and forearm had been amputated. The difference that learning to paint made to his mental well-being made her determined to help other men in a similar position. As Annie continued to work with the men at Wharncliffe, she got them to make a range of textile items, including dresses, scarves, handkerchiefs, furnishing fabrics, ecclesiastical work and even theatrical curtains and backdrops, which they decorated with painted stencilling. After the Armistice, Annie set up workshops in the centre of Sheffield where a few men could work. Local people supported the scheme financially. In 1923, the United Services Fund bought part of an old army camp at Norton Woodseats and then leased the premises to the new company Annie and her colleagues had set up. It was called Painted Fabrics Ltd.

By the time that the Princess Royal formally opened the company, in 1925, there were twenty-nine employees, some of whom lived with their families in huts on the site. One of their publicity leaflets announced that the forty-seven veterans only had fifty-seven undamaged arms and fifty undamaged legs between them. Other workers had suffered gunshot wounds or were shell-shocked. While they worked at Painted Fabrics the men were paid at least a shilling an hour and were guaranteed thirty hours work a week. They lived and worked, with their families, in peaceful, secure surroundings. The residents must have been very aware how fortunate they were to have been taken on by the company. In 1928, ten new houses, adapted to meet the men's specific needs, were built on the site as Haig Memorial Homes. Much of their work was sold through exhibitions in town halls or similar venues or at specially arranged 'at homes' in the houses of many of Annie Carter's aristocratic contacts. Many of the goods they made were aimed at the luxury market. They had an annual exhibition at Claridges, in London, and one year Queen Elizabeth bought two dresses for Princess Elizabeth. They also sold items to Liberty of London. Some of their finest articles were specially commissioned wedding dresses as well as evening dresses and dressing gowns.

Some people who wanted to help disabled veterans fell prey to inept fraudster Richie Gill. He registered a company called the Heroes Poultry Farms (Limited) which, he claimed, would give employment to disabled veterans and would also supply eggs to military hospitals. He had big plans and claimed to be raising 5,000,000 shillings and that the farms would eventually cover 100 acres. When two women complained, he was arrested for trying to procure charitable donations by fraud and admitted that there were, in fact, no farms. He was fined £25.

The United Services Fund was set up under Royal Charter in 1920 to administer a share of the profits from canteens, for the benefit of serviceman, their widows and families. One of their activities was setting up local clubs where veterans could develop a social life.

The Southport Soldier's Club, which had been run by Miss Willets during the war, continued to operate for some time after the Armistice as a free social centre for demobbed veterans. The people who ran small clubs of this kind were sensitive to the ongoing needs of recently demobbed men, and the lack of other provision for them, so they continued for as long as they could raise the necessary funds.

The first Kitchener House Club for Wounded Soldiers and Sailors opened in London in February 1917 and was modelled on the California House for Wounded Belgian Soldiers. Kitchener House Clubs were near hospitals where wounded servicemen were treated. They were meant to provide a safe refuge where men could come and go freely, under hospital rules, and where the men could be stimulated and could be helped to find a new livelihood. The clubs were open every day from 10 a.m. to 6 p.m. Classes were held every afternoon and the subjects on offer included languages, woodworking, arts and crafts, embroidery, and music. Free dinner and tea was always on offer. A second club was opened, in the Regents Park area of London, followed by one for officers in the upmarket Grosvenor Place.

The Not Forgotten Association has become one of the best-known British charities for veterans. However, most people do not realise that it was created to help deal with the human fallout of the First World War. American soprano Marta Cunningham had been involved with canteen and charity work during the war. In 1919 she visited a Ministry of Pensions hospital and asked the matron whether they still cared for any wounded servicemen. When the matron responded that 600 of her patients fell into this category Marta Cunningham decided to see how widespread this situation was. When she found that the same circumstances were replicated throughout the country, she felt compelled to try to help the men by giving them something positive to look forward to. She mobilised a number of her friends, persuading them to invite the men out for tea and entertainment. In August 1920, this work was formalised by the creation of the Not Forgotten Association. The Association's aims were 'the cheer and entertainment' of men who had been wounded during the war. The scale of both the need and Marta Cunningham's efforts were soon clear and 10,000 men were helped in the first year of the Association's existence.

Many officers were in a particularly bad position, as the Government still acted as thought they were all gentlemen with private means and would not, therefore, need any help finding work. In reality, the sheer scale of the war combined with the appallingly high death rate among young subalterns, meant that many officers were conscripts, who had been promoted in the field. They desperately needed access to Labour Exchanges and other help and some of them suffered extreme poverty and became homeless. An officer was seen by one of his former men, wearing the ribbon of the Military Cross and standing in the gutter trying to sell matches and shoelaces.

Sylvia Newell was born in Blackheath, South London, in 1928, nine years after the end of the war. She vividly recalls poverty-struck veterans trying to make a living during the Depression in the 1930s. There were men who had lost a limb leading others who had been blinded. They would sit on the pavement, near the station, holding pieces of card on which they had scrawled 'Wounded at Ypres' or other, similar phrases. They were dressed in filthy rags and begging. Her mother, who had been a VAD during the war, would give the children a penny to drop in the men's cap. On the other side of the road there were men who had managed to scrape together enough money to buy twelve boxes of matches, which they pushed together to form a question mark. They then sold the boxes of matches for a penny, which was a halfpenny less than the shops charged. Scenes like these were replicated all over the country.

Just a few weeks after the start of the War, Lord Kitchener, Secretary of State for War, asked for volunteers to search for soldiers who were missing, and who might be wandering around in the chaos after a battle had finished. As a result of his appeal, a group of civilians, known as the British Red Cross Mobile Unit, started driving around when fighting stopped, looking for lost soldiers and collecting wounded men. One of these volunteers was Fabian Ware, a former editor of the *Morning Post*, who started to note the details and location of all the British graves they saw. He later persuaded the military authorities that this work should have the backing of the War Office and this led to the creation of the Graves Registration Committee in March 1915. Ware became a major and continued his work for the committee. By October, he and his colleagues had registered more than 31,000 graves and marked them with wooden crosses. The Imperial (later Commonwealth) War Graves Commission grew out of Ware's instinctive, voluntary efforts.

With the decision not to repatriate the remains of the dead, even where they could be identified, thousands of people were determined to visit their loved one's grave. Shortly after the Armistice, the Salvation Army set up the War Graves Visitation Department under Mrs Commissioner Higgins to escort relatives on 'Pilgrimages of Remembrance'. They were based at the Red Shield Hostel for Graves Visitation in Arras. Workers would go to England, meet a group of relatives, and then escort them to France where they stayed in a 'Hostel of Consolation' near the cemeteries. Staff would help them find their relative's grave. When relatives were unable to visit the cemeteries themselves, staff would find the grave, lay flowers on it, and send a photograph, with a card and a few pressed petals from the flowers to the family in Britain. Other religious organisations also took groups of bereaved relatives to France. Charities helped finance the visits for people unable to afford to cover their own expenses. The St Barnabas Society was founded by a clergyman in 1919 with the specific aim of subsidising travel for those who could not afford to go with commercial travel companies. Between November 1919 and June 1920, the Church Army alone took 5,000 people to visit war graves. By 1923, the Salvation Army and the YMCA had taken 78,500 people on visits to France and Belgium.

As the bodies of dead servicemen were buried overseas most local communities decided to erect some kind of permanent memorial to local men who had died. Funding these memorials was another matter. After four years of incessant fundraising for one cause or another, many people were too tired and worn, and short of money, to get excited about another campaign. In some communities the initial, grandiose plans, had to be scaled down to match the available resources. In others, people were very keen indeed and launched their fundraising campaigns with renewed energy. Many workplace memorials were paid for by the workers who had not gone to fight.

In many communities, people wanted a say in how the money was actually spent with fierce debates raging over the relative merits of a stone memorial or something more practical. Within a very few years 38,213 public war memorials of one kind and another had been erected. These included 431 memorial halls, 185 clock towers, 90 sports fields and 431 church organs or bits of organs. Major landowners were sometimes persuaded to donate land where a memorial could be built. After the war, some voluntary hospitals were often very short of money so contributions towards a memorial ward were very welcome. Veterans often felt that their wishes were ignored and some objected to the effusive language employed in the memorial inscriptions glorifying the dead and their 'glorious, willing sacrifice.' Since many of the dead were conscripts who would much rather have stayed at home, and since the survivors were aware that dead had not died gloriously, the generally accepted texts for memorials suited civilians more than veterans.

Many people favoured practical, rather than monumental, memorials. The National Federation of Discharged and Demobilised Sailors and Soldiers often supported utilitarian memorials such as the maternity home in Bethnal Green and Cottage Hospitals in a number of towns. Veterans in the small village of Bosham in Sussex built their simple and touching memorial to their dead comrades with their own hands, using materials that they had persuaded local people to donate.

Conflict between civic officials and local people came to a head in
Fulstow in Lincolnshire. Officials refused to include Private Charles
Kirman's name on the memorial because he had been executed for
cowardice in 1917. Local people felt that this was unjust, as Private
Kirman had been a soldier for nine years, and had been wounded and
had suffered from malaria before both his mind and body had had
enough and he could not continue fighting. When the officials stood firm
local people were so angry that they refused to let any other names be
included and the village therefore had no memorial until 2005.

***

The legacy of the First World War included a number of organisations set
up by veterans to try to improve their own situation. This kind of self-help
was a new aspect of British charitable work and their efforts included
lobbying for improved pensions and disability and unemployment
allowances. These organisations, and many of the local branches, were
quick to register under the War Charities Act. There was a considerable
amount of disagreement and squabbling between the groups. The first of
these organisations was the National Association of Discharged Soldiers
and Sailors (the Association), which was set up in September 1916 and
which had strong links to the Labour and Trades Union movements.
Membership was open to veterans of all ranks.

The Association was followed in April 1917 by the National Federation
of Discharged and Demobilised Sailors and Soldiers (the Federation).
Membership was restricted to men who had served in, or risen from,
the ranks. It had links with the Liberal Party. Although its members
came from all over the country they were most numerous in central and
eastern London.

In response to Establishment fears that the Association and the
Federation would ferment a Russian-style revolution, a third group was
formed in August 1917, without any political affiliation. The Comrades
of the Great War (the Comrades) was not officially sponsored by the
Government but did have its unofficial approval and the open support of
Lord Derby, Secretary of State for War. Two of the founders were MPs,
who were former colonels, and the launch of the organisation included
sending a letter to every Lord Lieutenant in the country. Membership was
boosted when Captain Towse, VC, a charismatic national hero who had
been blinded during the Boer War, toured camps in France encouraging
men to join. Towse later became the chairman. The Comrades flourished
and got some support from rank and file servicemen even though
its structure and attitude were paternalistic. It was well resourced
and guaranteed positive and extensive press coverage as its sponsors
included the Duke of Westminster and press barons Lords Rothermere
and Northcliffe and Major Gavin Astor, whose family owned *The Times*.

The most radical of all the veterans' organisations was the National Union of Ex-Servicemen, known as NUX. It was founded in 1918 by John Beckett, a former soldier who was a committed member of the International Labour Party. He believed that the only way for ex-servicemen's organisations to flourish was to affiliate themselves to other workers' organisations with similar aims.

In the summer of 1919, MPs were very worried when the Federation assembled 10,000 protestors in Hyde Park. The demonstrators demanded that unemployed veterans should be found work without delay, at trades union wages, or should have their unemployment benefit raised to £1 8s a week for a single man or £2 a week for men with children. The demonstration turned violent. Members of Parliament were increasingly nervous and heard the Federation, with its 2,000,000 members, described as 'a huge shapeless and menacing mass, on the verge of collapse into anarchy.'

The first suggestion of uniting these organisations came from the Association in 1918 but the others rejected the idea. Both the Association and the Federation changed after the war. The Federation opened its membership to commissioned, as well as non-commissioned, officers and the Association began to loosen its links with the unions and Labour. As positions became less entrenched, there were suggestions that the organisations should work together, or possibly merge. When Churchill became Secretary of State for War, he suggested that the Comrades and the Federation should join together but the proposal was rejected. Each organisation was very sensitive to what they saw as outside interference.

During the war, the Expeditionary Force Canteens, the Navy and the Army Canteen Board had built up a considerable balance of funds, which the service authorities wanted to use for benevolent work. In February 1919, they consulted the three organisations over how this money should be distributed, apparently hoping that they would join together in an officially sponsored, Empire Services League. The Comrades thought this was a good idea but members of the Association and Federation disagreed. As the three groups could not agree on a way forward, the authorities set up a Royal Navy Benevolent fund and a United Services Fund (for soldiers and airmen) and split the money between them.

In August 1920, representatives from the Federation, Association, Comrades, NUX, and the newly formed Officers' Association, held a conference to discuss uniting. It was chaired by T. F. Lister from the Federation, who believed they had to abandon any political affiliations in order that they could lobby more effectively. The representatives from NUX opposed uniting and left the conference. Not long afterwards, NUX was disbanded. Members of the Officers' Association were also suspicious. They had recently raised more than £600,000, which they did not want to share. It later came out that they had already applied for a Royal Charter, which would protect their funds.

Throughout the negotiations, Lister was the voice of reason, drawing the others together even when any alliance seemed like an impossible dream. Delegates managed to agree to draw up a constitution for a joint organisation that would be discussed at a further conference in December. Various names were suggested for the new, joint, organisation but the British Legion was selected, as delegates felt it was strong, but not too imperialistic or military. The creation of the British Legion was formalised at a three-day conference at the Queen's Hall in London in May 1921. The conference started with the observation of a silence for the dead and ended with a service at the Cenotaph. Earl Haig was the first president and the Prince of Wales became the British Legion's first patron. Lister was the first chairman.

Throughout the 1920s, the British Legion consolidated its position as the main charity working to improve conditions for veterans. It campaigned for employers to give preference to ex-servicemen; for women, who were not breadwinners or dependants of servicemen, to give up their jobs; for money to help people start businesses, provision for retraining for those who had not been able to go back to their old jobs, decent living allowances; special help for disabled veterans, and preferential treatment for veterans over transport and admission to places of entertainment.

Naturally enough, it was some time before all the members of the old organisations transferred their allegiance to the new British Legion. For administrative reasons the British Legion divided England into ten areas and Wales into three. They also kept close links with Irish veterans both north and south of the new border. To everyone's surprise, Scottish veterans decided to go their own way. On 18 June 1921, just two weeks before the official establishment of the British Legion, a Scottish Legion was set up at a meeting in Edinburgh. Members of the National Executive Committee initially assumed that the Scottish organisation was simply a regional group within the overall British Legion. This was not the case and the Scottish group steadfastly refused to pay any affiliation fees to the London office.

By end of 1921 there were 1,500 branches of the British Legion. After a membership campaign, the number of branches rose to more than 1,800, but still, only one in twenty-five veterans had joined. Ordinary members of Legion had to have served in the forces for at least seven days. From 1922 women who had served were allowed to join but conscientious objectors, even if they had served with the Red Cross, were barred. The initial membership of 18,206 rose quickly, to 116,426 by the end of 1922, and 312,506 by the end of the decade. Membership of the French equivalent of the British Legion reached 3,000,000 members in the time it took the British Legion to reach 500,000.

As well as the money from the Federation, Association and Comrades, the British Legion took over various other funds, including £157,000 from the National Relief Fund. Most of its income came from subscriptions and fundraising events and, in 1921, a national appeal in various newspapers. Their greatest single source of income came to be Poppy Day.

The use of red poppies as a symbol of remembrance originated in the USA, where poppies, made in France, were sold to raise money for French children who had been badly affected by the war. When the General Secretary of the British Legion was shown samples of the paper poppies he gingerly ordered a large number, to be sold to the public and worn on Armistice Day in 1921. Demand so exceeded the number of poppies that he had ordered that staff at the British Legion's headquarters had to make more, although the paper they used was pink, rather than red.

Approximately 8,000,000 poppies were worn that year, raising £106,000. The poppies had cost £21,000. After expenses had been deducted, ninety per cent of the profit went to the Benevolent Fund and the remaining ten per cent to the general administration of the British Legion. Branches could bid for half the money they had raised, providing they could show how previous grants had been used and that they needed the money.

The Appeals Department then invested in materials and equipment and invited applications from hospitals and other organisations to make poppies for future years. They stipulated that as many poppies as possible should be made by disabled ex-servicemen.

One response came from Major George Howson who had launched the Disabled Society, mainly to improve the quality and supply of artificial limbs. He got a grant of £2,000 from the British Legion to set up a factory just off the Old Kent Road in south London. By August 1922, forty-one disabled ex-servicemen were employed there, many of whom had been unemployed for a long time. They worked a five-day week (less than normal) and were each expected to make 1,000 poppies a day. All the employees were single or double amputees.

The Poppy Factory, as it came to be called, was initially run by a joint committee, with representatives from the British Legion and the Disabled Society and chaired by Major Howson. It later moved from the Old Kent Road to Richmond Hill, where a well-wisher had donated a disused brewery that was converted into a factory. An adjoining estate was bought by the British Legion to set up flats and a club for workers and their families. By the time it was completed in 1925, there were more than 190 workers with another 300 on a waiting list. Distributing the vast number of poppies was a challenge. They rented a warehouse, where the poppies were stored. They then asked hauliers, whose vans were returning empty from London, to transport the poppies to regional distribution centres. From 1923, the wreaths laid on the Cenotaph by the king and members of the royal family were made by the British Legion from paper poppies.

The British Legion Clubs made money to help fund the core work of helping veterans and their families. However, this did not always run smoothly. There were issues with clubs allowing out of hours drinking and gambling, and of managers who failed to pay the Intoxicating Liquor Tax. Some clubs were very simple. Members of the Plumpton and East Chiltington branch in Sussex physically built their own clubhouse. To raise the £200 they then needed to get the club up and running they bought bonds at 10s each, effectively lending the money to the club. They got a return of six per cent on their investment. Ex-servicemen in Heavitree and Wonford, Exeter, got a grant for buying materials and then they also constructed their own club. At the other extreme, the Windsor branch was given a headquarters building and clubhouse by Mr Djunibhoy Bomanji of Windsor and Bombay. The building was opened by no less a dignitary than Earl Haig himself, and facilities included a concert hall, a billiard room with four tables, two lounge bars a reading room and a library; it was valued at £5,000.

Practical help was as important a part of the British Legion's work as lobbying for improved pensions or employment for veterans. In the winter of 1923–4, the Luton branch bought a bullock, which they cut up into joints to be given to the families of the unemployed. In Birmingham, the Windmill Street's free canteen for ex-servicemen served 300,000 meals in 1927. In Bethnal Green, in 1929, the branch gave 300 children of poor ex-servicemen in the borough a Christmas dinner of roast beef, Yorkshire pudding, vegetables, and Christmas pudding with custard.

In spite of the British Legion's efforts, many veterans and their families remained in extreme poverty. In 1924, there were 35,000 ex-service family members in workhouses in mainland Britain and the situation was even worse in Ireland, where there was little or no local relief. Branches even helped pay for the funerals of veterans who were paupers.

* * *

Returning POWs were also veterans and many were in poor health but the quality of their reception varied. In some cases, they were blamed for the amount of time they had spent away from the fighting, as though they had chosen to be taken prisoner as an easy option. This discrimination became so bad that the War Office, king and queen issued them with documents absolving them of any blame. Former POWS at least had the support of veterans' organisations and the authorities. Civilian

internees returning from Ruhleben and Holland received little support
or sympathy. Their careers, families and normal lives had been suspended
for the duration of the war and many of them were suffering from
'barbed wire disease' and yet even the charity sector ignored their plight.
Their problems were all thought to have evaporated on their release.

In the context of war, the term 'veteran' is usually assumed to apply
only to people who have served in the armed forces. This assumption is a
slight to the civilian volunteers, many of whom had worked in appalling
conditions in various theatres of war, often close to the front lines. Almost
nothing was done to help them. Most had worked without recompense
and to the detriment of their own finances. No matter how damaged they
were, physically or mentally, or how difficult they found it to fit back
into Britain after the war, they got no help for their on-going problems.
In many quarters, it was not even thought appropriate to discuss their
experiences. The Commonwealth War Graves Commission recognises
650 women among the war dead, some of them charity workers and
volunteers. There are no doubt others, aid workers among them, who
died during their war service from diseases such as typhoid, in the flu
pandemic or from the injuries they received, and who have never had
official recognition. A significant number also died earlier than might
have been anticipated. They were worn down by their experiences, like
Lady Dorothie Feilding, who died of heart failure in 1935 at the relatively
young age of forty-six.

Lady Ampthill, who had been chairman of the Joint Women's VAD
Department of the Order of St John and the British Red Cross Society,
recognised the need for somewhere where VADs could meet each
other and where the comradeship many of them had experienced and
valued could be continued. She thought that the way to achieve this
was to set up a 'first class ladies' club' in London for all VADs, past or
present. Realising that many VADs only had a moderate income she was
determined that membership charges should also be moderate.

She launched an appeal, aiming to raise the necessary finance through
the sale of individual shares costing £2. Members of the Red Cross and
the Order of St John bought 14,000 shares, thereby raising £28,000.
The management committee, chaired by Lady Ampthill, then bought a
999-year lease on 28 Cavendish Street for £25,000. Much of the work to
get the building ready for its new role was done by military veterans who
were keen to show their gratitude to the VADs who had worked so hard
for them during the war.

The New Cavendish Club opened on 14 June 1920. Queen Mary was
its patron and Princess Mary, who had been Commandant of a Volunteer
Aid Detachment, was made an honorary member. Lady Ampthill's belief
in the need for the club was quickly vindicated and even before it opened

its doors, it had 2,500 members. The country subscription was one guinea a year and the town subscription was two guineas. A single room cost 6s 6d a night. Lunch cost from 1s 3d and the six-course club dinner was 4s 6d. Even these 'modest' rates will have put membership beyond the reach of many former VADs and, of course, there was nothing similar in other parts of the country.

The dining room was staffed by former VADs who wanted to be in London and whose parents wanted them to be somewhere respectable. What they really thought of waiting on their better-off former colleagues is not known. They wore VAD uniforms including caps and aprons and slept in staff accommodation nearby, three to a bedroom, getting one weekend a month off and earning 50s a month.

It is a shame membership was not extended to women who had served in other roles, many of whom must have felt very isolated when they tried to return to their ordinary lives. A number never did return, continuing to work in the countries where they had served during the war, working in hospitals, setting up orphanages or finding some other way of prolonging their self-imposed exile. Some of them presumably found that the thought of returning to the restricted world and relative idleness of a middle or upper-class life in Britain was intolerable after all they had experienced.

* * *

Both the triumph and the enduring tragedy of the many organisations that were set up to help servicemen during and after the war is that the need persists and will never go away. People no longer collect moss for dressings or eggs, vegetables or cigarettes for the sick and wounded. They no longer knit socks, sew shrouds for soldiers or nurse the sick and wounded; but charities and volunteers are still essential. Organisations that were set up with the expectation that the need for their services would be brief are still working hard. In some cases, they are working harder than ever after 100 years and constantly adapting to meet changing needs. The Not Forgotten Association still helps about 10,000 men a year.

Charity fundraising and spending time as a volunteer are entrenched in British society. Britain is consistently about the sixth most generous nation in the world when it comes to donating money or time to charities. It ranks well above some of the biggest economies in the world and all of its European neighbours.

No longer dominated by groups helping those caught up in wars, the range of charities, at least partly supported by volunteers, is enormous. There may be scores of well-paid professional fundraisers who arrange high profile events and campaigns but when it comes down to it, many – or even most – charities depend on the efforts of people who are sponsored to run races such as the London Marathon, jump out of planes or abseil down tall buildings, who bake and sell cakes, or knit blankets and clothes for refugees, who rattle collection boxes at us and who give their time and energy to helping those in need. It is the efforts of individuals and small groups that make events such as Comic Relief, Band Aid and Children in Need such a spectacular success. With the advent of mass media and, not least, the internet, individual efforts are often publicly lauded. We should, however, remember that the groundwork for this kind of responsive and inclusive charity and voluntary effort, rather than upper-class benevolence, was well and truly prepared by the hundreds of thousands of people who made whatever contribution they could during, and just after, the First World War.

Acknowledgements

I would like to thank staff at Barrow Archive and Local History Centre, Barrow-in-Furness; Bexhill Library; Tracey Cooper at the Blue Cross; Mary Painter at Blackburn with Darwen Library and Information Service; Brighton History Centre; Bristol Record Office; Cheshire Archives, Chester; Simon Butler and the Dartmoor Archive; Eastbourne Library; Hastings Library; Imperial War Museum Library; Kent History and Library Centre, Maidstone; Lancashire Archives (Preston); London Borough of Barnet Archives; London Metropolitan Archives; Matlock Library; Seaford Library; Sheffield City Archives and Local Studies Collection; Melissa Atkinson and the Library of the Society of Friends Library; The Keep (East Sussex Record Office and Brighton History Centre); University of Kent Library, Canterbury; University of Leeds, Department of Manuscripts and Special Collections, Brotherton Library; University of Sussex Library; Worthing Library.

I am grateful to everyone in Britain and France who responded to my search for information about the British League of Help for the Devastated Areas of France, to Luc Philament for help approaching staff in French archives, to Andrew Maunder of the University of Hertfordshire for introducing me to First World War propaganda plays, to Dr Peter Grant for access to his unpublished thesis, to Fiona Davison of the Royal Horticultural Society for a copy of the Society's booklet about Ruhleben, and to Michael Gallagher for a copy of the Glasgow refugee database.

Edward Besly provided encouragement and commented on selected chapters, providing cogent comments and suggestions.

In the last few years countless people have researched how the First World War affected their family or community and have generously made this information available through the internet. I have benefitted hugely from their efforts.

I would like to thank the following for permission to reproduce illustrations: the Imperial War Museum (1, 2, 3, 4, 5, 8, 10, 11, 12, 13, 14, 15, 16, 17, 18, 19, 20, 21, 22, 23, 25, 28, 31, 34, 35); The Blue Cross (24); Warwickshire County Record Office (8, 9); The Religious Society of Friends (Quakers) Britain (26, 27, 29, 33); Darwen Library and Information Service, Blackburn (32).

Select Bibliography

Books and Articles

Adie, Kate, *Fighting on the Home Front. The Legacy of Women in World War One* (London: Hodder and Stoughton, 2013)

Aitkin, Jonathan, *A War of Individuals. Bloomsbury Attitudes to the Great War* (Manchester: Manchester University Press, 2002)

Amara, Michael, *Des Belges à l'épreuve de l'Exil. Les réfugiés de la Première Guerre Mondiale* (Brussels: Editions de l'Université de Bruxelles, 2008)

Anglo-German Family History Society, *An insight into civilian internment in Britain during WWI. From the diary of Richard Noschke and a short essay by Rudolf Rocker* (Maidenhead: Anglo-German History Society, 1998)

Arscott, David, *Chailey Heritage. A Hundred Years* (Seaford: SB publications, 2003)

Arthur, Max, *Forgotten Voices of the Great War* (London: Ebury Press, 1988); *We will remember them. Voices from the aftermath of the Great War* (London: Weidenfeld and Nicholson, 2009)

Atkinson, Diane, *Elsie and Mairi go to War. Two Extraordinary Women on the Western Front* (London: Arrow Books, 2010)

Baily, Leslie, *Craftsman and Quaker: The Story of James T Baily 1876–1957* (London: Allen & Unwin Ltd, 1959)

Beckett, Ian F. W., *The Home Front 1914–18. How Britain Survived the Great War* (London: National Archives, 2006)

Bell, Julian (ed.), *We Did Not Fight 1914–18 Experiences of War Resistance* (London: Cobden-Sanderson, 1935)

Beresford, Charles, *The Bath at War. A Derbyshire Community and the Great War* (Bakewell: Country Books/Ashridge Press, 2007)

Bilborough, Ethel M., *My War Diary 1914–1918* (London: Ebury Press, 2014)

Binyon, Laurence, *For Dauntless France. An Account of Britain's Aid to the French Wounded and Victims of War* (London: Hodder and Stoughton, 1918)

Bower, Thekla, *The Story of British V.A.D. Work in the Great War* (London: IWM Department of Printed Books, 2003)

Bridger, Geoff, *Great War Handbook* (Barnsley: Pen and Sword Books, 2009)

Britten, Vera, *Testament of Youth* (London: Fontana Paperbacks, 1979)

Brown, Malcolm, *The Imperial War Museum Book of 1918 Year of Victory* (London: Sidgwick and Jackson, 1998)

Bushaway, Bob, 'Name upon Name: The Great War and Remembrance', pp.136–167, in Roy Porter (ed.) *Myths of the English,* Cambridge: Polity Press, 1992

Bygate, John G., *Of Arms and Heroes. The Story of the 'Birtley Belgians'* (Durham: The History of Education Project, 2005)

Chambon, Pascal, *Les Soissonais dans la Grande Guerre* (Stroud: Alan Sutton, 2011)

Clouet, Hugh, *After the Ruins* (Exeter: University of Exeter Press, 1996)

Clouet, H. D., 'Rural Revival in Marne 1914–30', *Agricultural History Review,* Vol. 42, II, pp. 140–155, 1994

Cohen, Susan, *Medical Services in the First World War* (London: Shire Publications, 2014)

Cohen-Portheim, Paul, *Time Stood Still. My Internment in England 1914–18* (London: Duckworth, 1931)

Cowen, Ruth (ed.), *War Diaries. A Nurse at the Front. The First World War Diaries of Sister Edith Appleton* (London: IWM with Simon and Schuster, 2012)

Cresswell, Yvonne M. (ed.), *Living with the Wire. Civilian Internment in the Isle of Man during the two World Wars.* (Douglas, Isle of Man: National Heritage, 1994)

Crofton, Eileen, *The Women of Royaumont. A Scottish Women's Hospital on the Western Front.* (Phantassie, E. Lothian: Tuckwell Press Ltd, 1997)

De T'Serclaes M.M., Baroness, *Flanders and other Fields. Memoirs of the Baroness de T'Serclaes* (London: George G. Harrap & Co Ltd, 1964)

Dropsy, Henriette, *Le journal d'Henriette Dropsy. Deux ans de guerre en Transloy de juillet 1914 à août 1916* (Montreuge: Bayard Service Edition, 2003)

Dyer, Geoff, *The Missing of the Somme* (London: Orion, 1994)

Farnborough, Florence, *Nurse at the Russian Front. A Diary 1914–18* (London: Constable, 1974)

Farrar, Martin J., *News from the Front. War Correspondents on the Western Front 1914–18 (Stroud:* Alan Sutton, 1998)

Fiennes, Peter, *To War with God. The Army Chaplain Who Lost His Faith* (Edinburgh: Mainstream Publishing Ltd, 2011)

Fowler, Simon, 'Charity Begins at Home', *History Today,* Vol. 49 No.9, pp. 17–23, September 1999

Fry, Ruth, *A Quaker Adventure, the Story of Nine Years' Relief and Reconstruction* (London: Nisbet, 1926)

Graham, Wootton, T*he Official History of the British Legion* (London: Macdonald and Evans, 1956)

Grant, Peter Russell, 'Mobilising Charity: Non-uniformed Voluntary Action during the First World War' (Unpublished Doctoral thesis, City University London, 2012)

Graves, Robert, *Goodbye to All That* (London: Penguin Modern Classics, 2000)

Gregory, Adrian, *The Silence of Memory: Armistice Day, 1919–1946* (London: Bloomsbury Academic, 2014); *The Last Great War. British Society and the First World War* (Cambridge: Cambridge University Press, 2008)

Gregson, A. S., 'The British League of Help for the Devastated Areas of France: A Forgotten Memorial to the Great War', *'Stand to'* Western Front Association No. 66, January 2003

Grieves, Keith, *Sussex in the Great War* (Lewes: Sussex Record Society Vol. 84, 2004)

Griffith, Paddy, *The Great War on the Western Front. A Short History* (Barnsley: Pen and Sword Books, 2008)

Hallam, Andrew and Nicola (eds.), *Lady under Fire on the Western Front. The Great War Letters of Lady Dorothie Feilding* (Pen and Sword Books, 2011)

Harding, Brian, *Keeping Faith. The History of the Royal British Legion* (Barnsley: Leo Cooper, 2001)

Harris, Janet, *Alexandra Palace. A Hidden History* (Stroud: History Press, 2013)

Hattersley, Roy, *Borrowed Time* (London: Little Brown, 2007)

Heron, Pat, *Guests of the Nation. The Story of Ilford's Belgian Refugees 1914–1919* (Ilford: Purple White and Green, 2010)

Kripper, Monica, *The Quality of Mercy. Women at War, Serbia 1915–18* (London: David and Charles, 1980)

La Motte, Ellen N., *The Backwash of War* (London: Conway Publishing, 2014)

Lee, Janet, *War Girls. The First Aid Nursing Yeomanry in the First World War* (Manchester: Manchester University Press, 2005)

Lemaitre, Jean-Michel & Marie Christine, *1914–18 Dans La Somme Occupée. Memoire en Images,* (Saint-Cyr-sur-Loire: Edition Alan Sutton, 2007)

Leneman, Leah, *Elsie Inglis. Founder of Battlefield Hospitals Run Entirely by Women,* (Edinburgh: NMS Publishing, 1998)

Lewis, Bryan F., 'The Contribution of the British League of Help for the Devastated Areas of France following the First World War' (Unpublished M.A. Thesis, University of Kent, Canterbury, 2002)

Lewis-Stempel, John, *The War Behind the Wire. The Life, Death and Glory of British Prisoners of War 1914–18* (London: Weidenfeld & Nicholson, 2014)

Liddle, Peter, *Testimony of War 1914–1918* (Wilby, Norfolk: Michael Russell, 1979); *The Voice of War* (London: Leo Cooper, 1998)

Macdonald, Lyn, *The Roses of No Man's Land* (London: Penguin Books, 1980)

McPhail, Helen, *The Long Silence. Civilian Life under the German occupation of Northern France 1914–18* (London and New York: I B Tauris, 2001)

Marlow, Joyce (ed.), *The Virago Book of Women and the Great War 1914–18* (London: Virago Press, 1998)

Martin, Benjamin F., *France and the Après Guerre 1918–24. Illusions and Disillusionment,* (Baton Rouge: Louisiana State University Press, 1999)

Marwick, Arthur, *The Deluge. British Society and the First World War* (Harmondsworth: Penguin, 1967); *Women at War 1914–1918* (London: Fontana, 1977)

Masefield, John, *The Old Front Line* (Barnsley: Pen and Sword Military Classics, 2003)

Mayhew, Emily, *Wounded: From Battlefield to Blighty 1914–18* (London: The Bodley Head, 2013)

Miller, Louise, *A Fine Brother. The Life of Captain Flora Sandes* (London: Alma Books, 2012)

Mitton, G. E., *The Cellar House of Pervyse: The Incredible Account of Two Nurses on the Western Front during the Great War* (Leonaur, 2011)

Munson, James (Ed.), *Echoes of the Great War. The Diary of the Reverend Andrew Clark 1914–19* (Oxford: Oxford University Press, 1985)

Nicholson, Juliet, *The Great Silence 1918–20. Living in the Shadow of the Great War* (London: John Murray, 2009)

Osborne, Brian S., 'In the Shadows of Monuments: The British League for the Reconstruction of the Devastated Areas of France', *International Journal of Heritage Studies,* Vol. 7, No. 1, pp. 59–82, 2001

Panayi, Panikos, *The Enemy in our Midst, Germans in Britain during the First World War* (Oxford: Berg, 1991)

Parker, Peter, *The Last Veteran. Harry Patch and the Legacy of War* (London: Fourth Estate, 2010)

Pederson, Sarah, '"A Surfeit of socks".The Impact of the First World War on Women Correspondents to Daily Newspapers', *Scottish Economic and Social History,* Vol 22, No 1, pp.50 – 72, 2002

Peel, Mrs C. S., *How We Lived Then* (London: Bodley Head, 1929)

Powell, Anne, *Women in the War Zone. Hospital Service in the First World War* (Stroud: The History Press, 2009)

Pugh, Martin, *We Danced All Night. A Social History of Britain Between the Wars.* (London: Vintage Books, 2009)

Pye, Edith M. (ed.), *War and its Aftermath: Letters from Hilda Clark from France, Austria and the Near East, 1914–24* (Wells: Clare, Son & Co, 1956)

Rathbone, Irene, *We That Were Young* (New York: The Feminist Press at the City University of New York, 1989)

Remarque, Erich Maria, (trans. Brian Murdoch), *All Quiet on the Western Front* (London: Vintage Books, 1996)

Reznick, Jeffrey S., *Healing the Nation. Soldiers and the Culture of Caregiving in Britain During the Great War* (Manchester: Manchester University Press, 2004)

Robinson, Maude, '"Lest We Forget". A memory of the Society of Friends in the War Years (1914–18)', *The Friends' Quarterly Examiner,* Vol. 66, pp. 91–104 and pp.158–172, 1932

Ross, Ishobel, *Little Grey Partridge. First World War Diary of Ishobel Ross who Served with the Scottish Women's Hospitals Unit in Serbia, with an Introduction by Jess Dixon* (Aberdeen: Aberdeen University Press, 1988)

Royal Horticultural Society, 'Horticulture and the First War', *RHS Occasional Papers from the RHS Lindley Library,* Vol. 12, September 2014, London.

Roynon, Gavin, *The Massacre of the Innocents. The Crofton Diaries, Ypres 1914–15* (Stroud: Sutton Publishing, 2004)

Stibbe, Matthew, *British Civilian Internees in Germany. The Ruhleben Camp, 1914–18* (Manchester: Manchester University Press, 2008)

Storey Neil R. & Housego, Molly, *Women in the First World War* (London: Shire Publications, 2010)

Storr, Katherine, *Excluded from the Record: Women, Refugees and Relief, 1914–1929* (Oxford: Peter Lang, 2009)

Summerfield, Muriel and Bellingham, Ann, *Violetta Thurstan – a Celebration* (Newlyn: Jemeson Library, 1993)

Taylor, Keith, *Matlock and the Great War 1914–1919. The Sacrifice Made by the Families of a Provincial Town* (Bakewell, Country Books, 2010)

Thurstan, Violetta, *The Hounds of War Unleashed. A Nurse's Account of Life on the Eastern Front During the 1914–1918 War* (Cornwall: United Writers, 1978)

Todman, Dan, *The Great War, Myth and Memory* (London: Hambledon, 2005)

Van Emden, Richard, *The Quick and the Dead. Fallen Soldiers and Their Families in the Great War* (London: Bloomsbury, 2011); *Meeting the Enemy. The Human Face of the Great War* (London: Bloomsbury, 2014)

Van Emden, Richard & Humphries, Steve, *Veterans. The Last Survivors of the Great* War. (Barnsley: Leo Cooper, 1998)

Watson, Janet S. K., 'Fighting Different Wars: Experience, Memory, and the First World War in Britain' in *Studies in the Social and Cultural History of Modern Warfare,* ed. J Winter (Cambridge: Cambridge University Press, 2004)

Wharton, Edith, *Fighting France: from Dunkerque to Belfort* (London: Hesperus Press Ltd, 2010)

White, Sally, Worthing, 'Richebourg and the League of Help for the Devastated Areas of France: The Rediscovery of an Adoption', *Sussex Archaeological Collections,* Vol. 140, pp. 125–38, 2002; 'Forgotten Philanthropy', *History Today, Vol. 63, No. 7, pp. 22–8 July 2013*

Wilson, Keith (ed.), *The Rasp of War. The Letters of H. A. Gwynne to the Countess Bathurst 1914–18* (London: Sidgwick and Jackson, 1988)

Winter, Jay, *Sites of Memory, Sites of Mourning* (Cambridge: Cambridge University Press, 1995)

Books, periodicals and theses on the Internet

Adkins, Barbra, Banbury Rest Station and Canteen 1914–1919, *Cake & Cockhorse, Banbury Historical Society*, Vol. 8., pp13–16, Autumn 1979. www.banburymuseum.org/Cake-and-Cockhorse-archive/

Anon, *The Condition of Belgian Workmen now Refugees in England* (London: T. Fisher Unwin Ltd, 1917). https://archive.org/details/conditionsof belgi00unse

Cahalan, Peter James, *The Treatment of Belgian Refugees in England during the Great War*, McMaster University Open dissertations and Theses, 1977 Blue Cross: https://www.bluecross.org.uk/

Carlile, John Charles, (ed), *Folkestone During the War: a Record of the Town's Life and Work*. (Folkestone: F J Parsons Ltd, original publication date unknown) https://archive.org/stream/folkestoneduring00darliala/folkestoneduring00carliala_djvu.txt

Corporation of Croydon Libraries Committee, *Croydon and the Great War; the Official History of the War Work of the Borough and its Citizens from 1914 to 1919, together with the Croydon Roll of Honour*: .https://archive.org/stream/croydongreatwaro00moor/

Dearmer, Mabel, *Letters from a Field Hospital* (London: Macmillan & Co, 1915) www.archive.org/details/lettersfromfield000dear

Dixon, Agnes Margaret Powell, *The Canteeners*, (London: J Murray, 1917) https://archive.org/details/canteeners00dixo

Edgington, M A., *Bournemouth and the First World War. The Evergreen Valley 1914–1919* (Bournemouth: Bournemouth Local Studies Publications 675, 1985) www.edgww1.jp137.com/edgww1.pdf

Gatrell, Peter. Europe on the Move: Refugees and World War One: https://www.bl.uk/world-war-one/articles/refugees-europe-on-the-move

Gerard, James W., *My Four Years in Germany* (New York: Grosset & Dunlap, 1917) https://archive.org/details/fouryearsgermany00gera

Gordon, Mr & Mrs Jan, *The Luck of Thirteen. Wanderings and Flight through Montenegro and Serbia* (New York: E. P. Dutton and Co, 1916) http:/wwwgutenberg.org/files/17291/17291-h/17291-h.htm

Grant, Peter, *Mobilizing Charity – Voluntary Action in the First World War. Financial Capital/Social Capital*. Presentation at the Voluntary History Society Seminar 11 November 2006. www.vahs.org.uk/content/uploads/2006/12/voluntary_action_in_first_world_war.pdf

Mobilizing Charity: Non-uniformed Voluntary Action during the First World War (London: Unpublished Doctoral thesis, City University.2012) http://openaccess.city.ac.uk/2075/

Hasted, Rachel, *Domestic Housing for Disabled Veterans, 1900–2014* (Historic England, 2016) https://historicengland.org.uk/images-books/publications/iha-domestic-housing-for-disabled-veterans-1900–2014/

Betty Keays-Young (Ed), *My War Experiences in Two Continents by Sarah McNaughtan* (London: John Murray, 1919) www.gutenberg.org/files/18364/18364-h/18364-h.htm

Kushner, Tony, Local Heroes: Belgian refugees in Britain during the First World War. In *Immigrants and Minorities. Historical Studies in Ethnicity, Migration and Diaspora*, Vol 18, Issue 1 pp. 1–28, 1999, www.tansfonline.com

Levy, Angela, *Belgian Refugees: Worthing's 'Guests'*. www.westsussexpast.org.uk

MacDonald, William, *Reconstruction in France* (London: The Macmillan Company, 1922). https://archive.org/details/reconstructionin00macduoft

Mack, Louise, *A Woman's Experiences in the Great War* (London: T. Fisher Unwin Ltd, 1915). https://archive.org/details/womansexperience00mackrich

Gordon Massey, *Hendon and the Outbreak of World War I*, Unpublished undergraduate dissertation, Middle University (Tottenham), 1998. Dissertation. Gordon Massey.

Mitton, G. E. (ed.), *The Cellar House of Pervyse a tale of uncommon things from the journals and letters of the Baroness T'Serclaes and Mairi Chisholm* (London: A & C Black, 1917). https://archive.org/details/cellarhouseofper00mittuoft

Sheffield Libraries, Archives and Information, *Painted Fabrics Ltd 1915 – 1959* (originally produced by Sheffield Archives in conjunction with the then City Museum and Mappin Art Gallery and Sheffield Hallam University, 1998) https://sheffield.gov.uk/libraries/archives-and-local-studies/research-guides/painted-fabrics.html

Picton, Harold, *The Better Germany in War Time. Being Some Facts Towards Fellowship.* (London and Manchester: The National Labour Press, Ltd., 1918). www.gutenberg.org/files/24810/24810-h/24810-h.htm

Picot, Lieut.-Colonel H P CBE, *The British Interned in Switzerland* (London: Edward Arnold, 1919). https://archive.org/details/britishinternedi00pico

Powell, Joseph and Gribble, Francis, *The History of Ruhleben: A Record of British Organisation in a Prison Camp in Germany* (London: W. Collins Sons & Company Ltd, 1919). https://archive.org/stream/historyofruhlene00poweuoft,historyofruhlebe00poweuoft_djvu.txt

Stanley, Monica M., *My Diary in Serbia April 1, 1915–Nov. 1 1915* (London: Simpkin, Marshall, Hamilton, Kent & Co, 1915). https://archive.org/stream/mydiaryinserbiaa00stanrich/mydiaryinserbiaa00stanrich_djvu.txt

Stobart, Mrs St Clair, *War and Women. From Experience in the Balkans and Elsewhere* (London: G Ball & Sons Ltd, 1919). www.archive.org/details/warwomenfromexpe00stobrich

Violet Cross's Journey from Dorset Vicarage to Croix de Guerre in the First World War. Somerset Live, 11 January 2014: http://www.somersetlive.co/uk/violet-cross-croix-de-guerre/story-20430885-detail/story.html

Thomas, Anna Braithwaite, (compiler), *St Stephens House: Friends' Emergency Work in England 1914–1920* (London: Emergency Committee for the Assistance of Germans, Austrians and Hungarians in Distress). www.isle-of-man.com.manxnotebook/fulltext/sh1920/

Wade, Linda 'By Diggers Defended, By Victorians Mended': Mateship at Villers-Bretonneux. *Eras* Edition 8, November 2006: www.arts.monash.edu.au/eras.

Walbrook, H. M., *Hove and the Great War. A Record and a Review, together with the Roll of Honour and List of Distinctions* (Hove: 1920). https://archive.org/details/hovegreatwarreco00walbiala

A War Nurse's Diary. www.greatwardifferent.com/Great_War/Furnes_Nurse_01.htm

Websites of particular interest

Australian newspapers online: http://trove.nla.gov.au/newspaper/#

BBC: www.bbc.co.uk/charityappeals/amounts-raised

Bank of England's Online Inflation Calculator: www.bankofengland.co.uk/education/Pages/resources/inflationtools/calculator/index1.aspx

Belgian Refugees. Online Centre for Research on Belgian Refugees: http://belgianrefugees.blogspot.co.uk/

Belgian Refugees in Glasgow 1914–1920: www.glasgowlife.org.uk/libraries/the-mitchell-library/archive/collections/belgian-refugees/pages/default.aspx

Select Bibliography

Belgian Refugees in Lincolnshire and Hull 1914–1919, Katherine Storr: www.yourpod.co.uk/library/refugees.htm, 2011

Belgian Refugees in Rhyl: https://refugeesinrhyl.wordpress.com/

Belgian Refugees in West Cumbria during World War I: www.cumbria.gov.uk/eLibrary/Content/Internet/542/795/6637/4193214157.pdf

Birmingham: 'Godmother' of Albert in Picardy: http://www.alantuckerfirstworldwarpages.co.uk/birmingham-as-the-godmother-of-albert-in-picardy

Birtley Belgians: https://en.wikipedia.org/wiki/The-Birtley-Belgians

Blackburn: www.cottontown.org/

Erskine. A brief history of Erskine Hospital
http://clydeside-images-blogspot.co.uk/2011/12/history-of-erskine-hospital.html

Glasgow. *Belgian Refugees, 1914–1920* http://glasgowlife.org.uk/libraries/the-mitchell-library/archives/collections/belgian-refugees/pages/default.aspx.

Guardian Newspaper Archive: http://archive.guardian.co.uk

Letchworth Recollections: www.ourletchworth.org.uk

Letchworth Garden City and the Belgians: www.gardencitymuseum.org/about_us/history_letchworth_gc/history/letchworth_garden_city_and_belgians

National Archives: http://nationalarchives.gov.uk/documentsonline

Newhaven: www.newhaventowncouncil.gov.uk/newhaven-in-the-first-world-war/

New Zealand newspaper online archive https://paperspast.natlib.govt.nz/newspapers/

Ossett and Belgian refugees: www.ossett.net/pages/belgian_refugees.jpg.htm

Quaker Strongrooms. A Blog from the Library of the Society of Friends. quakerstrongrooms.org/2015/01/26/friends-emergency-and-war-victims-relief-committee-cataloguing-project-relief-and-reconstruction-during-world-war-i-and-beyond/

Rhyl History Club: http://rhylhistoryclub.wordpress.com/2012/03/23/the-belgian-refugees

Rowntree, Colin: http://www.guise.me.ac/articles/familyatwar/colin/index.htm

The Royal British Legion. http://britishlegion.org.uk/about-us/our-history/

The Royal Star and Garter Homes. https://starandgarter.org/about-us/history/

The Ruhleben Story. The Prisoners of Ruhleben Civilian Internment camp 1914–1918 www.ruhleben.tripod.com

St Dunstan's: www.blindveterans.org.uk/about-us/our-history/

Save the Children: www.savethechildren.org.uk/about-us/history

Scarletfinders: www.scarletfinders.co.uk

RSPCA: www.rspca.org.uk/whatwedo/whoweare/history/firstworldwar

Society of Friends: www.quaker.org.uk/about-quakers/our-history/quakers-and-wwi

Times Archives: http://archive.timesonline.co.uk/tol/archive

The Times History of the War, London, 1914: https://archive.org/details/timeshistoryofwa03lond

YMCA. The Long, Long Trail. The British Army in the Great War of 1914–1918 www.longlongtrail.co.uk/army/other-aspects-of-order-of-battle/ymca-british-volunteer-organisations-1914–1918/

YMCA. On the Home Front: Mrs Churchill and the YMCA http://telegraph.co.uk/history/world-war-one/inside-first-world-war/part-three/10418471/ymca-volunteers-great-war.html

Index